THE REMEMBERED VILLAGE

This volume is sponsored by the
CENTER FOR SOUTH AND SOUTHEAST ASIA STUDIES
University of California, Berkeley

The Center for South and Southeast Asia Studies of the University of California is the coordinating center for research, teaching programs, and special projects relating to the South and Southeast Asia areas on the nine campuses of the University. The Center is the largest such research and teaching organization in the United States, with more than 150 related faculty representing all disciplines within the social sciences, languages, and humanities.

The Center publishes a Monograph series, an Occasional Papers series, and sponsors a series of books published by the University of California Press. Manuscripts for these publications have been selected with the highest standards of academic excellence, with emphasis on those studies and literary works that are pioneers in their fields, and that provide fresh insights into the life and culture of the great civilizations of South and Southeast Asia.

RECENT PUBLICATIONS OF THE
CENTER FOR SOUTH AND SOUTHEAST ASIA STUDIES

TOM G. KESSINGER

VILYATPUR, 1848–1968

*Social and Economic Change in
a North Indian Village*

MURRAY J. LEAF

*INFORMATION AND BEHAVIOR IN
A SIKH VILLAGE*

Social Organization Reconsidered

A. M. SHAH

*THE HOUSEHOLD DIMENSION OF
THE FAMILY IN INDIA*

SYLVIA VATUK

KINSHIP AND URBANIZATION

White-Collar Migrants in North India

THE REMEMBERED
VILLAGE

M. N. SRINIVAS

UNIVERSITY OF CALIFORNIA PRESS
BERKELEY • LOS ANGELES • LONDON

University of California Press
Berkeley and Los Angeles, California

University of California Press, Ltd.
London, England

Copyright © 1976 by M. N. Srinivas
ISBN 0–520–02997–6
Library of Congress Catalog Card No. 75–7203
Printed in the United States of America

Had not all the copies of my processed notes been burnt in the fire on 24 April 1970 at the Center for Advanced Study in the Behavioral Sciences, Stanford, I would not have thought of writing a book based entirely on my memory of my field-experience. I wish therefore to acknowledge the part played by the arsonists in the birth of this book.

The anthropologist has 'to be also a novelist able to evoke the life of a whole society'.

Marcel Mauss,
Manuel d'Ethnographie, edited by Denise Paulme,
Payot, Paris, 1947, p. 8

When we say that a social fact is total it does not mean only that everything which is observed is part of the observation; but also, and mostly, that in a science where the observer is of the same nature as his object, the observer is himself a part of his observation.

C. Lévi-Strauss,
Introduction à L'oeuvre de Marcel Mauss,
Sociologie et Anthropologie, p. XXVIII*

* I thank my friend Professor Georges Condominas for drawing my attention to these two passages and for translating them for me.

Foreword

The two short quotations preceding this Foreword say that ethnography is an art; and the book itself is an excellent exemplification. The notion is popular in anthropology, but its meaning has not been clearly specified. Since Professor Srinivas has done me the honour to ask for a Foreword to what is an important contribution to the subject, it seems worthwhile to write about different ways of conceiving ethnography.

As a new comparative, empirical science, anthropology had early success (for example in Frazer's *The Golden Bough*) in drawing psychological and historical conclusions from the fascinating variety of cultural practices added to the literature of ancient times by soldiers, explorers, and missionaries as Europeans expanded their world. These conclusions were soon faulted, among other reasons, for being based on data which were torn out of usually unknown contexts. But this was less a theoretical fault of method than of the use of data reported by others.

Anthropology came of age when theoretical anthropologists did first-hand fieldwork. The first monographs that resulted (e.g. Lewis H. Morgan's *The League of the Ho-dé-no-sau-nee, or Iroquois*, 1851; W. H. R. Rivers's *The Todas*, 1906) were not too different from others of the time (e.g. Spencer and Gillen's *The Arunta*, originally 1899) which were written by men who were not and did not come to be recognized as anthropologists. Indeed, there continue to appear excellent descriptions of peoples and cultures by non-anthropologists and the monographs of people who are labelled 'professional anthropologists' are often far from sensitive and perceptive enough to be useful. Nevertheless the best of the *genre* combine full and credible descriptions with closely related advances in theory in such a way that each seems to have preceded the other. Thus it was, even with Morgan's and Rivers's primordial studies. So also with such later classics as A. Radcliffe-Brown's *The Andaman Islanders* and Bronislaw Malinowski's *Argonauts of the Western Pacific*.

But with every gain there is a loss; and the pattern of the problem-oriented monograph, which has become fashionable, has virtually destroyed what was once the glory and value of the holistic monograph, in which the ethnographer submerges his own special professional interests to display the world of the bearers of the culture he has come to know. Professor Srinivas's present monograph is one of only about five per cent of those published in our generation which shares the glory of being holistic.

Please note the specification that the classic monograph submerges the special professional interests of its creator, not of course his or her personality. To attempt to submerge—even as a *tour de force* —differences in the minds, personalities, and skills of ethnographers would be useless and foolish. These differences, as much as those of the cultures described, account for the uniqueness of the monographs. Ethnography is an art in so far as it is a purposeful attempt to describe for outsiders how a society of necessarily heterogeneous persons see one another and their ideas and their behaviour collectively. It requires a highly sophisticated anthropologist to minimize unconscious intrusions of concepts and values from any other culture. It requires also a wise and sensitive person who strives to achieve that by using his mind and his values purposefully. The least likely ideal one imagines is the vacuum of a false 'objectivity' which is in fact polluted with all of the intrusions of the unconscious. A good ethnography must necessarily be a high art.

But however excellent the ethnographer, and however courageous, persistent, and creative the attempt, relative failure has been the result. Few ethnographies stand the test of time as true reflections of the peoples and the cultures they describe. Complex as any reality is for a painter or sculptor to interpret credibly, it is simple compared to a human cultural tradition which can be seen only through the minds of people who carry it—and their own artistic works, as they and others may interpret them. The only comparison is with the poet or novelist who brilliantly catches the truth of a nation, a civilization, an era. In this comparison, the ethnographer suffers the major disadvantage that in the process of learning he must himself collect the thousands of items of mundane data at a dozen levels of abstraction from which any eventual interpretation must be made. This process itself fogs the mind—the forest is lost in the trees; there follow years of stewing in the data for which the ethnographer is intellectually responsible. Professional and scientific resources come to the rescue. One now searches the data for items relevant to theoretical and comparative problems; instead of completing the ideal monograph, the ethnographer achieves and is rewarded for theoretical contributions which become then the remains of a forgotten culture.

Again, as so often in human affairs and in scholarly and scientific history, an accident opens the path to a solution. Professor Srinivas's monograph, based on the human mind's extraordinary capacity to bring forth significant details of the past, is a major ethnographic portrait woven from the warp of immersion in the sea of original data and the weft of purposeful seeking after a description of a village in its own terms. Its success will suggest not that we should all destroy our field-notes, but that we need not let them destroy our art!

SOL TAX

Chicago
29 July 1975

Preface

THIS book would not have been written but for a bizarre and tragic accident which occurred on 24 April 1970, when I was at the Center for Advanced Study in the Behavioral Sciences, Stanford, as a Fellow. I had gone in January of the same year with the aim of completing a much-postponed monograph on Rampura, a multi-caste village in princely Mysore (now part of Karnataka State). By a strange quirk of fate all the three copies of my fieldwork notes, processed over a period of eighteen years, were in my study at the Center when a fire was started by arsonists. My own study, and a neighbour's, were reduced to ashes in less than an hour, and only the steel pipes forming the framework stood out with odd bits of burnt and twisted redwood planks of the original wall sticking to them. My first impression was that all my processed notes were irrevocably lost, though that did not prevent me and my friends from rescuing every bit of paper on which some writing could be discerned. Luckily, I had left my original field-diaries and notes behind me in Delhi, but the task of processing the data once again from scratch was something I could not bear to contemplate.

This is not the place to narrate the story of the recovery of my processed notes. Suffice to say that a substantial part of them were recovered thanks to Mrs A. B., a lady who had specialized in the art of recovering documents from buildings hit by fire, and who insisted on remaining anonymous. It seemed a relatively simple technique but expensive in terms of resources, labour and time. Mrs A. B., assisted by several lady volunteers, wives of Center Fellows, and of the Stanford University faculty, inserted each slip of paper on which something had been written or typed into a plastic folder and this was photographed. In the meanwhile, the Ford Foundation in Delhi had on its own initiative contacted my department, and microfilmed my original field-notes, and airmailed the film-rolls to the Center. They also financed the travel and stay, for a period of nine months, of my student and research assistant, Mr V. S. Parthasarathy, who had helped me from 1954 onwards in the processing of my data. He had, in addition, accompanied me on short visits to Rampura. Mr Parthasarathy and I were able to recover a good part of the processed data by comparing the bits of writing on the recovered cards with the original notes, and supplemented by my own recollection of things and events. I must express my gratitude to Mr Parthasarathy for his wholehearted co-operation in the recovery of my data, and also for other help and support in that crisis-ridden year. I must thank the Ford Foundation for the promptness with which they came to my aid, and the Wenner-Gren Foundation, New York, for making financial grants to the Center to enable me to spend an extra four months there.

Two days after the fire, we were visited by our friends Professor and Mrs Sol Tax, and Professor Tax did not spend much time getting to the point. He told me that no social anthropologist, not even the most industrious, had ever published more than a small portion of his data. While the loss of my processed data was indeed a disaster, I should not forget that my colleagues valued my study not only because of the new material it provided on Indian rural life but because it was I who had done the fieldwork. My mind, and my entire personality, had been involved in that experience, and what did I remember of it? I should try and do a book on Rampura based solely on my memory. Indeed, I should forget that I had made any field-notes.

Professor Tax wanted to try and instil some hope and courage into me. He was my neighbour at the Center, his study being only two doors away. Being an anthropologist, he realized, perhaps more than others, what the loss of field-notes meant.

Professor Tax's advice and encouragement could not have come at a more opportune time. This book is the result of his advice and encouragement. He must, in all fairness, bear some responsibility for its inordinate length and highly personalized style.

A few days after Professor Tax's visit, sitting in another study provided for me by the Center's Director, Dr Meredith Wilson, I tried to recall what I knew about Rampura but was dismayed to find my brain refusing to co-operate. I tried again a day or two later, and this time, with better results. I wrote more or less steadily for three days from 10 a.m. till 5 p.m. I then arranged the notes into distinct themes. While working on each theme, I was able to recall additional information which was contextually relevant.

I tried to use a dictaphone in order to make up for lost time. I was also doubtful whether the idea of writing a book on Rampura based on my memory was a sound one, and if it was not, I did not want to waste much time on it. It seemed that I would have to abandon the dictaphone as my first two or three efforts at using it were most discouraging. But after a while I had some success which encouraged me to persist. Using a dictaphone saved me a tremendous amount of labour and time. Indeed, between May and November 1970 I had dictated a very rough draft of the present book.

Right at the beginning I had taken a decision to include in the book only those facts, incidents and impressions that I was able to remember. But that did not prevent me from checking against the field-diaries when I felt doubtful. Except in a very few cases, checking only confirmed what I had written. While preparing the final draft, however, I thought that I should give the exact figures on such matters as village population and the amount of available arable land, and these figures were worked up from the original notes. I have also quoted an extract from one of the diaries about an oracular consultation with the deity Basava. I did this in order to get the correct sequence of events and words. But for these, the book has been based entirely on my memory.

I should make it clear that this book is about Rampura as it was in 1948, the year when I first did fieldwork there. When a reference has been made to conditions obtaining at other times, the period has been usually specified.

I would like to acknowledge my sense of indebtedness to Mrs Joan Warmbrunn, who was my secretary at the Center, for accurately transcribing the tapes and for much other help. As she transcribed them, she developed a keen interest in the inhabitants of Rampura and their concerns and affairs, and this made me believe that my account would be of interest to others besides anthropologists. It also prompted me to aim at writing for the intelligent layman instead of for the specialist.

The fire posed a variety of problems which I shall not go into here; but they were real and difficult ones, and I would not have been able to cope with them but for the total support of the administrative staff of the Center. I gratefully acknowledge the help and kindness of the Executive Director, Dr O. Meredith Wilson, the Associate Director, Mr Preston Cutler, the Treasurer, Mrs Jane Kielsmeier, and the Business Manager, Mr Alan Henderson.

I must thank the University of Oxford, and the late Professor E. E. Evans-Pritchard, for permitting me to spend the first year of my appointment as University Lecturer in Indian Sociology at my field village of Rampura. A major reason for the unconscionable delay in publishing the results of my research has been my pre-occupation with teaching, administration and committees while in my own country. It was only when I was on research assignments abroad that I was able to work on my field-notes, do some essential reading on the region of my interest, and also try and catch up with new theoretical developments. In this connection I must thank the University of Manchester and the late Professor Max Gluckman for electing me to a Simon Senior Fellowship in the Department of Social Anthropology from June 1953 to March 1954; the Rockefeller Foundation for a fellowship during the academic year 1956–57; and the Center for Advanced Study in the Behavioral Sciences for awarding me a fellowship for the period January 1970 to June 1971. I am thankful to the University of Delhi for giving me leave of absence to accept the Center's invitation.

Finally, I must express my sincere thanks to the Indian Council of Social Science Research and Mr J. P. Naik, its Member-Secretary, for electing me a National Fellow from September 1971 to July 1974. I was able to devote a part of this period to completing the final draft of the present book.

I thank Professor Milton Singer, Dr S. Seshaiah, Mrs Veena Das and Mrs Judith Varadachar for reading part or all of the manuscript, and offering comments and suggestions; Mr Parthasarathy and Mrs Pushpamala Prasad for reading the typescript with a view to locating repetitions, and errors in spelling, and checking the references; Mr B. G. Kulkarni, in the Human Geography Unit at the Institute for Social and Economic Change for preparing the maps and sketches; Mr Kamal Kishore, Mr C. N. C. Unni and Mr S. Krishna Murthy for typing and secretarial help; and finally Miss S. Kulkarni for the index.

M. N. SRINIVAS

Institute for Social and Economic Change,
Bangalore

Contents

Illustrations

Between pages 136 and 137

Nandi, Shiva's vehicle—Chamundi Hill, Mysore

Feeder Canal off the Ramaswamy Canal

Feeder Canal, another section

Paddy field after being harvested

Jaggery-making

Harvesting

A bullock cart on the road along the Tank

Collecting alluvium from the Tank in summer

The Basava Temple

The deity Narasimha being taken in procession during the
annual festival at Harigolu village

Cheluvadi, hereditary Harijan servant of the high castes,
showing the symbol of his office

Ornamented door in a rich landowner's house (left);
a detail of the carving (below)

Maps and Diagrams

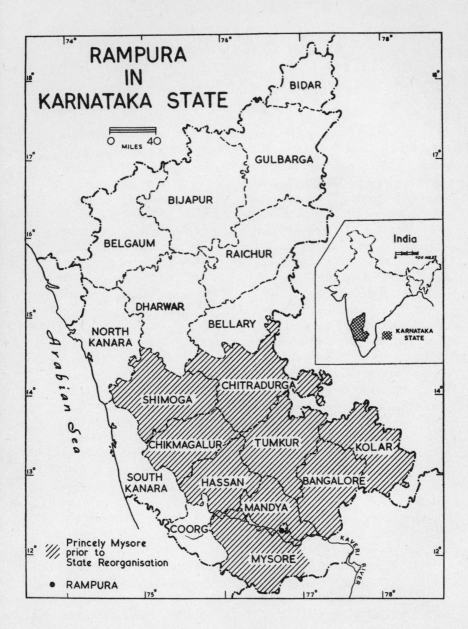

RAMPURA
IN
KARNATAKA STATE

0 MILES 40

BIDAR

GULBARGA

BIJAPUR

BELGAUM   RAICHUR

DHARWAR   BELLARY

NORTH
KANARA

SHIMOGA   CHITRADURGA

CHIKMAGALUR   TUMKUR   KOLAR

SOUTH
KANARA   HASSAN   BANGALORE

COORG   MANDYA

MYSORE

Arabian Sea

India

KARNATAKA
STATE

KAVERI RIVER

/// Princely Mysore
     prior to
     State Reorganisation

●   RAMPURA

CHAPTER I

How It All Began

THE SEEDS of my study of Rampura, a multi-caste village in Mysore District in Mysore State (recently renamed Karnataka) in South India, were sown in 1945–46 when I was a doctoral student in social anthropology at Oxford. It was Radcliffe-Brown's last academic year at Oxford, and on more than one occasion he talked to me about the scientific importance of making a field-study of a multi-caste community in India. While there was a great body of writing on caste, most of it was based on historical and literary material, and was concerned with the institution at the all-India or provincial level. Reliance on historical and literary material had resulted in a view of the caste system which was at variance with that obtained from, for instance, folk literature. Thus, there were many proverbs in the Indian languages making fun of the Brahmin, his greed, gluttony and pusillanimity, while in the sacred literature of the Hindus, mostly written by the Brahmins themselves, he had been portrayed as the apex of the caste system and as a deity on earth.

Even more important, according to Radcliffe-Brown, was the fact that the extant studies did not give an idea of the day-to-day social relations between members of diverse castes living in a small community. That could only be done through the intensive field-study of a multi-caste village or town by a trained social anthropologist. The importance of such a study could not be overstated as caste represented a unique form of social stratification, and millions of human beings had ordered their lives according to it for over two millennia. The institution was beginning to change fundamentally, and it should be studied before it changed totally. Time was of the essence of the matter.

The 1930s were a period when social anthropology was beginning to move out of its preoccupation with the study of relatively isolated primitive communities to undertake the study of villages and towns which formed an integral part of vast political and historic societies. This new tendency showed itself in both the United States and

England, and Radcliffe-Brown was friendly to it. This was only to be expected as he had spent the years 1930–37 in Chicago where Redfield, Sol Tax, John Embree and Horace Miner were all busy studying villages and towns in Guatemala, Japan and Canada. The Chinese anthropologist, Fei Hsiao-tung, had made a study of a Chinese village in the thirties.

Radcliffe-Brown's suggestion that I should make an intensive study of a multi-caste village appealed to me for several reasons, including of course the purely scientific one of adding to existing knowledge about the working of a uniquely hierarchical society which was on the threshold of far-reaching changes. For one thing, I felt that my previous field experience, diverse as it was, had not been sufficiently intensive. I had only made brief forays into rural areas from towns, and I had gathered information from a few individuals instead of participating intimately, over a period of time, in the day-to-day activities of the people I was observing. I had been converted during my year of studentship to Radcliffe-Brown's brand of functionalism (subsequently designated 'structural-functionalism' in the United States), and I was excited about its implications for field-work: I wanted to examine, first-hand, events and institutions in all their complex interrelationships.

I was one of Radcliffe-Brown's last students at Oxford, and after his retirement from the Chair in July 1946, I became a student of his successor, Evans-Pritchard. No two teachers were more different. I found it easy to establish contact with Evans-Pritchard. In fact, he took the initiative in establishing contact with me. His informality and charm, and his natural impulse to treat a student as an equal, made a profound impression on me. Evans-Pritchard's teaching methods were highly personal and unorthodox but effective. I found him most stimulating outside the classroom or even the formal supervision session, and when he was with a few close colleagues and students. He was generous with his time and ideas. It is possible that Evans-Pritchard may have singled me out for favoured treatment because of the good word which Radcliffe-Brown had put in for me. Evans-Pritchard's informality made it possible for me to talk to him about many other things besides anthropology.

Evans-Pritchard must have found my faith in functionalism very naive, and he proceeded, in his own way, to make me more sceptical towards it. He even tried to outrage me by saying that functionalism was nothing more than a way of organizing and presenting field data. There was a streak of scepticism in Evans-Pritchard's thinking: he distinguished between the heuristic value of an idea and its truth-value. This facilitated experimentation with all sorts of ideas while at the same time not being tied to, or bound by, them. In the context of functionalism, it meant that the institutions of a society were related to each other, that changes in one set of institutions led to changes in other sets, and finally, that each set of institutions had a contribution to make to the whole. This idea did lead to better field-work and analysis as it made the anthropologist more sensitive to connections between different areas of social life and culture. (It became closely linked with the method of 'participant observation', first practised by Malinowski, and which is now regarded as indispensable for anthropological training and analysis.) But whether even primitive societies are really wholes in which every institution is linked to every other is a debatable question. At some point in his career Evans-Pritchard had been influenced by Vahinger's *The Philosophy of 'As if'*.

Some time in July 1947, a few days prior to my departure from Oxford, Evans-Pritchard told me that there was the likelihood of a new post being created in the Department, viz. a University Lectureship in Indian Sociology, and did I want to be considered for it? I think he mentioned this while Radcliffe-Brown was on a brief visit to Oxford. Radcliffe-Brown told me how a few years at Oxford were necessary before I could return to India to teach. (I think he put it more bluntly!) I do not think that I showed appreciation of what Evans-Pritchard was planning for me, for at that moment I was overwhelmed to find that I was thought good enough to teach at Oxford. Also while it was no doubt a dream come true I was not ready for it. I was homesick, and eagerly looking forward to going home, and the prospect of returning to England in the immediate future went against my plans.

I returned home to Mysore in August 1947. It was a crucial and exciting month in the sub-continent's history: it became independent but, in the process, was divided into two sovereign countries, India and Pakistan. The partition of the sub-continent was marked by bloody and barbarous riots which eventually culminated in the assassination of Mahatma Gandhi on January 30, 1948. There was considerable confusion in the country, particularly in the north.

Before leaving Oxford I had applied for a research post in the Anthropological Survey of India but I did not hear from them for several weeks after my return. I was aware that the convulsions caused by the partition of the country would take time to settle down and only after something like normalcy had been restored would the Government turn to a minor chore such as filling posts in a research department. It was during the latter half of October 1947, I think, that I received a letter from the Government asking me to present myself for an interview at New Delhi on the date mentioned in the letter. (It was early in November, I think.) Delhi was still gripped by partition riots in November 1947, and the trains coming in from the Punjab literally overflowed with refugees with dozens of passengers perched on the roofs of the compartments. I left Delhi soon after the interview for the calmer and more familiar Bombay, and when I reached my host's home I found a letter from Evans-Pritchard telling me that the lecturership had been instituted, and asking me whether I would be willing to take it up. He also added that I could spend the first year of my job carrying out the field study which I wanted to do. It was an extraordinarily generous offer, though still not quite formal, and I was delighted. It was characteristic of Evans-Pritchard that he added the extra gift for a year's field work in a village. I replied accepting the offer and thanking him. I did not feel any sense of guilt in accepting Evans-Pritchard's offer as the Selection Committee in New Delhi had not given me a clue to their intentions. In fact, I had had a rough time with Dr B. S. Guha, the Director, and we did not have a single point of agreement. He was surprised that I regarded the annual Brahminical *shraddha* as ancestor-propitiation. He was a physical anthropologist, and was not familiar with modern social anthropology. Working with him would not have been easy.

I started looking around for a village as soon as I had official news of my appointment. I was required to return to Oxford during the first week of January 1949, and if to this was added three weeks for the journey, I would not have more than a maximum of eleven months for my stay in the village. I had therefore to find a village as soon as I could. This great constraint was responsible for helping me to decide on the language-area in which I would work. I could have worked in a village in any language-area in south India, but I had the utmost facility in Kannada which was the language of my street and school, though not of my home. I would have no need for interpreters, and I would also be able to go to such original documents as existed and did not need anyone's help to copy and decipher them. (However, I discovered subsequently that I needed considerable guidance and help before I was able to make use of the land records and other documents.)

If the time factor decided the language-area, sentiment decided the part of Mysore where I would select my village. Three or four generations ago my ancestors had migrated from neighbouring Tamil Nadu to settle down in rural southern Mysore. In studying a village in this region I would therefore be finding out about the kind of society which they had lived in, and obtained a living from. My study thus would enable me better to understand my personal cultural and social roots.

An important social process in Mysore, if not in South India as a whole, is the urbanization of Brahmins. This process has yet to be studied, and its many consequences and implications understood. It has gone on for a hundred years or so, and as with several other processes, its tempo has continued to accelerate since World War I. As a traditionally literary caste, whose members were frequently economically better off than many others, Brahmins were among the first to become aware of the opportunities opened up to those proficient in English. The new schools and colleges were located in the cities and those who wanted education had to migrate to them from their villages. Urbanization gradually spread to the other rural castes. I may add that this picture of urbanization is somewhat oversimplified inasmuch as, traditionally, cities in Mysore included a number of non-Brahmin trading, artisan and servicing castes. Besides, the development of Bangalore, the biggest city in the State, involved the immigration of a number of Hindu castes, Muslims, Christians and others from neighbouring linguistic areas, in particular, Tamil Nadu. But it is not necessary for me here to consider urbanization in all its complexity, and my statement that Brahmins were among the first to urbanize and that many other rural castes followed them later, remains broadly true.

My father had left his natal village and moved to Mysore before the beginning of World War I in order to be able to educate his children. It was not an easy decision for him as he was an only son, and by local standards he had a sizeable quantity of irrigated land on which he and his father had both worked hard alongside their tenants and servants. He obtained a job in the Mysore Power and Light (as the Department of Electricity was then called) but the bulk of his income continued to come from his ancestral land. Like many other landowning Brahmins, he visited his village every year at harvest to collect his share of the rice crop and sell the surplus to rice-millers in Mysore. Students of urbanization may be interested to note that landownership added to a person's social status even in Mysore city, and the fact that a man obtained the staple food grain of rice from his own land instead of buying it in the shops was mentioned with pride by those who owned land, and with envy by those who did not. An important symbol of landownership was the line of bullock carts, loaded with paddy, which stood before the landowner's house during the harvest month of January.

After having decided, on sentimental grounds, on the southern Mysore area, I looked about for villages which satisfied certain other criteria such as a multiplicity of castes, which grew rice as a major crop, were small enough to be studied by a single person, and finally, were not too 'progressive' or 'modern'. While the village had to be multi-caste in composition, I did not want the number to be so large that I would be unable to study inter-caste relationships in some detail and depth. It was also necessary that a sizeable proportion of the village population be Okkaligas who constituted the dominant, landowning and cultivating caste of this region (hereafter referred to as Peasants). I also wanted Harijans, and the essential artisan and servicing castes such as Smiths, Barbers, Potters, Washermen and Priests represented in my field village.

Rice cannot be grown without irrigation from tanks (artificial lakes), wells or canals, and irrigated villages are in a minority in Mysore State. But canal and tank irrigation is widespread in southern Mysore, and I had a feeling that the growing of rice would make my village more 'Asian' than it would be without rice.

Negatively, I wanted my village to be away from a main road, and to be without electricity and piped water. In 1948, very few villages had electricity and piped water, and it was necessary to avoid them. Location on a main road opened up a village to outside influences and there were a number of such villages.

I contacted several landowners in Mysore city and talked to them about their villages and others which they knew. I then made a list of likely villages. I also took a few trips to villages within a radius of thirty miles or so from Mysore. Gradually, I discovered that the kind of village I wanted was not easy to come by. One or more essential factors were found missing in each village on my list.

As I went about my search I discovered that I had overlooked certain mundane factors. For instance, accommodation was difficult to find. Houses were built in villages for living and not for renting. The few houses which fell vacant for one reason or another were occupied by lesser officials such as school teachers, police constables and doctors. It became clear to me that I would not be able to rent an entire house for my exclusive use. I then thought of renting at least a couple of rooms in a house but even for that I needed the patronage of a local landowner.

The availability of good drinking water was another practical consideration. After my experience in Coorg, I was keen, in fact anxious, that my field-work should not be disturbed by illness. Finally, while villages away from the main road were ideal, the problem of maintaining a constant supply of groceries and vegetables, all to be sent regularly from Mysore, meant that I could not turn down a village merely because it was on a bus road. In fact, dilapidated war-time buses, powered by charcoal gas, were so liable to break down that even a village on a bus route presented difficulties. During the period of my stay in Rampura, I did not undertake many bus journeys which were free from breakdowns.

Luck came my way after a few weeks of searching. A friend, whose brother-in-law owned land in Rampura, wrote to the headman, and I was told that they would be able to give me a place to live in. As soon as I learnt of this, I caught the first available bus and presented myself at the headman's house. The headman was away in Tirupati on his annual pilgrimage, and I met his eldest son, Rame Gowda. I asked him a few questions about the village. By way of recommending it to me, he said that unlike neighbouring villages, it was free from factional politics, and that it was also 'progressive'. As evidence, he mentioned the fact that sometime in the 1930s the Village Panchayat had ordered the inhabitants not to burn precious cowdung for fuel but to use it only for manure. And this order was being obeyed. As far as accommodation was concerned, there were two houses, both belonging to the headman, one in which he received his important guests ('office house') and the other where his bullocks were stalled ('bullock house'). I would be provided accommodation in one or the other. Could I visit the village after the headman returned from his pilgrimage?

I was excited by the prospect of being able to start my work soon, but I could not ignore the negative features of Rampura for my field-work. First, it was located on the Mysore–Hogur bus road, and as such was likely to be more urbanized than interior villages. Second, it had a population, as I later discovered, of 1519, and I wondered whether it was not too big to be studied by one man. Third, my ancestral village was too close to it—six miles by bus and a little over three miles by footpath. Further, Rampura's alleged faction-lessness, and its 'progressive' character added to my doubts about its typicality.

I bade goodbye to Rame Gowda saying that I would return as soon as I had word from him and walked down to the brick and mortar platform built around the trunk of the huge peepul (*Ficus religiosa*) tree, to wait for the bus to Mysore. The bus took some time coming. As I sat on the platform, I could not help looking towards the east, the direction from which the bus was expected. The Mysore–Hogur road snaked its way up towards Gudda village which occupied the crest of the rise. Gudda itself was not visible— the road, after zigzagging for a while like a drunk, disappeared into a blue sky flecked with white, cottonwoolly clouds. A furlong from where I sat was the Big Tank, a stretch of shimmering silver and blue, walled in on the south by a huge stone-and-earth embankment whose flattened top was the bus road. Around the tank were orchards growing coconut, arecanut, mango, banana, and other favourite trees. The silver and blue of the tank, and the blue-flecked-with-white of the sky, the green of the orchards somehow blended with the brown of the terraced plots where paddy had been harvested only two or three weeks ago. Someone was making jaggery in a nearby field—a smell compounded of boiling sugarcane juice and of cane tops being burned for fuel reached me. It was a beautiful morning, sunny but not too warm, typical of January in this part of Mysore. I then and there decided that Rampura was the village for me. Rame Gowda appeared friendly, and he had promised me accommodation. It did not matter very much that Rampura was on a bus road. More serious was its unity and progressiveness but luckily for me they later proved to be an exaggeration.

I feel self-conscious to mention that my decision to choose Ram-pura was based on aesthetic rather than rational considerations. However, it was in line with my earlier decision to select the southern Mysore region on sentimental grounds. But the alternative of men-tioning only the 'rational' criteria while ignoring the 'non-rational' ones would be dishonest.

Back in Mysore, I attended to a number of things which I had to get done before moving into Rampura. I needed furniture, medical supplies, groceries, lamps, torches and many other articles. I saw the Deputy Commissioner of Mysore District to secure from him a letter which would allow me access to official documents in the village and *taluk* (the administrative division comprising a number of villages and presided over by an official called *amildar*). Such a letter was essential though not always enough. Luckily for me, I had other connections to use: the Amildar of Sangama Taluk was the father-in-law of an acquaintance of mine, and he wrote on my behalf. I later discovered that the Revenue Inspector (head of the *hobli*, an administrative unit lower than the *taluk*) of Hogur was a friend of a friend, and he was also helpful.

The Deputy Commissioner also gave me a permit for a tin of kerosene every month to keep my hurricane lanterns going—kerosene was scarce and was supplied in minuscule quantities against ration cards. It was almost unobtainable in the villages, and most villagers in Rampura in 1948 obtained such light as they could from small earthen lamps in which cotton wicks burned using sesame or groundnut oil.

I started looking around for a cook but finding one seemed extremely difficult. Not only were cooks scarce, but cooks prepared to work in a village seemed practically nonexistent. I realized to my surprise how dependent cooks were on such urban facilities as piped water and electricity. I thought of having my food supplied by the teashop in Rampura but it was far too unhygienic a place for my liking. The other alternative was to cook my own food but I feared that it would take up too much of my time. At this point one of my knowledgeable friends warned me against taking anyone who was likely to get me into trouble in the village by his amorousness, quarrelsomeness, or some other quality. An ability to withstand rural conditions and behave in such a way that no problems were created for me seemed to be even more important than cooking. After much searching, I found such a person in our domestic cook's younger brother, a young man barely out of his teens, who wanted to earn some money while waiting for a job. Everyone assured me that he was a 'good boy', and he was willing to learn how to cook. It was also pointed out to me that he was a Brahmin from an orthodox family and this was helpful as elderly villagers would expect me to behave like a Brahmin. I discovered later that the advice given to me was extremely sound—Nachcha, my cook, was a social success with the men who mattered, and they found even the soups he cooked to their liking. I frequently heard tributes to his conduct and abilities. Sometimes I even felt that the villagers liked him better than me, which was all to the good.

I thought I would pay another visit to the village to find out when I could move in. However, on 30 January 1948, Gandhiji was assassinated, and in common with millions of other Indians, I could not think of my own work for a few days. And when I did visit Rampura I was told to come after the mourning period of thirteen days had ended. I was slightly upset to hear this as I did not see immediately the connection between Gandhi's death and my moving into Rampura. I even wondered whether the villagers were only putting me off. But after a while I told myself that the villagers did not want me to start an auspicious piece of work (my research) during an inauspicious period just as no one would have thought of starting the construction of a house during mourning.

The villagers commemorated the thirteenth day of Gandhi's death with a meeting, group photograph, and snacks. At first sight it looked like a strange way of expressing their sorrow at the death, but traditionally the ending of the period of mourning was marked by a feast. Only the photograph was a new addition.

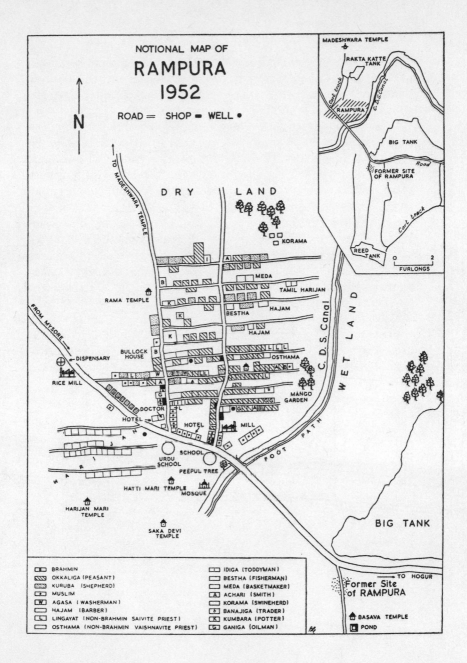

NOTIONAL MAP OF

RAMPURA
1952

ROAD = SHOP ▬ WELL ●

N

MADESHWARA TEMPLE

RAKTA KATTE
TANK

C.D.S.Canal

RAMPURA

BIG TANK

Cart track

Road

FORMER SITE
OF RAMPURA

REED
TANK

0   2

FURLONGS

TO MADESHWARA TEMPLE

D R Y   L A N D

KORAMA

MEDA

TAMIL HARIJAN

RAMA TEMPLE

BESTHA

HAJAM

HAJAM

FROM MYSORE

DISPENSARY

BULLOCK
HOUSE

OSTHAMA

RICE MILL

C. D. S. Canal

W E T   L A N D

MANGO
GARDEN

DOCTOR

HOTEL

HOTEL

MILL

H
A
R
I
J
A
N

SCHOOL

URDU
SCHOOL

PEEPUL TREE

FOOT   PATH

HATTI MARI TEMPLE

MOSQUE

HARIJAN MARI
TEMPLE

SAKA DEVI
TEMPLE

BIG TANK

TO HOGUR

Former Site
of RAMPURA

BASAVA TEMPLE

POND

▭▭ BRAHMIN
▨▨ OKKALIGA (PEASANT)
▦ KURUBA (SHEPHERD)
▪ MUSLIM
W AGASA (WASHERMAN)
H HAJAM (BARBER)
L LINGAYAT (NON-BRAHMIN SAIVITE PRIEST)
▭ OSTHAMA (NON-BRAHMIN VAISHNAVITE PRIEST)

▭▭ IDIGA (TODDYMAN)
▭ BESTHA (FISHERMAN)
▭ MEDA (BASKETMAKER)
A ACHARI (SMITH)
▭ KORAMA (SWINEHERD)
b BANAJIGA (TRADER)
K KUMBARA (POTTER)
G GANIGA (OILMAN)

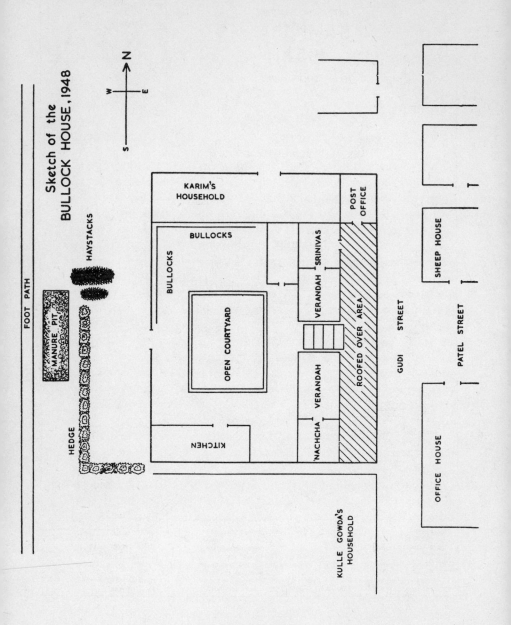

Sketch of the
BULLOCK HOUSE, 1948

FOOT PATH

HEDGE

MANURE PIT

HAYSTACKS

KARIM'S HOUSEHOLD

BULLOCKS

BULLOCKS

BULLOCKS

OPEN COURTYARD

KITCHEN

NACHCHA

VERANDAH

VERANDAH SRINIVAS

POST OFFICE

ROOFED OVER AREA

KULLE GOWDA'S HOUSEHOLD

GUDI STREET

OFFICE HOUSE

PATEL STREET

SHEEP HOUSE

CHAPTER II

The Field Situation

1 *The Bullock House and Its Inhabitants*

AFTER what appeared to me to be a long period of waiting, I moved into the village with Nachcha, my cook, and twenty-six pieces of luggage. The bus deposited me at the point where Gudi Street cut into the Mysore–Hogur road, and the Bullock House, where the headman had decided I should stay, was only a hundred yards away. As the bus neared Rampura I wondered how we were going to transport my luggage from the bus stop to the house as some of it was too heavy for one person to carry. I need not have worried. Some villagers who happened to be there helped Nachcha to carry our goods to the house. They made it a point to snatch away from me any article I tried to carry. I was a respected guest and therefore above carrying my own things even when they were not heavy. In contrast, Nachcha was allowed to, though he too was relieved of unwieldy and heavy articles. As we walked up the street, there was some good-humoured comment on the number of things a single man needed for a temporary stay in the village. A large number of villagers lived their entire lives possessing much less.

The headman had set aside for us three rooms in the Bullock House, one of the five houses he owned in Rampura. It was a large house on the western flank of Gudi Street, and Patel Street, running east to west, terminated at its entrance. The other four houses were located at the western end of Patel Street, so that all the five formed a cluster. Thus the western walls of the headman's Office House and Sheep House stood on the eastern flank of Gudi Street (see sketch).

The Bullock House was typical of the better houses in this part of rural Mysore. The two main features of such houses were an inner, rectangular courtyard open to the sky, and a narrow, covered verandah (*jagali*) in the front running almost the entire width of the house except for the space where the front door was located. There was no fixed point for the door—it could be at either end or in the middle. In the case of the Bullock House the door was in the middle bisecting the verandah into two. A small, poky room with a barred window opening on to the street marked either end of the verandah. I occupied the northern room and Nachcha the southern.

The height of the front verandah varied from house to house even on the same street. But all houses, including the smallest, had a verandah. (I shall discuss later the uses of the verandah.) The Bullock House, however, had a second and subsidiary verandah, which was unpaved, and almost at street level. The northern end of the lower verandah terminated in a room which was used as the village post office. A taciturn local Brahmin, Rao, was the postmaster.

The principle of the covered verandah was also used inside the building. The central courtyard was sunk a foot or more below floor level, and paved with granite slabs. Roofs on all the four inner sides sloped towards the courtyard and a tunnel running beneath the floor carried rain and bath water to the street outside. There were two rooms on the edge of the southern verandah and one of the two served as our kitchen. It was dark even when it was bright out-side, and the kitchen door had to be kept at least partially open during the day in order to see the food served on the plate. Such ventilation as the kitchen had, came from a gap between the top part of its southern wall and the roof. This gap also served as a chimney. Smoke from the stove had painted the wall above it a shiny black while elsewhere it was varying shades of brown.

The roofed portion to the north and west of the courtyard was used as a cattle-shed. (The division of the inner living space between human beings and livestock was widespread in this part.) The head-man's eleven bullocks were stalled here when not working. Five pairs of matched animals were used for cultivation while one short animal (*gidda*, literally 'shorty') drew a small cart in which the headman's older son, Rame Gowda, travelled every day to the field.

The continuity of the inner verandah was broken on the eastern side by a room which was used for storing some tools, and odds and ends. A door in the western wall of the Bullock House opened on to a small yard at the back. But all the land beyond the backyard was also the headman's. Just beyond the backyard was a huge straw-stack from which small bundles were taken every day for feeding the animals, and beyond the stack was an immense manure pit which when full provided nearly 500 cartloads of organic manure for the headman's 114-odd acres of land. The first duty of the headman's servants in the morning was to sweep the Bullock House, Sheep

House and Cow House and empty the sweepings into the manure pit. Small as the backyard was, it was ploughed along with other land after the monsoon rains in June, and planted with sorghum or gingelly or some other 'dry' (unirrigated) crop. The headman was a careful farmer, and he did not allow one square foot of land to go unused.

The Bullock House seemed to have been built with a view to accommodating a large household. It was also likely that additional rooms had been built as and when the need had arisen. The secondary verandah with a room at the end had been built probably to meet such a need. Similarly, a small strip of land on the northern side of the northern wall had been converted into a semi-detached house with a separate entrance from the north. This house could not have had more than three rooms, including the kitchen, and in it lived Karim, a Muslim client of the headman's, his wife and two sons, and his brother Nasar and his newly-married wife. Luckily for this household, their door overlooked a vacant plot of land, giving them a sense of space. On the southern side, however, the Bullock House was separated from its immediate neighbour by a narrow lane not more than three feet wide. The slanting roofs of the two houses almost met above the lane making it dark even during the day.

Three of the headman's *jita*[1] servants, all boys under sixteen, slept at night on one of the outer verandahs of the Bullock House. These boys slept late for villagers. They were the last to be fed in the headman's house and their masters made it certain that they had completed all their chores before they were given dinner. They came in between 9 and 10 p.m., smoked *bidis* (Indian, leaf-wrapped ciga-

[1] 'Jita servantship may be termed "contractual" servantship, to mark it off from traditional servantship. Under it a poor man contracts to serve a wealthier man for one to three years. The terms of the service, including the wages to be paid by the master, are usually reduced to writing. The master advances, at the beginning of the service, a certain sum of money to the servant or his guardian, and this is worked off by the servant. Usually no interest is charged on the advance unless the servant tries to run away or otherwise break the contract. The sum paid is exclusive of food and clothing, which it is the master's duty to provide. Frequently, before the period of the service runs out, the servant or his guardian borrows another sum of money and thus prolongs the service. Formerly it was not unknown for a man to spend all his working life between ten and seventy years of age in the service of one master.' (From Srinivas, M. N., 'The Social System of a Mysore Village', in McKim Marriott (ed.), *Village India*, Chicago, 1967, pp. 27-8.)

rettes), and curled up to sleep on torn reed-mats. The thin mats were spread on the verandah floor and the boys had only their *kamblis* (coarse, woollen blankets woven by shepherds) to cover themselves with. A towel or sheet rolled into a ball served as a pillow, and often, even this was missing. But the boys were so tired that they were soundly asleep within minutes of lying down. One of the things I can never forget is the cheerfulness of these boys at the end of a long day's work and nagging.

In 1948, the institution of the 'village watch' (*kavalu donne*, literally 'watch staff') was functioning, after a fashion, though even then it had become something of a joke. It was therefore not surprising to find that it had become defunct by the summer of 1952 when I revisited the village. In 1948, villagers were expected to take turns in sleeping on the Bullock House verandah. There was a roster of houses with the headman, and each morning one of the Harijan village servants (*chakras* as they were called) deposited a long staff, one in each of the two houses whose turn it was to send a representative that night. Traditionally, however, the watchmen were expected to go round the village every few hours, alerting people to keep awake and be on the look-out for thieves. They were expected to lie down on the verandah of the council house (*chavadi*) or Mari temple and not on the headman's verandah. The 'village watch' as it functioned in 1948 probably represented an attempt on the part of the headman to use a traditional institution to his advantage. Its unlamented death put an end to an inconvenience to the villagers.

2   *The Urban Tenant*

The stench of cow-dung and cow-urine hung about the Bullock House as it did in most village houses: only a few rich men could afford separate houses for their animals. It assailed my nostrils during the first few weeks of my moving in but after a while I found that I did not notice it except when I returned to Rampura after a brief absence in Mysore. Very few who have worked in the rural areas of southern Mysore could have missed the fragrance of the hedges but the smell of cowdung and manure heaps is clearly a different matter. But eventually all came to symbolize for me a way of life which was not only different and fascinating but attractive.

What I never got used to, though, was the rich and varied insect life of the Bullock House. Many of them, including the beige-coloured paddy-insect with soft, silky wings, had a nasty sting. There were also other live things such as cockroaches, centipedes, scorpions, lizards, snakes, and rats, all of which evoked in me loathing if not fear. A snake was once killed between the front door and the central courtyard, and another time, I just missed stepping on a purple-coloured snake. It was in my backyard and I only became aware of it when it shot away, in a flash, from my descending foot and disappeared in the tall grass. Like most village houses, crevices abounded in the Bullock House, and the roof which had a structure of split bamboos overlaid with country-tiles provided ideal runways for the many rats which came into their own at night. I kept awake many a night, listening to those rodents chasing each other in the roof above, making sharp, staccato noises with their teeth as they raced along. A camp cot and a mosquito net protected me from them but I was always afraid that one of them might miss its foothold and land on top of me. I knew that I could not mention this to any villager for fear of being laughed at. Many a poor villager hunted field-rats (*toda*) after the harvest and ate them after collecting the paddy they had stored in their burrows. Occasionally, boys, or even adults, enjoyed hunting a bandicoot or rat which was known for stealing their grain.

Water, especially drinking water, was a problem, though Rampura was better off in this respect than many other villages of the region. My nearest well was in the headman's main house, and Nachcha, along with many others in the neighbourhood, drew water from it. It was a deep and perennial well, and there was always a queue of users for it, especially in the mornings. The users of the well were usually women, and each woman carried her own rope along with her brass vessel. There was a reluctance to share a rope and a fear that it would be stolen if left unguarded. This delayed everyone and led to frequent argument. The women were tough and aggressive, and the gentle Nachcha was no match for them. But he did have a status as a Brahmin if not as my cook. On those occasions when he had been made to wait a long time either one of the women or someone from the headman's household intervened on his behalf.

Nachcha had instructions to filter and boil all drinking water. This water was then cooled in a mud pot and a lemon was squeezed into it to take out the brackish taste. Lakshmana, the headman's second son, thought that this fussiness was typical of Brahmins to whom no trouble was too great where food and drink were concerned. But thanks to my mosquito net and filtered and boiled water, I maintained good health throughout my stay. My constant walking must also have helped.

Within a day or two of my arrival, Rame Gowda, the headman's eldest son to whom his father had already passed on the official headship of the village, told me, quite casually and before a few people, that there was a big tree, a *Ficus indica*, about two hundred yards behind the Bullock House, and I should answer calls of nature under its protective shade. Incidentally, he commented on the virtues of the tree and of the spot he had commended. I knew that the land and the tree both belonged to the headman. But I was astonished that Rame Gowda could so matter-of-factly discuss such a personal matter with a relative stranger like me. Incidentally, this was the first of many occasions when I ran up against the total but implicit acceptance of the biological dimension of life which characterized rural culture.

Two hundred yards to the *Ficus* tree was not always easy, and especially when it was very hot or raining. There was also the chance of meeting someone on the way with the certain prospect that the exchange of courtesies would take a few minutes. (I remember reading somewhere that farmers in Elizabethan England made it a point to defecate on their own land even when it was at some distance.) Villagers, even casual strangers, experienced no shyness in asking me what time of the day I answered calls of nature. If they saw me taking my bucket (of water) more than once they would ask me why I was visiting the backyard frequently. A full and patient answer was expected. Exhibiting concern for my health was a friendly act just as a full reply meant that I reciprocated their friendship.

Like most other houses in the village, the Bullock House did not have a separate bathroom. Excepting the richest villagers, and the Brahmins and Lingayats, the others took their bath in the central courtyard. Only a small number had a daily bath while the others were content with a weekly bath, perhaps on a day (Saturday, Monday or Friday) sacred to their domestic, caste or sectarian deity. A copper cauldron was kept on a stove, improvised with three stones, and a fire was started with dried pats of cow-dung (*berani*) and lengths of wood. When the water was hot enough, the bather bailed it out with a small vessel and poured it over his body. If the water was too hot, it was first bailed into another vessel where enough cold water was added to it. Men bathers wore at least a loin cloth while bathing, while women usually kept on their saris though not blouses. The use of soap was becoming popular, though for the elaborate 'oil bath', the powder of the pods of *sheegekayi* (*Acacia concinna*) continued to be used. It was more efficient than soap for removing oil from the skin and hair.

I found it uncomfortable to have a bath while the *jita* servants and others wandered in and out of the house. Knowing the villagers, I thought it not unlikely that one or the other would try to involve me in a conversation while I was engaged in what to me was the purely private act of washing myself. I therefore instructed Nachcha to close the front and back doors of the Bullock House while I had my bath in the central courtyard. The servants did not like this as it delayed their cleaning work. They must have complained to the headman or his sons, for I was asked by one of them why I could not have a bath like other people. When I replied that I liked to be by myself when having a bath I was asked whether I was in the habit of being nude while bathing. I confessed to the depravity but in order to remove inconvenience to the servants I decided on having a booth of woven, split bamboo erected in the courtyard. The idea was at once pronounced prodigal though typical of me. I had my way, though, and one of the attractions of the idea was that it brought me into contact with the Medas (Basketry-makers) in Rampura.

The villagers I talked to were unanimous that the Basketry-makers were unreliable and given to drink. Not infrequently, they disappeared along with the advance which they invariably demanded. But I was determined, and my friend, Nadu Gowda, one of the most respected men in the village and a great friend of the headman, decided to help me out in this matter. He sent for one of the Basketry-makers, haggled with him not only over the rates but also over measurements—the latter was possible since the unit of measurement was the cubit and this varied from person to person—decided on the amount of the advance, and warned the Basketry-maker about the dire punishment (unspecified) that would follow if the screens were not delivered on the agreed day. The screens did arrive eventually, though not on the agreed day, and I could have my warm baths without the servants pounding the doors while I was doing so.

My daily shave also drew comment from the villagers. Most of them shaved only once a week or fortnight, and they had to be shaved by one of the village Barbers. The Barber did not ply his craft on inauspicious days—Tuesdays, full moon and new moon, for instance—and besides, the frequency of his visit was directly related to the wealth of his patron, and the amount of grain that was paid him at harvest. (However, a hair-cutting saloon, operating on a cash basis, had been recently opened on the main bus road by one of the younger Barbers.) Besides, the removal of hair as well as the Barber's touch polluted a member of the higher castes, and not only was he required to have a bath immediately after the shave, and change into pure clothes, but the spot where he had sat down with the Barber—it was usually on the outer verandah—had to be purified with that ubiquitous purifier, a solution of cowdung.

Contact with the Barber rendered a Brahmin or other high caste men impure, and this resulted in shaving being associated with impurity. There was therefore a resistance to using the safety razor among the orthodox. For instance, the headman's widowed mother, a highly respected and pious lady, had banned its use in her house. Rame Gowda confessed to me that the inconveniences of having to wait for the Barber had occasionally made him think of buying a safety razor but he had desisted out of respect for his grandmother. The Old Matriarch had, however, permitted Bharata, her grandson who was a graduate and employed in the Government, the use of the safety razor on his rare visits to the village. But he was permitted to use the polluting instrument only in the 'Office House' and not in the adjoining main house where icons and lithographs of the household gods had been kept in a separate room called *devara mane* (gods' room).

It was only in the village that I realized how far I (and my family) had travelled away from tradition. The morning shave had been a habit with me for several years, and I generally shaved before my bath. One morning, however, I had to reverse the order though I cannot recall why. Perhaps the water was getting cold and Nachcha urged me to have the bath before it became too cold. Anyway, I was shaving when the headman walked in. He asked me at once why I was shaving after my bath. I do not remember what I told him but he told me firmly that it was better that I finished shaving every day before my bath. The fact that I was a Brahmin made my disregard for the rules more culpable. I took care never again to shave after a bath. I had gone to Rampura to study it and I did not want to do anything to jeopardize that.

3 *I Try to Win Friends*

It was necessary for me to be able to talk to everyone in the village, irrespective of religion, caste, class, sex and age. It was also equally necessary that the villagers felt comfortable with me. Otherwise I would not be able to obtain their spontaneous reactions and views to my queries. I tried hard to make myself liked by one and all, and I found that this meant that I had to suppress frequently my own reactions and views. Sometimes I even went further: I gave expression to ideas and views which I thought the villagers would like to hear. In fact, I started doing this with such ease and 'spontaneity' that I became concerned. Did one have to become a hypocrite to do field-work? Did I have no convictions of my own?

Like every other anthropologist I had taken a medicine chest with me to the village, and it proved to be a boon. I dispensed medicines to villagers complaining of headache, flu or malaria, and I had a supply of ointments and bandages for those suffering from cuts, bruises and boils. A few villagers complimented me on the 'power' of my medicines and added that the Village Doctor did not have them. Their preferring me to the Doctor was at least partly due to my not charging them a fee. In contrast, the Doctor treated patients only after initial discussion as to the amount that had to be paid to him as fee. The patient had to bear the 'cost' of the medicines, and also pay a suitable sum as reward if the disease was cured. The Doctor had been trained in the Indian system of medicine (*ayurveda*), considerably modified, though, by the incorporation of many elements and techniques and drugs from Western medicine. He was an appointee of the Mysore District Board and was liable to be transferred to any village in the District. Generally, no doctor was allowed to stay in a village for more than three years. This was the rule for all officials of the State, and the District Board followed the State in this and many other matters.

I liked playing doctor to the villagers who came to me and it did not occur to me that the Village Doctor might take a dim view of my activities. He was a friend of the headman and Nadu Gowda, and once in a while all of us went together for a walk along the embankment of the tank. We did talk to each other on such occasions, and also when we met on the headman's verandah. But our relationship never became close. The Doctor seemed keen on maintaining some distance from me though he claimed to know some of my relatives. His coolness towards me evoked a similar reaction in me. Besides, some of my close companions in the village were hostile to the Doctor. They thought that he paid attention to only a few rich villagers such as the headman and Nadu Gowda and neglected the poor. My friend, neighbour and assistant, Kulle Gowda, made no secret of his dislike for the Doctor.

My camera also contributed to my popularity. I was a poor photographer but I made up for my lack of skill by my enthusiasm and willingness to 'snap' everything I saw. A small percentage of my photographs were, however, successful, and I proudly showed them around. Generally, the villagers loved being photographed, and the examination of the prints provoked much laughter and comment. Somebody had spread the myth that the photographs would be shown abroad, and this added to the pleasure of being photographed. In short, the camera became a passport to every place. Men and women digging the bed of an irrigation canal or repairing a road at the height of summer, or transplanting rice seedlings in the wind and rain of July, all enthusiastically posed for me. (The photography also broke the monotony of their work.) The camera enabled me even to cross barriers imposed by my bachelorhood. Some months after I had moved into the village, wealthy landowners invited me home to take pictures of their wives, daughters and daughters-in-law. The fact that I did not accept money for taking pictures and that I was taking them all the time added to my reputation for prodigality. Many a villager knew me as the camera man—only they transformed 'camera' into 'chamara' which in Kannada means the fly-whisk made from the long hair of yak tails. Traditionally, servants whisked flies from the persons of Rajas, and temple priests used it on the icons during *puja*.

I spent the first few weeks in the village collecting genealogies, and carrying out a census-survey of households. I had assumed that these would be regarded as innocuous activities unlike the collection of data about landownership or the quantum of grain and other produce grown on each plot of land. To my pleasant surprise, the collection of genealogies proved to be popular with the villagers. And Kulle Gowda, who had appointed himself my assistant, proved to be highly accomplished in handling the villagers and collecting information from them. After I had collected genealogical information, he accompanied me on my round of village houses for securing census-data.

The genealogies and the household census made village faces familiar to me, and made me familiar to them. When later I recognized someone as from such-and-such a house, he felt pleased, and if I did not, he explained to me who he was and how I had gone to his house the other day with Kulle Gowda. Censuses and genealogies are not only means of collecting data. They are among the easiest ways of establishing social bonds with the people the anthropologist is studying.

Nachcha's popularity with the important men of the village was also a factor in my success as a field worker. The headman and his sons, Kulle Gowda, and a few others, thought that he made tasty soups (*saru*) and curries, and occasionally there were requests from one or the other of these men for a bowl of soup. I was happy that I was able to acknowledge in a small way the kindness and hospitality of the villagers, and I encouraged Nachcha to be generous in this respect. Indeed when he had cooked something which I fancied, I took the initiative in sending a little of it to the headman or Nadu Gowda or Kulle Gowda. Once in a while, on returning home from my evening walk, I found two or three empty bowls lined up outside the kitchen threshold. Either my friends had gone to Nachcha directly or Nachcha himself had asked them to send bowls that night. Either was all right. The empty bowls were a symbol of our being accepted by the village. Nachcha, like my assistant Kulle Gowda, was a find.

Cooking for me did not prove to be too arduous or time-consuming for Nachcha, as the headman soon discovered. One day he asked me whether Nachcha could spend an hour or two every day teaching his grandchildren. It did not occur to me to say anything but 'yes'. And when Nachcha was asked, he was found to be willing. (It was not at all unlikely that Nachcha had been sounded before I was asked.) From then on, Rame Gowda's eleven-year-old daughter Akki, and one or two other children were closeted with Nachcha every day for a couple of hours. It was not always easy to adjust our varying schedule to find two hours when the children were free but I did not mind some inconvenience to myself. And Nachcha seemed to enjoy his new role as teacher. It enhanced his standing in the village, and especially with the men who mattered. On more than one occasion I heard the sound of a bamboo stick descending sharply on an unfortunate child, and this was followed by a cry of pain if not weeping. My first impulse was to jump to the rescue of the child but I restrained myself. Once, after what I thought was a rougher-than-usual use of the bamboo, Rame Gowda spoke to me appreciatively of Nachcha's teaching methods: 'He does not hesitate to use the rod when necessary. The children have a healthy fear of him. He is not soft like you.'

Nachcha basked in the sunshine of the appreciation of the headman, his sons, and Nadu Gowda. Later in the year the headman and his sons mentioned several times that Nachcha was a good and deserving person (*yogya*), and that I should find him a permanent job in an office or factory. Nachcha was already on my conscience but factory or office jobs were not at all easy to come by for a person with Nachcha's qualifications or lack of them. The villagers' repeated recommendations of Nachcha irritated me. They seemed to imply that I was not exerting myself. Eventually, Nachcha found his way to a big factory in Bangalore and I vaguely remember that the links established in the village played a part in his getting the job.

4 The Right to Move Around

Within the first few days of my moving into the village, I ran into a somewhat unpleasant incident. It was afternoon and I had gone to the Brahmin teashop for a cup of tea. Inside, I found a dark and handsome young man in a white *jubba* and dhoti, both of handspun khadi. The dress was typical of rural politicos though it was the first time that I had encountered one in Rampura which was, in 1948, little politicized in comparison with a neighbouring village such as Kere or Hogur. I sat down on the bench in the dark and smoky interior of the teashop, and the young man at once asked me what I was doing in the village. (The question was only intended to start a conversation for, in all probability, he knew what I was doing.) I told him what I proposed to do, and he seemed to become tense as he listened. Even before I had finished what I had to say he came out with his criticism: If I wanted to study the people and their problems, I should move with all sections of the village and not confine myself to a few persons and believe what they said was true of the entire village. It was obvious that the young man was having a dig at me for staying in the Bullock House and becoming insensibly part of the headman's entourage. I was annoyed at the charge but tried to conceal my annoyance. I assured him, as calmly as I could, that I wanted to meet and talk to everyone in the village. I was going to spend the rest of the year in Rampura and I hoped that I would have the benefit of occasionally discussing village affairs with him. He had probably expected me to react angrily and my calm reply seemed to pacify him. Perhaps he was even disappointed. Anyway I left the teashop after expressing the hope that I would soon have an opportunity to meet him.

The young man was Putte Gowda and he was then the only member of the Indian National Congress Party in Rampura. He visited the post office the following morning and after finishing whatever business he had there, walked up to my verandah and sat on the bench there. (I wonder if he did this because he was uncomfortable about the way he had talked to me on the previous afternoon.) Our talk this time, brief as it was, was pleasant, but I saw that the headman and his sons were watching us from their verandah. I felt that Putte Gowda's visit to my house was not to their liking though I had no idea then of the seriousness of the breach between the two. It was just as well. In any case, it was the politico who had visited me and not me him. But the headman might have concluded that Putte Gowda was only repaying an earlier visit by me to his house.

The two incidents, one following the other, were an implicit repudiation of the claim repeatedly made by the Establishment that Rampura, unlike neighbouring villages, was unified and free from factions. As the headman's sons put it, 'We are all one here and there is no party [feeling].' In this connection I could not help recalling the statement of Lakshmana that they (the headman's household) as respected people could not afford to frequent the teashops where all and sundry gathered together and exchanged gossip. Visiting the teashop meant rubbing shoulders with the *hoi polloi* on equal terms. I suspect that Lakshmana mentioned this to make me aware how the headman would view my visits to the teashop. I was likely to pick up all kinds of gossip there which it was not necessary for me to know. But then the headman and his sons did not know that it was part of my business to pick up gossip. Even if a good deal of the gossip was untrue it provided valuable leads in my quest for information. The individuals and themes which were regarded as worthy of gossip would help me in understanding local culture.

Whenever I returned home after a tour of the village, either the headman or one of his sons would ask me where I had gone, what I had seen and whom I had met. Such questioning was not necessary as someone or other would have reported seeing or meeting me somewhere in the village. My activities and encounters aroused the villagers' interest and were discussed widely. I could not keep them secret even if I wanted to.

The collection of genealogies and the carrying out of a census of households must have made it clear to the headman that I had to move about freely in the course of collecting information and participating in local activities. But I did not realize soon enough that the headman and his sons did not like my becoming too friendly with several young men who were opposed to them and who had nearly prevented, a few months before, the headman from becoming the first elected chairman of the official village panchayat (council). The wound was still raw, and the young men in question had earned the wrath of the headman's faction. I was ignorant of all this and it made me run risks which could have put a premature end to my field-work. But then awareness might have made me either inhibited in my contacts or choose another village. The latter would have not been a solution as there is no faction-free village. Factions are an integral part of rural life.

While collecting genealogies and household censuses, I deliberately excluded the Harijan ward as I thought that I should approach the Harijans through the headman both as a gesture of respect to him and also to make sure that I got the maximum co-operation from them. Otherwise I might rouse their suspicion. I told him what I wanted to do and sought his help. He replied that he would send for Kullayya, an old man whom the headman and others regarded as the leader of the Harijans. Kullayya was a Harijan of the old school. He was respectful of the high castes and he was conscientious in performing his duties as a hereditary village servant (*chakra*). In addition, he was priest (*gudda*) at a local Harijan temple, and in that capacity was particular about observing the rules of purity and pollution. His leadership of his caste had been recognized by his nomination to the official panchayat of the village.

I waited for a few days before reminding the headman of my need to meet Kullayya. I received the same reply as before. After a while I discovered that the headman was too preoccupied with his own work, and that I would have to make an independent move to contact Harijans. But I was not at all certain how the headman would react to my taking matters into my own hands. He might interpret this as an expression of my dissatisfaction with him. And this would add to his annoyance with me over the visit of Putte Gowda.

These doubts nagged me. But the solution came one morning naturally and easily. I talked to Kulle Gowda about my failure to meet the Harijans. My work had fallen behind schedule, and besides, how could I claim to be making a study of a village and ignore the Harijans? I told Kulle Gowda, 'Why don't we just walk over to their area?' Kulle Gowda had no objection at all. However, he insisted on carrying my reed mat and portable writing desk with him to the Harijan area. He probably thought that both were necessary symbols of my status. The Harijans were delighted to find that I had gone to them myself. One of them snatched the mat from Kulle Gowda and spread it on a sunny verandah. The verandah was open, and narrow, the mat being too wide for it. Soon there was a cluster of men of all ages around me and information flowed freely and fast. More important, I had established contact with the Harijans. From the point of view of earning their friendship and co-operation, I could not have done a better thing. I had not at all been comfortable about the headman's idea of sending for Kullayya. My visit to the Harijan ward did create a small stir. Young politicos would not be able to accuse me any more of listening to a few people only.

I went about the village freely. In retrospect, however, it occurs to me that I did not go to the Harijan area frequently enough though I came to know several individual Harijans reasonably well. I made it a point to spend some time occasionally sitting on a bench in front of one of the several shops talking to villagers who came in to buy something. This enabled me to establish links with Traders and Muslims (a few of whom kept shops) among others. It did not take me long to realize that such visits served to create goodwill for me. Word must have gone round that I did not consider myself too high to mix with poor villagers. I also enjoyed such contact especially as it usually generated much laughter. I was able, in such encounters, to obtain the views of the poorer villagers. Only occasionally did I worry over whether the desire to be a successful field-worker had eliminated all my naturalness and I had become an actor playing a role. I sensed in myself a capacity to dissemble that I had not suspected. But such moments of introspection were not too frequent. I was too busy most of the time.

One of my favourite shops in the village was kept by Karagu, the third and husky son of my friend Nadu Gowda. Karagu was a pleasant young man, always with a smile of welcome on his face, and I enjoyed sitting before his shop. His was a popular shop and it was patronized by villagers many of whom only rarely visited the part of the village where the Bullock House was located. On a few occasions I took Karagu's place as vendor and sold the villagers a few pies (a pie was 1/192 of a rupee) worth of *bidis*, bananas, betel leaves, etc. The villagers found the idea of my playing the role of shopman absurd and comical. A small crowd used to collect on such occasions and there was laughter and comment. It made many friends for me among the poor. Karagu welcomed these interruptions as they broke the monotony of his long day, and perhaps also attracted some customers. I do not know, however, what the headman thought of all this. To tell the truth, I did not worry about it. I do not know why.

5   The Villagers' Curiosity

I found the villagers were curious about me, and strange as it may seem, I had not anticipated it. It usually showed itself in their asking me direct questions. For instance, a few children from the headman's household watched me eat my first lunch in the village. I had taken my food in a tiffin-carrier and it included a large tomato. The children watched me from outside the window, grasping the window bars with their hands while their feet rested on a ledge in the wall. They talked to each other as I plunged my teeth into the tomato—I had not taken a knife with me. I tried to shoo them away but I was not successful. A few days later I was surprised to find Rame Gowda asking me, with wonder on his face, how I could eat a big, raw tomato as part of my meal. Salads were not commonly eaten except for raw onions or on certain festivals when cucumber was garnished with spices and coconut-bits. Only children ate raw vegetables when they were being sliced for cooking.

I was also asked how I could subsist on the little food I ate during my meals, and this knowledge again was obtained by watching me eat till I mustered enough courage to shut the kitchen door. I must add here that the villagers' idea of a satisfactory meal was one where a person ate till he could not stuff in any more. The usual phrase was 'to eat till the stomach could hold no more', the belch which followed such eating being regarded as symbolic of the eater's satisfaction. My concept of a meal, on the other hand, was to get up when I was still feeling hungry. No wonder I was so thin. Thinness was almost synonymous with weakness and ill-health while stoutness was equated with good health. A slim man was described as desiccated (*onuthukondu*), likely to be blown away by a strong wind. A stout man was described as full, strong and healthy. However, a very fat man who tired easily was regarded as unhealthy. He was also a figure of fun.

It annoyed me to find that such personal matters as answering calls of nature and the daily bath were not outside the 'public domain'. I became accustomed to shaving while one or two villagers looked on, and but for the bamboo cubicle, the daily bath would have been a public act. My bachelorhood was also a subject of frequent comment. By village standards, I should have been a father of several years' standing. Why had I remained single? I tried to explain that I had not thought of marriage till I had completed my studies and obtained a job. A man needed a job to maintain a wife and children. But the villagers were amused that a man whose family owned a good quantity of rice land (according to them), and who was educated should trot out an excuse such as not having a job in defence of his remaining single. The more sophisticated suspected that I was keeping from them my secret love life. Who knew what I had been up to in England? Westerners were free and easy in their sex life. Men and women kissed each other shamelessly in public, even on the platforms of crowded railway stations. The dancing together of the sexes was another expression of their lack of morals. Westerners were also given to drinking.

I was questioned many a time about getting married, and the villagers found my answers evasive. Once my friend Nadu Gowda was so annoyed with my replies that he asked if everything was all right with me. A few villagers even suggested possible brides for me. In the summer of 1952, when I revisited the village, Akbar Sab, a Muslim leader, was shocked to find that I was still a bachelor, and he informed me that there was a good bride, belonging to my caste, in the town of Nanjangud. The girl's mother was a widow, and had property worth three lakhs of rupees. I would become a rich man if I married the girl as she was an only daughter. When I remarked that he regarded marriage as no different from the paddy-trade in which he was engaged, he replied blandly that marriage was also a kind of trade (*vyapara*).

The villagers were also curious about my work—what was I trying to do and why was I doing it? I told them that I was collecting information about their way of life and would later lecture on the material to students in England. While they were flattered at the idea that their life was important enough to interest foreigners, they were also puzzled that I should be paid a salary to collect information about such ordinary things as agriculture, the diet of the people, festivals, gods, etc. It is likely that a few sophisticated villagers did not believe me, and thought that I was concealing my real aim. I think I was partly responsible for different people understanding and interpreting my work differently—my answers were not always uniform and this must have roused the suspicion of a few.

Early during my stay the headman asked me why I was collecting information about the village. I answered him by saying that I wanted to present an account of traditional social life and culture which would be of interest, for instance, to the headman's grandsons. Conditions were changing so rapidly that if the information was not collected immediately, it would be lost forever. I was taken aback by the headman's reply. He told me that my work was similar to that of the Chinese travellers who had visited India several hundred years ago and had left accounts of the conditions prevalent then. These accounts were an important source of information about life in ancient India. The headman had only had a few years' schooling in a traditional one-teacher school (*kooli matha*) which existed in Rampura during his boyhood, but the ease with which he grasped the significance of what I was doing astonished me. Nadu Gowda, my friend, was similarly quick to understand: he told me that while other people were going in for perishable goods (*chara*, the term for movable property) I was going in for imperishable property (*sthira*, immovable property, also meaning permanent). Nadu Gowda was given to flamboyance. In the few letters he wrote to me after I left Rampura he used to address me as *Vedamurti*, which caused me some embarrassment as I was not a Sanskritist, let alone a specialist in the Vedas.

In some respects the villagers were the proverbial frogs in a well. Even so intelligent a person as Nadu Gowda believed that all intelligence and beauty were concentrated in Mysore State as it then existed. He listed the names of some famed administrators of Mysore, forgetting conveniently that some of them had come from neighbouring states. In support of his view that Mysoreans were better-looking than their neighbours he told me that as one neared the borders of the State people became darker and uglier. Another articulate villager asked me whether Kannada was not spoken in England.

But what was surprising was that there existed along with this frog-in-the-well mentality an intense curiosity about England and the English (synonymous with all Westerners). Some villagers were of course more curious than others, and the headman was even prepared to spend money to go on a tour of England, provided of course that I was his guide. English food, dress, customs, etc. fascinated the villagers, and I was plied with questions about them. Putte Gowda, the politico, had received a letter from a distant relative who was a student in England and he had described how the British had to have meat at every meal—pig-meat (bacon) first thing in the morning, flesh of the cow or sheep at lunch and meat again at night. The villagers thought the English looked so red (in the tropical sun) because of all the meat they ate everyday. That chillies and spices were absent from English food, and that pepper and salt had to be added by each person to the food on his plate gave rise to hilarious laughter.

The size, strength and health of the British were admired but not their beauty. The villagers thought that European skins were blotched, and blue eyes and blonde hair appeared odd if not grotesque in the noonday sun. I heard this view expressed several times, and I was so irritated by it that I tried to point out that there were many beautiful men and women in England. But it was no use: some villagers had seen middle-aged or elderly Englishmen who had probably spent years in the tropics, and they chose to believe in their eyes rather than in my words.

A few intelligent children understood what I was trying to do, and I discovered that they could be valuable sources of information. A twelve-year-old son of the headman asked me to join a group of boys playing village games so that I could describe them in my notebooks. He even offered to steal a fowl belonging to an old widow in order to provoke her to display her mastery over the vocabulary of curse and abuse. Several women were known to have a good repertoire of abuse and curses, but this one was the best of them all. She could abuse for hours, and after a while, the abuse assumed the form of a rhythmic dirge, and then went on and on. The same boy asked me to be on the lookout for certain features of an approaching festival of a village deity. He told me, for instance, that one villager would be possessed by the deity and walk on sandals which had sharp nails in them.

As the days went by, my verandah became a favourite stopping place for villagers. Any villager who was walking along Gudi Street, or any of my neighbours who felt time hanging on his hands, stopped to spend a while with me. More likely than not he would find a few villagers engaged in the animated discussion of a dispute, custom or usage while I listened with a notebook and pen in my hands. It was not unusual for a passer-by to join the discussion, forgetting whatever work he had planned to do. By and large, villagers took an intellectual interest in their culture. Only a few young men who had been to school dismissed customs and ritual as the product of ignorance. A few old men would occasionally comment on the futility of discussing customs which had gone out or were about to disappear.

Some of my visitors were regulars. Nadu Gowda, who had left the day-to-day supervision of cultivation to his grown sons, came at least once a day and spent an hour or more answering my questions. Kulle Gowda, my assistant, spent most of the working day on my verandah copying information from land records or other official documents. Even the headman wandered in occasionally to spend a little time, though one part of his mind seemed always to be engaged in getting something or the other done. He was rarely as relaxed as Nadu Gowda. The headman's sons also spent some time with me though not when their father was giving me his company. Rame Gowda and Lakshmana seemed to take turns in visiting me.

There were several others who visited me whenever they wished. Some were frequent visitors. Once the headman remarked on the attraction which my verandah held for the villagers. He said it with a side glance at his old friend Nadu Gowda who happened then to be sitting on the verandah. The headman added that whereas formerly people visited me because I was close to the headman, nowadays they visited the headman because he was close to me. It was a compliment of sorts to me and a dig at his friend.

The villagers went to bed early, and I took advantage of this to bring my notes up to date. After an early dinner, I sat in my room, writing by the light of two hurricane lamps which, however, attracted many insects. But insects or no insects, I had to finish my notes and entries for the day. This was the ideal, however, and occasionally I accumulated arrears. I disliked the task as I did not trust my memory, and also my sleep was troubled if some fact or event which I thought important had not been recorded. On many a night, before going to bed, I made a list of items which had not been entered in my diary so that I did not forget them. There was also the likelihood that failure to list unrecorded items would result in disturbed sleep. I generally woke up in the early hours of the morning and an unrecorded item was certain to prevent my falling asleep again.

Very occasionally, however, I was kept awake by a late visitor. One such intrusion is still fresh in my mind. I had had a long day, and, feeling very tired, I retired to bed at about 10 p.m., hoping for a good night's rest. I was about to drop off when I heard a familiar voice calling me. '*Ayyanōré, Ayyanōré!*' ('Oh, Brahmin, Oh, Brahmin!'). It was my neighbour Shive Gowda, the youngest of three peasant brothers. He was a very tall and bony villager who sported a huge moustache twirled at either end. I could see his face pressed against the bars of my window, in the dim light of the lantern which was kept low throughout the night. (I did this because of my fear of creeping, crawling and running things.) I was not at all in a mood for company so late in the day. I decided to start snoring in order to discourage my visitor. (It was perhaps a wrong move.) He ignored the snoring and persisted in his efforts to wake me up. After a while he became impatient, and shouted, 'Are you asleep?' I said, 'Yes.' 'Why don't you get up? I want to talk to you.' I gave up the struggle and got out of bed. I was annoyed, but I thought that the man had come because of an emergency. He might be in need of medicine. I removed the door chain from its hook, and opened the two doorhalves and got out.

'What is the matter?' I must have sounded angry or worried. 'Oh, nothing. I was feeling lonely and bored and I thought I would visit you.'

He did. He talked of various things—how big the headman's father's thigh was, for instance. Then there was an old Brahmin who was very dark and had an immense, hooked nose—he held out his broad wrist and said the nose was even bigger than his wrist. All villagers admired size, especially in dead and defunct things. (There was an implication that we were living in inferior times.) He bared his thigh to show how big the python was which he had killed a few months ago. He had killed it on his land with a spade. He had to hit it hard several times before killing it. Then he went on to his wrestling days. Blabbermouth that I was, I admitted to having heard about the famous wrestling match between Koppalu Basava and Jani Pahelwan. Basava was the local hero of Mysore and Jani was the outsider. The match had taken place in the late 1920s and had been discussed for years by wrestling fans in Mysore. One of my relations was a fan and that was how I had heard of it. Jani Pahelwan came with a great reputation but the local hero beat him, decisively and soon. Shive Gowda demonstrated to me the trick which Basava used to defeat his opponent. He held me up above his head but, luckily for me, remembered to bring me down gently. Eventually he left, satisfied that he had spent a sociable evening.

The lack of privacy, the pervasive curiosity of the villagers and the perpetual need to be on my best behaviour frequently made me feel claustrophobic. After several days of continuous field work I felt the need to be by myself for a few hours at least. The only way to achieve privacy was to go for a long walk by myself. The Accountant in Kere was known to me and he was always hospitable. Besides, I enjoyed walking along the Rampura-Kere lane which went past the village of Gudi. Parts of it were beautiful and typically rural. The market in Hogur was another place which I visited occasionally. I could buy vegetables, fruit and provisions there. Besides, it was a longer walk than that to Kere. I enjoyed the rolling countryside, the occasional water tanks, the crops, hedges, birds and smells. A long solitary walk in the country restored my spirits and prepared me for another bout of intensive socializing.

But it was not easy to go on a walk by myself. One or another friend was likely to get to know about it and offer to keep me company, if I decided to go by bus. The bus was cheap and got me there much faster than walking did. I felt it rude to tell my friends that I wanted to be alone. They would not have understood. I resorted to trickery: I kept the proposed visit a closely-guarded secret, and left early in the morning. (Nachcha had to be privy to this trickery.) My friends were puzzled by such excursions. Why did I not tell them? They would have gone with me, cancelling whatever work they had. Their solicitousness deepened my feeling that I was being mean.

I generally visited Mysore city for two or three days after every four or five weeks' stay in the village. I did not keep much money with me, and I ran out of whatever I had in about a month or so. Besides, all my big shopping was done in Mysore. I also discovered that I could not take more than four or five weeks of field-work at a stretch. I worked from morning till night when I was in the village, and I was always working according to a plan which had to be revised frequently, taking note of contingencies that had arisen in the meanwhile. All this meant that I had to be on the alert continuously. It would not be an exaggeration to say that I drove myself as hard as I could. But after a period of continuous activity my nights became restless, and I felt stale and tired in the morning. My days became less and less productive. It was then that I took off for Mysore. It was pleasant to get back to electric lights, piped water, good food, and above all, privacy. It was delightful to walk around without having to be asking questions and making notes. It was equally if not more delightful that I did not have to answer questions all the time.

I could not keep my Mysore visits secret from my friends, and especially from Kulle Gowda. My friends were eager to visit my home and meet my people, and perhaps even go to a movie with me. But the last thing I wanted to do in Mysore was to spend time with my village friends.

I was a refugee from the village on those brief visits to Mysore. I was determined to prevent my village friends from visiting me in Mysore. I invented all kinds of lies to tell them that I did not have a minute to spare. I felt mean about shutting them out but I argued that my entire work would be ruined if I did not have two or three days to myself once in a while. I was aware that my friends would find my behaviour puzzling, to say the least—I was a hail-fellow-well-met in the village but I did not want to have anything to do with them in Mysore. I tried to make up for this by being extra nice to them after returning from each trip to Mysore. I invited them home and treated them to snacks and coffee. I even took small gifts to the headman, Nadu Gowda and Kulle Gowda. But I could not shake off a nagging sense of guilt.

6   The Anthropologist as Brahmin

As far as the villagers were concerned, I was primarily a Brahmin whose joint family owned land in a neighbouring village and they expected me to behave like one. This was not at all easy for me as my family were lay (*loukika*), and not orthodox (*vaidika*), Brahmins. In addition, my natal family and kin-group included members who had rebelled against many customs and usages of the Brahmins. I was, therefore, ill-suited for the role cast for me by the villagers. To make matters more complicated, a few young blades in the village, who were my friends, expected me to be emancipated from such traditional customs as vegetarianism and teetotalism. Luckily for me, I did not have time to speculate about the villagers' expectations of me. I reacted to situations as they arose, and the only rule which I observed was to be as nice as possible to the villagers while I did what was most convenient or natural to me.

I was an odd kind of Brahmin though I expected that in Mysore in 1948 there were hundreds like me. I did not perform the daily rituals which the more traditional among the lay Brahmins performed. I had given up, in common with my brothers, the custom of painting the *namam* (caste-symbol of the Iyengars or Sri Vaishnava Brahmins) on my forehead every morning after a bath. I had discarded the wearing of the sacred thread long ago, and while in England I had broken the dietary rules of vegetarianism and teetotalism. I did not conceal any of this from the villagers who asked me about them though I did not shout out my nonconformity from the rooftops.

I have already narrated how the headman ticked me off for daring to shave after my bath instead of before it. This incident may be regarded as typical of others in which the village leaders kept reminding me of the fact that I was a Brahmin. Thus Nadu Gowda tried to convince me once that I should paint the *namam* on my forehead after the daily bath. I must explain here that the *namam* consists of a U painted on the forehead with diluted *kaolin* (china clay) with a vertical red line in the middle of the U, painted with *kumkum* (vermilion). Nadu Gowda thought that I was probably too modern to wear the panoply of the full *namam*—even the single red line was enough (a simplification which the more modern Iyengars had adopted). According to him, the forehead looked bare without even a single *namam*. He was trying to convince me of the need for an attenuated *namam* on aesthetic grounds. I had first heard this argument many years before when I was a boy. I saw no point, however, in arguing the matter with Nadu Gowda—I just kept to my habit of not painting any caste mark.

The headman's second son Lakshmana wanted me to have the kitchen of the Bullock House purified with the ritual of *punyaha* (which he called *punya*). We were already using it but Lakshmana argued that the ritual should be performed because of the possibility that my mother might one day visit me in the village. The villagers had told me more than once that I should invite my mother and other relatives to the village, and I had replied that I would do so when I had done enough work. At Lakshmana's insistence I got the Brahmin priest of the Rama temple to purify the kitchen.

The villagers laughed among themselves at the kind of Brahmin I was. They, Peasants, had to keep urging me to behave like a Brahmin! Akki, Rame Gowda's daughter, was scandalized by my indifference to the rules of pollution and purity, and reported accordingly to her father. Akki was then being tutored by her grandmother in those complex rules. For instance, it was Akki's job to clean the puja room on Fridays when the household deity of Lakshmi, the Goddess of Wealth, was worshipped by the women members of the headman's household. The room was swept and then purified with a solution of cow-dung. Designs were drawn before the altar with *rangoli*, whitish powder from a soft stone found in southern Mysore. The puja vessels and lamps were scrubbed clean. After she had performed these tasks, she took a bath and did puja to Lakshmi. She broke her fast after completing the puja. Rame Gowda was proud of his daughter's religiosity.

I attended weddings in the village without bothering to be invited. I simply could not afford to miss weddings, funerals, etc., amongst the various groups and classes in the village. And on such occasions I was treated as a Brahmin. However poor the host, I was given a green coconut and a cash-gift (*dakshina*) of eight annas or a rupee. The gift was placed on a deck of betel leaves and arecanuts and given to me before everyone else. I did not like to receive the gift from the poor, especially when I had gone without being invited. But the poor had their pride and sense of propriety—I was a Brahmin and a guest, and I had to be treated like one. I tried to ease my conscience by giving a return gift on a suitable occasion, but it did not always present itself.

At the wedding of the village Washerman's son I was given the usual coconut and cash-gift before everyone else, including the Brahmin priest who was conducting the ritual. I remember that the priest of the Rama temple was officiating on this occasion for the Brahmin *purohita* (or domestic priest) who regularly officiated at weddings and other life-cycle ceremonies among the high castes. The Rama priest was annoyed at having been forced to concede precedence to me and protested. But Kulle Gowda who had taken me to the wedding house shouted at him: 'Do you think you will be overlooked? You will get your *vilya* (collective term for betel leaves, arecanuts, etc., given on ritual occasions) in good time. Can't you wait while a distinguished guest from outside is being honoured with *vilya*?' The priest, outshouted, kept quiet. My efforts to intervene on his behalf were ignored. My sympathies were with him but I was in a minority, or so it seemed.

The Rama Navami, or the festival of the birth of Rama, the hero of the epic Ramayana, and believed to be an incarnation (*avatar*) of Vishnu, was a grand festival in the village especially as the local Rama temple was one of the most important. There was a colourful procession on the ninth day of the festival, in the evening, when a portable platform on which the deity, his wife Sita, younger brother Lakshmana, and his faithful servant Hanuman, were carried along the main streets. After the procession had returned to the temple, the villagers sat down to a collective dinner which was cooked by Peasants.

It was the custom to send, on the ninth morning, the raw ingredients of a meal to households from castes that did not eat cooked food prepared by Peasants. Accordingly, a villager brought me the ingredients of a meal arranged, as was the custom, on a winnow fan of split bamboo. He deposited the winnow fan on the verandah and told me to ask my cook to take it and return the empty winnow fan. I had not expected the gift and I told the villager that it was possibly a mistake as such a gift was only given to a poor and practising Brahmin and not to someone like me. I asked him to take the gift back.

After a while the headman strode into my verandah and asked me, somewhat sternly, why I had returned the winnow fan. I repeated my reasons. He was not convinced. He told me, somewhat harshly, that if I wanted to be regarded as a member of the village I should accept the gift. My rejection of it would mean that I did not want to be so regarded. Thus presented, I had no choice but to accept the gift. I salved my conscience by making a suitable subscription to the expenses of the festival, which I was allowed to make.

One afternoon during the Rama Navami festival I visited the temple along with my friends, the headman and Nadu Gowda, to watch the puja being performed to the deity. I stood with my Peasant friends in the main hall of the temple, just beyond the *garbha gudi* (*sanctum sanctorum*). As the puja began, the headman and Nadu Gowda asked me to go into the *sanctum sanctorum* where the priest's wife and one or two other Brahmins were standing. I did not like the idea of leaving my friends behind. But the *puja* was in full swing, and it was not the moment for an argument. I crossed the threshold into the *garbha gudi*.

Towards the latter half of my stay, the Adult Literary Council of Mysore visited Rampura, at my instance, to show some educational films. In the Council's van were the driver and a commentator—the films were all silent, and a commentator was necessary for explaining to illiterate villagers what the film meant. Some time after the van's arrival the headman came to my house and told me that I would have to feed the commentator while he would look after the driver. He added, by way of explanation, that he did not want to play host to a Brahmin even if he was keen to eat in his house. I was taken aback by this remark. The headman had already discovered the castes of the driver and commentator, and that the latter belonged to a progressive, reformist type. I did not know all this, and I was the anthropologist!

As I have said earlier, my young friends in the village did not make things any the easier for me in expecting me to behave like a few emancipated urban Brahmins whom they knew. They kept asking me whether I would like chicken or mutton curry to be made for me. They were keen to play host. Apart from the fact that this was likely to get me into trouble with the headman and Nadu Gowda, I was a vegetarian by habit and inclination, I did not feel an urge to eat meat. Besides, I had a queasy stomach and it could not take the rich and highly spiced curries which the villagers liked. Food was repeatedly thrust before the guest, and he was forced to eat even when he felt that he had had enough. A guest with a small appetite was likely to be misunderstood.

Food was also cooked without any awareness of the existence of bacteria and this was particularly true of the huge dinners which were prepared by men volunteers during weddings and village festivals. I remember paying a sudden and unplanned visit to Rampura in the summer of 1964 and it happened to be the day on which Nadu Gowda was celebrating the weddings of two of his grand-daughters. An immense *pandal* (temporary awning erected with bamboo poles and a roof of woven coconut fronds) covering three streets which met to form a T, had been erected. In the centre of the *pandal* were two beautiful, decorated booths, each one occupied by a bridal pair, The guests sat on carpets spread on the street, and the colour, music.

noise and confusion were typical of rich weddings in this region. I was welcomed effusively by Nadu Gowda's sons, and after I had spent some time in the *pandal*, I told my hosts that I had to leave as I had an appointment in Mysore, later in the day. They would not hear of my leaving without eating the wedding dinner. I expressed the fear that it would mean my breaking my appointment. They told me that the first batch of guests would be eating in a little while, but I need not wait even for them. I could eat ahead of everyone—I was touched by this symbol of affection, even though it was some years since I had visited the village. I was hustled into a long dark hall where I saw huge mounds of rice piled up on mats of woven leaves of the toddy palm (*Phoenix sylvestris*). Several huge cauldrons contained steaming curries. Beyond, the cooks and their assistants were still busy cooking the rice and the various dishes. (Four thousand guests were sitting down to dinner, involving the cooking of thirteen bags of rice, each containing a hundred seers.) A leaf was produced for me, and Nadu Gowda's second son, Kempu, himself supervised the serving of food. The sight of those immense mounds of rice around which flies buzzed, and the noise, confusion and messiness of the cooking beyond were not exactly stimulators of appetite. I did my best, though I knew it was hopelessly inadequate. Kempu made fun of my appetite but was appreciative of my intentions. I bade 'goodbye' to my hosts and caught my bus. I could not then help reflecting how I had been sticking to my own food preferences when I was doing field-work. The headman was conservative in social and religious matters but he could stretch his rules when he had good reason to do so. Thus he had no objection to having non-vegetarian food prepared in his house for the benefit of the members of an influential urban Brahmin family which owned land in Rampura and with whom he was friendly. The food, however, was served in the Office House and not in the main house where the headman's mother lived. As I have said earlier, she was orthodox and would have disapproved strongly of Brahmins who wanted to break the vegetarian rule. She would also have regarded it as sinful for Peasants to encourage such Brahmins.

The headman's natural conservatism had asserted itself with regard to the commentator from the Adult Literary Council of Mysore but he was able to overcome his conservatism to please his influential Brahmin friends. He had found their friendship prestigious and profitable. In fairness to him, however, it must be stated that a normal or habitual conservatism which, on occasion, is stretched to meet a new situation or type of situation is a feature of the life-style of many sectors of Indian society.

The contextual variation of rules governing intercaste relations was a feature of social life though occasionally it produced in me a feeling of bewilderment. For instance, at my first visit to the Madeshwara temple I stretched out my cupped hand to receive the *thirtha* (sanctified water used in worship) before drinking it but the Lingayat priest Sannu emptied the water into his own right hand and sprinkled my face and head with it. I asked him why he did it. He replied that it was the custom to sprinkle the sanctified water on the head and face of a Brahmin devotee. It was a temple which had Lingayat priests, and perhaps, not all Brahmin devotees were ready to drink *thirtha* served by them. The Lingayats are a non-Brahmin priestly caste who have always claimed equality with Brahmins though the latter have refused to concede the claim.

Some time later Sannu visited my house with some Peasant friends. I offered all my guests coffee but Sannu refused to drink it. He explained that as a priest of the Madeshwara temple he had to be particular about how he behaved in the village. Otherwise villagers would talk about him. However, when he was in Mysore city, he went to restaurants freely without bothering about the caste of those who cooked the food.

I knew that Sannu had to be particular within the village but what surprised me was his feeling that he could not accept even coffee from my cook, an orthodox Brahmin, unless the fact that the coffee was served in cups from which I had drunk made them too polluted for Sannu. Besides, he had to be extra careful in view of the proximity of my landlord. Months later, during the Deepavali festival, Sannu sent an urgent request to me to go over to his house to meet a relative of his from Bangalore. I went, and the relative, after the usual but effusive questions about my background and relatives, discovered that he knew some of them. He proceeded to explain, eloquently and at length, how intimate he was with them, and how fortunate it was that he had run into me in Rampura. The closeness of his ties with my relatives established a bridge between him and me which gave much pleasure to my beaming hosts who felt that their own links with me and their important guest had become stronger. An occasion has an ethos and the guest seized upon it and developed it. He was obviously a past master at handling such a situation. He had given us all pleasure and soon we were breakfasting on hot, delicious *idlis* (steamed, rice-flour cakes eaten with a hot chutney and butter) and coffee. Sannu's hospitality on this occasion contrasted with his sprinkling *thirtha* over me instead of giving it to me to drink. It was true that the temple and home were two different places, but it was also likely that all of us were temporarily living in an urban ambience generated by the presence of the important guest from Bangalore. The rules and conventions which came into play on this occasion were different from those which came into play at the temple and in the headman's Bullock House. What was remarkable was the effortless switching of rules as demanded by the occasion. Only I was slow in figuring out when each set of rules applied.

7 The Anthropologist as Respected Outsider

To the villagers, I was not only a Brahmin but a respected outsider and guest. This meant that things which did not redound to the village's credit were hidden from me. During the first week or so of my stay I found Rame Gowda discussing, more than once, certain incidents with one or another fellow villager, but as I was present at these discussions, the names of the persons involved were not mentioned and there were tantalizing smiles, innuendoes and references to events and personalities. Good manners required me not to ask direct questions—I had readily assumed my other role, viz. outsider and guest, though I did not realize it then. But the ill-concealed attempt to keep me out strengthened my determination to find out the facts for myself. I did succeed eventually though not in all the detail I wanted.

The first incident discussed was about a villager who had jumped over the back wall of his house to escape the summons which a bailiff from the law courts in Mysore had come to serve. A desperate creditor in Mysore had tried unsuccessfully to realize his loan from the villager who was given to borrowing money without any intention of returning it. The debtor seemed to have a dubious reputation in other areas also. I later discovered that the hero of the escapade was none other than Kulle Gowda. The incident was characteristic of him, as I came to find out gradually.

The second was a case of arson in which a straw-rick belonging to a villager had been burnt down by a tenant from the neighbouring village of Bihalli. The inhabitants of Bihalli were known for hard work and combativeness. They had also discovered a distinctive technique of arson—a lighted incense stick was stuck into a straw-rick, a device which allowed the arsonist to make good his escape while the stick slowly burned down to ignite the straw. The victim in this case was a poor man and his misfortune aroused widespread sympathy. Several villagers contributed a headload of straw each to the victim who ended up by having more straw than he had lost.

The third 'incident' was a complaint by a widow, Devi, that she had been 'defamed' by another widow, Siddavva. Several days previous to the complaint, Devi was sleeping on her verandah when she felt that a man was 'pulling her by the hand'. In the non-verbal language of the village it meant that the man was inviting her to sleep with him. Devi raised an outcry and everyone came to hear about what had happened. Several villagers wondered why she had chosen to raise an outcry as Devi did not have a reputation for meanness with her affections. Siddavva said bluntly that everyone knew Devi, and that, as likely as not, she was complaining because the man had refused her advances. Siddavva had a reason for being angry with Devi as it was her son-in-law whom Devi had accused of trying to pull her by the hand. Devi complained that Siddavva had publicly accused her of immorality. The panchayat had to take notice of the complaint and imposed a fine, though a nominal one, on Siddavva for defaming Devi.

Others besides Rame Gowda also tried to hide unpleasant facts about the village from me. Even Nadu Gowda, who patiently gave me a vast amount of information on a variety of matters and took me to weddings and funerals, kept me away from disputes which came to him for arbitration. Indeed I did not know that he frequently heard cases till he casually told me one day that whenever he had to decide cases involving adultery, pre-marital sex, divorce, etc., he heard the parties not on his verandah but in his vacant, second house adjoining his son's grocery shop. He did not want his family to have to hear all that 'dirt' (*hesige*). Once again, I knew that I could not request him to allow me to sit in on the cases with him. The parties to the dispute would not like an outsider to be present while they discussed such sensitive matters. My presence was also bound to cramp Nadu Gowda's style. Besides, my friendship with him had not reached the point where I could freely express to him my interest in 'dirt': I would have been misunderstood.

One effect of the efforts of villagers to keep disputes from me was to force me to pay greater attention to them. It was at these disputes that facts normally hidden surfaced, and even reached kinsmen, friends and neighbours. Again, the passion which was ignited during the heat of a dispute led the disputants to say and do things which revealed motivations and relationships with the clarity with which lightning illumines, albeit momentarily, the surroundings on a dark night. Perhaps even the disputants themselves obtained new insights into each other during disputes. Disputes roused people's memories and led to the citing and examination of precedents. Again, it was at disputes that parties were often asked to establish certain facts by the production of evidence. Disputes, then, were a rich mine of data which the anthropologist could not ignore.

Disputes were going on all the time. One particular type of dispute, namely that concerning the partition of the ancestral property among a dead man's heirs, dragged on for weeks if not months. I found two or three partition disputes going on simultaneously and I had to watch their progress as closely as I could. They involved different individuals, and one man's version was different from another's. And disputes were only one of my several irons in the fire. Sometimes, other disputes, shorter-lived than partition disputes, flared up and I had to give them priority over partition disputes. Such a situation usually resulted in my trying to drive myself so hard that I could not sleep at night. Even my normal collection of data was affected and I had to go away to Mysore to allow my brain to simmer down.

A dispute meant at least one public outburst where the disputants argued and shouted at each other, casting aside normal restraints. Sometimes there were even fisticuffs and the drawing of blood. (At one dispute, two Muslims, related to each other, shouted and fought vigorously, and the one who had the worst of the exchange, a burly and bearded man, came to my verandah and broke down like a child, unable to bear his public humilitation.) This part of the dispute could not be concealed from neighbours and friends. But every outburst was preceded and followed by conflict which occurred in a lower key and only a few confidants came to hear about it.

During the latter part of my stay I felt confident enough to question my friends closely about disputes which were going on or had occurred a little while before. When I revisited the village in 1952 I told my friends that I wanted to watch a few disputes to learn how the disputants and the arbitrators behaved, and the principles, if any, which guided the arbitrators in settling disputes of various kinds. My young friends sent word to me when a dispute occurred, and I was able to watch its progress notebook in hand. On a few occasions, my friends turned the tables against me by asking me how I would settle such-and-such an issue which had arisen in the dispute. I had only to propound a solution for it to be shot down instantly as it had not taken into account facts which, incidentally, were brought up only after I had given my verdict! My friends did not play fair and they enjoyed making a fool of me. I did not mind it as long as I learnt something in the process.

But there was another side to the matter of which I was only dimly, very dimly, aware. Those who were watching the dispute, and sometimes even the disputants, were distracted by the discussions which went on between the young arbitrators and me. We became a secondary attraction which occasionally even threatened to become the major attraction. That we should be discussing and laughing at matters which were moving the disputants to violent argument, shouting, tears and even fighting, sounds somewhat callous in retrospect. In my eagerness to understand how disputes were settled, I had become insensitive to the feelings of my villagers.

Sex and money were areas where it was particularly difficult to come by reliable information. I found the villagers given to making wild allegations about everyone's sex life. In fact, many villagers calmly expressed the view that only one village elder was faithful to his wife. I thought they were probably pulling my leg but I later discovered that they were serious—I heard it on several occasions and from the most unlikely persons. And they did not seem to think that they were giving expression to anything out of the ordinary. I lacked the courage, at least during the first few months, to tell them that I did not believe them. That would have been rude, and asking for evidence was likely to be mistaken for nosiness on my part into the dirty side of village life. It would have resulted in damaging the confidence that was developing between me and the villagers. That confidence was the foundation on which my entire work rested. It not only meant that I would get good information. I wanted to understand the villagers, their institutions, relationships, beliefs, ideas and values. Mutual trust, affection and respect were indispensable. I was not going to risk all this by a premature display of curiosity about sensitive areas of personal and social life. It is possible that I erred on the side of caution but I have no regrets about it.

There was a conspicuous lack of privacy in the village. And this was coupled with a tendency to gossip. It followed from these two conditions that any man who was concerned about his reputation had to walk a straight and narrow path as far as his sex life was concerned. It was not easy to ignore the opinion of kinsfolk and castefolk in a small, face-to-face community in which people were bound to each other by a multiplicity of ties. Most important of all, the wife or husband and the children of the guilty party would be bound to express their resentment of the liaison.

Of course, a chance encounter between a man and woman was possible on the field, and during a pilgrimage or festival when people were forced to sleep *en masse* wherever they could, on the verandahs of houses, hospices, etc. A few young men, and several older villagers during their youth, had visited prostitutes in urban areas. In such cases, either the man himself told me about his adventures, or about his having to pay for the treatment of a son or nephew afflicted with V.D.

Liaisons within the household also occurred, and in two of the three cases reported to me, the evidence could not be easily set aside. In one of the two cases, a young man was supposed to be having friendly relations with his father's newly-acquired mistress, who was also living in the same house. I asked my friend how he knew about it. He said that a single, thin wall separated his house from the young man's and he could not help overhearing a bedroom conversation which came through the usual crevices between the top of the wall and the country-tiled roof. I had also been told earlier by another informant that the young man and his father's mistress talked to each other like an amorous couple, and not at all like 'mother' or 'stepmother' and son. The father in that case was past seventy.

However, intra-household liaisons were certain to rouse deep conflicts among the members as they fell within the area of prohibited relationships and were regarded as incestuous. They were rare, and they roused sharp condemnation.

It was enduring liaisons between men and women who lived in different houses and streets that I found difficult to believe without strong evidence, especially when one or both parties to the liaison was living with a spouse and children. I spent a considerable amount of time and energy checking on each such reported liaison and in the majority of cases I was only able to report that several villagers believed in their existence. Only in a few cases was anything like circumstantial evidence available.

My attempt to collect information about sex relationships emphasized once again the importance of disputes. Only very rarely were the parties to a liaison caught *in flagrante delicto*, and the matter was then promptly reported to the headman for the awarding of suitable punishment. Sometimes, a woman or her husband complained that so-and-so had tried to rape her, or had pulled her 'by the hand' while she was alone in the fields. The matter was inquired into and the accused punished or let off for lack of evidence. Documents about sex and marital disputes which had occurred in Rampura and neighbouring villages were therefore of importance to me. I did not come across any such documents in Rampura but I was luckier in the neighbouring village of Kere. There, the head of a prestigious Peasant lineage had a small collection of documents, and I was able, after much effort, to persuade him to lend them to me. In Rampura itself, I had to rest content with oral reports about disputes which had occurred—that is, apart from the ones which I had myself witnessed.

Another area where I could not obtain reliable information was money. I knew how much land every landowner in the village owned, and how much of it was wet (irrigated), dry (unirrigated) and garden (irrigated). I also knew about the other immovable property which they owned. But I could not get facts about cash transactions. I was eager to know the assets and liabilities of the village leaders as it was indispensable to me, among other things, for obtaining an idea of the number of people in the village and elsewhere who were obliged to them. I often heard it said that the headman had lent 1.5 lakhs of rupees to people in thirty villages, including Rampura while smaller figures were mentioned for other landowners such as Nadu Gowda and Millayya. These reports did not seem wild to me, unlike reports about illicit sex activities, but here again evidence was unobtainable.

There was a strong sense of secrecy about money especially among the village rich, and direct questioning about financial transactions would have not only not procured any information but would have earned ill-will for me which could have expressed itself in disagreeable ways including making my continued stay in the village difficult if not impossible.

I knew that the prevailing rates of interest in the village varied from a low of 12 per cent to a high of 24 or 30 per cent. I am ignoring here a few moneylenders who lent small sums of money to poor traders and others at 50 or 75 per cent. These men were highly unpopular and they were known to resort to abuse and violence in the course of realizing their loans. The high rates of interest were undoubtedly a factor in keeping loans secret, especially as there was a moneylender's act prescribing the maximum rate of interest payable.[1]

Even respectable moneylenders kept their transactions confidential. They were afraid of pressures being brought upon them to lend to all and sundry. Understandably, a man wanted to lend to those whom he considered safe. Otherwise he was likely to be pestered by poor relatives and clients for loans.

There was also a long and ingrown tradition of concealment of personal financial condition, a legacy from the politically uncertain, pre-British days when a rich man was likely to be mulcted both by the Raja and by commanders of invading troops. A rich man invested his money in land, cattle, gold and precious stones, and money-lending. He lived a simple even miserly life, cutting down his wants to a minimum except during weddings and funerals when ostentatious spending was prescribed by tradition.

All this was brought home to me in dramatic fashion when one afternoon in the summer of 1948 an old man got down from a bullock cart which stopped in front of the headman's house. He wore a narrow, almost a mini-dhoti which covered him only from waist to knee. Suspended from his neck was an ancient iron pestle and mortar to pound betel leaf and arecanut to a paste before putting it into his toothless mouth.

I was told by Lakshmana that the man was a rich moneylender from Oddur which everyone in Rampura considered backward. They wore no shorts and shirt, they travelled by bullock cart, their speech was rough and so on. The point which I would like to emphasize here, however, is that no one in Rampura who did not know the old man well would have suspected him to be rich. In the towns he would have been mistaken for a very poor villager.

It was not difficult, however, to get information from the poor about their financial condition. Through the influence of one or another friend, I was able to obtain accounts of expenses incurred

---

[1] The maximum interest permitted was 9 per cent for secured, and 12 per cent for unsecured, loans, under *The Mysore Money-Lenders' Act, 1939* (Act No. XIII of 1939), Ch. IV, Sections 14 and 15.

by a few poor men at weddings and funerals. They also talked to me about the debts they had incurred and from whom.

8 Some Failures

It is clear from the previous section that I was dissatisfied with the information I was able to collect about extra-marital sex relations and the financial activities of the richer villagers. This does not, however, mean that I was totally satisfied with my performance in other areas. Like many other fieldworkers, I have often regretted that I did not do better with the opportunities that I had. But my aim here is not to indulge (for it is nothing less than an indulgence) in breast-beating but to record a few of my more important failures in the areas where I wanted more information.

While I cannot help feeling relieved that I maintained, on the whole, good relations with the villagers during each one of my visits to Rampura, I feel that I erred on the side of caution. It did not even occur to me to do anything which might get me into trouble with the village establishment. I accepted the limitations and tried to work within them.

My respect and admiration for the villagers increased as my knowledge of village life and culture grew. I was impressed by their agricultural knowledge and skills, common sense, sense of humour, and the stoicism with which they accepted disaster which was as frequent as it was sudden. After a while I found myself talking enthusiastically about the skill involved in traditional agriculture, etc. I genuinely believed in what I was saying but I was also aware that the villagers liked to have compliments paid to them. The facility with which I said and did what was to the villagers' liking created a vague disturbance in me. Was I being a hypocrite?

The Bullock House was indeed a good place to observe the village for a variety of reasons. Gudi Street on which it was located was an important road used by many villagers, and also by people in Gudi. Everyone in Rampura and Gudi who had work in the Post Office, be it only dropping a card into the post box, had to visit the Bullock House. The daily visit of two 'Watchmen' to the Bullock House verandah also provided a source of contact with the poorer villagers. Most of all, from my verandah I had a 'ringside seat' for observing the innumerable activities which continuously went on in the headman's verandahs and on his street. Villagers who had to see the headman on some matter or other gradually developed the habit of dropping in on me before or after their work with him. My contacts with the headman and his sons, grandchildren and relatives, friends and servants were all invaluable for understanding village structure and social relations. Any study of the village which did not accord a central place to the headman would have distorted reality. He was involved in every important collective activity.

But there were also several minuses to my stay in the Bullock House. I knew that I was under continuous observation and this was responsible for my failure to develop close relations with the men whom the headman disliked. I also came to know later that many villagers avoided Gudi Street because they did not want to be seen by the headman—the popularity of the footpath behind the Bullock House was proof of this avoidance. Several young men, a few of whom had some education, avoided my part of the village because they felt that the headman had been arrogant to them. Thus Siddu, a lawyer friend of mine, was bitter about having been criticized by the headman for having dared to have his head croppeu. He came from a priestly family and the headman had asked him sarcastically if the villagers would accept *thirtha* (sanctified water) from him after he had got rid of that symbol of orthodoxy, the tuft on the crown of the head. Another educated man, who had joined the police force, complained that he had been insulted by the headman. He was at pains to convince me that he liked to visit me and talk to me but found it impossible because of my living in the Bullock House. I found both Siddu and the policeman pleasant persons and I wanted to know them much better than I did.

Even Nadu Gowda's eldest son, Swamy, experienced some reluctance in visiting the Bullock House. In fact, it was easier for me to visit him in Nadu Gowda's vacant house which he and his brothers used during the day, and it was there that I had talks with Siddu whenever he visited the village. Once Swamy offered to place his house at my disposal—it was in a different corner of the village and it would have enabled me to get to know not only those living there but everyone else who did not like to meet me in the Bullock House. It would also have brought me into closer touch with Muslims, and with many poor people. I thought long about the offer and finally rejected it as I was certain that my movement would be attributed by the village gossips to my unhappiness with the headman. In his own way, the headman had been friendly and helpful, and I appre-

ciated it, though occasionally I was made to realize the disadvantages
of staying in the Bullock House. There was also another aspect to
the matter: my movement would have placed Nadu Gowda in a false
position *vis-à-vis* the headman. The latter would have wondered
whether Nadu Gowda had not himself invited me to shift. Indeed,
I could not dismiss the possibility that Nadu Gowda, for all his
liking of me, would have been angry with me for messing up his
relations with the headman. He and the headman were friends since
their childhood. I was a bird of passage, and I should have more
sense than to upset an old and valued friendship.

I wondered whether it would be less difficult for me to stay in
Nadu Gowda's house during a second field-visit. I was already
planning such a visit. I could write to the headman explaining that
I should study the village from another base in order to get to know
better those individuals whom I could not get to know during my first
stay. But when in Oxford, I received a touching letter from the headman telling me how much everyone liked me, and that the Bullock
House would always be available for me whenever I decided to
return. And to the Bullock House I returned in the summer of 1952
to everyone's satisfaction. I realized that I was not a ruthless enough
anthropologist to sacrifice good relations for better field-work.

I have no doubt that I would have obtained a somewhat different
picture of the village from Nadu Gowda's house. The members of
Nadu Gowda's lineage, the biggest in the village, were concentrated
in the area where his houses were situated, and I was keen to know
them more intimately than I did. There was an old tradition of
rivalry between the headman's lineage and Nadu Gowda's, and in
1948, some of the bitterest critics of the headman were several young
men from Nadu Gowda's lineage. While I had pleasant relations
with these men, I did not become really close to them as they did not
like to visit me in the Bullock House. I did meet them occasionally
in the village and the knowledge that my meetings were reported
back to the headman was inhibitive of spontaneity on my side. I
would have felt freer if I had been living in Nadu Gowda's house.

Though I knew several Muslims and Harijans well, I did not know
these two sections of village society as intimately as I wanted to. I
would have obtained a new angle on the village if I had spent more
time in their areas. I must, however, add that while the Harijans
were concentrated in one compact area, the Muslims were far too
scattered. They were also factionalized.

I must also list other failures. I could never muster enough courage to watch the actual slaughter of an animal. I told myself that this was a weakness and that I should overcome it. But I never did. Once I told Siddavva, the proud owner of two goats, one of which was a magnificent billy goat, that I would take photographs of them while they were being slaughtered for the feast she was giving on the occasion of her son's wedding. I had watched the two animals for months as they often grazed in the fields near the Bullock House. The billy goat was a tall and well-built animal, with a sheen on its beautiful brown and white coat. Everyone in the village stopped to admire the animal when they saw it feeding from a hedge. I had occasionally talked to Siddavva about her animal. She was very fond of it, but she was raising it for her son's wedding dinner. She sent word to me on the day before the slaughter and I told myself that I would photograph the slaughter and watch the animals being cut up for curry. But when the morning came, I just could not bring myself to go.

However, my reluctance was only in witnessing the actual killing. Cruelty which did not involve killing did not affect me much. I remember, for instance, photographing the castration of a splendid bull calf by the village castrator, Goolayya. The method of castration was barbarous in the extreme. The poor animal was brought down by two villagers who held it down while Goolayya proceeded to place its scrotum on a wooden pestle and pound it with the rounded side of an axe-blade. The animal writhed in pain while the pounding went on. A young psychologist from Mysore was with me when I was photographing the castration and he later told me that he was horrified to find me so indifferent to the animal's pain. He said that I even exchanged pleasantries with the men while they went about their gruesome job.

There was a toddy-shop in the village—a hut under a big *hippe* (*Bassia latifolia*) tree situated where the Mysore–Hogur Road forked, one fork proceeding to Rampura and Hogur and the other to Gudi. I knew that the toddy-shop had a regular clientele from Rampura, Gudi and one or two other nearby villages. The thought of visiting it did occur to me but I dismissed it as it would have been hopelessly inconsistent with the role assigned to me in the village. Even my progressive young friends would not have understood my visiting it. It was the haunt of Harijans and other drinking castes. A few members of the higher castes did drink toddy but when they felt the urge they visited a toddy-shop in Hogur, where they were not likely to meet respectable villagers from Rampura. My young friends were not averse to the idea of visiting an urban bar with me to drink 'Western' beer or whisky, but certainly they would not patronize a local toddy-shop and drink low-status toddy.

A few villagers were given to smoking *bhang* (*Canabis indica*) regularly. These individuals were well known and roused only the pity if not the contempt of the more respectable villagers. All of them were on the downward economic slope, and in the process of losing such assets as they had inherited from their ancestors. Most villagers were acquisitive and the idea of a man liquidating his ancestral estate in drink, *bhang* and women was regarded as wicked and foolish if not impious by them. I have no doubt that the *bhang*-smokers were acutely aware of the fact that they were looked down upon by everyone.

I once attended a *bhang*-smoking session. It was in Shepherd Chikkava's house, which was close to the headman's Office House. It was a strange meeting. The men sat in a circle on their haunches on the bare cow-dunged floor. An earthen pipe held in its bowl a ball of *bhang* which was placed above a burning ember. Each man took the pipe in his cupped hands, drew a deep puff, taking care to see that his spittle did not pollute the pipe-stem, and then handed it over to the next man. Chikkava went out after each pipe for a few minutes and I was told that it was his habit to have a fried *vade* or other snack between puffs. It was believed that some smokers became ravenously hungry. But all of them remained silent throughout the session. It is possible that the silence was due to the presence of the 'respected stranger' in their midst but I am not wholly convinced by the explanation. I found the silence eerie, and was glad to get out after a while. It did not occur to me to take a puff.

Anthropologists, like other scholars, write primarily for the members of their profession, and a convention has grown in the discipline to present an impersonal account of the community studied. The profession is interested in the community and not in the relationships which the anthropologist had with its members. But then the anthropologist learns about the community through his relationships with individual members. The assumptions he makes about social relationships, his initial mistakes and the gradual diminishing of mutual bewilderment are essential steps in the anthropologist's knowledge. To leave out all this may make for economy of presentation but it also means the removal of a dimension of reality. How can one be sure that this does not subtract from the reader's understanding of the community if not distort it? At the very least there is a loss in vividness and a failure to communicate the 'feel' of social relationships in the community studied.

CHAPTER III

Three Important Men

LOOKING back upon my field experience, I cannot help thinking that three individuals, the headman, Kulle Gowda and Nadu Gowda, contributed significantly to my understanding of village life and culture. This should not, however, be taken to mean that they were the only ones to whom I am indebted. Everyone, from the very old to young boys and girls, took a hand in trying to lessen my ignorance, vast as it was. Indeed, it would not be an exaggeration to state that the entire village participated in the education of one urban adult. But the three men mentioned above, each in his own way, taught me a great deal about village life, and it would be true to say that I saw the village principally through them and their activities. Two of the three, the headman and Nadu Gowda, were rich and powerful while the third, Kulle Gowda, was neither. But all three left an indelible impression upon me, and even after twenty-six years since I first set foot in Rampura, I cannot think of the village without simultaneously thinking of those three men, each so different from the other. Since they were all crucial, I feel that I owe it to my readers to present brief sketches of them and of my relations with each one.

1 The Headman

The first thing that struck me about the headman was that he looked like one. He was tall, well and muscularly built, and his face seemed as though it had been carved out of the dark granite boulders which were dotted about the countryside. He was well past sixty in 1948 but he looked younger than his age. There was a marked absence of fat on his body and this was partly due to his perpetual activity. He gave the impression of power held in reserve, and this was enhanced by his serious mien and habitual taciturnity.

He was always simply dressed in a full-sleeved shirt without a collar, and a dhoti tied the Brahminical way with the two lower ends taken between the legs to be tucked in at the back of the waist. This mode of tying the dhoti revealed his thick white shorts which came down to his knees. The normal dress of the villager was a shirt and shorts but the headman and his friend Nadu Gowda both wore the dhoti, Brahminical style, above the shorts. The manner in which he wore the dhoti symbolized his conservatism in social and religious matters.

However, on important occasions such as the visit of the Finance Minister in the State Government, the headman donned a close-collared silk coat, a white turban with a big band of gold on it, and a gold-laced upper cloth (*uttariya*), folded several times over, one end coming down in front while the other came down at the back after going round the neck. The headman received the Minister at the decorated arch at the entrance to the village. The headman looked very distinguished, even regal, and it was difficult to believe that he was not the more distinguished of the two men who greeted each other with folded hands.

The headman was the wealthiest man in the village. The members of his household, including his widowed mother, owned about 114 acres of different kinds of land, wet, garden, and dry. The headman also managed the land of several absentee landowners, and this was also a source of profit, power and influence to him. As stated earlier, he was reputed to be a big moneylender. In fact, one of his Muslim clients, Nasar, the younger brother of Karim, spent much of his time going from village to village reminding debtors to be prompt with their payments towards the principal and interest.

The office of headman was a source of power and influence, and everyone was aware of this. It may be recalled that in 1948 the official headman of the village was Rame Gowda, the headman's eldest son. Rame Gowda put his name to all the documents, and did all the running around, but when anyone in the village referred to the headman (*patel*) he meant the father and not the son. This division also enabled each to shift the responsibility for an unpleasant decision to the other and to the bewilderment of the suppliant. I should not be surprised if the transfer of the office had been effected to keep this advantage, among others, in mind. The headman and his sons showed great sophistication in their handling of situations involving power.

The headman presided over a large and complex household which included his old mother, his second wife and her unmarried children, his two married sons by his deceased wife and their wives and children, and a maid servant who looked after his mother. He had several *jita* servants who worked in his house as well as on his estate from early morning till bedtime. His youngest son by the first wife, Bharata, lived in Mysore as an employee of the Government, and his house was really treated as an extension of the main house in the village. The headman had four sons-in-law living in nearby villages and towns, and there was frequent coming and going as was usual with affinés. There were also numerous other relatives and castefolk anyone of whom might arrive in Rampura at any moment of the day or night.

Like the other rich landowners in the village, the headman kept open house. But, as was only to be expected, he had more guests dropping in on him than the others. Any guest from Peasant or equivalent caste would be invited to take pot luck if he came at meal time. If the guest was a Brahmin or Lingayat he would be given fruit, milk or tea, and if he was particularly close or important, arrangements would be made at a Brahmin or Lingayat house for his meals. Visitors were more frequent during the summer months —it was usual for relatives in other villages to come during summer for several days' stay, and special food was cooked in their honour. They were not allowed to depart easily. The host had to press the guest to extend his stay and the guest had to produce really serious reasons why he had to return home early. The failure to exert such pressure showed a lack of hospitality and both host and guest were aware of this.

The headman played host to others as well. For instance, some time before my arrival, the Food Depot Clerk from the Peasant caste ate all his meals at the headman's house for several months. He was a bachelor, and the headman had given him a room in the Bullock House. Guests who stayed only for a few days were put up in the 'Office House' if they were not close enough to be accommodated in the Main House.

Others besides castefolk were helped by the headman. Thus, as described earlier, his Muslim client Karim and his joint family stayed in a part of the Bullock House without paying any rent. Sometime after moving into the Bullock House, I broached the subject of paying a monthly rent but the headman would not even hear of it. I tried to show my appreciation of the headman's kindness by presenting him with fruits and vegetables after each trip to Mysore. This only prompted him to make occasional gifts to me.

The management of the large and complex household called not only for considerable resources but for managerial skills. The headman lacked neither. What was even more impressive was the manner in which he had educated the members of his vast household, especially his two grown sons, in orchestrating the manifold activities in such a way that each one contributed to the growing wealth, power and influence of the household as a whole. However, occasionally, very occasionally, someone or the other struck a discordant note, but the surprise was not that this occurred but that it was not more frequent. I am not here reporting only my impression —everyone in the village admired the unity and cohesiveness of the headman's household. Only once in 1948 did discord rear its head, when Lakshmana had a quarrel with his stepmother when the headman was away visiting a son-in-law. Lakshmana, it was rumoured, had even written to his father asking for partition of the family property. Several villagers came to hear of it, and a young and intelligent man informed me that it was the first time that a 'fork' (*kavalu*) had appeared in the headman's household. The crisis passed after a while. Everyone resumed working towards increasing the resources and influence of the huge household. The juggernaut had resumed its onward march.

The efficiency and smoothness with which the innumerable activities were co-ordinated never ceased to surprise me. If Lakshmana went to one field to supervise the work that was to be done there, Rame Gowda went to another. Frequently, one or the other of them had to go to the *taluk* headquarters in Sangama or the district headquarters in Mysore for some work or the other. There were also a variety of other duties—guests and visiting officials and friends had to be looked after, weddings in Rampura and elsewhere among kinsfolk and castefolk had to be attended by at least one member of the household, and so on. The members were constantly on the move, catching buses, travelling in bullock carts, and sending baskets and letters to relatives and others.

The comings and goings increased sharply when the headman began, in 1948, to extend his interests and activities. Thus he was busy building a few houses for renting in the swiftly-expanding town of Mandya. He also acquired a site in Mysore and became the mortgagee of a house. Later, after I left Rampura, he acquired two bus lines and was planning to acquire a third. His youngest son Bharata resigned his job, and took over the management of the new enterprises. Sons and grandsons in their early teens supervised the collection of cash from passengers and gradually learnt how to prevent conductors and drivers from acting in collusion to cheat the owner. And everything continued as before, functioning without a hitch. I could not help marvelling at the machine which the headman had built. He was a superb organizer. He did not fuss or complain except for an occasional remark about the carelessness, inefficiency or corruption of employees. He drove himself hard and he thought others working for him should do the same. If they did not, it only meant that the supervision of their work was inefficient.

The headman had realized that the ultimate source of his prosperity was his land and he and his sons worked ceaselessly at the supervision of its cultivation. The land was not in one piece but in several, and each piece differed from the others in its fertility, in the kind of crops grown on it, etc. It is only fair to add here that the headman's father was also a good agriculturist, but under the headman's leadership the family agriculture reached a new level of excellence. The headman annually put in over 500 carts of farmyard manure mixed with rotting paddy husk to his fields. The family owned a long and narrow strip of land on the edge of the river Kaveri. All kinds of trees had grown on this fertile strip, and great pits were dug to store the leaves which rotted with rain to produce excellent manure which was then removed in bullock carts to different parts of the estate. The headman owned a pond in the village and during summer when it dried, the alluvium was dug up for spreading on rice-land before transplanting. Every year the Department of Agriculture in Mysore bought over 500 *khandies* (a *khandi* = 180 seers) of paddy from the headman to sell as seed to other agriculturists all over the district. The headman was alive to new techniques, new modes of cultivation, and since he was the main link in the village for the experts, the latter leaned heavily on him to popularize anything that was new. Here again he was not overwhelmed by expertise but always took care to see how it accorded with his own experience. He and his sons were aware of their leadership in agriculture and sensible experts showed them the respect that was their due.

The transfer of the official headmanship to Rame Gowda was a symbol of the headman's desire to shed as many activities as he could. He rarely went to the main part of his estate and had left the day-to-day supervision of cultivation to his sons. The headman stayed at home most of the time when he was in the village. But he was far from being inactive, let alone lazy, and his contribution to domestic agriculture and other economic activity was significant. For instance, he was up by 5 or 5.30 every morning, and he came over to the Bullock House and paced the shaded area in front of the post office while he shouted out a constant stream of instructions to the *jita* servants. (This was one of those occasions when his taciturnity left him.) The three houses where animals had been quartered, Bullock House, Cow House, and Sheep House, had to be swept, and the sweepings emptied into the huge manure pit. A thin layer of paddy husk was spread on the floor of these houses immediately after sweeping in order to catch the animals' urine and dung. Then the cows and bullocks had to be given water and straw. Later, one of the *jita* servants drove the sheep and cows to some pasture-land a couple of miles away. He returned only in the evening.

The *jita* servants had other duties as well. They had to fill an immense cauldron and other vessels in the bathroom with water from the well, and then keep a fire going in the stove. Fuel had to be used economically, and the fire started with *gobli* (*Acacia arabica*) twigs bristling with long, sharp thorns. The servants who had to drive the sheep and cows to pasture, and those who worked on the estate, were then given a breakfast of overnight *ragi* balls and a red chilli relish. But one if not two boys always remained to attend to the myriad tasks that needed to be done in the house.

The animals had to be given water and straw again in the evening. The sheep and small cows drank water out of big wooden containers while the bullocks were usually taken to the canal, tank, or the headman's Red Pond. Frequently, the stems (both green as well as dry) of *jowar* (*Holcus sorghum*) plants, and the tops of sugarcane were given to the bullocks after a servant had cut them to suitable lengths.

In short, the *jita* servants were kept busy from about 5 or 5.30 a.m. till 8 or 9 p.m., and this required constant supervision of the activities of each one of them, and it was the headman who did most of the supervising when the servants were working in and around the house. Over the years the headman had evolved a special mode of supervision which he had communicated to his sons. His voice took on, automatically, a raspy quality when talking to servants—each task would be spelled out, paying attention to any likely lapse, however slight, in its performance. The instructions were sprinkled with abuse when the headman's voice rose sharply and suddenly.

The headman's early morning instructions to servants made it unnecessary for me to have an alarm clock. Both Nachcha and I woke up to the headman giving instructions in the raspy tone reserved for them. Occasionally there was a burst of abuse including the usual obscenities. It was not the best way of being woken up. Nachcha, like every good Hindu, said a few prayers on waking up, and he found it difficult to concentrate on God and his attributes while someone outside was shouting out his intention to sleep with the bumbling servant's mother or wife. But we did not complain.

In 1948, the headman had six or seven *jita* servants, three adults and the rest boys, but they did not fully meet his need for labour. He seemed always to be in need of an extra man or two for doing all manner of odd jobs. Anyone who was walking near his house was liable to be diverted from his job to do something for him. For instance, a villager on his way to his field with a spade on his shoulder would be called by him and asked to take a tiffin-carrier of food to one of his sons who had forgotten to carry it with him. Or he might be sent to someone to borrow an additional pick-axe or spade. If the poor man protested that he was already late, he would be told that the job, whatever it was, would not take him more than a few minutes. On such occasions the rasp in the voice was replaced by honey. The poor man was being given a chance to oblige the headman—the tone and the words used suggested intimacy and affection. How could a poor villager resist such a request from the headman? The cleverer villagers anticipated being lassoed suddenly for the headman's errands and they avoided Gudi Street even though they lived near it. But they were likely to be told, 'It is so rare to see you these days. You only think of me when you want something, don't you?' The man addressed understood the message. He was avoiding the headman and the latter knew it. And when he approached the headman for a favour as he would, one day, he would be told a few home-truths.

I have mentioned earlier that one or other of the hereditary servants of the village came every morning to the headman's house to find out whose turn it was to act as watchmen that night and leave a staff in the home of each of them. It was usual for the servant to be asked to do a few other jobs besides the one he had come for. Occasionally, an old Harijan widow called Doni came up to the headman's house to take the staves and she was also given additional jobs. She complained that she was frequently asked by the women-folk to clean up the lavatory and she resented it. The Harijans in Rampura worked as agricultural labourers and never as scavengers. They were particularly sensitive about the matter as professional scavengers were regarded as occupying the lowest rung in the caste ladder.

Doni asked me once in a way for small sums of cash to buy betel leaves and arecanuts, and I would give her the money. I teased her about her love of toddy and on a few occasions I even gave her money to buy herself a drink. This gave her much pleasure, and when she saw me she folded her hands above her head in *namaskar*, to express her gratitude.

The leading Peasant households in Rampura were envious at the zeal with which servants worked for the headman. They never tired of contrasting it with the work of their own servants. They paid their servants twice the wages which the headman paid, and they treated their servants better. They should have known that it was the headman's general political and economic power which secured for him such efficient service and this was in spite of the poor wages and harsh treatment. A poor villager was often given an acre or two of the land owned or otherwise controlled by the headman, to culti-vate as tenant or sharecropper, on condition that he allowed his son or younger brother or nephew to work as *jita* servant in the headman's house for a few years. The tenancy was the real prize in such a case. Again the headman could, through the influence he had, secure for a villager a contract to repair a section of the Mysore–Hogur road, or deepen a section of one of the canals, etc.

I was friendly with the servant boys who slept on the Bullock House verandahs. I could not help watching how they were being treated and the more I watched the more I realized how wretched their condition was. One night, for instance, I found two servant boys sitting on my verandah looking woebegone, and I could not help asking them what the matter was. They replied that they had been told that no food would be served to them till they had brought enough straw from the rick for the bullocks. They had forgotten to perform this chore earlier, and the headman was angry. They were scared to remove bundles of straw from the rick in the dark as cobras were known to seek shelter in ricks. A few months ago a servant in a neighbouring village had been bitten to death by a cobra when on a similar errand. I gave the boys my lanterns, and they left at once to fetch the straw.

Later, Nachcha asked Rame Gowda whether it was safe to send the boys to the rick without a lantern. Rame Gowda replied that if one servant was bitten the others would learn to complete their jobs in time. Nachcha was horrified and begged Rame Gowda not to say such a thing even in jest. Nachcha was gentleness itself except when he was teaching.

There was a Harijan servant by the name of Ninga who had grown old in the headman's service—it was difficult to tell his age. No one knew it, including himself. He was small, thin, and had a face as sharp as an eagle's, and with an aquiline nose. Once, when Rame Gowda and I were walking on a part of the headman's land where Ninga was working, he told us that he had seen a huge python the previous evening when he was busy checking whether the supply of water to the different rice plots was adequate. (Ninga was regarded as an expert on the amount of water which rice plants needed at different stages of their growth.) The report about the python drove Rame Gowda to sudden rage, and he screamed that Ninga must have imagined it. He asked Ninga to shut up and mind his work. I later told Rame Gowda that I did not understand why he had reacted so violently to an innocent piece of news. He replied that once the servants came to learn about the python they would avoid that part of the estate which meant neglecting the crop there. His sharp reaction was calculated to nip the rumour in the bud.

The *jīta* servants were all scared of the headman though some showed it more than the others. They had signed a contract of service which was enforceable in a court of law. When a servant found conditions intolerable he tried to run away but a determined master pursued him. The master was afraid that if he did not go after the fleeing servant, he might be tempting other servants also to run away. In such a case, the master did not hesitate to complain to the police that the servant had absconded after stealing money or jewelry. He then became a suspected thief and the police had to make a serious effort to catch him. The master was spared the bother of finding and bringing him back. It also taught the other servants to behave.

When a Harijan servant of the headman objected to my photographing him (incidentally, one of the only two men who objected to having their pictures taken), I asked him why, and he replied, after much hesitation, that a photograph enabled the police to identify a runaway servant. He did not ever want to be photographed. The servant's reply gave me an idea of what he thought about his work, his hopes and his fears.

The boys also disliked *jita* service and they looked forward to the day when their terms expired. Sometimes a boy who went home for a festival showed reluctance to return and pressure had to be brought to bear on his guardian to send him back. Once I told Mariya and Dyava that the third servant boy, Muga, had very nearly got three of the headman's sheep run over by a cart. One of the two replied, 'Three sheep, that means another eight years as *jita* servant!' All the three exploded with laughter at the remark.

The headman was also able to get more out of his tenants than other landowners. He managed to obtain the best agriculturists as tenants, and as mentioned earlier, their ability to spare a younger relative for service in the headman's household was often a factor in their being awarded tenancies. A tenant was also required to contribute his labour on at least two days in the year: during summer, he was required to contribute his labour and cart to the transfer of alluvium from the tank-bed to various parts of the estate, and just before transplanting, he had to help plough rice-land. There was an acute shortage of labour during the transplanting season. Everyone felt the shortage, including the richest. The headman had made certain of one day's free labour from each of his tenants when the scarcity was at its worst. It was only one of several methods employed by him to assure himself of the labour he needed.

While other landowners collected their share of the crop immediately after the harvest, the headman's tenants were required to store his share also in their granaries till he wanted them to be produced. Generally, the price for rice was highest a month or two before harvest, and it was then that the headman preferred to sell. His tenants were required to give him his share at that time, and this meant that they were responsible for all the losses in storage: rats always managed to get at stored grain, and besides, dehydration resulted in a decrease in the quantity.

During the years when rationing prevailed, storage by tenants offered additional advantages. All private trade in foodgrains had been forbidden by the government which meant that the surplus which had not been surrendered to it under its procurement programme had to be stored, and disposed of, covertly. As a big landowner, the headman naturally attracted the officials' attention. He was entitled legally to keep only such quantities as were essential for feeding members of his household and servants, for paying labourers and artisans, and finally, for use as seed-grain at the next sowing.

In reality, however, most village landowners surrendered to the government only a portion of their surplus. Prices were much higher in the black market, and most landowners tried to sell as much as they could in it. This was not easy as officials had powers enabling them to inspect stocks of grain in granaries and rice mills which stored and milled rice under permits. Storing one's grain with one's tenants provided a way out for some landowners.

The headman's servants and tenants were so scared of him that none of them really looked him in the face while talking to him. They showed him all the symbols of respect if not self-abasement. Even those who were not servants or tenants displayed respect if not fear towards him. They did not hesitate to say things behind his back, but when they stood before him, they looked down or averted their eyes.

The headman had a clear idea of his interests, and pursued them over a long period of time. And, as I have said earlier, he had communicated both these qualities to the other members of his household, and especially to his first two sons. I could not help marvelling at the way in which he discovered a profitable use for Nachcha's spare time. In the petition which the headman, in his role as Chairman of the official panchayat of the village, presented to the Finance Minister, he had listed the village's needs which included electricity, facility to hire at a cheap rate a government-owned bulldozer and tractor, a hospital, etc. Later, I asked him why he had asked for electricity and he replied that it would enable some industries to be started locally. He was not specific about the industries, perhaps because he was afraid of my talking to others. What interested me was that he did not mention the use of electricity for lighting the home or streets or for the pleasure of listening to the radio.

In the summer of 1952, a government bulldozer was busy levelling a knoll, five acres in extent, on the headman's estate—the flattening out of the knoll enabled it to become valuable rice-land. Electricity had come to the village, and powered two rice mills. The headman's enthusiasm for electric power and the bulldozer contrasted with his feeling that a new building for a 'complete' middle school was not important, to say the least. 'A school will only teach the poor to be arrogant', he told me. Many other villagers, including the young men who were opposed to him, felt that he did not want a school because it would shut off the supply of cheap and obedient labour.

Gaining his ends was important to the headman, and if, in the process, he hurt someone or broke a rule, that could not be helped. For instance, the villager who was supplying me with milk for my morning coffee failed to appear one day, and when I met him later in the day, he did not even offer an explanation for his non-appearance. I was annoyed and told him that the least I expected from him was an explanation for his absence. After much hesitation, he came out with what had happened. He had, as usual, started for my house with the milk but on the way he had run into the headman who told him that he needed the milk for an infant in his house. The milkman was a poor relative of the headman and he dared not say 'no'. The headman did not feel any embarrassment in diverting the milk that was intended for me. Nor did he bother to tell me that he had taken the milk because an infant needed it. If this was the consideration I got from him, I could imagine how he would behave towards poor and illiterate villagers.

I once bought fifty mangoes from Chenna, a villager who had leased an orchard belonging to the headman, and he brought the basket to me with great secrecy and requested me many times not to reveal the transaction to anyone. He was afraid that the headman might infer wrongly that Chenna had had a good crop. Also, the headman ought to have been given a gift of the first fruits before they were sold to an outsider. There is a tradition in this area of presenting the first fruits to one's favourite deity or king or patron.

One night, a *jita* servant of the headman rushed over to me and asked me for my lanterns, a demand which usually upset me. Why could not the headman keep a few lanterns? But this time there was an emergency caused by the lack of supply of water to a part of the headman's estate growing rice. There was the risk that the young seedlings might die for lack of water. A party of villagers left at once, carrying my lanterns, to the C.D.S. Canal. After walking for over a mile we reached the canal lock controlling the supply of water to the affected part of the estate. Someone produced a duplicate key and two sturdy *jita* servants of the headman, one a Peasant and the other a Harijan, were able to open the rusty lock after much effort. The gush of water to the feeder channel was loudly cheered by all those present. A task had been accomplished and the parched seedlings were going to receive water in about fifteen minutes.

On another occasion, Rame Gowda narrated to me how he put in a pipe to another canal to draw much-needed water for a part of the estate which was not getting enough water for growing irrigated crops. He had applied to the irrigation department for permission and he had also met and requested the concerned officials to expedite the laying of the pipe. But, as usual, there was delay. So one afternoon he started laying the pipe on his own. But halfway through the work an inspector arrived at the estate and saw what was happening. Rame Gowda was taken aback as he had been told that the inspector would not be able to visit Rampura owing to work elsewhere. However, he was a discreet man, and knew when to turn a blind eye. Rame Gowda greeted him effusively, took him to the farm house, and had green coconuts brought down from a tree to quench his thirst. The inspector left after slaking his thirst. 'A very good man', was Rame Gowda's comment.

While the headman was an enthusiast for modern technology, he was conservative in social and religious matters—in this, perhaps, he was typical of millions of his countrymen. I have already contrasted his lack of interest in a new school building with his enthusiasm for electricity, etc. On more than one occasion he asked me whether I thought that Harijans should be admitted to temples, and when I replied in the affirmative he expressed his disagreement with me. He mentioned their eating beef as a reason for excluding them, and then added that in the case of private temples at least, the right of exclusion and inclusion should rest with the owners. He regarded the Rama temple as a private temple. (There were temples for which the government had a direct responsibility but none of the temples in Rampura were included in them.)

Every year, during summer, a big vegetarian feast (*para*) was cooked in honour of Madeshwara and Basava deities. The consecrated feast was then eaten by the villagers in the shady groves adjoining the temples. The feasts, then, were also picnics and hundreds of villagers looked forward to them. The cooking arrangements on these occasions were necessarily complicated as they had to take note of the rules governing inter-dining between castes. The Peasants cooked a gargantuan dinner for themselves and all equivalent and inferior castes. Since both the temples had Lingayat priests, the priestly families cooked another dinner for themselves and others (Traders, Smiths, etc.) who would not eat from Peasants. The Brahmins and Muslims were left out of these dinners. (The

Brahmins, however, were given the uncooked ingredients of a meal at the Rama Navami festival.)

At the feast in honour of Basava in the summer of 1948, the dinner for Lingayats was cooked by the women members of the lineage priests to the Madeshwara temple. They were very particular about the rules of purity and pollution both because they were members of a priestly lineage, and Madeshwara was a strict deity who showed his wrath to those who violated the rules of purity. As the cooking was going on, the two mistresses whom the old Basava priest had acquired a few months previously, from the 'southern country' (*tenka sime*), tried to join in and help. The acceptance of the proffered help would have meant that they were Lingayats. But the women of the Madeshwara priestly lineage had their own doubts regarding the caste of each mistress. Both of them were known to have led loose lives and their accompanying the old priest to Rampura was itself evidence of their lack of morals. The feast was going to be offered to a strict god and then eaten by orthodox Lingayats. They could not afford to offend the deity or pollute good and respected members of the caste. Sannu's mother asked the two intruders to keep out and she had her way.

A day or two later Sannu gave an account of the incident to the headman and requested him to tell the Basava priest to keep his women away on occasions such as the Madeshwara feast. If necessary, there could be two cooking units for Lingayats. The headman agreed to speak to the Basava priest.

Some time prior to the above incident I asked the headman how it was that he tolerated loose living on the part of the Basava priest. Some villagers believed that the protracted drought during the summer of 1948 was due at least partly to the priest's improper conduct, and did not the headman have a responsibility in the matter? In reply, the headman answered that Basava was none other than the Nandi bull, the animal on which Shiva rode. And the Basava priest was like the deity he worshipped: a bull which mounted any cow, not bothering whether it was mother, sister or wife.

I was taken aback by the headman's reply as he laughed only very rarely. His sense of humour showed itself in odd places, and on this occasion, his reply was even blasphemous. But the villagers treated their deities as they treated their friends and neighbours though some deities such as Madeshwara roused in them much fear.

The headman was a typical patron who intervened to protect the interests of his dependents. However, he was a somewhat fastidious patron and he expected his clients to behave properly. A client who was consistently deferential and carried out the jobs entrusted to him was praised for his loyalty (*niyat*). Karim, for instance, was such a client. It was true that there were moments when he was dissatisfied with even Karim, but, by and large, he trusted Karim and protected and helped him.

He was also a good friend though his general taciturnity and his inability to articulate his affections misled people into thinking that he was a cold man who did something only after calculating the pros and cons of a course of action. Calculation did enter into everything he did including his friendships but the important thing was that he had a few friends of whom Nadu Gowda was the closest. He liked Nadu Gowda's company, and he persuaded Nadu Gowda to accompany him not only on his pilgrimages but also on his visits to his affinés in nearby towns and villages. The two were seen together everywhere. If there was a feast in the headman's house, it was not unusual for Nadu Gowda to be invited to join in the meal. The headman himself rarely went out in the village to eat and a relative or close friend who had a special dish cooked in his house usually took it to him. His invitations were commands while the gifts given to him were tributes.

The headman was also an implacable enemy. He did not easily forgive or forget. He had power, influence and money, and he had the ability to plan his moves, keeping a long time-perspective in mind. The fact that a handful of irresponsible young men from Nadu Gowda's lineage, and their friends, had the audacity to oppose him for the elective chairmanship of the official panchayat of the village, was something he could not forget. Once, after someone had informed him that I had spent some time with these young men, he showed great anger. 'Who were they after all, and what was their standing? They are not equal to my pubic hair,' he shouted. I was reminded of the Kannada saying that an elephant becomes distraught when an ant gets lodged in its trunk.

The older villagers told me that the headman had been a model son. He never sat in his father's presence, nor did he speak unless his father asked him a question. He stood leaning against a pillar on the verandah with a towel tied round his waist, the picture of filial obedience, while his father held court.

The headman's father, who had died in 1930 (*circa*), was a mythogenic personality. He was large, far stouter than the headman and cut an impressive figure. He had a magnificent moustache with twirled ends which the older villagers regarded as a symbol of beauty as well as manliness. He was most particular about his food and water. His taste approved of the water from only one pond, about a mile away from Rampura, in the direction of Mysore. His drinking water had always to come from this pond. He was, of course, fond of mangoes. And so on.

Like a few other top landowners in this area, the headman's father had kept a victoria ('low, light four-wheeled carriage with seat for two and raised driver's seat and with falling top', *Oxford English Dictionary*). I may add here that keeping a victoria was a symbol of high status before motor cars became popular, and high officials usually kept a victoria and horse. A coachman and often another boy who worked as groom were incidental to keeping a coach. The headman's father had persuaded Karim's father to migrate to Rampura to become coachman and groom. Karim's father was provided with a house to stay in, and the crop growing on a few plots on the headman's estate was given to him as salary. Thus began a long relationship between the headman's and Karim's households.

The style of life of the headman's father was more ostentatious than that of his much richer and more frugal son. The old man was fond of shooting duck in the Big Tank, and occasionally an Englishman, most likely an official, came down to Rampura to enjoy the sport with him. The headman's mother was, however, opposed to the slaughter of these birds on religious grounds. Eventually, she had her way.

The headman's father was generous, as the older villagers were fond of repeating to me. Six acres of rice-land had been designated as *devaru gadde* (god's field) and their produce was given to the poor every year. The manner in which it was given shed light on the father's personality. When the crop was ready for cutting, he would invite the poor to assemble outside the field, and at a given signal, they all rushed in, each taking away as much as he could. The headman's father enjoyed the scramble among the contenders for a share of the crop.

Like many other rich men, the headman's father had employed a poor relative, Uddayya's father, as a servant. He was a devoted servant and his long and faithful service was rewarded by allowing him to be buried in the family graveyard on the estate. Uddayya's father had several children, but he and his grown sons lived in the headman's house. But after the headman's father's death, he told Uddayya and his brothers to move elsewhere. The headman himself was heading a large and growing family and he needed space.

The headman put an end to the domestic custom of the annual distribution of the produce of six acres among the sturdy poor. He cut down all unnecessary expenditure. The coach and horse disappeared along with other symbols of ostentatious living. He discharged all debts which were supported by documentary evidence. Everyone knew that a new master had taken over, and that he stood no nonsense. In 1948, eighteen years after the headman's father's death, the villagers contrasted the two life-styles to the headman's disadvantage. This may have been due at least partly to the villagers' tendency to glorify the past. They also admired generosity and ostentatious living in a rich man.

The headman's father was a typical village leader of the old days. In fact, he recalled the local chieftains (*palegars*) of South India, who periodically reared their heads and tried to assert their independence whenever the king or Raja showed weakness. The headman's father was, like other leaders, a staunch patron and he was opposed by other patrons both within and without the village. In Rampura, for instance, he was opposed by Nadu Gowda's father and two or three other leaders of God's House lineage, and by Melkote Sr., a Peasant leader who had acquired familiarity with the law courts and lawyers, and who used his knowledge to harass his enemies.

Fighting each other was absorbing as well as time-consuming and it left no time for the less interesting work of improving the village. But an unexpected event changed the attitude of village leaders to each other. Soon after the end of World War I, a former servant of the headman's father was alleged to have committed a triple murder in Mysore, and this created a big stir. It also brought the city police in numbers to Rampura to investigate the servant's background and history. The investigative techniques of the police produced general panic, and all the leaders decided to present a united front in the interests of everyone.

Nadu Gowda and others were of the opinion that unity resulting from common dread of the police had signalled a change in the fortunes of the village. The panchayat expressed itself against ostentatious expenditure at weddings and funerals. More attention began to be paid to agriculture. Gradually, the villagers began clearing their debts. In the early 1920s creditors from Mysore used to appear during harvest collecting a substantial share of the crop as interest on their loans but this disappeared gradually.

Nadu Gowda was the headman's senior by a few years but both of them had studied together under the same teacher in the traditional village school. They became friends but their parents, who were enemies, did not like this. They tried to discourage the boys' friendship but without success. By 1920 they were men in the prime of life, and slowly but steadily their influence increased for the good of the village.

The increased prices for agricultural products since World War II was a crucial factor in the economic betterment of the village. The introduction of rationing and controls gave rise to a black market, and everyone tried to sell as much as he could in it. Naturally, the bigger landowners were able to sell far more than the poor. Activity in the black market brought about prosperity, and provided the capital for investment in new enterprises.

The headman's father died in 1930. Rame Gowda piously recalled that a *garuda* or brahmini kite (*Haliastur indicus*), the bird which serves as the vehicle of Vishnu in Hindu mythology, settled down on a coconut tree opposite the headman's house soon after the corpse was removed to the verandah. It waited there till the corpse was bathed and dressed, and followed the cortège to the family graveyard on the estate. The brahmini kite disappeared after the corpse had been buried, and then a star came down from the sky. The heavens had witnessed to the greatness of the departed leader.

The headman's mother was alive in 1948. She was very old and had to be supported by a sturdy maid who accompanied her everywhere inside the house. The old woman was widely respected for her piety. She was undoubtedly an important factor in the scrupulousness with which festivals and other periodical rituals were performed in the headman's household, in particular the ritual of the annual *shraddha* in honour of her dead husband. It was because of her that everyone in the house had been drilled in the complicated rules of pollution and purity, and which led little children of the headman's to laugh at my indifference to those rules. The old lady also disapproved strongly of Brahmins who departed from their traditional way of life. She set the religious tone of the household.

The headman's mother was unable, in 1948, to visit personally the temples but she loved to sit and watch a religious procession from a chair on the verandah of her house. She also liked to listen to readings from the epics, Ramayana and Mahabharata. The priest of the Rama temple occasionally went to her to speak about problems which were bothering him.

The headman never once spoke to me about his mother or father. I did not ever see him fondling his children or grandchildren. In this, he was different from the other villagers who were demonstrative fathers and doting as grandfathers. It was not that he was desiccated. It was merely that he was not given to exhibiting his affection for those closest to him. The only occasion when he was visibly moved was when he had to leave his house for the hospital in Mysore to get treated for a persistent bronchial infection. Dozens of villagers went to him in his house to express their concern at his ill-health. The headman suddenly looked old and tired, and as he neared the door he turned back and saluted the pictures of the deities on the wall, and then his mother. No one said a word but everyone, including the headman, was moved to tears. He quickly got into the waiting taxi outside.

The dedication with which the headman had worked for the prosperity of his household was recognized by one and all. Even more remarkable was the devotion to the common cause which he had inspired in every other member of the household. In a household as large as the headman's, there were always forces which pulled in diverse directions. While each person worked for the household, he had also his distinctive interests which clashed with those of the others. Villagers did occasionally talk about how each member had stashed away a large amount of cash unknown to the others, and how each woman had her own economic transactions. But even the gossips agreed that the headman's household presented a remarkable instance of unity and no other household in the village could compete with it in this respect. Under his leadership, the village had climbed from poverty to prosperity, or at least that is how many villagers saw the situation. He also gave the village peace and order such as it had not experienced previously.

2 Kulle Gowda

My first 'meeting' with Kulle Gowda was odd even by Rampura standards. It was auditory and not visual, and occurred when I paid a brief visit to Rampura prior to moving in with Nachcha. It was night and I must have already lain down to sleep when I heard someone trying to talk to me from the verandah. It was not a pleasant voice but throaty and cracked. It was interrupted frequently by a vicious, phlegmy cough. I forgot the details of what the voice was saying but the trend was ominous: poor people like him (the owner of the voice) had no alternative but to live in the shelter (*ashraya*) of important men. The speaker used a high-flown Sanskritized Kannada as befitted an educated villager, and I became uneasy about what the man wanted. Was it only a small loan or was there a suggestion that I should support him during my stay in Rampura? How to say 'no' without making an enemy of him? While my mind thought about these possibilities the visitor added that he had been ill for the last several days and that was why he could not present himself before me earlier. I think I tried to take a look at him through a chink in my door. That door, like other village doors made by a local carpenter, was liberally supplied with chinks and holes, but I only saw a vague shape covered by what I inferred to be a *kambli*, one of those rough, prickly blankets woven by Shepherds. I had to postpone the pleasure of identifying the owner of that distinctive voice to a future occasion. Little did I know then that my life in the village was going to be bound up intimately with my visitor's, and that I would spend some of my time in the village and even later, thinking about him and his doings, and their impact on me. It was indeed a momentous meeting, though I had no idea of it at that time.

Considering the unfavourable impression which Kulle Gowda had made on me initially, no one was more surprised than I to find that, within a matter of a week or two, he had made himself a part of my entourage. At this distance of time I am not clear about the precise steps which led to this. But he did achieve what he had set out to do though it was not exactly clear who was living in whose shelter. The physical shelter was, however, the Bullock House and Kulle Gowda was on my verandah from morning till evening except for a brief break for his midday meal. He was so helpful to me in my work that I felt I could not carry on without him at my side. Just as I had no choice in the selection of where I lived in the village, I had no choice about who I wanted to assist me in my work. Kulle Gowda had selected himself and joined me.

Kulle Gowda's appearance was as, or perhaps even more, unprepossessing than his voice. He was a small and emaciated man and he had a pronounced stoop. His face was lined like a walnut kernel, and he was bald everywhere except for a narrow crescent of hair beginning from either ear, and a few tiny wisps in front. He also had a prominent, bulbous nose, and when he wore his workaday spectacles, he looked like a studious gnome. He dressed in a dirty shirt and a dirty dhoti, and I can picture him even now, walking from his house to mine, carrying one of the front ends of his dhoti in one hand, his bald pate shining in the sun.

It may be inferred from the foregoing that Kulle Gowda was totally indifferent about his appearance. This was true, however, only within the village. If he wanted to go out to Mysore, or when he had to meet an important visitor, he transformed himself. The perpetual stubble on that lined face would be removed by the Barber, and then Kulle Gowda would have a hot bath, cleaning himself with soap. (Incidentally, Kulle Gowda had a safety razor which he no longer used—like other villagers he was entirely dependent upon the Barber.) He donned a white *jubba*, wrapped a dhoti of fine mull around his waist and legs, and a white upper cloth, folded many times over along its length, was thrown over his shoulder. His ordinary spectacles gave way to gold-rimmed ones.

The first occasion I saw Kulle Gowda transform himself was during the Minister's visit, and I could not help thinking that he looked like a sophisticated village politician who stood out from the others. He was so vain that, after his transformation, he came and stood on my verandah waiting for us to comment on his appearance. Rame Gowda said, 'Look at the Colonel, how can anyone miss him?' Kulle Gowda's walnut face broke into a grin and he said, 'What kind of a Colonel? I don't have even three pice in my pocket for *bidis*.' I discovered that he liked to be called 'Colonel' (pronounced 'kurnallu') by the headman's sons. Whenever they wanted him to do anything they called him Colonel before mentioning the work —draft a petition, or build a *mantap* for taking out an icon in procession, or something else. Kulle Gowda, who was all guile in many matters, succumbed to flattery like a child.

There was a photograph of Kulle Gowda, framed and hung on the wall, of which he was very proud. It was taken before time had wrought its havoc on his face—it was unlined and adorned by a Charlie Chaplin moustache. The face was crowned by an ample, gold-laced turban, and below the neck was a Western jacket and tie. If the visitor said that he did not know whose photograph it was,

Kulle Gowda felt highly complimented. It was a memento from the world of his vanished youth, money and status.

One of the first things I wanted to do in the village was to collect genealogies covering everyone living there. Information regarding landownership was vital for me but I decided to try and collect it only after I had established myself. I also wanted to carry out a census of households and find out the interrelationship between residents in each, but even that I wanted to attempt after making sure that I was not unwelcome. I mentioned my intention to my friends and I was told that there was already a list of households in the village. Why did I not get the 'H. S. Lists'? I was asked. The Harvest Scheme Lists were prepared as part of the rationing system introduced during World War II. In order to enforce rationing of essential foodgrains the surplus had to be collected from the growers and distributed among the non-agricultural population as well as agriculturists who did not grow enough. The foodgrains were procured immediately after the harvest at rates prescribed by the government. The implementation of the programme made it necessary to divide the rural population into three categories, viz., those who grew more than their needs, those who grew just enough, and others who either grew less than their needs or, like landless labourers, did not grow any grain at all. The surplus was calculated after deducting the quantity of grain needed for feeding the members of the household, for seed purposes, and finally, paying artisans, members of the servicing castes, and labourers. The household included servants, if any, for calculating the amount of grain needed. Each villager was regarded as a manual worker, and he was entitled to receive twice the quantity allotted to a non-manual worker while a child counted as half. The H. S. Lists would not only tell me about the composition of households but give me an idea of the economic position of the landed families in the village.

I approached the Accountant whose duty it was to compile the H. S. Lists. In 1948, the Village Accountant was Bhatta, a native of Hogur, who came to Rampura only when he had work. Bhatta was the *purohit* or domestic priest of Rampura, and this meant that he had to officiate at the weddings of high caste villagers excluding Lingayats. The chaplaincy of over 65 villages around Hogur was hereditary in Bhatta's lineage, and Bhatta and his brothers and cousins had divided the villages among themselves very much as the descendants of a landowner divided ancestral land. Bhatta also owned a certain amount of land in Rampura. Bhatta was regarded as well off, with income from his priestly duties, his land, and the interest he got on the money he had lent to people. It was in view of his old connections with Rampura that he had been given the Accountantship of the village. The hereditary office of Accountant, however, belonged to another lineage which had long ago left Rampura. But a scion of this lineage came to Rampura in 1949 and successfully reclaimed his office. At that time, there was a discussion in political circles that hereditary offices should be abolished, and the posts of headman and accountant be filled like other government jobs on the basis of competition among qualified candidates.

It was not easy to meet Bhatta. He was a busy man, and his comings and goings were uncertain. I had to bring pressure to bear on him through the headman to lend me his registers including the H. S. Lists. When I looked at the slim volume on which was written H. S. Lists, I recognized Kulle Gowda's handwriting. Perhaps Kulle Gowda had prepared it at the instance of the headman. And characteristically, he had obliged a number of people in the process of preparing the list. He had included casual visitors, temporary relatives, and sometimes had even given a servant or two to some households in the village in order that they might keep to themselves a greater share of the crop grown. Every landowner wanted to surrender to the government as little as he could in view of the high rates obtaining in the black market. Kulle Gowda sympathized with this desire especially when he got a tip for his efforts. But he could also be honest in the cause of science: he told me that he knew where exactly he had inflated the lists. He would prepare for me a 'purified' (*shuddhimadida*) list in which he would weed out all fictitious servants and temporary visitors. I went through the volume with him and he was able to point out who were the genuine members and who the fictitious ones. I marvelled at the intimacy of Kulle Gowda's knowledge of the village. He also brought the lists demographically up to date by removing persons who had died since the compilation, and by adding those who had been born since.

Kulle Gowda was also helpful in the collection of genealogies. My idea was that I should go to everybody's house and record their genealogy. But things worked out differently. Villagers walking on Gudi and Patel streets, and those who visited the post office were commandeered by Nadu Gowda and Kulle Gowda to step onto my verandah to give me the information I wanted. Several others were sent for. I had to visit homes only in a small number of cases.

I must not fail to mention here that the collection of genealogies proved to be a popular pastime. When passers-by saw me pumping an informant for the names of his various relatives, they stopped to watch the fun. Sometimes they were able to prompt the informant if not even correct him. Arguments developed occasionally about the name of a particular relative, and sometimes about such a matter as whether he was the third or fourth child of his parents. I was surprised to find that several villagers did not even know the names of their own children—it was usual to address children by their pet names or nicknames and this occasionally meant that their formal names were forgotten. As I went about my job I noticed that villagers got some fun out of the game of collecting genealogies. I am certain that the news of my collecting the genealogies of villagers spread not only to everyone in the village but to others in neighbouring villages, and I think it helped in making people become accustomed to my role as a collector of information about old customs and beliefs. Perhaps even more important was the fact that I was making friends in the process of collecting information and it is a pity that this fact does not find mention in textbooks on research methods. I am certain that these early encounters with villagers paved the way for later inquiries into areas of life which were sensitive.

Kulle Gowda was with me when I was recording the genealogies, and he also accompanied me on my visits to everyone in the village in the course of my collection of information regarding household composition, occupation, education and literacy, etc. He was extremely well-informed about a great many people, and I was surprised to find that his knowledge was not confined to members of a particular caste or class, or to his neighbours. The work he had done to compile the H. S. Lists, and his popularity as a scribe were both factors contributing to that knowledge. Even more remarkable was the ease with which he communicated with all kinds of people, especially the poor, women, and little boys and girls. He would stand near the front door, or on the street and shout for the owner. If he was not in, and his wife or mother came out, he would ask gruffly, 'Where is that no-good husband (son) of yours?' If the unfortunate woman replied, 'work', he countered it with a string of profanities expressing his disbelief and this rarely failed to bring out a smile or grin. If he did not think that the woman was able to give us the information we wanted, he would instruct her to ensure that her husband stayed home in the evening, or came to my verandah. During these visits he asked several villagers a question about an application or letter or other transaction which was of importance to them. If anyone replied that something had not been done, he asked them to see him in a day or two. He would speak to X or Y, or send a reminder to an official. He said all this with authority and conviction, and the man's demeanour showed that he appreciated the favour that was being done to him.

Usually Kulle Gowda caught me when I was performing my ablutions. He got up early like all villagers, and was in my house as soon as he saw that the headman had gone home after supervising the servants' work. Kulle Gowda had the villagers' readiness to participate in social life immediately on waking up. If I was having a bath, he would ask me from outside the bamboo screens, 'Are you having a bath?' If I was shaving, the question frequently was, 'Aren't you tired of scraping the chin every morning?' Or, 'I suppose you like a smooth cheek'. Worse, if I had just returned from a trip to the ficus tree, 'Had you been to the backyard? Aren't you somewhat late today?'

The only peace I had was when I was having my breakfast. When my kitchen door was three-fourths shut—total shutting meant darkness—my visitors understood that I wanted to be left alone. Even this was not always successful. And Kulle Gowda had his own technique for annoying me. He would stand in the verandah outside the kitchen and shout at Nachcha: 'It is already late. Please open the door of your room so that I can take out the registers, stationery and the writing desk.' Nachcha had to go out and give the things Kulle Gowda had asked for. Kulle Gowda would comment on the dust on the verandah and ask Nachcha to sweep it before spreading the mat on it. Kulle Gowda's voice went up as he talked—he wanted everyone, including me, to know that he was anxious about *my* work. Nachcha returned to the kitchen, complaining that Kulle Gowda was bossy and rude.

But Kulle Gowda's voice and the manner of talk changed a little later when Nachcha gave him breakfast. Kulle Gowda usually had breakfast and tiffin (afternoon snack and coffee) in the Bullock House. I don't know how this had come about but as soon as I came to the verandah after breakfast or tiffin, Kulle Gowda went in and had his, sitting outside the kitchen. He then exchanged pleasantries with Nachcha and complimented him upon his cooking.

When he finally returned to the outer verandah he would tell me, 'There is a lot of work to be done. At this rate I don't know when we are going to finish.'

Kulle Gowda liked to write. The act of writing gave him an aesthetic delight. He asked me for special stationery for copying the information in the big land register that I had borrowed from the Accountant. I got him red and blue ink, and hard-bound notebooks which were lined, and Kulle Gowda loved devising various columns in red ink. He then proceeded to fill the pages with information in a small, rounded hand which was more decorative than clear. He obtained much satisfaction from filling a page with his writing. He worked with concentration, and he had a sense of tidiness when it came to writing. He liked to have one or two spectators while he was working and their appreciation was a tonic to him. He frequently asked me for my opinion and I had to turn aside from whatever I was doing and admire his handiwork. He demanded attention and praise.

As he was copying the land records, he instructed me about the meanings of the various columns, and the difference between the information in the different registers which each accountant was required to keep. As important, was the information he passed on to me about individual landowners. For instance, such-and-such a landowner had partitioned his land among his sons, but this had not been recorded in the register. I would ask him the reason for the discrepancy and he would explain that the mere act of partition was not enough. It had to be followed by an application to the government requesting that the partition be recorded, and that the new owners of the fragmented shares each be supplied with a title deed (*patta*) to their land. This resulted in a single survey number being split among the heirs. Thus, for instance, survey number 323 was divided among the three heirs into 323-1, 323-2, and 323-3.

The partition of land or its sale had to be entered in the accountant's registers. Such entries were regarded as evidence in courts of law. The accountant was usually paid a fee for entering the information. Failure to pay meant delay in entering it. Sometimes, when a powerful person was involved and he brought pressure on the accountant to withhold recording a piece of information, the latter delayed as long as he could. Very occasionally the accountant suppressed his knowledge of the fact that a powerful landowner was growing an irrigated crop on what was officially dry land. The landowner was stealing the water from a canal without paying the fee for conversion and the higher tax on irrigated land. All this became clear to me as I watched Kulle Gowda. Sometimes I did the copying myself asking questions of Kulle Gowda as I went along. After a while I found that the registers made sense to me. This gave me satisfaction and my friends complimented me upon my intelligence.

But once I knew what was in the registers, I was content to leave the mechanical work of copying to Kulle Gowda who continued his job on the verandah, to the admiration of one or two people who were always watching him, while I went out of the house with my camera and notebook to meet someone in the village with whom I had an appointment for the day. My morning and evening rounds in the village were indispensable to me, to keep track of the various things that were going on. Occasionally, Kulle Gowda would comment sarcastically, 'So, you are going out, are you, to talk to your friends while I sit here and wear my eyes and fingers out?' I usually countered it with a crack at his love of red and blue ink. But sometimes I found it irritating: he was certain to make a big fuss when visitors were present. He wanted everyone to know that *he* was doing the work.

It was not only in calligraphy that Kulle Gowda's artistic impulse expressed itself. He was skilled with his hands, and he enjoyed a local reputation for the beauty of *mantaps* he made and decorated. A *mantap* was a shrine-like structure made with split bamboo and cloth or cardboard, and decorated with intricate designs cut out from papers of various colours. Icons were carried in *mantaps* on ritual occasions, and the richer landowners got *mantaps* made at weddings to seat the bride and groom.

When Kulle Gowda was requested to make a *mantap*, he threw himself into the task with enthusiasm and energy spending long hours over it. I was puzzled by his zeal especially as I knew that he was not going to be paid for his labours. The man who had commissioned him to make the *mantap* would be lavish with praise and that was what Kulle Gowda wanted most. He also enjoyed a sense of importance such a commission brought him—several people asked him about the progress of the *mantap* and he liked nothing better than talking about the problems which he was facing and the amount of time it was eating up. He had so many important things to do and he was not able to attend to them because of the *mantap*.

Kulle Gowda was indispensable for any drama that was put on

in the village. He was then busy making cardboard crowns, and bows and arrows with split bamboo and string, and improvising the many articles needed for the mythological characters figuring in the play. He also helped in make up. During his Mysore days, Kulle Gowda had witnessed many plays put on by the companies there and he told me more than once that he had written several plays all based on some story taken from one or other of the two epics. Once or twice he told me that he had been up all night writing or finishing a particular play, but he did not show me the manuscript. I did not ask him to show it either.

Kulle Gowda also claimed proficiency in another traditional art, the reading of the Mahabharata epic. Kannada versions of both the Ramayana and Mahabharata exist. The poignant moments in each epic were brought home to rural audiences in such readings and in words which they had heard since childhood. Besides, listening to such readings was not only entertainment but productive of religious merit. The elderly and the orthodox made it a point to attend them.

Sometime in the summer of 1948 there arrived in Rampura a visitor, Kuder, who claimed to have been, in his younger and slimmer days, an actor in the Chamundeshwari Nataka Company, a dramatic troupe in Mysore. He had retired from the stage and was living in his natal village twenty miles or so to the southwest of Mysore city. He went to the headman's house, and after a while I was asked to join the group on the headman's verandah. We talked about the dramas staged by his company and the well-known actors of the old days; everyone present enjoyed the collective reminiscing. In the course of the talk it turned out that Kuder had had some training in the art of reading the epic Mahabharata (or Bharata as it is usually referred to). The headman requested Kuder to read an incident from the epic, adding that it would give great pleasure to his old mother. Kuder agreed readily. But he was going to do it later in the day, after the sun had gone down a little.

Several villagers assembled for the late afternoon reading. The headman's mother, if I remember right, sat in a chair placed on the street, before the main house door, while her sturdy and dark maid stood at her side. Kuder read sonorously in a bass voice, and everyone enjoyed the reading.

When Kulle Gowda found all of us praising Kuder's voice and the sincere feeling which he had brought to the reading he decided to give a demonstration of his skill. He did it a day or two later. The contrast between the two could not have been sharper. Kulle Gowda's throat had been subjected to continuous ill-treatment since he was a boy of ten or twelve when he started smoking *bidis*. His voice was cracked, and even normally he had to leave my verandah several times a day to spit out blobs of phlegm into the gutter outside. No sooner had he started reading the verses than a vicious cough broke out and it took time to subside. Then he discovered that he was not the master of his voice. He would begin a verse at a particular pitch, and suddenly, after a minute or two, it would degenerate into a squeak. He made all kinds of noises in his throat in an effort to control his voice, but there was rebellion inside as soon as he started reading. Altogether, it was a disaster, and Kulle Gowda was forced to recognize that his Bharata-reading days, like several other things, had ended long ago.

Those who knew Kulle Gowda well said that very few in the village could cut grass with his skill. I wondered how grass-cutting could call for skill, and one day Kulle Gowda showed me how. The patch where he had cut grass with the sickle was smooth but where the others had, was uneven, with clumps sticking out. It was obvious that Kulle Gowda was more dextrous than the others.

Kulle Gowda was interested not only in mastering traditional skills but in modern ones involving machines. It was this which led to his learning, in the late 1920s, how to ride a cycle. He proudly recalled that he was the first in Rampura to own a cycle. Again, he was one of the first in the village to own and operate a primus stove. He also knew how to sew on a sewing machine.

Kulle Gowda differed from most other villagers in his lack of interest in agriculture and acquiring land. In fact, he had been steadily mortgaging or selling bits and pieces of ancestral land instead of trying to add to it like the others. During the years he spent studying in Mysore, he had acquired urban tastes which the older villagers considered unnecessary and wasteful if not wrong. He liked going to restaurants, cinemas and plays. He was friendly with a rich and younger Peasant from a neighbouring village who had liquidated his sizeable fortune to indulge in his love of women, liquor and gambling. In 1948, however, I did not see Kulle Gowda showing any great liking for gambling and liquor, but those who had known him longer were of the opinion that I was only witnessing a fire which was on its way out. He had been a gay bird in his younger days and there was no doubt about it. As the villagers expressed it, 'He had played a great deal' (*bahala āta ādidavaru*).

On the subject of women, however, Kulle Gowda himself told me that he had seen many women, and that after visiting a harlot in Rampura he had an excruciating attack of VD. He gave me a vivid and technicolour account of it and the long and painful treatment he had to undergo.

Parting with ancestral land was a serious matter under any circumstances, and selling or mortgaging it to indulge in one's taste for women, gambling and liquor was regarded as a heinous offence against those closest to the wrong-doer. Respectable village opinion had turned against Kulle Gowda. His father and younger brother had given him up as a lost cause long ago, and their problem was to contain him and minimize the damage he could still cause to his family. To make matters worse, Kulle Gowda was the eldest son, and in the village context, the eldest son had frequently to take on the role of the father on the latter's death. Instead of doing that, Kulle Gowda had become the axe busily hacking away at the trunk of the family tree.

The ancestral land and house had to be divided between the father and Kulle Gowda and his younger brother, Chadi, but this gave Kulle Gowda freedom to borrow money on his share of the land. His father and Chadi alerted Kulle Gowda's sons to what their father was doing and they persuaded them to press for the division of the property he had inherited. They succeeded, and a year or two prior to my arrival in Rampura, Kulle Gowda's property had been divided among his four sons by the first wife, who was no more, and his second wife. The first three sons took their shares while the fourth who was only fifteen or sixteen did not. Kulle Gowda was managing, if that is indeed the word for what he was doing, his wife's and youngest son's shares. The boy Rami was a good agriculturist, and he did all the work on his and his stepmother's land leaving Kulle Gowda free to do what he liked with his time.

Even when he was a student in Mysore Kulle Gowda had started playing the role of a 'broker', a broker between the villagers and shopmen in Mysore. He was entrusted with buying saris and jewelry by villagers who were celebrating weddings and he usually managed to collect a commission. But the villagers did not know about it. And as, over the years, his fortunes declined, he was forced to do a number of things to obtain such small sums of cash of which he was in need perennially: he accompanied villagers to Mysore not only when they shopped for a wedding but when they needed the services of a lawyer or doctor, or wanted to meet an official to get something done.

He was performing such services even in 1948. Thus when one of his daughters-in-law was ill he admitted her to a nursing home in Mysore while he stayed in a nearby hotel. To be fair to him, however, he did not try to collect any commission from her. Indeed, he was not then in need of a commission. He had just sold his jaggery cubes, and the cash was burning in his pockets. During this trip he did himself well visiting restaurants, cinemas, and a Western-style hotel where he had chicken and beer. He returned to Rampura when his pockets were empty. As a villager put it, when he had cash he went to Mysore and had a good time, and when he did not have any, he sat on his verandah wrapped up in his blanket.

On another occasion he accompanied a poor villager from Gudi, and a few others from Rampura, all of whom had to go to Nanjangud. The Gudi man had land near the Madeshwara temple and the government wanted to acquire it to provide a burial ground for Muslims. But the owner did not want his land to be acquired, and Kulle Gowda offered to take him to an official who he thought had the power to cancel the acquisition. Kulle Gowda said he had made certain of the cancellation by bribing a clerk with twenty rupees. It is not known whether he actually bribed a clerk, and if he did, whether he paid twenty rupees or less.

Kulle Gowda made another trip to Mysore, this time to persuade a lawyer who owned dry land near Gudi to lease it out to someone from that village. No doubt the latter had to pay the expenses of the trip which in all probability included a visit to one of his favourite eating places.

Either in the summer of 1952 or 1954, Kulle Gowda presented himself in my house in Mysore accompanied by a boy in his teens. Needless to say, I was surprised to see my old friend and after we had spent some time exchanging courtesies and information, Kulle Gowda asked the boy to go out for a few minutes. He then asked me whether my eldest brother was in Mysore. I said 'Yes'. Kulle Gowda then proceeded to explain that the boy was poor, and came from a good family. He had appeared for some university examination and had done well in all subjects excepting English. Kulle Gowda had come to know that my brother was marking his answer script. Would I recommend the unfortunate boy's case? Kulle Gowda took care to add that the boy was a Brahmin. I was about to embark on a discourse on the ethical implications of his request when I realized that he would only interpret it to mean that I lacked sympathy for the poor boy, and ignored the plea of a friend. I took a cowardly way out. I went inside the house for a while and returned to Kulle Gowda to tell him that he had been misinformed. That boy's script had not come to my brother.

Kulle Gowda's freedom from scruples was widely recognized as extraordinary. For instance, he had held, for a few months only, in 1946 and 1947, the post of food depot clerk and this required him to be responsible for the rice which the government collected in Rampura under its procurement programme. The rice was measured into gunny-sacks which were then sewn and stored in the rooms in the Bullock House. Each sack held a hundred seers of paddy, and it was Kulle Gowda's duty to check his stock frequently to make sure it was all right. No one else had keys to the rooms in which the sacks were stored. When the time came to move the sacks to a mill, it was discovered that they held much less than what they should have. Kulle Gowda blamed the rats for the loss. He was told that his sacks held too little even after allowing for the rats. When this happened more than once, he was relieved of his job.

But what was surprising was that he again managed to become depot clerk in 1950 in Millayya's mill. And he even improved upon his past record as depot clerk. Sannu told me that Kulle Gowda was transferred to another village after he was found short by a few hundred bags. But he continued his depredations in the new village also. He was dismissed and narrowly escaped being prosecuted for his misdeeds.

Living as he did, Kulle Gowda was frequently struck by disaster but he had enormous resilience. A few days of sitting on the verandah, wrapped in his blanket (or a dirty cotton sheet in the hot weather), and then he was back in business. He was also capable of altering the scale of his operations. If he could not make a few hundred rupees in a single operation he turned to the steadier occupation of earning a rupee or two writing a sale, partition or marriage settlement deed. But the writing of the deed gave him valuable information which his extraordinary sensitivity to possibilities and his knowledge of the villagers and the intermeshing of their interests, enabled him to extract a few more rupees, and maybe also a trip to Mysore. Kulle Gowda was acutely aware of the serendipitous effects of his activities as scribe. He was not above telling a party that he had added or omitted a particular fact of which he could later take advantage in a court of law.

Kulle Gowda's ability to perceive an advantage to himself in all kinds of unlikely places and among all persons once moved the headman to remark, with admiration as well as exasperation, 'He has sensed a crack [in someone's affairs] and moved in.' Once Kulle Gowda and I were walking near the Pattabhi pond when we saw the Muslim tailor, Mamusil, bathing in it after washing his clothes. It was Friday, and the tailor was preparing himself for his evening visit to the mosque. At once Kulle Gowda informed Mamusil that the Revenue Inspector was visiting Rampura on the following day. If it was true Kulle Gowda had not mentioned it to me and I wondered why he had chosen to convey it to Mamusil. I got my answer sooner than expected. Mamusil asked, 'Do you think I will be allotted a site?' Apparently there had been some local talk about officials visiting Rampura to allot house sites on land near the Madeshwara temple. Kulle Gowda: 'Yes. It is only for people like you. Not for the well-to-do.' Mamusil: 'Supposing they say that you are living in your father-in-law's house?' Mamusil lived with his father-in-law, an old man who was considered well off as he had land and a house. Kulle Gowda: 'That argument will not work. ... I have a jacket, a tweed one, and it needs to be repaired.' Mamusil: 'If it is woollen, you should take it to a city tailor. I can't do it.' Kulle Gowda: 'Didn't you learn how to sew woollen clothes?' Mamusil: 'I did, but I have forgotten. ... That site, you must somehow get it for me.' Kulle Gowda: 'I will come later with the jacket. See if you can do it.' Mamusil: 'I don't think I can. But please remember the site.'

Kulle Gowda's habit of making promises which he had very little intention of keeping, of utilizing every opportunity to make a few rupees for himself even if in the process he caused loss and worry to others, and his earlier uninhibited sex life, had all given him an unenviable reputation. The headman's sons warned me several times about the need to be on the alert in my relations with him. They cited several instances of his disregard for truth and his eye only for immediate gain. They expressed their horror at finding him calmly telling people whom he had met at a wedding in Kannambadi that he had a B.A. degree, and was employed as an official in the government. Worse, he had even told people that he was a member of the headman's lineage. He was related to the headman through his (Kulle Gowda's) mother but that did not make him a member of the headman's lineage. To me, both these instances appeared to be harmless boasting but the headman's sons saw them differently. According to them, if Kulle Gowda found that his audience accepted his stories as true, he was certain to exploit the fact to his advantage. He might attempt to borrow money on the strength of a mythical government job or equally mythical membership of the headman's lineage. The latter could give rise to other complications also and therefore his claim had to be nipped in the bud.

The headman warned me during the first few days of my moving in not to lend money to Kulle Gowda or to invite him to my house in Mysore. I was successful only with regard to the former. It was not difficult for me to regard all the payments I made him as money earned by him, or gift. Indeed, I wanted to pay a monthly salary to him as long as I was in Rampura. But Kulle Gowda was incapable of waiting for thirty days between two payments whatever the size of the payments. Money burned in his pockets. He could not rest till he had run through the cash he had come by. A restlessness possessed him and he thought of some excuse to catch a bus to Mysore. When he came back, his pockets were empty. Sometimes he brought sweets or some fried savouries for his wife and young children. He was for a good time, and he did not fret about the morrow.

When the cash with him was not enough for a visit to the city, Kulle Gowda rested content with sending one of his sons to buy a sitting hen in Edagai. He had the reputation of being a good cook and he liked cooking. One of his favourite dishes was fried chicken.

I had to conceal the money I paid Kulle Gowda from the headman and his sons. They thought I was hopelessly extravagant and advised me to pay what they thought was a sufficient wage. My problem was made more difficult by Kulle Gowda's tendency to exaggerate, many times over, the sums I paid him.

My reasons for wanting to keep Kulle Gowda away from my house in Mysore were different from those of the headman. First, I had no intention of inflicting my problems upon my people, and my experience of Kulle Gowda's adhesive qualities had convinced me that if I once let him in, my people would find it impossible to shake him off. But he did find his way to my house in Mysore once when I was not there. He was naturally received as my friend, and allowed to leave only after he had had his lunch. When we met in the village, a day or two later, Kulle Gowda took me to task for not being at home when he had called on me (unannounced), but added that my people had been extremely friendly and hospitable. I thought that his compliment to my people contained an unspoken criticism of my own behaviour but I may have imagined a slight where none was intended. Anyway, I let the remark pass, and then he tried to subject me to a long questionnaire on each resident of my house. I discovered a few days later that all my village friends had been informed about his visit to Mysore, and given descriptions of each member of the joint family and what they were doing. He must also have emphasized their friendliness and how much they had all liked him. They once again told me not to encourage him to visit my house.

During the latter part of my stay in Rampura, Kulle Gowda was under pressure from his youngest son, Rami, to give him his share of the land and house. As I said earlier, Rami was cultivating his as well as his stepmother's land. The boy worked hard and had the reputation of being a good agriculturist. He had grown sugarcane on a part of the land, and this was harvested, made into jaggery cubes and then sold to a middleman who specialized in jaggery trade. Unfortunately there had been a sudden and steep slump in jaggery prices in 1948, and the profits were low. But the moment Kulle Gowda received the money for jaggery he discovered an excuse to visit Mysore and returned only after he had run through it. This annoyed all his relatives—I remember his brother Chadi telling me that while he had to go to the rice land to look after the water supply his brother was enjoying himself in the city.

About this time, Kulle Gowda befriended the owner of the Brahmin teashop who was looking about for accommodation for his wife and two or three children. The man had been living alone for several months and he was anxious that his family join him. Despairing of finding a whole house for himself and his family, he was prepared to settle for a couple of rooms. Kulle Gowda stepped in to play the good samaritan. He offered the teashop man a room on his front verandah and the offer was gratefully accepted. And one day the wife and children arrived by bus with their bundles, steel trunks and baskets, and the entire family walked up Gudi Street with the father leading the procession. Everyone came out to the verandahs to stare at the new arrivals. Their entry into Kulle Gowda's house was noticed and doubtless commented upon. Characteristically, Kulle Gowda had not informed anyone in his house about the offer of his room to the teashop man, and this made his relatives and friends even more suspicious than usual about his motives. The house, though big, had many people living in it, and could not take in any more, especially strangers. Why had Kulle Gowda done this? Certainly not for money, as the teashop man was barely able to make a living. No one would believe that he had been moved by motives of kindness and generosity. Kulle Gowda's father, and Chadi, advised Rami to demand his share of the property immediately. Chadi harassed Kulle Gowda's wife by not allowing her to use the back door giving her access to the backyard. Kulle Gowda's wife could not have been enthusiastic about her husband's new tenants, especially as their arrival had not been announced and made everyone angry.

Kulle Gowda was upset by all this. He told me that he had not spoken to his father for over twenty years. His father had never liked him and the old man was now goading Rami to take his share away. Chadi was making things difficult in the house. One of Kulle Gowda's older sons had contracted VD while on a visit to Mysore and Kulle Gowda had to have him treated as his consummation ceremony (*osage*) was approaching. Kulle Gowda's eldest son, who was unmarried, was also a problem. The eldest son was not living with Kulle Gowda and he walked about everywhere looking preoccupied, and with only a pair of yellow shorts on. He had already borrowed money on his land. To cap it all, Kulle Gowda was finding his tenants dirty and noisy.

Kulle Gowda's wife was several years younger than him. She came from a landowning Peasant family in Harigolu, a village across the Kaveri. She was young, well-built and comely, a thorough contrast to her emaciated and shrunken husband. A few villagers felt that Kulle Gowda should have followed his younger brother Chadi's example and not married after becoming a widower. Villagers were broad-minded enough to be tolerant of liaisons which did not give rise to the complications which marriage did. The latter would have been wiser in view of Kulle Gowda's age, health, and lack of money.

Kulle Gowda was proud of his wife, of her background, looks and culinary skill. He once invited me to his house to meet her. She was stocky and short with high cheekbones, and was dressed in an orange-coloured silk sari with black and red checks, the kind favoured by richer village women for special occasions. She appeared for a brief minute only and then disappeared inside, no doubt overcome by shyness. Incidentally, he was the only villager to be urbanized enough to introduce me to his wife.

Kulle Gowda was an indulgent father to his little children. In 1948, his daughter was four or five years old, and she clung to her father who spoiled her by taking her, whenever he had cash, to the teashop or to a grocery shop where he bought her fried snacks. Four years later, when I revisited Rampura, her place had been taken by a small boy, Kulle Gowda's son. The boy had his mother's high cheek bones and a pug nose, resembling a bulldog. He had only a shirt on and he followed his father everywhere. He was also encouraged to buy snacks from the teashops whenever the father had cash. Kulle Gowda was one of the very few in the village to encourage his children to visit teashops. In fact, the other villagers had strong feelings about letting children spend cash to buy eatables made outside the home. All money given to them had to be put away in a box or pot, and when the sum became large enough, it was invested in a loan or a nanny-goat or ewe. They were taught to be petty capitalists from a tiny age.

When I left Rampura, I had the feeling that his many troubles were closing in on Kulle Gowda, but, as I said before, nothing could keep him depressed for long. He was always planning, scheming and plotting, and the aim of all that cogitation was to earn a few rupees the easy way. If in the process of earning the money he visited a town and restaurant, and met a few new people, life seemed a little more worth living.

Kulle Gowda informed me that, after I left the village, he would undertake on his own a survey of Gudi, the small village next door to Rampura, and I encouraged him. I told him I would pay the expenses, and even try to get his survey published somewhere. I knew that he had the ability and capacity for hard work to undertake a survey. I had become fond of him and I wanted to do him a good turn. Maybe if he did a survey, I could get him a regular job somewhere as collector of data.

But once I left the village, the idea of doing a survey of Gudi receded into the background. He was preoccupied with the day-to-day problem of raising petty cash. But he was there to welcome me effusively when I returned to Rampura in the summer of 1952. His walnut face split into a wide grin of welcome and he said, 'So you have come at last. Why didn't you write? How long are you going to stay this time? Are you still a bachelor?' And so on.

I knew that I had come home.

3 *Nadu Gowda*

I must begin by stating that my account of Nadu Gowda is likely to be biased in his favour. Our relation was characterized by mutual regard and affection, and strange as it may seem, it was totally free from occasional irritations and annoyance. In this respect it differed from my relations with the headman and Kulle Gowda. Perhaps the fact that Nadu Gowda did not have power over me, or try to keep a watch over my movements, or annoy me constantly in a variety of petty ways, was an important factor in our consistently friendly relations. In fact my affection and regard for him blinded me to his weaknesses till long after I had left Rampura. It is quite probable that another anthropologist studying Rampura at the same time as I might have seen Nadu Gowda (and also the headman and Kulle Gowda) differently from me. Nadu Gowda had a strong personality with definite views on a number of matters, and if the anthropologist's own views had run counter to Nadu Gowda's, he would have presented a picture of the leader markedly different from mine.

When I explained to Nadu Gowda what I was attempting to do he thought that it was important. He readily agreed to help me in my work, and he was generous with his time. He spent a few hours every day on my verandah teaching me what he knew about agriculture, ritual, custom, etc. The enormity of my ignorance only amused, but never irritated him. He took me under his wing, and I accompanied him to weddings, funerals and festivals. He showed me off to his relatives, castefellows and others, and spoke in superlative terms about my achievements and work. He always spoke in a grand idiom so that things appeared much more impressive than they really were. In the beginning, I felt acutely embarrassed to listen to Nadu Gowda's praise of me but I got used to it after a while. His liking for me was obvious and it was easy to reciprocate his warmth.

In 1948, Nadu Gowda, like the headman, had retired from active supervision of the agricultural work on his land, and this gave him leisure. But he was an important man, and there were always people wanting to see him. But he put aside his work to help me in mine. I got the impression that he enjoyed educating me. He also liked the sound of his voice and in this he was typical of his countrymen. He was given to flamboyance of speech but occasionally he could be pithy and epigrammatic, as for instance, when he said, 'When you educate a boy, you extern [*gadiphar*] him from the village.' He could be blunt on occasion, and here again he exaggerated. Thus at a wedding agreement when he was representing the bride-to-be, he turned to me and said loudly, 'You will now see that we will take the fat [out of their bottom].' The groom's representative perceived a slight in the statement. He wanted to make it clear that the groom's family was respectable and well off and could afford to give the girl enough jewelry and saris. 'We have enough fat,' he replied. But Nadu Gowda was gracious the next minute: 'We are not going to haggle over jewelry and saris. You look to our respectability (*maryade*) and yours, and do accordingly.' The groom's representative was humbled at once: 'It is a big responsibility you have placed on us. We will do the best we can [in the matter of jewelry].'

I visited Bharata's (the headman's educated son) house in Mysore one day in August 1948, soon after getting off the bus which had brought me from Rampura. I think I wanted to find out how the headman was faring at the hospital in Mysore. Two other villagers accompanied me to Bharata's house and as we got in through the small door, we saw Nadu Gowda sitting on a mat. After we had talked for a few minutes, I casually informed Nadu Gowda that the transplantation of rice seedlings on his land had been successful and smooth. In the course of giving me information on rice cultivation, Nadu Gowda had stressed the complexity of the operations involved in transplantation, and how it was particularly difficult for the landowners. He had grandiloquently compared transplantation to a wedding in which anxious parents heave a sigh of relief when the groom ties the marriage badge at the auspicious moment fixed by the astrologer.

My news brought relief and pleasure to Nadu Gowda. (I knew that he would be worrying about it.) His face broke into a big grin, and then he went into a panegyric about my intelligence and thoughtfulness in giving him the news. He turned to the two unfortunate villagers who had accompanied me and soundly berated them for failing to think of giving the news to him. They had spent all their

lives in agriculture whereas I had started learning about rice cultivation only a few months ago. Look at the difference between them
and me. And so on.

Nadu Gowda had dignity but I did not find it forbidding as I did
the headman's. He told me stories, occasionally risqué ones, and he
laughed heartily at his own stories, showing the few remaining teeth
in his mouth. It was nice to see an old man enjoying his stories with
such gusto. I looked forward to his arrival and to his stories, and
he told me that he felt odd if he missed seeing me for a day or two.

Like the headman, Nadu Gowda was of large build, but he seemed
heavier and less bony. He also looked much older than the headman.
When both of them went out on one of their frequent walks, they
looked not only important but bigger than everybody else.

Nadu Gowda was one of the rich landowners in the village with
about forty-five acres of land. A few years previously he had planted
a few thousand casuarina saplings on six acres of sandy waste near
the Kaveri, and they had come up well. They were going to fetch
him a good sum of money later when they were full-grown. (In 1964
he was offered eighteen rupees per tree but had refused to sell for
less than twenty-two.) Like other landowners, he had lent money at
the usual high rates of interest. He also owned a grocery shop which
was popular.

In 1948 Nadu Gowda was the acknowledged leader of God's
House lineage, the largest Peasant lineage in the village. While the
headman's lineage included only seven or eight households, God's
lineage included over thirty. The members of the latter lineage had
a feeling of unity especially in relation to the headman's lineage
which, though numerically small, was rich and influential thanks to
the office of headship.

Nadu Gowda owed his leadership of God's House lineage to a
variety of factors such as age, wealth, and his reputation for honesty,
and rigid sex code. Even his opponents respected him for the last-
mentioned virtue. Apparently it was a scarce enough commodity for
it to be valued highly.

There was at least one member of God's House lineage who was
in his eighties but he was too old to be its leader. Again, Millayya
was probably richer than Nadu Gowda but he was much younger,
and looked up to the older man as an elder brother if not an uncle.
Indeed, one of the younger brothers of Millayya was angry with
him for the deference he showed to Nadu Gowda.

Nadu Gowda owed his leadership, to some extent, to his father. His father had begun life as a middle-level landowner but over the years had been able to buy up good rice-land at cheap prices principally from absentee Brahmins who were under the pressure to sell. Both Nadu Gowda and his father were the only sons in their families, and this had enabled the accumulation of land over generations. As Nadu Gowda's father's wealth and prestige increased, the members of his lineage and their clients increasingly took their disputes to him for settlement. He became an important leader and he assumed the title of 'caste headman' (*nadu gowda*), and after his death, his son took it over.

I should mention here that traditionally only the leader of the dominant Peasant caste living in a *hobli* had the title of Nadu Gowda. A *hobli* is a large village, much larger than Rampura, and it is the administrative capital for all the villages included in it. Thus Rampura was included, along with twenty-five other villages, in Hogur *hobli*, and the leader of the Peasant caste in Hogur was the proper Nadu Gowda for his area. I knew the Peasant caste headman living in Kere and he had scoffed at the idea that my friend had the right to the title. According to him, the title of *nadu gowda* was not an ancient one in my friend's lineage. Nadu Gowda's father had called himself Nadu Gowda and no one had objected. That was all.[1]

Anyway, my friend spent a good part of his time settling disputes which were taken to him by the members of his lineage or their clients or others. Generally, the disputes referred to such matters as adultery and divorce while disputes regarding stealing vegetables or fodder, or a fight between villagers were taken to the headman. But the headman was so busy with his multifarious activities that he let his old friend handle whatever he could. The settling of disputes added to Nadu Gowda's prestige though occasionally it earned him the hostility of people who were displeased by his decisions, or with his manner of dispensing justice. A few villagers complained to me about his rudeness and arrogance. They contrasted the headman's restraint and taciturnity with Nadu Gowda's lack of restraint.

Nadu Gowda was socially and religiously conservative like the headman. This made them the twin pillars of the old order—both of them did indeed look like pillars, substantial ones at that. They worked together at the Rama Navami, Madeshwara and other village

[1] See in this connection my 'The Dominant Caste in Rampura', *American Anthropologist*, Vol. 61, February 1959, pp. 1–16.

festivals. They were the most important men in the panchayat of the village, and no decision could be arrived at without both of them agreeing to it. Indeed, the two knew each other's mind so well that prior consultation was not usually necessary. It was only when the interests of the two or those whom they represented, diverged sharply that such consultation was called for.

During the summer of 1948 the headman and Nadu Gowda spent a few days in the mountain resort of Ootacamund staying with an affine of the headman. The affine owned a coffee plantation and the two visitors had been taken round it. After their return, Nadu Gowda complained that the introduction of prohibition had led to deterioration in the work done by labourers on the tea and coffee estates. The work was hard and had to be carried out in cold and frequently very wet weather. The labourers needed toddy or arrack at the end of a long day's work. Nadu Gowda complained that prohibition had brought down the labourers' efficiency. Our ancestors of the Vedic days knew that those who did heavy manual work needed liquor and this was why drink had been permitted to the castes which did such work. Modern Indian leaders did not have the wisdom of their Vedic forbears. He ended his argument with a rhetorical flourish stating that pigs had to have their food and not that of human beings. The statement jarred on me, even after allowing for rhetorical exaggeration. I realized that Nadu Gowda was capable of deeply hurting people in the course of making a point.

There was a young Harijan, Pijja, who had been a servant of Nadu Gowda's for a few years. After the contract had expired, he had collected some twigs from one of Nadu Gowda's trees for feeding his sheep. Pijja's action was technically theft as he did not have Nadu Gowda's permission. Nadu Gowda wanted him to be fined one hundred rupees but the headman thought a fine of ten rupees was enough. Nadu Gowda was very angry with Pijja and said that Pijja would be reduced to ashes if he (Nadu Gowda) merely opened his eyes. Pijja was a new type of Harijan, assertive of his rights. He was also talented, and had a knowledge of Hindu mythology. He asked me, 'Does Nadu Gowda think that he is the god Shiva for me to be burnt when he opens his eyes? Everyone knows that he is rich today because his father was able to buy up cheaply the land of absentee Brahmins.'

The god Shiva was deep in meditation when Kama, the God of

Passion, tried to distract him, and the angered Shiva opened his third eye, reducing Kama to ashes in a trice. Nadu Gowda's comparing himself to Shiva appeared absurd to Pijja. To emphasize the absurdity, Pijja had called him a parvenu. Wealth sits easy on a person when it has been in his lineage for a long time. Newfound wealth expresses itself in unpleasant ways. Pijja was giving expression to a popular view.

The Harijans of Rampura were all agricultural labourers and village servants. However, each Harijan household had the traditional duty of removing the carcass of any dead bullock, cow or buffalo in their patron's household.[1] The animal was skinned and its meat eaten, and both these were regarded as a symbol as well as a source of untouchability. But no Harijan in Rampura worked as a scavenger, as the occupation involved constant contact with ordure which was considered defiling. Scavenging was the hereditary occupation of only a sub-caste among the Harijans, and these were traditionally regarded as the lowest among them. Rampura had imported a scavenger from the Tamil country and the panchayat paid him a monthly salary.

While ordure is polluting, villagers are aware of its value as manure. The richer villagers, especially the women-folk, used the open backyard as their lavatory. Ashes and paddy husk were spread on the waste, and this was allowed to accumulate for several months when the scavenger removed it to the fields.

Nadu Gowda told me that the scavenger had been called to his house to remove the backyard manure. He had come with his cart, and after loading it with manure, had sat in the driver's seat, and then proceeded to take out a betel leaf and arecanut which he put into his mouth after spreading lime paste onto the back of the leaf. How could the scavenger have used his hands to chew betel when he was sitting in the manure cart? He had not washed his hands, feet and face after handling the manure. It was ordure even though it looked like ordinary farmyard manure. Nadu Gowda had laughed aloud at the scavenger's insensitivity to ordure. There was no sympathy for the unfortunate who had to earn his living as a scavenger. He had merely given expression to his bewilderment. However, I am certain that many others in the village shared this bewilderment. I remember a young Peasant boy who was critical of the Rama

[1] See my 'The Social System of a Mysore Village' in *Village India*, McKim Marriott (ed.), University of Chicago Press, Chicago, 1955, p. 27.

priest for carrying a basket of farmyard manure on his head to his field. Farmyard manure was not defiling—in fact, cowdung was commonly used for cleaning and purifying—but the idea of a Brahmin priest carrying manure on his head had appeared odd if not improper. If, however, the manure included the droppings of fowls, it would be regarded as defiling. It was only since the late fifties that modern poultry-farms started becoming popular in the region.

However, Nadu Gowda did have a soft heart and could not bear to see people suffer even when he was convinced that they had done something particularly immoral. One morning, for instance, a dark and attractive woman in her thirties walked to the Bullock House and said she wanted to meet Nadu Gowda. She had been directed to my verandah by someone acquainted with Nadu Gowda's routine. Nadu Gowda asked her what it was that she wanted to see him about. She had a pathetic tale to tell. She was one of the two women whom the seventy-year-old Basava priest had brought to the village a few months ago. The priest had gone out of the village with his other mistress, and in his absence, his younger son was abusing and beating her. She had been beaten that morning. She was convinced that she had made a serious mistake in leaving her people for the old man. But she could not leave now as she was three months advanced in pregnancy. She could not even think of writing to her brothers about her condition: they would be furious with her.

Nadu Gowda listened with growing distaste to the woman and her unvarnished narration of facts. In retrospect, it occurs to me that as a seasoned arbitrator in marital disputes, he should have been much less squeamish. (Perhaps my presence had made a difference.) However, controlling himself with difficulty, he told the woman that arrangements could be made for her to stay in the village till she had given birth to her baby and she could leave later. But she did not want to have the baby. She wanted an abortion. At that point I intervened and said that her life might be in jeopardy if she went to a local quack. Nadu Gowda advised her against going to an abortionist but she said she had no alternative. She left us soon after. But the point I wish to make here is that Nadu Gowda offered to help the woman even though he found her story and her life revolting. The more common attitude was that she was a loose woman and had brought the misfortune upon herself.

Every year, on the ninth day (*Mahanavami*) in the dark half of the lunar month of *bhadrapada* (September–October), Nadu Gowda distributed about twenty-two *pallas* (*palla* = 100 *seers*) of paddy among the poor of the village. Non-Brahmin castes in southern Mysore have a feast in honour of their dead ancestors during the *Mahanavami* (or *Marnoumi* as it is popularly called). Nadu Gowda sat on his verandah and personally distributed the grain to the poor. The ancestors had developed and enlarged the family estate and if a part of what was grown was not given on the occasion of their annual propitiation, the land would not continue to be the profitable proposition which it was. Giving to the poor satisfied the ancestors and assured continued happiness and prosperity for the descendants. Anyway, this was how Nadu Gowda explained his annual act of charity to me. There were several other rich landowners in the village but they did not follow Nadu Gowda in his generosity.

Nadu Gowda was not only deeply religious but he could not conceive of how anyone could live without a belief in god. The only occasion when I came near to annoying him was when instead of giving him a straightforward answer about my religious beliefs I tried to be clever and asked him whether God really existed. Nadu Gowda's first response was bewilderment which soon gave place to annoyance. I felt that he was beginning to revise his opinion of me: I was not the god-fearing man he thought I was but an unbeliever, a real wolf in sheep's clothing. Belief in the existence of god was universal in the village and I did not meet a single atheist or agnostic during my stay. Indeed, even to talk about belief in the existence of god was, in a way, to make remote, if not distort, the villager's state of mind. One might as well talk of 'belief' in the existence of wet land, bullocks, goats, etc.

Nadu Gowda narrated how he owed his eldest son Swamy to the kindness of the god Rama. Before Swamy's arrival, his wife had had the mortification of seeing her babies die soon after birth. Both Nadu Gowda and his wife became deeply worried about it, and mentioned their distress to a Brahmin couple, the Kumars, with whom they were on friendly terms. The couple owned land in Rampura and came every year to collect their share of the harvest. They were Sri Vaishnavas (or Iyengars) by sub-caste, and devotees of Vishnu in all his forms. Mrs Kumar assured Nadu Gowda that his next child would live long and he should name the boy after Vishnu. Sure enough, Nadu Gowda's wife had a baby boy, and he survived, unlike the earlier babies. He was named after Vishnu in gratitude.

The above incident deepened Nadu Gowda's liking for Iyengars.

Some of the warmth he felt for me was probably due to my being an Iyengar. The birth of the baby boy was probably a factor in Nadu Gowda's father paying for the site of the present temple of Rama (an incarnation of Vishnu). The headman's father paid for the building. Stone icons of Rama, Sita, Lakshmana and Hanuman were installed in the temple in 1924. Nadu Gowda described at length the splendour of the installation ceremony. The Iyengar temple-priest who performed the complicated ritual of installation of the icons was a master of temple ritual, and it was a delight to hear him chanting the sacred verses. The present Rama priest was a nincompoop by comparison.

Nadu Gowda's orientation towards Vaishnavism had increased in subsequent years when he and the headman started making annual visits to the temple of Srinivasa in Tirupati. In common with millions of other Hindus, Nadu Gowda was a staunch devotee of Srinivasa. In 1950, Nadu Gowda undertook a pilgrimage to the pilgrim centres in north India. On the eve of his journey, his daughter-in-law, Mrs Swamy, who was expecting a child, became seriously ill, and suggestions were made to him to postpone the pilgrimage. But his reply was unequivocal. He was going, come what may. If the girl died, they should dispose of the corpse and not inform him. When he returned from his tour, the girl had completely recovered. Faith had triumphed.

I have referred earlier to the great friendship between the headman and Nadu Gowda, and how it had contributed to the stability of the village. As far as Nadu Gowda was concerned, that friendship had frequently placed him in conflict with members of the God's House lineage. There was a history of conflict between the headman's and God's House lineages, and Nadu Gowda was under pressure from the militants in his lineage to take up positions opposed to the headman's. This came out sharply in the 1947 election to the chairmanship of the Village Panchayat. Nadu Gowda was asked to support a youthful candidate from his lineage against the headman, an idea which appeared absurd to him. But the young militants had worked on the resentment which many had against the headman, and also appealed to lineage loyalty. It looked as if they were going to defeat the headman. At this point Nadu Gowda went before the young men with folded hands and said, 'You protect our honour this time' (*namma maryade ulisi e sala*). The young men relented and the headman won.

The Reed Tank was acquired in 1949 by an outside official under the government's 'Grow More Food' campaign. It was made out that the land was marshy, and that it could be brought under cultivation if enough capital was invested. The truth, however, was that the Reed Tank was a reservoir providing water for many acres of land owned principally by men from the God's House lineage. It was argued that the tank could not have been acquired without the headman's knowledge and consent, and Nadu Gowda was criticized for not protecting the interests of his lineage men. Why had Nadu Gowda allowed this to happen? The villagers concluded that he had stood to gain in some way by not opposing the headman.

Nadu Gowda, even more than other Peasant leaders in Rampura, tried to emulate the headman in every respect. He admired to the point of envy the agricultural expertise and the organizational ability of the headman and his two able sons. He made no secret of the fact that when he saw the excellent way in which the headman's land was cultivated, he felt a 'fire in his stomach'. His success in planting casuarina saplings on six acres of unproductive land was particularly relished by him—he had done it on his own and not by imitating as usual.

Again, his consenting to his second son starting a rice mill, small though it was in comparison to Millayya's, meant that he too had got his foot in the new and exciting world of commerce and industry, and away from agriculture. He much later bought a petrol bunk in Mysore and this was strategically located. His youngest son obtained two university degrees, and made a brilliant marriage from the point of view of furthering his and his family's fortunes. His older brother, Karagu, had married a grand-daughter of the headman, and as a result of these marriages, and the family's entrepreneurial activities, Nadu Gowda's fortunes kept growing throughout the 1950s. He had every right to feel that he had kept true to the spirit of his ancestors and had done well by his descendants.

Nadu Gowda was a devoted husband. I saw his wife only a few times, and each time, briefly—she was small-made, her face was lined with age, and her forehead was decorated with the red mark of *kumkum*, which was different from that painted by Brahmin wives in that it was bigger and oval-shaped. (The large *kumkum* mark made one take note of the face.) She greeted me with folded hands and then asked me whether she could give me some milk and fruit to which I said 'no'. Nadu Gowda told me that one needed a wife especially in one's old age and it is not unlikely that he was telling me indirectly to plan for my old age. His sons respected him greatly but I had the feeling that fear was not far removed from the respect. Once his eldest son Swamy asked a boy to go and buy a box of matches from the family shop. He told the boy not to tell anyone that it was for Swamy. Nadu Gowda was sitting on the verandah in front of the shop. I asked him whether his father was ignorant of his smoking. He laughingly replied that he would be sent out of the house if his father came to know about it. He commented that his life was a miserable one—he scratched the land a bit (derogatory reference to agriculture), ate, slept and reproduced, that was all. He lived in fear of his father. There were hundreds of others like Swamy in Rampura and neighbouring villages, young men who were husbands and fathers, but who had to behave like children before the head of the family. They increasingly resented their dependence.

I got the impression that Nadu Gowda was a stern grandfather when he told me that he had not allowed two of his grandsons, neither over twelve years of age, to sit in the family shop and sell goods after he had learnt that they had stolen petty sums from the till. I had, however, to change my view when one afternoon both of us encountered his deceased daughter's son, aged about twelve, returning home from an outing. Nadu Gowda asked him gruffly, 'Where have you been?' I concluded that he was angry to find the grandson wandering around instead of being at home. The boy replied in a tone reserved for an equal, 'To get your wife . . . ed.' Needless to say, I was not prepared for the reply, and I expected thunder and lightning to strike the foul-mouthed urchin. Nadu Gowda stopped in his tracks at once and laughed loudly and uncontrollably. I knew that joking relationships between grandparents and grandchildren were widespread but I was taken aback both by the obscenity of the boy's reply and reaction which it provoked in his grandfather.

Nadu Gowda was a sensitive and proud man, and he did not put up with a slight from anyone. For instance, when Chennappa, a powerful Peasant politician of Mysore, showed impatience with Nadu Gowda, he was firmly told that he was not dealing with a nobody but a respectable local leader. Chennappa may have settled thousands of disputes but Nadu Gowda had settled hundreds. Nadu Gowda's anger had the desired effect and the politician remained courteous and attentive for the remainder of the interview.

As I have narrated earlier, my last visit to Rampura was in the summer of 1964, and on the day Nadu Gowda was performing the wedding of two of his grand-daughters. Nadu Gowda was very glad that my visit had coincided with the joyous occasion, and it was interpreted as a symbol of my affection for him. I sat near him and the headman, watching the bridal couples, the guests, the progress of the ritual, and the various other activities incidental to a wedding. But somewhere at the back of my mind I felt that I should have chosen another day for my visit as it was not possible to talk to anyone for even a few minutes at a stretch. Distractions were the order of the day.

Nadu Gowda seemed preoccupied, though there was no reason why he should have been. His sons were capable of looking after everything. But I suppose he was unable to shed the feeling that he was responsible for everything that happened in his house. He was then in his eighties. He still looked sturdy but his eyes had a faraway look. He sat there clutching a long, thin bamboo cane in his hands. As the orderly confusion of the wedding progressed, he suddenly got up and brought the cane down with a swish on the back of a poor mongrel which was prowling around looking for scraps to eat. It yelped in pain and ran away stepping on the startled wedding guests sitting on the carpeted street. Nadu Gowda slowly returned to his chair and sat down, breathing heavily and resumed his faraway look. I felt uncomfortable. The poor mongrel! And it looked as though time had caught up with my dear friend and mentor.

CHAPTER IV

The Universe of Agriculture

1 The Dominant Activity

RAMPURA, in common with thousands of other villages, represented to its inhabitants a distinct universe of interests. There was a general preoccupation with agriculture, land, and other objects or events either incidental to, or derived from, agriculture. Most villagers were either wholly or partly dependent upon agriculture in one or more of the following roles, viz.: landowner, tenant, sharecropper, labourer, and servant. The members of the artisan, servicing, labouring and and trading castes earned their livelihood by providing goods and services to the agriculturists. Many members of the non-agriculturist castes also owned land though in small quantities.

The dominance of agriculture resulted in a biased perspective for large numbers of the people. For instance, in Rampura, as in other villages of the region, the Smiths performed a double job: blacksmithy as well as carpentry. They made and repaired all agricultural tools in return for which they were paid by their patrons an agreed number of bundles of paddy-with-straw at harvest. The agriculturists did admit that the Smiths performed a useful if not essential service but they were convinced that no work was as important as agriculture. Everyone was kept alive as a result of their efforts but there was little appreciation of this obvious fact among the city-dwellers. They could be called visceral determinists. If they did not grow the food how could anyone do his work? The primacy of agriculture was derived from the primacy of food.

In my discussions with them, I tried to point out that officials, at least some of them, had important contributions to make to collective prosperity, but I do not think that I won any converts. They did not believe that some officials were dedicated and worked hard. In answer to my defence of some officials, they invariably invoked the picture of the agriculturist who dug away with his shovel in the pitiless heat of the afternoon sun, with no sandals on his feet or cap on his head. In contrast, there was the turbaned official, sitting in

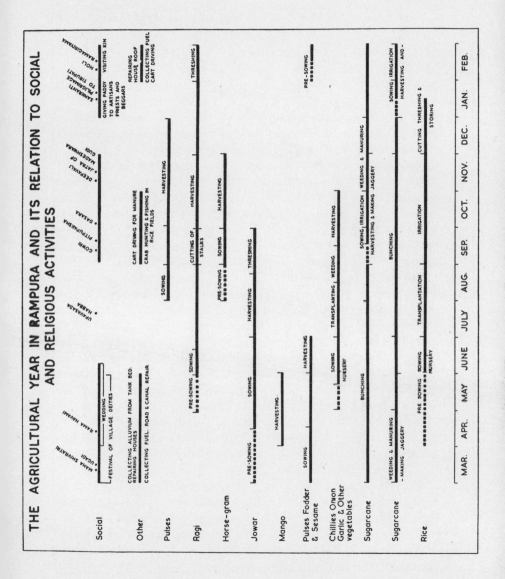

THE AGRICULTURAL YEAR IN RAMPURA AND ITS RELATION TO SOCIAL AND RELIGIOUS ACTIVITIES

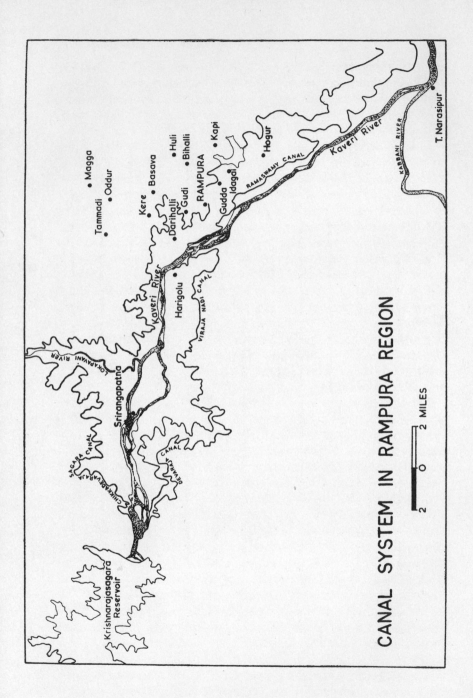

CANAL SYSTEM IN RAMPURA REGION

2   O   2 MILES

his upholstered chair while a big electric fan whirred above his head, and he had only to press a button for a liveried servant to appear and carry away a file or bring a cup of coffee. They would not be convinced of the importance of brain-work, and in this they were Tolstoians, without having had to take the trouble to read him.

Lakshmana once told me that many young Peasants had begun to ask the question, 'Why should we have to work so hard in all kinds of weather while the officials have it so easy?' Lakshmana was referring to the phenomenon of the dominance of the bureaucracy in Mysore (and other parts of South India as well) by Brahmins and how this was viewed by the Peasant and other non-Brahmin castes. Rural-urban differences acquired caste overtones as the higher non-Brahmin castes became increasingly aware that Brahmins were represented, out of all proportion to their numbers, in bureaucracy and professions. A movement to displace them began in the 1920s and gathered momentum in the succeeding decades. Lakshmana, who was sensitive to the political winds blowing outside the village, was giving expression to a sentiment that was widespread among the leaders of the non-Brahmin castes in the 1940s. However, the movement did not come in the way of the existence of strong friendships between individual Brahmins and non-Brahmins.

The crucial economic activity of the village, the cultivation of rice, determined how most villagers spent their time during any part of the year. The beginning of the active cultivation of rice was dramatized by the opening of the gates of the irrigation channels on 10 June just as its end was indicated by their closure on 10 January. Irrigated land owned by the villagers lay under two old channels, the CDS (Chikkadevarajasagara, after the ruler, Chikkadevaraya, who ruled Mysore from 1673 to 1704) and Ramaswamy (built by Dewan Purnayya, chief minister to Tippu Sultan). It took three days for the water in the CDS channel to reach Rampura whereas it took only several hours in the Ramaswamy channel. The main locks in the latter were about three miles upstream from the village. The arrival of the waters was greeted with excitement and joy. From then on till the completion of rice transplantation, agriculturists could not afford to look right or left. It was a period of total preoccupation with rice crop.

The rice season was from June to January no doubt, but the cultivation of summer crops was supportive of rice in several ways. Thus the legumes (blackgram, horsegram and chickpeas) were ploughed in after collecting the pods, and they were an important source of green manure. Jowar was also a summer crop, and its stalks provided some variety to bullocks whose staple was rice straw.

The agriculturist's tools and implements had to be in good condition to be able to do the heavy work of getting the fields ready for rice transplantation, and this meant that all repair and maintenance work had to be completed earlier. Sometimes the owner felt that he had to replace an old implement with a new one but he had to convince the Smith that it was necessary. The Smith was naturally reluctant and tried to argue that the implement could be repaired for the work of another season. He probably had to be promised an extra bundle of rice-with-straw to induce him to make a new implement. While the duties as well as payments were definite and known there was some room for argument and negotiation, and each party naturally tried to take advantage of the other.

Bullock carts had also to be kept fit for transporting manure and alluvium, and careful agriculturists attended to this work immediately after the harvest. The regular Smith did not do cart work which called for special skills. Two or three villagers, one of them a Muslim, set up sheds during the dry season for the making and repairing of carts. These men worked strictly for cash unlike the regular Smith.

New bullocks were bought or exchanged during the post-harvest months. Incidentally, this part of the year was well known for the elaborate festivals (*jatre*) of local deities, and at some of these festivals large numbers of cattle were customarily sold or exchanged. This enterprise brought in money to the village or town holding the festival, and therefore enjoyed enthusiastic local support. The villager who went to one of these *jatres* to buy or exchange bullocks had not only the satisfaction of making a good bargain and earning religious merit which followed a visit to the temple but also of having a brief holiday. A *jatre* invariably attracted cinemas, dramatic troupes, gambling booths, sweet-stalls, restaurants, ferris wheels, itinerant traders, and many other things to distract and amuse the villagers.

Rice cultivation was accompanied by considerable anxiety, and agriculturists tried to postpone all other work to the post-harvest months. The rice season was also the rainy season, and it was only around harvest time that the peasant did not need rain. A good agriculturist believed in continuous supervision of his plants and he did not like to be away from his village till he had safely gathered his crop in and built his straw-ricks. The time for travel was after harvest. The sale of surplus rice was the most important if not the sole source of cash for rice-growers, and anything that involved the spending of some money got postponed to the post-harvest period. Many households were on an annual shopping cycle: clothing, vessels, jewelry and other articles were bought after the sale of rice. My friends loved to contrast their plight with the prosperity of the salaried official who was paid on the first of every month, whether he did any work or not, whereas they themselves had to produce and sell grain before they could have any cash. It gradually dawned on me that a monthly salary appeared as a way out of the hazards and difficulties of agriculture to many villagers, and every village youth who graduated from high school was eager to exchange the back-breaking shovel and plough for the clerical pen. I must add that this was in 1948 before leading villagers plunged into commerce and industry.

In contrast to the rainy, agricultural season, the post-harvest months were a period of intense social activity: it appeared as though villagers wanted to make the most of the four months or so before they became involved with the summer crops which were a prelude to as well as a part of rice cultivation. Weddings were usually celebrated in the summer months and attendance at them was important for all invitees. Attendance varied from active participation in the organization of the numerous activities incidental to them to sending a junior member to make the customary cash contribution of *muyyi* (equivalent return).

A variety of other activities, social and religious, were performed during the post-harvest months. Pilgrimages to one's lineage deities (*mane devaru*) were usually undertaken then. The services of certain outside artisans such as brick-makers, tilers and sawyers were only available during summer. The sawyers were seasonal immigrants from the Tamil-speaking plains in the south. They were themselves agriculturists and wanted to return to their village before the onset of the south-west monsoon in the last week of May. Itinerant entertainers also visited the Rampura area during summer. Two of them, for instance, were agriculturists from the Bangalore region, and they played wind instruments by blowing through their nostrils. That is, the tip of each instrument was stuck into a nostril while the fingers manipulated the holes in the flute-like attachment to the gourd above. The instruments resembled those used by snake charmers. The novelty of their technique impressed the villagers while I found the entire idea unaesthetic. But the point I wish to emphasize is that it was agriculture which determined how people spent their time during various parts of the year. And as stated earlier, even several members of the artisan and servicing castes were part-time agriculturists, and this helped to enforce on all a common pattern of activity.

Fuel was extremely scarce in Rampura and neighbouring villages. The thoughtful villager had to make sure that he had at least enough fuel to last him during the busiest part of the rice season, when he would have no time to attend to any other activity. The rich had trees on their land, and they took care to have them trimmed during summer. A few big branches were also lopped off, if necessary, to provide enough fuel for the rainy months. The poor literally broke off every dry twig from their hedges (the goats ate off the green ones), and collected everything else that could be burned. They bought tiny bundles of fuel, generally of very poor quality, in the weekly markets (*sante*) nearby. Some hardy villagers crossed the river Kaveri and hacked the scrub growing on the southern bank to make up immense bundles which were then carried home. The hacking was done during the hottest hours, and the men perspired profusely from their exertions. The bundles were then carried on their heads. The men knew exactly where they could ford the river which was over a hundred yards wide. At places they had to wade in the water, and at others they had to walk on the granite boulders smoothed and polished by centuries of water-flow. The loads were so heavy that the men could only look straight ahead, while their feet negotiated the river by the feel. The torn, buttonless shirts of the men, wet with perspiration, stuck to their bodies, and their faces were beaded with perspiration. After they had successfully crossed the river, the men put down their bundles and sat for a while recovering their breath. The last lap of their journey was the walk back to their homes in the village, nearly three miles away, on pebble-strewn footpaths.

It was not only that the activities performed by villagers during different seasons were determined by agriculture, but the dominant occupation generated concerns and interests marking off those who practised it from the others. This meant that all agriculturists, irrespective of caste or religion, had certain common interests. They were doing more or less the same thing at any given month. For instance, during the summer all of them were busy collecting alluvium (*godu*) from the tank-bed, and ploughing their land after every decent shower of rain. The richer landowners did not themselves do the work but supervised the work of servants and labourers. They also did many other things as a result of their extensive contacts in the region. But there were also a few individuals who were odd and their actions and movements were different from those of everyone else. Villagers referred to such men as *eda gorasu. Gorasu* referred to the split in the hoofs of cattle while *eda* meant left. The expression may be translated as 'left-hander', bearing in mind the fact that right-handedness was equated with normalcy. The use of a bovine idiom to characterize human behaviour provides an eloquent comment on the place of agriculture in village life and thought.

Agriculture was not only a means of earning a livelihood but a way of life. While it required consistent hard work, and its rewards were uncertain and always small, at least according to those who practised it, it was the only one available to the villagers, and there-fore had an air of inevitability about it. It was also a vital one for it fed everyone. It was a manly occupation, the only one in fact. City-dwellers were softies and parasites living on the toil of poor villagers. That those who espoused these views were not often famous for their kindness towards their servants and labourers did not make them any the less passionate when it came to condemning the urban parasites. The cities with their wide, tarred roads, their big buildings, hospitals, schools, colleges and other amenities had battened them-selves on the labour of the poor agriculturists. These remarks were usually made in jest and to tease me, but they did reveal a basic element in the villagers' make-up and thought.

2 Land as a Value

It does not take long for a visitor to Rampura to discover that the villagers were preoccupied, if not obsessed, with land. It was seen, for instance, in daily talk and conversation. Everyone wanted to acquire land, and as much of it as he could. It was the object of endless conflict. According to an old Kannada saying, women (*hennu*), gold (*honnu*) and land (*mannu*, literally, soil) were the three things about which men were so greedy that it led to self-destruction. It was an oft-quoted saying though it seemed to be singularly in-effective in influencing conduct. That brothers all of whom came out of the same womb (literally, *hotte*, stomach) should fight each other for ancestral land was tragic but only too frequent. Among the smaller landowners ancestral land was usually divided soon after the death of the father, and the presence of the widow-mother did not seem to have much effect in delaying partition. Indeed, sometimes the mother hastened the breaking up of the joint family by dis- criminating in favour of her daughters as against her daughters-in- law, or between one daughter-in-law and another. Even after land had been divided among the heirs, the latter were at loggerheads with each other over the boundaries of their respective plots, over rights of passage across each other's land, and other matters. Just before the transplanting of rice, the ridges separating one plot from another were trimmed as part of the process of getting the plots ready for the crucial operation. Divided brothers usually had some boundary-ridges in common and when a brother started trimming the ridge from his end, the other complained of encroachment. Some- times this led to fighting and even death.

Grown brothers frequently were not on speaking terms with each other. I once found two men, who seemed to resemble each other a little, not exchanging a word even though they had been sitting on my verandah for some time. After a while I told them, 'You must be brothers for you are not talking to each other.' A burst of laughter greeted my remarks: they were indeed brothers who had quarrelled over land.

There was a basic distinction between arable land (*jamin* or *bhumi*) and other kinds. Every village included traditionally a certain quan- tity of pasture-land (*gomala*) and waste-land (*banjar*). Village cattle and sheep had the right to graze on the pasture-land, and the waste- land provided fuel. Even in 1948, villages in the dry or non-irrigated parts of the State had retained some pasture- and waste-land. Arable land was extremely valuable in irrigated villages, and there was a temptation to bring as much land under the plough as possible, with the result that pasture- and waste-lands were practically non-existent.

There was a hierarchy in arable land. Land which did not enjoy an assured source of water constituted the lowest kind: only the millets and other 'dry' crops were grown on it, and that too only if there was rainfall at various stages of their growth. Unirrigated or 'dry' land (*khushki* or *hola*) was valued at Rs. 1000 per acre where- as irrigated or 'wet' land (*tari* or *gadde*) fetched at least between Rs. 3000–4000 per acre. Wet land which enjoyed seepage from a perennial tank or river was valued highly as the moisture enabled

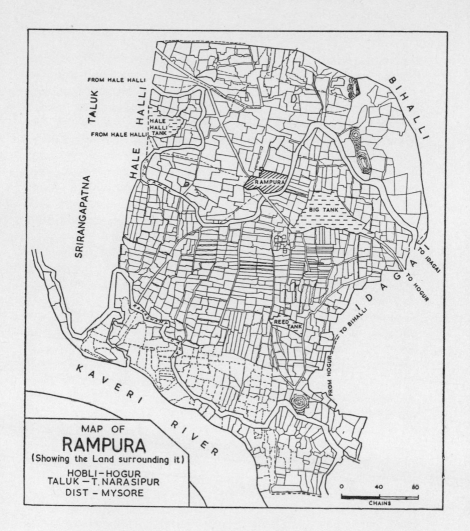

FROM HALE HALLI

TALUK

HALE HALLI

FROM HALE HALLI

HALE
HALLI
TANK

SRIRANGAPATNA

RAMPURA

BIG TANK

BIHALLI

TO IDAGAI

TO HOGUR

I D A G A

REED
TANK

TO BIHALLI

FROM HOGUR

KAVERI

RIVER

MAP OF
RAMPURA
(Showing the Land surrounding it)
HOBLI – HOGUR
TALUK – T. NARASIPUR
DIST – MYSORE

0   40   80
CHAINS

sugarcane, or a secondary crop of pulses, to be grown during summer. Orchard land (*bagayat* or *thota*) was the most valued of all kinds of land as it usually had considerable moisture and a high water-table which made it possible to lift water from a shallow well. Needless to say, the presence of such trees as coconut, arecanut, mango, tamarind and jack added to the value of the orchard.

A piece of land which was at the head of the feeder-canal system was prized by villagers as it ensured undisputed access to water, and eliminated the possibility of conflict with neighbours. In 1948, a small piece of strategically located rice land in Edagai was sold at the rate of Rs 10,000 per acre. I also came across other instances of strategically located land fetching unusually high prices. Competition for such land was intense.

There was a certain amount of unirrigated land in Rampura, apart from waste- and pasture-land, but that was small compared to the total quantity of irrigated land. The two artificial lakes in Rampura, Big Tank and Reed Tank, had been both included in the CDS canal irrigation system. Each tank was used as a reservoir and this meant that it was able to provide a certain amount of water for agriculture even after water had been shut off in the canals. It also meant the presence of more moisture in the seepage area of each tank.

I found a great emphasis on acquisitiveness in village society, and land was the most important object of acquisition. Villagers stinted and saved for years, denying themselves the barest necessities, in the hope of acquiring, after several years, an acre of land. Frugality and saving were more than habits; they were virtues. Correspondingly, the loss of land was associated with a non-virtuous life involving gambling, drinking, women or marijuana.

The desire to own land was nearly universal and not confined to any caste or religion. Even city-dwellers liked to own some arable land. Over a hundred years ago, L. B. Bowring, who was Chief Commissioner of Mysore from 1862 to 1870, remarked upon the difficulty of introducing land reforms because of the widespread tendency among officials, nine-tenths of whom were Brahmins, to own land.[1] It was usual for officials to buy some land to assure

---

[1] 'Again, the landed aristocracy, which existed prior to the ascendancy of the Mysore Rajahs and the usurpation of Hyder Ali, is absolutely extinct, so that neither land nor money conveys that right which should give importance to the possessor. The result is that the commercial and agricultural communities are as

themselves of the supply of good rice and other farm products, if not as part of insurance for old age. As officials they were strategically placed to obtain knowledge of good land coming into the market and they had enough influence to beat their rivals. It was only after India's becoming independent in August 1947 that land gradually became an unattractive field for investment excepting for those who were acquiring it for cultivating it themselves. Even they had to be careful not to own beyond the ceiling of twenty-four standard acres prescribed by the State government. The headman, a man of unusual foresight, told me as far back as 1948 that he was not interested in adding an acre of land to his estate. He had decided to invest his savings in commerce and industry.

Landownership meant not only wealth and status but power over people. Given the simple technology, which obtained even in 1948, a landowner could only cultivate a certain amount of land. Status considerations were an additional constraint, preventing the richer landowners from personally handling the plough or shovel. Further, servants and labourers were not easily available. Though there was no limit in theory to the amount of land that could be cultivated through servants and labourers, very few villagers were willing to work in these roles. Indeed, a landowner often obtained a servant by leasing his father an acre or two of land. Another device was to give the servant or labourer the crop growing on a few plots of land in addition to a cash salary. In brief, the biggest landowners cultivated some of their land through servants and labourers and the rest through tenants and sharecroppers. The smaller landowners had no inhibitions about working on the land—during transplantation and harvest even their womenfolk worked.

The ownership of land was also the best-understood road to personal and familial prestige. A man's importance was measured by the acres of arable land he owned, number of bullock teams, and the size of his manure heap. Such a man could play host to visiting

a bundle of sticks, the whole of the authority of the province being in the hands of the officials nine-tenths of whom are Brahmins. Many of these are men of great ability, and some bear a very [great] reputation for integrity and zeal in the service of government, but as they all, to a man, hold land, it is obviously difficult to carry out any measures of reform which may affect their interests in the soil. In many parts of India, native officials are prohibited from holding land in the districts they serve, but such a prohibition is impossible in Mysore, where the practice is universal and a declaration only of the fact is therefore exacted.'— *Eastern Experiences*, London, 1872, p. 16.

officials, important castemen, religious mendicants and others. He could also perform acts of charity such as building or renovating a temple or pond, or feeding so many poor people during a festival or other occasion. Villagers liked to say that so-and-so was well off (*anukoolastha*), owned so many acres of different kinds of land, and had lent so many thousand rupees (*levadevi*) to others. He was a weighty person (*tooki manushya*). If he was also capable of long silences, then he acquired a reputation for sagacity, and maybe even wisdom. He would be invited to settle disputes.

I have mentioned earlier that villagers were expected to make contributions in cash and kind towards the celebration of such festivals as the Ramanavami. The contributors were divided into four ranked categories: the top category was formed by five Peasant lineages each of whom contributed Rs 2.50 and a specified quantity of rice and other provisions. Households included in the second category contributed less than those included in the first and more than those in the third. The fourth category consisted of those who were too poor to make a contribution. Many of them lived on the verandahs of houses owned by others.

The above categorization was based solely on the ability to contribute to festivals, and it cut across caste distinctions. Thus, the second category included a Toddyman household which owned some land, a toddy-shop in Hogur, and a fifty per cent interest in a cloth shop in Rampura. The fact that the traditional occupation of the caste was a ritually low one, the making and selling of toddy, had not prevented a Toddyman being assigned to the second category. Land-ownership and wealth were occasionally able to mitigate if not overcome the effects of birth in a ritually low caste.

No wonder, then, that there was a general scramble for land. The rich competed among themselves to acquire more land, for a variety of reasons, economic, political and social. When the rich belonged to the same caste, competition was compounded by inter-lineage rivalry. It was not enough to keep up with the Joneses but be one up on them. The poor, and the low castes, wanted land for it meant freedom from hunger and bondage to patron, and also self-respect.

There was another aspect of landownership: a man was acquiring land not only for himself but for his descendants. This assumed, of course, that the descendants would have enough sense to look after their patrimony which, however, was frequently untrue. Villagers reeled off the names of improvident descendants who had become paupers after running through their inheritance. But land was not easy to dispose of: even if a descendant lacked prudence, he may have piety towards his ancestors who had acquired or improved the land. And his wife was certain to object to the sale. There were also kinsmen who would tell him that he was being a fool. And so on.

While a man may have had his descendants in mind when buying land he also knew that it would be divided after his death. Big estates were more usually built up through the accident of single sons in more than one generation. It was significant that both the headman and Nadu Gowda and their respective fathers were single sons. But even worse than division of land among descendants was not having any. That meant the end of the lineage (*vamsha, kula*), a disaster which no one liked even to contemplate.

Then there was the burden of contingent expenditure which affected everyone. Conspicuous consumption was prescribed at weddings and funerals, and a rich man was certain to be accused of lacking filial piety if he did not have a lavish funeral for his dead father or mother, and of meanness, if he did not celebrate the weddings of his sons and daughters in style. In either case, his reputation suffered among his equals (*sarikaru*), clients, officials and others. 'Is he going to carry his wealth on his head when he dies?' was a frequent comment. The grandeur of weddings and funerals performed by others, some of them not as rich, would be cited to highlight the contrast. It required unusual insensitivity to local opinion to resist the pressure to spend on such occasions, especially when the pressure was exerted by one's castefolk, kinsfolk, and even one's own wife and children. Even those who were habitually tight-fisted let themselves go on such occasions.

Small landowners were also not exempt from the compulsion to spend lavishly at weddings and funerals. In fact, one of the common reasons for land to come into the market was expenditure at weddings and funerals. Typically, a small landowner mortgaged his land, or a part of it, to obtain the cash necessary to perform a wedding (or funeral) and over the years he discovered that he was unable to clear the debt especially in view of the high rate of interest which had to be paid. He then ended up by selling his patrimony to the mortgagee. Many a rich landowner had acquired the land of poorer villagers in this manner as the village gossips loved to recall. But while an able, lucky and unscrupulous individual acquired a sizeable estate during his lifetime, it usually split into several small shares among his descendants. One or more of the latter might even lose their land through foolishness or improvident living and such land was likely to be bought by a few able men whose stars were on the ascendant. The rise and fall of lineages was commented upon *ad nauseam* by local moralists.

While even the most careful could lose their land under the weight of contingent expenditure, men given to gambling, drinking, marijuana-smoking or prostitutes were certain to part company with theirs sooner than others. Village gossips loved to tell how wealth acquired over generations by men who had denied themselves an extra set of clothes or a good meal was liquidated in a few years by a profligate descendant. During the 1930s, a few rich Peasants from the Rampura region had lost their fortunes in the whore-houses and gambling dens of Mysore. These men were roundly condemned for not only losing their ancestral wealth but disgracing their lineages. The description of the downhill journey of the wicked rich gave satisfaction if not pleasure to the gossips.

My discussions and talks with friends made me realize, with something akin to shock, that they regarded Mysore as an evil place, full of wicked temptations for the rural innocents. I had assumed Mysore to be a sleepy city whose inhabitants were notorious for their lack of drive and enterprise. The upper sections of Mysore were only a step removed from the village with many of them annually visiting their ancestral village to collect their share of the harvest. But my Rampura friends saw Mysore differently, as Sodom and Gomorrah combined. One elderly villager told me how he was horrified to find students in a hostel playing cards (gambling!) in the afternoon and talking about visiting prostitutes in the evening. He withdrew his son at once from the hostel. I was also told about how a Kere man had lost nearly Rs 10,000 in a single night in a gambling den in the lanes of Mysore. I found it incredible and I told my friends so. But it only prompted them to list the names of a few others who had lost several hundred rupees in the course of a night's gambling. Another friend told me with conviction that he shuddered with fright when he learnt of the 'goings on' in some 'respectable' homes in Mysore. Yet another narrated his adventures during his student days: he was staying with some relations, and he had been seduced by several housewives when their husbands were away working. My incredulousness confirmed to my friends that I was pitifully lacking in knowledge of the real world. They were too polite to say anything more.

The city, then, had its temptations to which the wicked and weak succumbed. The virtuous and wise avoided the temptations, but there was one temptation, a relatively new one, which was in some ways as bad as the old ones, the law courts. The villagers did not understand the law or justice which was dispensed in them. The legal system appeared to many as a complicated and half-understood game which litigants played by hiring lawyers who were supposed to know the rules. Some lawyers knew and manipulated the rules better than others and this enabled them to win their clients' cases. The institution of appellate courts, and the fact that occasionally a man who had lost his case in a lower court managed to win on appeal, stirred the gambler and vengeance-seeker in each litigant. The loss of a suit in a lower court only induced a litigant to hire a cleverer (and more expensive) lawyer to argue in the appellate court. That was all. Some villagers who had come into protracted contact with lawyers and law courts used their knowledge to their economic advantage, and to harass their enemies. Melkote (Sr.), for instance, was such a man. Many an old villager told me that Melkote (Sr.) had such proficiency in law and legal procedure that he liked to argue his cases himself. He used his knowledge of the law to harass his enemies, principally the headman's father. Melkote (Sr.) was a creature of 'two worlds' —after a morning's work in the law courts in Mysore, he got off the bus near the Big Tank, proceeded to his land, hung his dhoti, close-collared coat, and turban on a wooden post, and put in a few hours' work before calling it a day. There was admiration for his versatility.

One day, when travelling in the bus from Mysore to Rampura, a passenger pointed to a ten-foot stump of a Nerale tree (*Eugenia jambolana*) and said that he has lost Rs 2000 over it in a lawsuit. There was not the faintest regret in the man's voice as he said it. Indeed, I thought I even detected a trace of pride in it. The fuel in the stump was not worth more than Rs 50 but the important thing in a fight was not the value of the prize available to the winner, but the fact of victory itself.

Responsible and sober village opinion recognized that the law courts could destroy families, and there was a sentiment in favour of settling disputes at the village level. Many a villager declared, in the course of proving his respectability, that he had never set foot in a law court. Only the shameless (*managettavaru*) were habitués of the law courts. A villager once moralized that the victor in a law suit suffered defeat while the defeated suffered death (*geddavanu sota, sotavanu satta*). The victor lost financially, while the loser lost financially as well as morally. He could not, unlike the winner, even crow from his housetop.

There were a few agriculturists in Rampura who had dropped out of the race to acquire more land. My friend Kulle Gowda was such a dropout and so were the marijuana-smokers. None of these men was respected and they knew they were not. By and large they were ignored and very rarely did someone refer to their downfall.

Men and women each had different relationships with land. Typically, a boy began paying regular visits to his ancestral land at the age of nine or ten. I knew of two Shepherd boys, aged twelve and nine, both of whom visited their land regularly, the older boy even doing the ploughing. One reason why the poorer villagers did not send their young boys to the school was because their labour was needed on the land. I knew one poor Shepherd who was putting his son through the middle school and he was hoping, somewhat simple-mindedly, that his son would get a job in the government after he had passed the lower secondary examination. He did not know that passing the final high school examination (the S.S.C.) was the minimum requirement for obtaining a clerical post in the government or in one of its many agencies.

By the time they reached fourteen or fifteen years of age, boys were full-fledged agriculturists doing practically every job on the land. Working for several hours every day, except probably for three months after the rice harvest, they came to know their land as intimately as the faces of their friends and neighbours. Even during the summer months many of them were engaged in work supportive of agriculture. Thus they would be gathering alluvium from a tank-bed, collecting fuel or manure, or accompanying their fathers to buy a pair of bullocks for the coming agricultural season.

In south India, unlike in the north, a person is buried after death except among Brahmins and a few others who cremate their dead. In rural Mysore, most castes buried their dead on their ancestral land. The place where the dead were buried was not cultivated for a few years but over the years even that came under the plough. Rice land was too scarce and valuable to be left alone. Only rich landowners such as the headman and Nadu Gowda could afford to leave alone land where their ancestors had been buried. Nadu Gowda's father had built a small shrine over the graves of his father, mother and wife and he himself was buried there after death.

There was something peculiarly apposite in a man being buried in his ancestral land—it had been the scene of his activity all his life, and the object of his hopes, dreams, anxieties and heartbreaks. In course of time he became a part of the manure that enriched the soil. Pious sons and grandsons felt that their dead ancestors watched over the prosperity of the land, and the annual sacrifice made to them on the eve of the *dasara* festival was meant to keep them content, for dissatisfied ancestors made trouble for the living. Thus a man's body contributed to the enrichment of the soil after death while his spirit kept an eye on the descendants, their good conduct and their happiness and prosperity. It was interesting that while the dead father or father's father was mentioned in connection with the lineage and land the dead mother and father's mother were not mentioned. The ancestresses who were also buried along with their husbands did not seem to have any function.

In contrast to a boy, a girl worked in the house, especially in and around the kitchen, helping her mother. She also milked a buffalo or cow or ran errands for her mother. She occasionally followed her mother to the family land to bring home some vegetables or grain or fodder. But a girl did not develop an association with land in her natal household. At her marriage, she was given gifts of jewelry and clothing both by her parents and her affines but rarely land. Sometimes a cow or buffalo was also given her to take with her to her husband's house. That was all.

It was in her husband's house that a woman developed a permanent association with land. This was perhaps more marked among the poor whose households were small and nuclear in character. Further, women were not prevented by status considerations from working on land. They hired themselves out at certain periods of the year, and a few women even helped their husbands on the farm. The wife of a Shepherd neighbour of mine worked alongside her husband most afternoons and returned home in the evenings with a headload of fodder.

When grown sons divided their ancestral land after their father's death, a piece of land called *ajjipalu* (grandmother's share) was set apart for the widow mother. She had the exclusive right to what was grown on this land but after her death it was distributed among the male heirs. Traditionally, a woman could only have a life-interest in land. There was fierce agnatism as far as land and ancestor propitiation were concerned. A woman came into the picture only as wife or mother and never as daughter or sister. Land was identified with mother earth (*bhumi tayi*). Villagers were fond of saying that if an agriculturist worked hard mother earth rarely failed to respond. The rice crop went through several shades of green before it started to ripen, turning from yellow to beige. Nadu Gowda was eloquent about the beauty of land under rice at various stages of the crop's growth. He described it as mother earth wearing a sari of one shade of green before discarding it for another. Most people shared his sense of beauty and no one who travelled in this part of Mysore during September to December could fail to be impressed by the beauty of fields carpeted with rice plants bowing in response to the gentlest breeze. The feeder canals sparkled and gurgled as they flowed to the waste weirs which eventually reached the expanse of the river Kaveri at the bottom of the valley.

For an agriculturist, there was no greater tragedy than loss of land. It meant the loss of security, status, and even membership of the village community. I remember witnessing the sale of his patrimony by a Shepherd who wanted to leave Rampura and settle down with his affines in another village. The buyer was a local Peasant and he was represented in the transaction by an articulate affine from another village. As the transaction was about to be concluded, the buyer's representative said that he did not want his affine to be accused later of having deprived the seller of the membership of the village. They would like him to keep a piece of his land, or even a manure heap, to symbolize the continuance of his relationship with his natal village. But no one paid attention to the noble sentiment. Everyone was preoccupied with the various aspects of the transaction. But I felt that the representative had given expression to an abiding sentiment.

The lineage in which the hereditary accountantship of Rampura was vested were once its biggest landowners but in 1948 they did not have any land in the village. Indeed, they had migrated to Mysore during World War I, and the land had been sold, bit by bit, to meet the expenses of daughters' marriages, and sons' education and marriage. In 1948 the lineage did not even own a 'cow's foot' (*go pada*) of land in Rampura. The man who had worked as accountant in 1948 was not a member of the accountant's lineage but an outsider, none other than the hereditary priest (*purohita*) of the village. However, in 1950, the youngest son of the accountant's lineage went to Rampura to reclaim the office and he was successful. The headman housed him in the Bullock House, and the entire village contributed cash and rice to rehabilitate the young man and to get him married. There was a great deal of sympathy for him. Many a villager told me, and before the embarrassed young man, how rich his lineage had been and how it had come down in the world. Everyone felt that he had to do something to rehabilitate the representative of the prodigal lineage.

3   The Thirst for Water

As an irrigated village, Rampura was only indirectly and secondarily dependent upon rain, and the villagers were aware of this. Rampura, in common with other neighbouring villages, was irrigated by the CDS and Ramaswamy canals, both of which issued from stone *anicuts* (or indigenous dams) erected across the Kaveri. Agriculturists took it for granted that water would always be available, during the season, for rice-cultivation. The certainty of canal water contrasted with the fickleness of the monsoon.

While the canals had made Rampura a rice-growing village, rains were essential at certain stages of the crop's growth. Thus heavy rains in August and September kept down weeds and made weeding less difficult and expensive. Again rains were needed when the rice plants put forth ears in early November. Without them the ears would not fill with sap (which the villagers referred to as *halu* or milk).

The summer crops were entirely dependent upon rain; they included the legumes, plants yielding oil-seeds such as gingelly (*achchellu, Sesamum orientale*) and wild gingelly (*huchchellu, Guizotea oleifera*), and a variety of jute, *sanabu* (*Creotolarea juncea*), the stalks of which were used for making rope. (The fibrous husk of the coconut, and the broad, sword-like leaves of the hedge plant, agave (*bhutale*), were also used for rope-making. *Sanabu* was the least important of the three as a source of rope.) Many villagers also grew *jola* or jowar but primarily for fodder. Some of this fodder was consumed when green while the rest was stored after drying.

The summer crops were grown mixed together, unlike rice. As far as the small landowner was concerned the quantity of legumes (*hesaru, Phaseolus mungo; uddu, Phaseolus minimus*; and *tadugani, Dolichos catiang*) harvested was negligible but welcome as a base for the soups (*saru*) in which each morsel of cooked ragi flour was dipped before being eaten. Villagers would perhaps have liked to grow only legumes but they needed some green fodder for their cattle during summer. The smaller landowners grew only the legumes and sorghum while the bigger ones tried to be as self-sufficient as they could.

As I have said, the summer crops were entirely rain-based, and villagers cast anxious eyes at the sky from the beginning of March. The Kannada New Year Festival of *Ugadi* on the first day in the lunar month of Chaitra fell in March–April, and rains were expected around then. They were referred to as *dharmada kalada male*, i.e., rains which occurred at the proper time if people were moral and God-fearing.

There was a long drought during the summer of 1948. The first rains were late, delaying the planting of the summer crops, and then followed another period of long drought which killed the sorghum and damaged other crops. (And when the southwest monsoon eventually broke, the rains were so heavy that the water-logged fields could not be ploughed for several days.) It was a blistering Ugadi, and I remember how a pitiless sun beat down on us as we returned to the village after a refreshing bath in the cool waters of the Kaveri. Some concern was expressed by the returning villagers at the absence of rain on Ugadi. The days which followed were no better: the sky continued to be a monotonous blue during the day, and the heat grew worse. Gusts of hot wind carried street dust into every part of the house. A thick coating of dust covered the floors and all articles of furniture. The evenings were marked by continuous lightning coming out of a cloudless sky (*bara sidilu*). Ninga, the old *jita* servant of the headman, had a reputation for being able to forecast rain and he was asked more than once whether the lightning portended rain. Ninga said 'no' decisively. Only when there was lightning in the north-eastern sky did it indicate rain. Not otherwise. I had the feeling that Ninga almost liked to disappoint those who asked him. He was a Harijan, invariably at the receiving end of orders, instructions and abuse. But the protracted drought had conferred some importance on him. His opinion was sought eagerly, and by his masters, among others. He would have pleased everyone if only he had told them it would rain in the next day or two. But he preferred to read the signs honestly.

To add insult to injury, clouds appeared in the Rampura sky on a few evenings only to move over to neighbouring villages before coming down. The villagers seemed outraged. They listed the names

I

of the neighbouring villages which had showers during the previous few days. Why was Rampura excluded? Why indeed? I tried to joke with the villagers: 'What else can you expect when everyone is selling grain in the black market?' My joke was not appreciated. Someone said that rains had failed because a dead man, who had suffered from leucoderma during his lifetime, had been buried instead of being exposed to vultures. In such cases the corpse was taken to a hilltop, placed in a sitting posture, while stones were placed around and above it (*kallu seve*, stone disposal). This method of disposal avoided defiling the earth. Some years previously, a Fisherman suffering from leucoderma had been buried and there was a drought. Some villagers wanted to have the corpse exhumed but the headman had strongly disapproved of the idea.

The crucial importance of rain for agriculture was acknowledged at Ugadi when the Brahmin priest of the locally important temple, or an astrologer, read out from the almanac (*panchanga*) the predictions for the coming year on such matters as the quantum of rainfall, the prospects for different crops, and the likelihood or otherwise of drought, flood, pestilence, disease and war. This rite was called *panchanga shravana*, or 'listening to the almanac' but it was not observed in Rampura in 1948. My guess is that the institution had disappeared with the emigration of Brahmins from the village.

The year is divided, in the Hindu calendar, into 27 named asterisms (*nakshatra*—the term also means a 'star'), and rain is believed to occur at some of them. Elderly villagers knew the names of those asterisms under which rain was certain to occur, or essential, or both and sometimes the expectations had crystallized into adages. For instance, rains under the asterism *hasta* were believed to be so certain that they insured the crop from disaster. Appropriately enough, the *hasta* rains were compared to the *abhayahasta* (right hand held with the palm outwards and the fingers pointing downwards) of Vishnu. (*Hastada male raitanige abhaya hasta kottide: hasta* rains have given *abhayahasta* to cultivators.)

When a spell of dry weather was broken by a shower, it was usually the subject of a critical discussion much like critics discussing a play. It was either too little or too much, or it did not come down the proper way. During the summer of 1948, I made the mistake of telling Chenna, one of the servant-boys of the headman, that the previous night's shower had been good. It was a heavy shower and it had cooled things down. The earth smelt fragrant. I had stopped perspiring and had enjoyed several hours of undisturbed sleep. But Chenna punctured big holes in my evaluation of the shower. It was a heavy shower no doubt, but it had come down too fast, washing away the precious topsoil. Rain, to be useful to the agriculturist, should come down gently, and over a period of time, so that it penetrated the soil. I felt foolish at being corrected by a small boy but my brash statement invited repudiation.

Only occasionally did the villagers admit that the previous day's rain had been good. There was a term for describing such rain: *tayi hada*. The word *hada* meant degree, quantum or level, and *tayi* was of course 'mother'. The mother was a common symbol of protection, affection and kindness. The cool shade of the *honge* (*pongamia glabra*), for instance, was compared to the mother's lap (*tayi madalu*). For a shower to qualify itself to be *tayi hada*, it had to come down slowly and in sufficient quantity to penetrate the dry top layer of soil and reach the moisture-impregnated level below. In rice land this varied from about two to eight or ten feet depending upon whether the plot in question enjoyed seepage (*vasthi* or *aruwasi*) from a tank or canal. *Tayi hada* varied therefore from one landowner to another. After such an ideal shower, the land was ready for ploughing. Ploughing was hard, back-breaking work but welcome as indicating the resumption of agriculture.

Rain could also be unwelcome on occasion. The villagers believed that rain towards the end of October meant maggots in the crop which were only washed away by a heavy shower sometime later. And rain was a disaster after the crop was ready for harvesting. The crop, already bending under the weight of the grain, lay down in the mire as a result of heavy rain and the landowner's yield was considerably decreased owing to the difficulty of retrieving it. Rain around harvest time was a particularly difficult pill to swallow as it came on the eve of success. But the last kick of the northeast monsoon (*hingaru*) often came just before the cutting of the crop.

Before the completion of the Krishnarajasagar dam in 1931, impounding about 49 square miles of water, upstream from Rampura, floods were frequent in the Kaveri valley. The building of the dam constituted a landmark in the development of agriculture in the two districts of Mandya and Mysore in southern Mysore. Agriculture became more predictable. The engineer and statesman who had worked unremittingly at this dam for two decades, Sir M. Visweswarayya, was revered by the villagers in these districts.

When in a humorous and self-critical mood, villagers did recognize that they were hard to please. 'The agriculturist is always blaming god or the government,' they used to say. God was blamed for drought, unseasonable showers, insects or other pests while the government was blamed for taxes, bad officials, controls and tortuous bureaucratic procedures.

4 The Cultivation of Rice and Other Crops

Preoccupation with rice cultivation resulted in a number of domestic and social activities being packed into about five months between the completion of its harvest and the beginning of the rainy season in late May.

Rice was a commercial or cash crop for the majority of villagers. Ragi or finger millet was their staple diet, and only a minority of rich landowners, and Brahmins, ate rice regularly. Before rationing was introduced early during World War II, resulting in a ban on the private sale of food grains, it was usual for a few villagers to go, after harvest, to nearby ragi-growing villages to barter cartloads of rice for ragi. After the introduction of rationing, however, villagers sold their surplus rice to the government at rates fixed by it, and bought ragi against ration cards from licensed dealers in Rampura.

The eating of rice was prestigious, and there was a reluctance to admit to eating ragi. Thus even though the richer landowners habitually ate a ball of cooked ragi dough at their meals they did not like to mention it. Only rarely would they say that while rice was a tasty grain it did not 'stay' in the stomach like ragi. They had therefore to eat a little ragi—after all, they had to be physically active. Only the Brahmins ate rice to the exclusion of other grains, and rice-eating by the other castes was part of the general phenomenon of emulating the Brahmins.

The hectic period in rice cultivation was marked by the opening of the canal locks on 10 June, and it ended on 10 January when the locks were shut. The summer crops were harvested early in June so that farmers were free to concentrate on rice. The release of water in the canals marked the beginning of a very anxious period in the agricultural year which was referred to as 'slushy fields' (*kesaru gadde*). The term connoted both intense activity and anxiety. The culminating activity of this period was the transplantation (*nati*) of rice seedlings, which villagers compared to a wedding (*lagna*). The rice plots had to be prepared for transplantation, and this required that several arduous jobs be completed in quick succession. First of all, the nursery plot (*age pati*) had to be prepared for the planting of the seed. The selected plot did not come under the plough for summer crops, and was tilled several times over so that the top layer was well aired 'and powdery. It was also mixed with a good deal of tank-bed alluvium (*godu*) and cattle-shed manure (*gobbara*). Growing the seedlings in the nursery enabled the farmer to care for the seedlings better, and to protect them from heat as well as heavy rain. The seedlings were transplanted after they had grown for about four to six weeks.

Every landowner and big tenant reserved one plot in his rice-field for growing chillies and a few vegetables, chiefly gourds and squashes, egg-plant and okra. The chilli plot was called *menasi madi*, and it was fenced all round to prevent thefts. But in order to be able to grow chillies, the agriculturist had to have seedlings ready for transplantation by July. Many villagers had chilli nurseries in their backyards in order to be able to look after them properly. Those who did not grow their own chilli-seedlings borrowed them from the others.

The hedges had to be attended to soon after the monsoon rains had started in earnest. Gaps (*kanna*) in the hedges had to be planted with new hedge plants—the careful agriculturist tried to keep out stray cattle, goats, sheep and human beings from his land.

Village agriculture distinguished between low-lying land with much moisture in it (*halla gadde*) and high-level land with little moisture (*dada gadde*). Summer crops were cultivated in low-lying land not only for fodder and green manure but also for such yield as could be obtained in pulses, sesame, jowar and jute. Sugarcane could be grown only on low-lying land.

Low-lying land was much less dependent upon summer rains than high-level land. For instance, summer crops were sown on the former without having to wait for rain. (Since all such land was situated within the seepage area of a tank, water could be taken from the tiny canal which issued out of its sluice.) It was also harvested earlier. Rice, the principal crop, was sown, transplanted and harvested earlier on low-lying land than on the higher. In short, the timing of the crucial agricultural operations varied according to the type of land.

Soon after the release of the water in the main irrigation canals, the rice plots were flooded for a day or two. The pulses which had stood there after the pods had been collected rotted with the sun and water when they were ploughed in.

Water was again let into the plots and allowed to stand there for eight to ten days. When the plots gave forth a powerful stink it was time to start the important work of cleaning them up (*achchu kattu*) for transplantation. The land was ploughed again and then levelled by a twelve-toothed harrow (*halube*) which was drawn by a pair of bullocks, with the driver standing on the flat top of the harrow. Those who did not have a harrow used a hoe with a broad blade (*ele guddali*, hoe with a leaf shaped blade) for levelling. The corners were dug with the hoe, the ridges were trimmed to a knife-edge, and any rat or crab holes in them closed. A good farmer was proud of the way he had trimmed the ridges and the corners of his plots. If while trimming the ridges enclosing a plot he stole a few inches of his neighbour's land he felt all the better.

Good farmers took care to see that each plot was of a uniform level. Without this, different parts of the plot got different amounts of water resulting in injury to those which were on a lower level which got flooded while the others on a higher level got little water. Every farmer knew that rice was finicky about water. It had to be given the precise amount, no more or no less, at each stage of its growth. The quantum needed was expressed in terms of so many finger-widths, each finger being placed horizontally. Four finger-widths at one stage, eight at another and so on. The quantum of water in each plot was controlled by widening or narrowing the inlet and outlet. The supply of the precise quantity of water caused continued anxiety to farmers. Occasionally, I came across farmers who were setting out for their fields after their evening meal in order to make sure that the plots were receiving enough water. They did not carry torches even though it was pitch dark, and sometimes they went barefoot. The imperative of 'seeing to water' (*niru noduvudu*) made them forget their fear of ghosts, and of creeping and crawling things.

The 'slushy fields' (*kesaru gadde*) season was also characterized by labour scarcity. And scarcity was greatest between 15 July and 15 August when transplanting (*nati*) was carried out. The only other comparable period was harvesting (15 December to 10 January). It is probable that the quantum of labour needed during harvesting (including a multitude of activities from cutting the sheaves to the storage of grain in the house and the building of straw-ricks) was greater than even that needed during transplanting but harvesting was made somewhat easier by the fact that the division of labour between the sexes was not as rigid. Thus both men and women could cut the sheaves, and thresh the grain whereas at *nati* only women did the actual transplanting. The men ploughed, harrowed, trimmed the corners and ridges but were excluded from plucking the seedlings from the nurseries and transplanting them in the plots. I must add, however, that even at harvesting certain tasks such as the measuring of rice, driving the loaded carts, and ricking the straw were exclusively male jobs. Another factor which eased the labour situation during harvesting was the availability of migrant labour from dry villages such as Chavalapura.

During the transplantation period, the village made use of the labour of every person it could. And as I have said earlier, transplantation had to be completed within a specified period of time which varied from a few hours for small farms to two or three days for the big ones. A number of factors went into the determination of the time for transplanting—the time of planting the seed in the nurseries, the readiness of the plots which received the seedlings, the availability of labour, paid as well as exchange, and, in some cases, the date and time fixed by the astrologer.

During transplanting, the women workers in each plot stood in a horizontal line planting the space in front of them and they moved back gradually till they reached the ridge. Each woman planted an area about four to five feet wide. The women stood barefoot in ankle-deep slush while planting, and frequently, a steady drizzle if not a heavy shower beat down on them. This part of the year was also known for its south-westerly winds. The working day varied from six to eight hours, usually in two equal shifts, and the women were bent double most of the time. When this position proved too tiring, they stood erect for a few minutes. It was generally recognized that transplanting was tough work which mere males were not equal to. The strain and drudgery of transplanting were somewhat lessened by the folksongs which the women sang while they were working. The headman was shrewd enough to have Karim present when transplanting was being carried out on his land: Karim not only helped by himself performing various minor tasks but he kept the women cheerful with his quips and jokes. The women retorted freely and there was a belief that they were 'hot' during this season. But the recognition of the arduousness of the work done by women did not lead to giving them the same wages as men. They were only paid half the rate for men. Nor was there any relief for them on the domestic front; they had to cook and feed their children and husbands. But the money earned was their own, and they treated themselves to snacks of slices of copra, jaggery, and roasted gram and peanuts during brief respites from work.

Each woman was part of a team with its own leader called *dabegati*, and a farmer dealt only with the leader. It was the leader's responsibility to bring her team along and to see that they did their work. The leaders were feared for their tongues and farmers were careful to be pleasant to them. The market conditions favoured the labourers, and farmers recognized the fact. A leader who was rude to a landowner or made a risqué retort was even admired.

Every farmer heaved a sigh of relief when his transplantation had been completed successfully. His next period of similar anxiety was harvest, at least four months distant. But he could not afford to take things easy during the intervening period. He had to be vigilant about the supply of requisite amounts of water at various stages in the crop's growth. He had to inspect the ridges every day for crabs and rodents which continually burrowed holes. A single big gap was enough to throw a farmer's carefully controlled water supply out of gear, flooding some plots and depriving some others. A powerful or greedy neighbour was inclined to steal water from others, but luckily this did not assume serious proportions in Rampura where the leaders of the village were respected. But very rarely did an enemy damage the crop by making a few selected breaches in the ridges, or by diverting water from the feeder canal into the plots.

The first weeding came soon after transplantation. These were weeds put forth by the summer crops (*hala satte*) which had been ploughed in. A few weeks later came the nasty, narrow-bladed *nojhe* grass which grew around the rice seedlings, and was likely to choke them if not removed in time. One of the main aims of an adequate supply of water was to prevent the sprouting of *nojhe* grass. Weeding was generally done by women.

The crop put forth ears (*hode kadiyuvudu*) in November, and, given suitable rains, they filled with sap. This was when farmers brought home the tops of sheaves and the lush grass growing on the ridges to hand-feed bullocks, their valued partners in farming. Many a farmer told me that the animals were overworked ploughing the slushy land prior to transplantation and that the season for feeding them (*dana meyisuvudu*) had arrived when the plants sprouted ears. They were convinced that the animals would not recover their strength without special attention. The more particular farmers woke up at four or five in the morning, if not even earlier, and thrust handfuls of sheaves into the reluctant mouths of the sleepy animals. This was repeated after the midday meal. In the evenings, a mash made of oilseed cake (*hindi*), cottonseed, and horsegram (*huruli, Dolichus uniflorus*) was given to the animals. Farmers were solicitous of their bullocks. But while the hard work which transplantation involved was acknowledged by men no one expressed great sympathy for the women workers, at least within my hearing. But then bullocks could not speak for themselves. They were *mooka prani* (dumb animals) while human beings could speak up for themselves.

The stoppage of water to the land before harvesting set new anxieties and problems. This was the season of thunderstorms, and a heavy shower, as already stated, made harvesting difficult and reduced the yield. Then there were human thieves. Many a farmer slept in his field at night. Sometimes, a few young men watched their crops together. This made the nights pleasant with bonfires, *bidis* and gossip.

Harvesting started with the cutting of the crop on the plot which was later used as a threshing-yard (*kala*). The stubble of the severed crop was beaten down and then sand was sprinkled over it. Stone weights were placed over coconut or palm mats, and dragged over the plot till it was firm and smooth. A wooden pole (*meti*) was fixed in the middle. Wooden planks were placed on the threshing-yard and men and women beat the sheaves against them. The grains were piled in a corner. The beaten sheaves, which still held some grains, were then laid on the ground and bullock-teams were driven over them repeatedly. Each bundle of sheaves was submitted to this dual threshing before the straw was separated from the grain. Heaps of grain were then winnowed from a height to separate solid grain from chaff and bits of straw. The grain was then measured, loaded into open carts, and driven home. The richer landowners had the grain stored in granary-rooms called *kanajas*, or had it packed in tough gunnysacks and sewed the edges. The sacks were then piled in a corner, one on top of another. The poorer landowners stored the grain in huge containers (*tombes*) made of split bamboo and plastered with a solution of cowdung. The mouths of the containers were sealed first with straw and then with mud.

Rice-straw was the most important source of fodder for cattle, and it was stacked either in the field or in the backyard. Stacking it on the field increased the chances of theft and arson but only rich landowners had backyards where it could be stacked. Also the tenants and small landowners did not have much straw to store. They had only enough straw for a few months at most and had to find fodder for the rest of the year.

In between the threshing-yard and the domestic granary, the grower parted with some of his crop in meeting the claims which many people had on him. In 1948, the government collected its share of the crop, in theory the entire marketable surplus. The grower was of course paid for the grain but at rates fixed by the government which were lower than the prices they fetched in the black market. The Madeshwara, Basava and Rama priests each collected a head-load of straw-with-grain from every grower. This grain went towards providing the temple deities with food everyday, food which was later eaten by the priest and worshippers as consecrated *prasada*. The members of the artisan and servicing castes who had served the grower during the previous year collected their dues (*adade*) on the threshing-yard alone. The Fisherman Dasi who held the office of *saudi* (waterman) collected his perquisite of a headload or two from every grower. This worthy had the keys to the canal locks, and the authority to operate them. As such, he was important, The threshing-yard also attracted other seekers of grain—religious mendicants and minstrels. Farmers could be excused for feeling that everyone was out to mulct them.

When the villagers were not busy trying to convince me how hard-working and exploited they were, they did admit that the harvest season (*suggi*) was a joyous one. The weather was beautiful, chilly in the morning and after sundown, and sunny during the rest of the day. The year's work was over, by and large, and the villagers looked forward to eating well and to their annual shopping. In the old days, there used to be harvest dances (*suggi kunitha*) of groups of men who sang and danced at threshing-yards in the hope of collecting some grain.

The conclusion of the harvest was marked by the festival of Sankranti. It was a three-day festival when the newly-harvested rice was ritually cooked and eaten. Ritual expressing a wish for abundance of the rice crop and increase of the herd was also part of Sankranti. Another element of the festival was the expression of thanks to cattle. Bullocks and cows (but not buffaloes) were washed clean, and their horns painted a variety of colours. Gold and silver paper was stuck on the horns, and turmeric paste (a symbol of auspiciousness) was rubbed on the animal's body. Some of the new rice which had been cooked was offered to cattle as also was sugarcane, banana and jaggery. In the evening, the animals were taken in procession with band and pipe, the beating of tom-toms, and lights. Small piles of straw were placed in a line and set on fire, and the animals were made to jump over the flames. They were then brought home in procession after being given sweet and savoury rice (*huggi*).

In 1948 sugarcane was only next in importance to rice in terms of the money it brought to the village as a whole. The price of jaggery had soared during the war years when sugar was scarce and could only be bought in limited quantities against ration cards. This resulted in more land coming under sugarcane. But then not all wet land was suitable for cane: only in land enjoying seepage could cane be grown, and this was the best quality land available. At Rs 300 per 1000 cubes of jaggery, an area of wet land under cane yielded far more than an area under rice. Sugarcane was a twelve-month crop, was more labour-intensive than rice, and required heavy inputs of fertilizers and oilseed cake. The grower's job did not end with harvesting, however. He had to have the juice pressed from the stalks, boiled, poured into wooden moulds, cooled, and finally, the cubes taken out. The cubes were then packed tidily in cane straw and sold to a middleman resident in the village. He was a native of Nagara and had migrated to Rampura during the early years of World War II. The quantum of business was enough to induce him to settle down in Rampura. (He had acquired for himself a local mistress.)

But there was an element of gambling in growing sugarcane. Jaggery prices were tied to sugar prices, and in 1948 the price of jaggery plummeted from about Rs 300 per thousand cubes to Rs 50. Those who had hoped to make huge profits by bringing more land under cane suffered heavy losses instead. The more conservative farmers who had stuck to rice felt that their caution had been justified, and they made no secret of their satisfaction at the distress of the cane-growers.

Only a small number of landowners had a few acres of dry land each. Several crops were grown on dry land and these were usually mixed. Apart from ragi, sorghum and sesame, villagers liked to grow the pulse *togari* (*Cajanus indica*) as it provided a base for their hot soups.

A few rich men also owned small orchards (*tota* or *bagayat*) where they grew a variety of trees such as coconut, arecanut, mango, banana and jack (*Aertocarpus integrifolia*). Orchards could only be raised on the best kind of land, and they increased a farmer's self-sufficiency. A landowner who owned several acres of rice land, and some orchard and dry land was said to be comfortably off. Affluence was a major factor in respectability in Rampura.

During the course of my field-work I gradually learnt that the agriculture of the villagers embodied tested knowledge, and a body of valuable skills transmitted over generations. In farming families, the domestic atmosphere was impregnated with agriculture and related skills, and the children absorbed it as they grew up. Traditionally, agriculture was but one element in a complicated ecological balance related to population, the inheritance system, etc. But that was beginning to be thrown out of joint by improvements in public health and communications. The farmers were intelligent, shrewd and sensitive to new opportunities, but they also knew, almost viscerally, that their economy did not permit them to take the slightest risk. The price of failure was starvation, a fact which officials concerned with the villagers' development did not always keep in mind.

The organization of agricultural activities called for careful planning. The problems of those who had big farms were more complex and difficult than those of the smaller farmers though the greater resources of the former mitigated their problems somewhat. Those who had different varieties of land, wet, dry and garden, had to be on the alert continuously, coordinating their diverse activities. It should be remembered here that the bigger farmers had all lent money and the collection of interest and capital was not always easy. Those who were moving into new enterprises were really inhabiting two economic and social universes and it must be said to their credit that they not only managed both successfully but strengthened their position in one area by their activity in the other. Thus a landowner obliged a candidate standing for elective office, or a bureaucrat, and obtained in return a permit to start a bus service or rice mill. Such men were very shrewd, acquisitive and competitive. They resented that anyone should regard himself as superior to them; at the same time they kept down inferiors who aspired to be their equals. They were firm believers in the idea of human inequality.

5 Animals and Trees

Agriculture could not be practised without caring for bullocks, and in some cases, even for cows. It also involved knowledge of the properties of certain essential plants. Farmers had their own classification of soils, and understanding of weeds, and insect and other pests.

Without a team of bullocks, a man was only a labourer or *jita* servant, occupying the lowest category in the rural economic hierarchy. He had to have a team of bullocks and plough (*ettu eru*) if he had to move into the next higher rung of tenants (*guttigedara*) and sharecroppers. Without being a tenant (or sharecropper) on good land for several years he could not hope to buy a little land. In other words, the ownership of a pair of bullocks, however small, was essential for economic and social mobility.

In southern Mysore and some other parts of southern India the bullock is the draught animal *par excellence*. The buffalo is rarely used for draught purposes. It probably never occurred to people that male buffaloes could be used for drawing ploughs and carts. Traditionally, they used to be sacrificed in large numbers, in very rare cases even in hundreds, to village deities during periodical festivals. The sacrificed animals were eaten by Harijans. All this came to an end, however, in the 1950s when animal sacrifice was forbidden in the State.

The female buffalo was more important as a milk-producer than the cow, its milk being much richer in fat. It made thicker curd, and thicker tea and coffee. And for those who sold milk, buffalo-milk had the advantage that it could be more easily diluted with water. Cow-milk, however, was preferred for use by infants and patients. The traditional Indian system of medicine, Ayurveda, had a preference for cow-milk and its products, and also a prejudice against buffalo-milk. This was probably a legacy from the Vedic period in Indian history.

The poorer landowners, and tenants, kept small bullocks. Even these cost about Rs 400 in 1948 and the careful farmer had always to think of the cost of replacement. The wooden ploughs which were in common use did not call for big bullocks—indeed one of the reasons advanced against the spread of the deep-ploughing iron plough was the inability of the ordinary farmer to afford big bullocks. Many of the plots were small, especially where the land descended sharply into a canal, waste-weir, river or tank, and big bullocks found it difficult to turn in them.

Only the richer farmers kept bigger bullocks: they owned better quality land, and they could afford the cost of levelling which made possible wider plots where bigger bullocks could move with ease. Their fodder resources were also greater, and they had servants to care for the animals. The loss of a bullock during the heavy agricultural season was an inconvenience but not a disaster for a rich farmer.

But a farmer had always to keep in mind the fact that bullocks were draught animals and not to be kept for purposes of show. Otherwise, bullocks became, to mix metaphors, white elephants. Villagers were sensitive to beauty in animals, especially cattle, and occasionally a farmer allowed his sense of beauty to prevail over his sense of utility. Besides, a man earned some prestige as the owner of a pair of big and beautiful bullocks: at the annual festivals of some neighbouring village deities there were bullock-cart races, and winning them enhanced a man's self-esteem.

Rampura had one farmer, Melkote (Jr.), who maintained two pairs of magnificent bullocks. They were much bigger than the bullocks kept by everyone else, had beautiful horns which curved symmetrically, and fine, shapely humps. The owner had paid about Rs 2000 for each pair, and he was obviously proud of them. They easily won the races they competed in. But the more cautious villagers pointed out that they cost a great deal to feed and maintain, and were they necessary for work on the farm? Melkote (Jr.) smoked marijuana, kept a mistress, and the two pairs of bullocks were of a piece with his unthrifty way of life. The day was not far off when he would lose his land. The dominant world-view, as I have said before, was an acquisitive one, and everything that did not promote acquisitiveness, except, to some extent, conspicuous spending at weddings and funerals, was useless if not worse. I for one admired Melkote's bullocks and I gave free expression to my liking. It was pleasant to come across a villager who indulged his fancy (*shoki*) instead of thinking all the time about increasing his income.

I have described in the previous section the trouble which farmers took to feed their bullocks after the heavy work in the rice-fields had been completed. And that was only one instance of the care which good farmers showed for their animals throughout the year. They gave only rice-straw in the cooler and wet months and *ragi*-straw during the summer as the former was 'hot' (*ushna*) while the latter was 'cool' (*tampu*). Farmers knew that their animals liked green fodder, and this was provided by the summer crops, especially sorghum, and the grass growing on the ridges during the rice season. Even a slight upset in their bullocks' digestion was noticed, and the few men who had a reputation for their knowledge of cattle were consulted about the remedy. The veterinary hospitals in one or other town nearby were used only during emergencies.

Very few villagers kept cows as milch animals, and indeed, there was a great shortage of milk in the village. This was no doubt related to the acute scarcity of pasture land. There was a widespread belief in the beneficent effects of drinking milk (especially freshly-milked, frothy milk) and in the consumption of milk products, but in spite of it milk was scarce. The richest landowners each kept fifteen or more small cows (*hudi dana*) but these animals were valued for the manure they produced and the milk they gave was less important though welcome. Small boys drove them a couple of miles every morning to a stretch of boulder-strewn wasteland where they were grazed. The low cost of maintaining them made it worth while to keep them for their manure.

There was a definite sentiment that cattle were sacred—I have commented in the earlier section on the occasional identification of bullocks with Nandi (or Basava), the bull on which Shiva rides. Monday was the day saved for Shiva's worship, and Shiva's animals were not tied to the plough on that day.

Killing a bullock, cow or bull was sacrilege for all Hindus including Harijans. No Harijan slaughtered a cow or bullock for its meat. Such beef as they ate was carcass meat. As mentioned earlier, the bull buffaloes sacrificed were eaten, but then buffaloes were sharply distinguished from cows. (Bull buffaloes were called *kona* and cow buffaloes, *emme* while bulls were *gooli*, cows were *dana* or *hasu*, and bullocks, *ettu*.)

The objection to the killing of cows and bullocks did not, however, mean that they were always treated kindly. Indeed non-killing was the important thing, and villagers were not sufficiently sensitive to the need for kindness towards animals, even cows and bullocks. Even the objection to killing was casuistically interpreted. Thus an owner who sold an old cow or bullock to a Muslim trader knowing full well that the latter would drive it to the slaughter-house did not feel that he was responsible. His responsibility had ended with the sale.

I must briefly describe here the institution of cattle exchange (*chati vyapara*) between owners and Muslim traders. Two or three traders went around villages exchanging the cattle they had with them for inferior animals. An owner gave an animal and some cash in exchange for a better one in the traders' herd. This made the traders combers of the countryside for decrepit cattle. The animals which were finally left with them were useless for the agriculturist. They then reached a slaughter-house and their meat was sold to non-Hindus.

Casuistical reasoning occurred elsewhere also. The people of Rampura, for instance, were boastful about the fact that unlike the less pious inhabitants elsewhere they did not make their bullocks plough on Mondays. The exemption, however, was only from *ploughing*; the bullocks were made to draw carts, work the sugarcane press, etc., if there was need for it. They were able to indulge in their sense of piety while at the same time they were not too severely inconvenienced by the rule.

Sometimes a villager dedicated a bull-calf to a deity in fulfilment of a vow. In such a case, the priest either directly took charge of the animal, or it roamed at will, feeding off hedges or any unguarded straw-rick. It even walked into cattlesheds and helped itself to the straw in the stalls. The animal benefited from the immunity, though not unlimited, that it enjoyed on account of its sacredness.

A bull which was directly looked after by the priest was better fed and groomed than the average domestic animal, the temple's resources being greater than a private owner's. But when a dedicated bull which roamed the streets was in good condition people attributed it to the fact of dedication. The Madeshwara bull, for instance, was a magnificent animal and it went where it wanted to. It was huge, milk-white in colour, and had a fine hump and beautifully shaped horns. It liked human company and had strong objection to being tethered. Occasionally it visited the Bullock House, standing in the covered areas beyond the verandahs, and allowed us to admire its good looks. During one such visit, Kari Honnu, my neighbour, talked to me about its virtues, and then going into the headman's Cow House, brought forth a bundle of straw and spread it before the animal. Some time later, Rame Gowda came in and asked where the straw had come from. He was indignant when he learned about what had happened and said that if people wanted to feed the bull they should feed it from their stock and not from the headman's. He left soon after, and Kari Honnu commented, more in sorrow than in anger, that he thought that a rich man like the headman would not mind sparing a handful of straw for Madeshwara's animal. He seemed wholly sincere when he made the statement and it did not occur to him that he was being kind to the animal at someone else's expense. The operative factors seemed to be that the bull was dedicated to Madeshwara, the headman was the richest landowner and his stock of straw was only thirty feet away.

The villagers were keen observers of the environment in which they lived, and in particular of the animals and plants with which they habitually came into contact. For instance, they knew a good deal about the behaviour of field-rats, crabs, water-snakes, egrets, and about the many uses of the plants around them. But sometimes their observation was influenced by religious and other considerations. For instance, when a dedicated bull nearly gored a villager at a festival in a neighbouring village, it was explained that the animal sensed that the man in question was ritually impure and that he was polluting everyone else by his presence.

One characteristic of the villagers' exploitation of their environment which was forcibly brought home to me, and repeatedly, was their excessive dependence on a few items in short supply. Thus, for instance, a tree whose shade was valued was stripped of leaves in June to provide green manure for the rice plots, and its twigs regularly broken off for fodder for sheep and goats. Every part of coconut, arecanut, mango, jack, *gobli* (*Acacia arabica*) trees and the banana was put to use in the house or farm, or in both places. Even the meanest twig was used as fuel after the sheep and goats had stripped it of leaves.[1]

There was general recognition of the value of trees and it was usual to calculate their value separately in land transactions. The planting of trees at suitable places on one's land was not only welcome from the point of view of agriculture and the domestic economy; it was regarded as an altruistic act especially if it was planted at a place where neighbours and passers-by could take advantage of its shade. A planter of such trees earned religious merit (*punya katti*

---

[1] See in this connection, 'Village Studies and Their Significance', in Srinivas, *Caste in Modern India*, Asia Publishing House, Bombay, 1962, pp. 120–35.

kolluttane). Rajas who built roads, rest-houses, planted avenue trees, and had ponds dug along roads were remembered as pious rulers by grateful citizens even though their main aim may have been better administration and increased revenue.

The cutting down of a tree was not only unfortunate but unethical and particularly so if the tree was a yielding one—*phala bido mara* meant a 'tree yielding fruits', and one who cut it down committed a sinful act (*papa*). I have referred earlier to the case of the Shepherd who sold all his land in Rampura to settle down in his wife's village. He had a small mango tree, just outside his land, and as the transaction was about to be finally concluded someone asked about it. Did it come along with the land or not? It did not. In fact the Rama priest had offered to buy it in order to augment his fuel supply. Someone in the group advised the seller against selling it to a man who wanted to cut it down. (In this instance, unlike the sale of an old bullock to a trader, the seller did not wash his hands of responsibility the moment the transaction was concluded.) The matter was put to an end when the buyer of the land agreed to pay Rs 50 for the tree. Later, Kulle Gowda was indignant that the Rama priest, a Brahmin and priest of an important temple, was infamous enough to think of cutting down a fruit-bearing tree. Kulle Gowda nursed a grudge against the priest and overlooked no opportunity to run him down.

The sentiment against cutting down a sacred tree such as the peepul (*Ficus religiosa*) or shami (*Prospis spicegara*) was even stronger. In fact, traditionally, a peepul tree was not cut down: it had to die a natural death and then a pious Brahmin was given the wood to burn. Kulle Gowda's third son, Machayya, once confided to me that all the troubles which were crowding in on him at that time were due to his having lopped off the branch of a dead peepul tree which overhung a troublesome neighbour's wall. After having lopped off the offending branch he had made use of it for fuel. He had realized that this was wrong and he wanted to atone for his sin by cutting down the rest of the tree and making a gift of it to a Brahmin. It was too big a job for him and he did not have the cash to pay a Smith to do it for him. Machayya's aim in mentioning it to me was probably to raise a loan. It was not unlikely that the money was going to be used for some other purpose. But even then I felt that he was feeling uneasy if not guilty at having lopped off the branch of a peepul tree and using it for his domestic needs.

Nandi, Shiva's vehicle—Chamundi Hill, Mysore

Feeder canal off the Ramaswamy Canal

Feeder canal, another section

Paddy field after harvest

Making jaggery

Harvesting

A bullock cart on the road skirting the tank

Collecting alluvium from the tank in summer

The Basava temple

The deity Narasimha being taken in procession during the annual festival at Harigolu village

Cheluvadi, hereditary Harijan servant of the high castes, exhibiting the symbol of his office.

Ornamented door
in a rich landowner's house
(left); a detail of the
carving (below)

CHAPTER V

The Sexes and the Household

1 Sexual Division of Labour and the Household

SEX difference provided an important basis for the division of labour, and this was true for all the castes. Among all the castes the kitchen was the recognized sphere of feminine activity but the extent of participation in man's traditional occupation varied from caste to caste, and even from household to household. The income of a household, and the degree to which its style of life was Sanskritized, were also significant in determining whether women participated in agricultural work or not. Generally, women from the richest households and the highest castes remained confined to their homes while women from the poorest households and lowest castes worked outside for cash wages.

It was the male head of the household who carried on the traditional caste occupation, be it agriculture, smithy, trade or priesthood. And there was an unstated assumption that his occupation was the important one, and that all other activities of the household were either supplementary or subordinate. This assumption was the principle on which the household's activities were organized. Thus, while it was the man's job to raise the crop, it was the woman's to look after his food and comfort.

Cooking was an exclusively feminine concern even when women periodically worked outside the house to earn cash wages as they did among the very poor. The husband took over kitchen duties for three days during the monthly periods of his wife: a woman was impure then, and she was required to sit in a corner by herself and eat the food given to her by her husband or daughter. If, however, she had a daughter who was twelve years or older, then the latter performed her mother's duties. She cooked, washed, served food to everyone and behaved generally like a mother. One of the most touching features of village life was the solicitude of an older sister towards her younger brothers and sisters. A daughter was trained to be a mother before she became a wife.

Very rarely, however, did a man cook his own food even when he was living with his wife or grown daughter. Such a situation arose as a result of religious considerations. For instance, a priest was often required to be a vegetarian and observe strictly the rules of purity and pollution while the other members of his household were non-vegetarian.

Cooking involved doing certain other incidental chores. While the man's job ended with bringing home the grain, it was the woman's duty to clean it, grind it into flour as in the case of the staple, *ragi*, or have it dehusked, as with paddy, before cooking. *Ragi* was ground on a stone quern which was operated by the wife either alone or with a partner. This was a monotonous chore, and when I started living in the village in February of 1948, I was occasionally awakened well before dawn by women singing songs while they operated the rotary quern. (There was a whole genre of folk-songs called 'ragi-grinding song'.)

When agricultural work was demanding, a wife had to carry food to her husband and other men (including servants) working on the family land. Not infrequently, this meant a long walk in the midday sun or wet weather.

It was the wife's duty to fetch water from the canal or well depending upon the season. Water was available in the canal from about 13 June to 13 January, and it was relatively easy to fetch it from there. The canal skirted the settlement area, and no house in the village was more than about 300 yards from it. There was no need to pull the water from the depths of a well, no need to queue up, no quarrels with other women over mutual precedence, and finally, no need to carry the heavy coil of coir rope on each trip. At the height of summer, when the water level was at its lowest, only one well in the village had water, and that was the headman's.

The ban on the use of cowdung for fuel, which was strictly enforced by the village leaders, meant that Rampura women were spared a time-consuming chore. In contrast, in the neighbouring villages women continued to collect and store the precious cowdung, and periodically pat it into cakes on their mud walls. These were removed after they had dried in the sun and used as kindling to light fuel for the kitchen stove.

During the post-harvest rain-free period, women busied themselves with making dried foods and pickles which brought some variety to the routine diet of cooked balls of *ragi* dough and hot sauce.

Strips of mutton were covered with a paste of spiced chillies and hung out to dry and then stored. These were roasted and eaten as a relish during summer when the appetites of even men working in the fields needed to be coaxed. *Happala* (Papads) and *sandige* (relishes made with cooked rice-flour), and green mango and lime pickles were made and stored in mud pots or stone jars. In the richer and upper caste households these activities consumed a considerable amount of the time and energy of the women-folk. Work parties of women and girls rolled out *papads* and made different kinds of *sandige* during summer afternoons. If there was going to be a wedding in the house, then these tasks were begun weeks ahead of the event.

It was the wife (or daughter or daughter-in-law) who washed the domestic clothes and this was done at the canal or tank. Villagers, excepting the poorest, generally possessed two sets of regular clothes, and an additional set of special clothes for festive occasions, and washing was done once a week or fortnight. Clothes were taken to the Washerman only rarely, at the approach of a festival or wedding, or on the eve of an important journey. The richer households, however, had a regular Washerman who was paid a stipulated quantity of grain after harvest.

While the wife regularly washed everyone's clothes, the husband washed only occasionally, and then only his and his young sons' clothes. It was unmanly for him to be seen washing his wife's sari and blouse, or even his daughter's skirt.

Again, it was the wife who swept the house and cattleshed, and carried the sweepings in a basket to the domestic manure heap. A sensible housewife would not let her husband handle the broom. Otherwise, she would be talked about. Boys who were *jita* servants were, however, expected to sweep the house and cattleshed. However, they would not be called upon to wash clothes or clean the lavatory where one existed.

Every morning, the wife swept a small patch of the street in front of her house, sprinkled it with a solution of cowdung, and drew simple designs (rangoli) with powder made from crushing a variety of soft stone. This was a ritual requirement, and the absence of the *rangoli* design before a house signified mourning. It was also omitted on the occasion of the annual *shraddha* (propitiation of dead ancestors).

The wife (or daughter) also lit the small earthen lamps in the evening. Among the higher castes, the wife cleaned the domestic altar (usually in or near the kitchen) every morning and lighted the lamps kept before lithographs and icons of the popular deities.

Bullocks and sheep and goats were looked after either by the male head of the household or one of his sons while cow buffaloes and fowls were cared for by the wife or her daughters. The income from the sale of milk, buttermilk, butter, *ghi*, eggs and fowls belonged to the wife. The money was lent at the usual high rates of interest to other women. Occasionally the wife turned pawnbroker (*aduvu ittu-kolluvudu*) advancing cash to neighbours and relatives against vessels or jewelry. Generally, the wife jealously guarded her money. If she lent it to her husband to meet a crisis, she expected him to pay her back later. She liked to keep some cash with her which she often spent in buying saris, vessels and jewelry and in gifts to a married daughter or son coming home from school.

The man had other jobs besides the work on the farm and caring for the bullocks, sheep and goats, He had to attend to all the maintenance and minor repair work in the house, bring fuel and chop it, do all the big shopping in the towns. If he had a teenage son, the latter relieved him of such jobs as taking the bullocks twice a day to the pond or canal, providing green fodder for the sheep and goats, and chopping dry sorghum stems for cattle fodder.

It was the man who exercised control over the domestic economy. He made the annual grain-payments at harvest to the members of the artisan and servicing castes who had worked for him during the year. The huge container (*tombe*) of split bamboo in which paddy was stored after harvest was sealed by him with straw and earth, and only he broke open the seal when necessary.

Women were given to selling quantities of paddy on the sly either to buy something they fancied or just to get some cash. There was a tendency to treat paddy as currency and this was perhaps linked to its being a cash crop with most villagers. Vegetables, betel leaves, small dried fish (*sigdi*), and even fruits, were locally bought with paddy. The scarcity of rice in urban areas had created a black market, and women who sold vegetables and other goods in the villages took advantage of this situation. For instance, the vegetable-seller from Hogur who visited Rampura twice or thrice a week accepted only rice in exchange for her vegetables. I had to bring rice from Mysore in order to be able to 'buy' vegetables from her. She knew of the difficulty I was put to but felt unable to make an exception in my favour.

There was a widespread belief that the male head of the household made all the crucial decisions. Women were thought to be incapable of understanding what went on outside the domestic walls. The husband was expected not to pay much attention to his wife's views in such matters as land, relations with officials, etc. If he was sufficiently 'male' he kept his wife and children under his control (*haddubastu*, literally, boundary stones marking off one man's land from his neighbour's). However, reality was somewhat different from belief. Women did exercise some influence on the men's decisions, though covertly, and the quantum of influence varied from household to household. Some men, for instance, were believed to be under the influence of their wives. They were lacking in 'manliness' and were the objects of ribald comment. Such comment, apart from giving satisfaction to the critics, served to conceal the fact that they were not uninfluenced by their wives. Otherwise it would be difficult to account for the widespread belief that joint families broke up because the incoming daughters-in-law wanted to form separate households with their husbands. Occasionally a man was heard saying that if he did a particular thing he would have trouble at home. Women had certain well-developed techniques for making known their views: they would go into long sulks, refuse food, nag continuously, appeal to elderly kinsmen over the head of the husband, and so on. Another evidence of the wife's influence was the occasional presence of her younger brother or sister in the household. After separating from his brothers, a man frequently developed friendly relations with his wife's natal kin. There was also the likelihood that his children would marry into his wife's natal household.

While it was unmanly to be influenced by the wife, it was a virtue to be influenced by the mother. I have already described the influence exercised by the headman's mother. There were others like the headman's mother though not as outstanding. I have a hunch that the mother's influence was much greater in the richer and the more Sanskritized households.

The bond between the mother and child was intimate and deep. It was often stated that the mother's lap (*tayi madalu*) was the place where a child enjoyed the utmost sense of security just as the most precious and natural food for an infant was breast-milk (*ede halu* or *tayi halu*). Bottle-feeding the infant was almost unknown in Rampura in 1948, and it was not unusual for a mother to give milk to her infant for twelve months or so. Among the poorer and lower caste villagers a mother did not consider it odd to breast-feed an infant even when a male stranger was present. But under normal circumstances, modesty required that a woman cover her breasts before everyone. Only the demands of motherhood overrode the restrictions dictated by modesty.

The mother–daughter bond appeared to be even more intimate than the mother–son bond. A mother knew, more than anyone else, that her daughter had a hard life before her. She would be uprooted when still in her teens from her natal home, where everyone loved her, to be sent off to live in her husband's house where she would be under the critical eye of her mother-in-law and her husband's sisters, and even her husband's brothers' wives. Parents were anxious that their daughter should be treated kindly in her conjugal home and then get absorbed into it. Her success redounded not only to the girl's credit but also to her parents' whereas her failure tarnished the household's, even the lineage's, reputation. A divorce was a disaster while widowhood was a misfortune. There was also anxiety that the girl should conceive soon, and give birth to a son. Since most childbirths occurred in the home, and villages were without hospitals or midwives, women ran grave risks at each delivery. The perils incidental to being a woman, and the pervasive discrimination against her in a male-dominated world, served to make the mother–daughter bond a close, tender and poignant one. Even the father expressed his tenderness towards his daughter.

A woman's natal home (*tavaru mane*) had a unique significance for her. During the early years of marriage, it was a haven, a refuge, from drudgery and constant fault-finding to which she was subject in her conjugal home. Her mother made a fuss over her when she came home, and it was customary for a girl to have her first two or three confinements (*herige*) in her natal home. This annoyed the daughters-in-law who felt discriminated against, and they complained to their husbands who were already beginning to see the world through the eyes of their wives. The expenses of the confinements had to be borne by the girl's father, and in his absence by the eldest brother. All this exacerbated the relations of the married sons with their sisters and mother. Seeds were being sown for the natal family's dissolution.

But the relations between married sons and their sisters did not have the explosive potential which relations among the former had. Conflict over land was always a possibility between brothers, and a possibility which existed even after partition. Fights over boundary-ridges, and rights of passage across each other's land, frequently resulted in bitter quarrels between brothers, their wives and sons. At such quarrels incidents would be recalled in which one or the other had behaved meanly if not outrageously, resulting in à reliving of past conflicts.

Village opinion recognized the need to 'cast a girl out of her natal home' in the interests of her future but marriage had always an element of sadness. The girl left her domestic nest to make a nest elsewhere. In a Kannada folksong a brother exclaims, on his sister's leaving the natal home for her conjugal one, 'Oh, if only you had been a boy, we could have stayed together in the same house and divided the ancestral land between ourselves.' He watches his sister, and the cow-buffalo she had been presented with, walk along the village path till the land dipped and both disappeared from view. (Perhaps the sister had married into the next village not more than five or six miles away.)

A brother certainly felt sorrow when his sister left for her husband's house but when she kept coming back for her periodical confinements, his view changed. However, the change was radical if he had been married and his wife was living with him. His mother bestowed all her care and tenderness on her pregnant daughter while she expected her daughter-in-law to do all the housework under her guidance. The daughter-in-law contrasted the way she was treated with that of her sister-in-law, and she complained, at night, to her husband who burned with a sense of injustice. (The situation was much worse when there was a plurality of married brothers and sisters.) But the irony of the situation was that when the daughter-in-law went to her natal home for confinement she expected her mother to discriminate in her favour against her brother's wife! And when the daughter-in-law became, in course of time, a mother, head of household and mother-in-law she discriminated between her daughter and daughter-in-law. The logic changed according to role and situation.

But over a period of years the daughter's visits to her natal home decreased and this coincided with the daughter-in-law's position becoming more secure. The daughter and daughter-in-law had each children of their own, and in accordance with the preference given to cross-cousin marriages, their children were likely to marry each other. Marriage between a man and his elder sister's daughter was also a preferred form in the Rampura area. All in all, one of the important results of cross-cousin, and cross-uncle-niece marriage was to mitigate the injustice which agnatic and virilocal principles inflicted on daughters.

It was not only a man's wife who had distinctive economic interests but also his son (or sons). As mentioned earlier, in many a household a son was given a ewe or nanny-goat to rear, and over a year or two the boy came to own a few animals which were sold after they had been reared, and the money was usually lent at high interest rates to build up a small capital for him.

In the better-off households, the children were each given a few measures of paddy at harvest, and this again was theirs to sell and invest in loans or animals. All in all, there was a deliberate effort to inculcate in a boy the qualities of thrift and saving. The money thus accumulated belonged to him and if the parents spent it, they had to make it good. I remember a dispute between Kari Honnu and his son Puttu which assumed serious proportions. Kari Honnu's wife had given Puttu a ram which the boy had reared, and when the ram was fully grown he sold it to a buyer who agreed to pay him Rs 96 for it. He was given an advance of Rs 30 with the promise that the balance would be paid later. The father took the money and spent it. Puttu was very angry and took the dispute to Lakshmana. He told the latter that the father was only entitled at best to a third of the money as the fodder had come from his land, the mother to another third as she had given him the ram originally, and he himself should get the remaining third. When his father did not give him the money, he ran away from home for several days, and after he returned, stayed in a relative's house. The incident so upset the boy that he eventually left the village for Mandya. He died in Mandya a couple of years later after contracting cholera.

The fostering of acquisitiveness from childhood was probably not the best kind of training for living in a joint family. It made each member sharply aware of his contribution to the domestic economy, and it made him ask whether the others were pulling their weight. I recall a dramatic moment in a partition dispute among four Peasant brothers when the youngest who was still in his teens suddenly broke down, complaining that he did not want to live any more with his eldest brother as he was being grossly overworked. Every part of his body ached with working continuously in slushy fields. He could not carry on. His sudden outburst put the eldest brother on the defensive. He appeared to the arbitrators as an exploiter of a young brother whom it was his duty to protect. The arbitrators decided that the youngest brother should form a separate household with his widow-mother.

In another case of partition, this time among Lingayats, there was a complaint that Sannu, after he became the head of the joint family consisting of himself and his younger brothers, began to be increasingly absent from the village. Sannu found visits to his wife's natal household particularly congenial—his wife's younger sister hung around him, gave him urban snacks, and was generally solicitous about his comfort. Sannu's younger brothers started asking, 'What was he contributing to farming? Why should they alone work?'

The eldest brother who succeeded to the headship of the joint family had to be extremely circumspect about his behaviour. In the first place, everyone had to be convinced that he always acted in the interests of the joint family as a whole. He had to husband its resources carefully, provide for expenditure on weddings and funerals, and invest the surplus in buying land, houses and cattle. Above all, his fairness and impartiality had to be beyond doubt. A head of a joint family was occasionally heard saying that he had refrained from fondling his children for fear of being misunderstood. I did not see any head of a joint family displaying great affection for any child in his household. Restraint and patience were essential qualities in a head of the household. In large households something or other always went wrong, and somebody or other frequently created a scene. The head had to put up with all that and take note only of serious outbursts. Such a head commanded the respect of the younger members who generally obeyed him.

The more urbanized villagers felt the authority of the head of the household too oppressive. A younger man did not have pocket money of his own to buy something for his wife or child, or even to buy his daily supply of *bidis*. A visitor from Kere, in his early thirties, told me that the refusal of the older heads of household to realize that the younger men needed some pocket money as well as mental elbow-room was a source of tension and conflict in every joint family. If the older people did not realize that the times had changed, joint families would not survive. One reason why educated youths wanted salaried jobs in urban areas was the need to get away from their natal families.

Among the artisan, servicing and trading castes, the extent of female participation in the traditional occupation varied from occupation to occupation. The common factor in each case, however, was that custom defined which tasks were to be performed by men, which by women, and which by both. For instance, women were excluded totally from the traditional occupation among Barbers but not so among Washermen. It was usually men who needed the services of the Barber, and the Barber came into close contact with the patron whose hair he was removing, and whose finger- and toe-nails he trimmed. The principle of the segregation of sexes worked here, and the idea of the Barber's wife shaving men was unthinkable.

The Barber had also a sinister connotation for Brahmin women among whom a widow had to have her head shaved periodically. One would have thought that given the principle of the segregation of the sexes the Barber's wife would shave the Brahmin widow. No, either the Barber's wife had a deep resistance to the job, as it was a reminder of the sad and inauspicious state which might befall any woman, or she lacked the skill. One of the many misfortunes which widowhood brought to a Brahmin woman was the periodical tonsure at the hands of the Barber, and a man at that. There was a taboo among Brahmins against using the Kannada word for 'Barber'.

Among washermen, on the other hand, the wife's participation was essential. No washerman would personally handle the menstrual sari which needed to be washed. It was his wife's job to collect the sari from the patron and wash it. This sari was carried at the end of a stick to which it was tied, and not mixed with the main bundle of dirty clothes. Menstrual saris, like trimmed hair and nails, defiled those who came into contact with them. They were washed by the Washerman's wife. The latter's services were also essential at child-birth: she cleaned the saris of the mother of the new-born infant. There was a customary fee and gift attached to these essential but polluting services.

The Potter made the pots and tiles, and his wife helped him only in such secondary jobs as keeping the fire going in the kiln, and a watchful eye on the pots, pans and tiles while they were being dried before firing.

Among Oilmen the men worked the bullock-drawn mill. The women came into the picture only when it came to selling oil, and selling hot, fried snacks which were relished greatly by the villagers. (Torches made with oil-soaked rags were sold by oilmen, both men and women, at festivals and fairs.) Thus Oilman Subba and his wife Lakshmi sold fried snacks at the Madeshwara fair in November 1948.

The two worked as a team, Lakshmi making small *pattis* out of the spiced dough while the husband fried them in a huge iron pan.

It was among Basketry-makers, though, that female participation was at its highest. It was the men who bought the bamboos from the urban market and did the primary job of splitting the stems. Both the men and women then took layer after layer from each split to weave baskets, fish-traps, winnow fans and screens.

I have said that the division of labour between the sexes was determined by custom. While this was true, personality factors were not utterly irrelevant. A wife who had a strong personality took over jobs which were not usually regarded as hers. But even she did not take over jobs which were exclusively men's.

2 Men and Women

As I have stated earlier I could not help being impressed by the villagers' acceptance of the body and its appetites. Such acceptance was regarded as not only natural but the only possible one for all human beings who were not *sanyasis*. All this was implicit in the sense that it had to be inferred from discrete acts of behaviour and occasional odd comment. It did not find expression as a coherent philosophy of life.

The villagers' acceptance of the body, its appetites, limitations and processes underlay their conception of proper behaviour for human beings, though living in society meant the imposition of some curbs on the body. One of the features of village life which I found striking was the unembarrassed discussion of bodily processes. I have earlier referred to Rame Gowda's advising me, loudly and at length, within a few hours of my arrival in the village, as to where I should defecate.

During my walks with my friends I found one or more suddenly hiving off to defecate near a bush and then clean himself in a pond, tank, or one of the canals. And gradually I found that it was not unusual for a man to request a friend to accompany him on a short walk at the end of which both of them defecated and even conversed with each other while smoking *bidis*. This was generally done at dusk or soon after: creeping and crawling things were about at this time and men did not like to be alone. I wondered how far this had been institutionalized and I even tried to compile a list of those who habitually defecated together.

Occasionally, during my cross-country walks, I came across two or more women answering calls of nature, sitting several yards away from each other. The need for companions was even greater in the case of women who had to take note of the possibility of coming across a rapist in a lonely field.

One morning, as I was standing on my verandah while waiting for my coffee, several men appeared on the street accompanied by a big, hefty bull and a puny cow. For reasons best known to themselves, they chose to have the cow served on the street, immediately opposite the post office. The cow was made to stand in a corner and it was firmly held by two men. Two other men were in charge of the bull, each holding tightly the free end of a leash made of twisted coir tied to the animal's collar. There was another man who acted as master of ceremonies.

A few children collected near the scene to watch the fun and it occurred to no elder to shoo them off. The men and women who had to use the street made a slight detour, walking on the vacant lot next to the Bullock House. The bull merely stood there for several minutes, refusing to be roused. Comments, some critical, some explanatory, were offered for the bull's refusal to cooperate. The master of ceremonies kept making a clicking noise with his tongue to coax the bull to mount the cow. The bull was finally roused and moved clumsily towards the miserable cow. But the latter collapsed as soon as the bull landed its front legs on its back, the two men holding the cow being taken completely by surprise. Once again, there was loud discussion among the men, and the master of ceremonies urged the two men in charge of the cow to give a firm support. The master of ceremonies then went back to his job of rousing the reluctant bull. After a long time it responded and mounted the cow. The master of ceremonies inserted the bull's member into the cow and then shouted in triumph, 'kobbu kadiyitu' ('the fat has come out'). Everyone expressed satisfaction, and the crowd disappeared from the street.

I must recall here that there were open fields behind the Bullock House, less than thirty yards from Gudi Street. But apparently it had occurred to no one to take advantage of the quiet of the fields. The bull might have been more forthcoming in a lonely field than in a busy street. Again, no one seemed to think that it was not proper or aesthetic to arrange for the serving of a cow at a place frequented by women and children. I could not help wondering that no one seemed to view the entire incident as anything except ordinary.

Many villagers kept one or two sheep, goats or buffaloes. And when these animals gave birth to their young, children were not only not told to keep away but asked to help. Again, considering the fact that in many houses the animals occupied one wing of the roofed inner quadrangle, while adults and children occupied the others, an important event like the birth of a calf or lamb could not be kept secret from the children, even if the elders wanted to. Village children learned the basic 'facts of life' by watching the animals around them.

The castration of a young bull, billy goat or ram was frequently carried out in the open street. And whether it was done on the street or inside the house, no attempt was made to keep the children out. Sannu, my friend, told me that sometimes a man castrated a billy goat or ram when it was very young. In such a case, he made a hole in the animal's scrotum with his teeth, and his children ate the testes after roasting them. 'As we eat roasted peanuts', Sannu said, to underline the barbarity of the act. Sannu, a Lingayat, was a vegetarian, and he felt that I, as another vegetarian, would see his point of view.

Sex was regarded as a primordial urge in the same manner as hunger. My friends frequently argued that the body which had consumed 'salty and sour' things (*uppu huli tinda deha*) also needed satisfaction of sex. No ordinary man could control his sexual urge except perhaps for brief periods.

The sex urge showed itself from a very young age. According to village opinion, a boy was ready for marriage as soon as he was strong enough to do a man's work on land, and hair had sprouted above his upper lip. And a girl was ready for marriage a year or two before attaining puberty. The consummation ceremony was generally held a few months after puberty. Among orthodox Brahmins, however, parents were required to get their daughters married before they came of age. Failure to do so meant not only incurring the wrath of relatives and castefolk but committing a sin.

A girl's coming of age was marked by elaborate ritual, and among the high castes, women were regarded as impure for three nights during their monthly periods. A woman in her periods sat in a corner of the house avoiding contact with others. She was freed from impurity only on the fourth morning after a purifying bath and change of clothes.

In other words, a girl's coming of age was a public event among the high castes. If she was as yet unmarried, her parents strove hard to obtain a groom for her. Otherwise tongues would wag, and there was also a danger of her going astray. Villagers were convinced that puberty was synonymous with maturity and a mature girl had to have her sex urge satisfied. It was folly to ignore this. I remember a conversation with Kulle Gowda about the marriage of his niece (deceased sister's daughter). She was small-made, and looked younger than her age. Kulle Gowda told me that the girl was going to be given in marriage to his younger brother's son, a husky youth. Unable to conceal my surprise, I exclaimed, 'Why, she is only a girl!' It was Kulle Gowda's turn to be surprised and he replied decisively, 'But she has come of age [*rutuwagiddale*].' Incidentally, men and women felt no awkwardness in mentioning, even before strangers, that so-and-so had come of age or was in her monthly periods.

The conviction that the sex urge was irresistible after puberty led the villagers to think that all bachelors and spinsters (including, if not especially, students in co-educational colleges) had a secret life of their own. The ease and conviction with which villagers commented on the loose morals of college-going girls annoyed me and I protested against speaking without evidence. My protests were generally brushed aside with the remarks, 'You think everybody is as innocent as you!' An obvious insult had been packed into the reply.

Among the non-Brahmin castes, it was customary for the parents of a boy to go about villages looking for a suitable bride just as among Brahmins the parents of a girl went about groom-hunting. (A preferred relative, acceptable to both the sides, was not always available.) The anxiety to obtain good brides was so great among Okkaliga parents that girls of ten or twelve were often 'booked' by the anxious parents of boys. In such cases, the wedding ceremony took place a few years later, about the time of the girl's puberty. The parents of both the parties entered into a solemn agreement before assembled relatives and others and betel leaves and arecanuts were exchanged to symbolize the agreement.

Laki, Rame Gowda's daughter, was not even twelve in 1948 but the parents of a few Okkaliga youths visited Rampura to take a look at her and 'book' her if possible. An alliance with the headman's lineage was a coveted thing and many influential landowners wanted it. (This was how marriage was viewed.) Rame Gowda used to tease his daughter, of whom he was extremely fond, about the visitors. Laki used to—or pretended to—get annoyed and gesture eloquently with her face and hands to express her dislike of the idea and her father. But it only stimulated her father to further teasing. Rame Gowda was, however, scared of his daughter's bursting into tears, and he took care to stop teasing well before he reached that point.

It was the accepted thing to tease boys and girls about their cross-cousins and the teased boy reacted with shyness or mock anger. The Kannada term for father-in-law is *mava* while that for the maternal uncle is *sodara mava*. The distinguishing prefix *sodara* [from the Sanskrit *Sahodara*, literally, 'from the same stomach (womb)'] was frequently omitted in ordinary conversation. More importantly, a man often married his maternal uncle's daughter with the result that his *sodara mava* became his *mava*.

A boy's behaviour towards his maternal uncle (and paternal aunt) was frequently singled out for good-humoured comment. If, for instance, he stood away from his maternal uncle at a wedding or festival, someone might say, 'He is showing great respect to his *mava* not to jeopardize his chances of marrying his cross-cousin.' And if the boy was less than normally shy he would be teased about the 'excess of informality' (*salige*). The net result of this teasing and the fact of obligatory attendance at the weddings of near kin, was to make village children regard marriage as something normal if not inevitable. Village society did not provide congenial soil for ascetics.

Manhood subsumed two ideas, maleness as well as the ability to provide for a family. I shall take up the latter idea first. As described earlier, a village boy was able to do practically all the work on the farm by the time he was fourteen or fifteen years old. If he had enough land, he could support a family by his labour before he was out of his teens.

Among the non-Brahmin castes, children, whether sons or daughters, were welcome, and not regarded as a burden. Sometimes an outsider had an interest in the fertility of a family: for instance, a rich person in need of cheap labour wanted his clients to have as many sons as they could. This was poignantly brought home to me one evening when I went out for a walk with the headman and Nadu Gowda. We saw Javarayi busily digging trenches on a patch of prime quality land on which sugarcane was being grown. This land belonged to a Brahmin who was resident in Bangalore, and it was managed for him by the headman. Javarayi had dug trenches at regular intervals of 18 inches and the trenches ran the entire length of the land measuring about 75 yards or so. He had done this with nothing but his hoe, and without using a measuring rod. We saw, or rather the headman spotted, the bare-backed Javarayi bent over his hoe at the far end of the patch of land. It was late and the sun was already sinking. A pleased smile cracked open the headman's granite face, and turning to his old friend, he said, 'Men like Javarayi should have a quick succession of sons, one, two, three, four. They will all be excellent cultivators.'

Another factor favoured fertility, though it was not verbalized. The high incidence of maternal and infant mortality, and the periodical visitation of the countryside by dreaded epidemics such as plague, cholera and smallpox, made large families welcome. The latter had better chances of survival than small ones.

As stated earlier, marriage was linked in villagers' minds with puberty. But while a girl's coming of age was marked with ritual, a boy's was not. When hair started sprouting on his upper lip, a boy was teased about his having become an adult, indicating his readiness for marriage. In the old days every man cultivated a moustache, and the more vain and hirsute among the landowners had big moustaches with fine tapering ends which were twirled and made to point upwards (*giralu mise*). A man who behaved in an unmanly way did not deserve to keep his moustache: 'Why does he carry a moustache?'

It was interesting that while the moustache was a symbol of masculinity, the beard was not. In the village, most adults had a few days' growth of stubble on their faces and this was due to the frequency with which the barber visited them. No villager had his face shaved more frequently than once a week. But a stubble was not a beard. A beard symbolized religiosity or mendicancy or both. When the beard was accompanied by long hair which had become matted and brown with neglect, and the forehead was adorned with *vibhuti* stripes or a *kumkum* dot, the association with religion and mendicancy was complete. Sometimes there was, in addition, the decisive symbol of the ochre robes.

Even in 1948, the younger and more urbanized villagers were showing a preference for a clean-shaven upper lip. Moustaches, especially the big or the handlebar variety, were ceasing to be symbols of masculinity and becoming instead symbols of antiquated rusticity. However, a few young bloods who spent the main part of the year in Mysore studying in high school or college sported a thin line of carefully-groomed hair just above the upper lip, in imitation of the film heroes.

The acceptance of the biological dimension of life did not, however, operate in a vacuum but was mediated through the culture. Thus, while it was recognized that sex was a powerful urge and demanded regular satisfaction from an early age, marriage was the proper institution through which satisfaction had to be sought. An important aim in marrying boys and girls early was to prevent them from 'taking to bad ways' (*ketta dari*, literally, 'bad road') or 'straying from the proper path' (*dari tappi hoguvudu*).

'Straying' was bad for boy as well as girl. But a girl paid a much higher price for it. A pregnancy could not be hushed up in the village, and it brought down not only the girl's reputation but her family's. No respectable man would be willing to marry the girl or her younger sisters. A girl who had strayed from the proper path made the members of her family hang their heads down in shame (*tale ettuva hagilla*).

The consequences of a boy's straying were nowhere as serious as a girl's. If a boy contracted veneral disease from visiting a loose woman or prostitute, his parents would be angry and hurt but their reaction would be qualitatively different from that to a girl's misconduct. It was another matter, however, if he regularly visited prostitutes. Veneral disease, drinking, gambling and neglect of agriculture, and loss of land and other forms of wealth were associated with visiting prostitutes. He became an enemy of his natal family.

The relation between husband and wife was conceived asymmetrically. While the married state was regarded as the only possible one for adults it had greater significance for women than men. A woman whose husband was alive was a *muttaide*, and the gold ornament *tali* which was tied round her neck by her husband was a symbol of the married state. There were also other symbols of being married such as the right to wear an oval (or circular) dot of *kumkum* on the forehead, and wearing flowers in the hair and glass bangles on the wrists. Among the more Sanskritized castes, only women whose husbands were living were entitled to wearing blouses.

While the married woman was regarded as an auspicious person the widow was inauspicious, her presence not being welcome at auspicious ritual, except when she had reached a great age and her son was devoted to her. Great age entitled a person to respect from younger people though an old widow was careful enough not to thrust herself to the forefront at a wedding or other auspicious occasion.

Among the higher castes a widow had to observe mourning for a year whereas a widower observed mourning for only thirteen days. Among the Brahmins, a widow was prohibited from marrying while among the others, an inferior form of marriage had been devised for her. No Brahmin priest officiated on such an occasion nor was an astrologer consulted. A widow's wedding usually took place after dark. (In South India, as distinct from the North, the crucial part of the wedding ritual is usually performed during an auspicious period of time before midday and never after sundown.) The widow sat on a broom behind a partially open door. Then the groom walked in opening the door fully, and lit an earthen lamp saying, 'I have come to light a lamp'. The presence of a few close relatives and caste elders gave public sanction to the alliance. The 'ritual' observed was an eloquent comment on the widow's status.

In contrast, however, a widower's marriage was celebrated like the marriage of a man and woman who were coming together for the first time. If, however, he was an old man with grown children, and the difference between his and the bride's age was great, he was expected to marry unostentatiously.

Singleness resulting from divorce was qualitatively different from widow- or widower-hood in that the latter was a misfortune, a condition brought about by an act of god, while both the partners were responsible in varying measures for divorce. Public opinion weighed the conduct of each partner and then apportioned the blame. If, for instance, the husband was impotent, given to drink or to constant wife-beating (as distinct from an occasional act of chastisement especially during the early years of marriage), gambling, visiting prostitutes, or failed to provide for his wife and children, then *he* was to blame. If, on the other hand, the wife was a loose woman, continually neglected her duties towards her husband and children, or repeatedly went to her natal home for long periods, then the blame was largely hers. A 'release agreement' (*bidugade patra*) was drafted before the assembled elders, and the wife returned the jewelry and bride-price (*tera*) which had been presented to her at the wedding. The kinsfolk of the partner who was to blame for the divorce had to pay a sum of money as damages to the injured partner. Each party was then free to remarry.

A husband who had been held responsible for his divorce found it difficult to secure another bride. He probably succeeded in getting only a widow or another divorcee, or a grown girl who, for various reasons, had not been able to find a husband. As stated earlier, much hard-headed calculation went into marriages including those among preferred relatives. The norms of kinship required setting aside 'rational' calculation but in practice it did enter. This was sharply brought home when one of two eligible relatives had to be selected. The parents of the rejected candidate naturally felt very upset.

A wife whose conduct had resulted in the dissolution of her marriage disgraced her family. The matter was far worse if she was guilty of loose conduct. Her relatives then looked frantically for someone to marry her. Only if she found a strong man who would control her was there any hope of her settling down, and of her sisters finding suitable husbands. However, a divorcee's offspring were regarded as belonging to a *koodavali vamsha* (literally, remarriage lineage), and as such, lower than the offspring of a proper marriage.

The sexual assumptions underlying marriage were complex. The ideal was that the husband and wife should be faithful to each other but villagers took a far more serious view of the wife's lapses. Occasionally, when in a confessional or boastful mood, my friends used to narrate their sexual adventures before or even after marriage. But I am certain that the same men would have behaved violently if they had learnt that their wives too had similar adventures.

A man could play around but not so a woman. A man's sense of private property in his wife's genital organs was as profound as in his ancestral land. And just as, traditionally, a wife lacked any right to land she lacked an exclusive right to her husband's sexual prowess. Polygyny and concubinage were both evidence of her lack of such rights. Men and women were separate and unequal.

A 'manly' husband kept his wife under control. She was not supposed to talk back to him or sulk or nag unduly. In the context of the joint family, she was expected to obey her parents-in-law, and in particular, her mother-in-law, and cooperate with her husband's brothers' wives, and her husband's sisters. A son or brother who demanded partition of the joint family's estate was likely to be accused of being under the influence of his wife or her relatives. If the wife was also attractive or light-skinned, then it would be mentioned as decisive evidence of the poor man's being under the spell of the charmer.

I am not suggesting that the villagers were unaware of the existence of conflicts among brothers which led to one or more of them asking for partition of the joint family's estate. But the wife who could not get on with her mother-in-law and her husband's brothers' wives, and who induced her husband to break away, was a convenient scapegoat. That each brother was himself influenced by his wife was conveniently forgotten unless someone mentioned it during the dispute.

The men permitted to themselves a roving eye. There were a few attractive women in the village and I found they were the subject of frequent discussion among my younger friends. Three of the women discussed had the reputation of being permissive if not loose. It was significant that all the three were the wives of poor men, and credited with undue influence over their husbands because of their good looks.

Extra-marital sex occurred as a result of either a chance encounter in a lonely field or corner, or assumed the semi-institutionalized form of a 'keep' (*madugikolluvudu* or *rakhavu*) relationship. Cases of rape or attempted rape were reported to the headman or Nadu Gowda for inquiry and the subsequent award of punishment. 'Keep' relationships, in contrast to chance encounters, were durable though not as durable as marriages. Either party to the relationship was in theory free to give up the existing partner and take on a new one. But as a matter of actual fact, a break in a 'keep' relationship was not easy, and gave rise to ill-feeling and bitterness in one or both the parties.

There were several cases of 'keep' relationships in Rampura in 1948, and they seem to have been even more common in the recent past. As the knowledgeable accountant of Kere explained to me, the phenomenon of 'this man keeping that man's wife and that man keeping this man's wife' was responsible for the atmosphere of violence and bloodshed which characterized rural life at the beginning of the century. For instance, even in 1948 elderly villagers recalled how a Brahmin leader of Kere had been murdered in 1910 (*circa*) and his body chopped up and thrown into the canal. And as I have already mentioned, before the end of World War I, a Peasant servant of a leader of Rampura was alleged to have murdered his wife and three children because she had become the mistress of a rich trader in Mysore.

Generally, it was the better-off landowners from the higher and dominant castes who kept mistresses. The latter did not always come from the same or equivalent castes, and when such relationships crossed the lines of caste, it was more common for the woman to come from a lower caste though the reverse type of relationship was not unknown. But the high caste man had to take care to see that his mistress came from a 'clean' caste. If, for instance, he took a Harijan mistress, he was likely to be outcasted.

A man from a low or non-dominant caste who developed a liaison with a woman from a high or dominant caste ran the risk of being punished by the men of the latter caste. There was an instance of such a liaison in Rampura in 1947. Kannur, a Lingayat youth, and Devi, a young Peasant divorcee, were having an affair. Some Peasant youths saw them together on one or two occasions, and warned Kannur to keep away from the girl. Kannur was contemptuous of the Peasants and replied, 'Let me see what you will pluck!' (*enu kittukolluttiro nodona!*), meaning that they could not do anything except pluck his pubic hair. We have seen earlier that comparing any object to, or bringing it in relation with, pubic hair, was to proclaim its utter worthlessness. The enraged Peasant youths were determined to teach Kannur a lesson which he would not easily forget. So when he next visited his girl friend he found the door suddenly bolted from the outside and locked. The matter was then reported to the headman who had Kannur tied to a pillar and flogged. He then called an emergency meeting of some elders including the head of the Mahadeshwara priestly lineage, a Lingayat.

The headman wanted to make an example of Kannur. He had not only had an affair with a Peasant girl but had insulted Peasants. The elders discussed various aspects of the matter till late at night but could not come to an agreed conclusion. The meeting was then adjourned to the following morning. But before the adjourned meeting could begin, the headman heard that a Peasant youth, who was agnatically related to him, had raped a girl whom he had encountered in the fields. Other factors being equal, rape was more serious than liaison between consenting adults, and the punishment awarded to a rapist ought to be more severe than that awarded to Kannur. But at the adjourned meeting, Kannur got away with a fine of fifty rupees, and Devi's guardian was urged to marry her off without delay.

As a caste, Lingayats occupy a higher ritual position than Peasants (Okkaligas) in the local hierarchy and Kannur's relationship with Devi was therefore a 'hypergamous' one. But Peasants were the dominant caste in Rampura and neighbouring villages, and they were more powerful and richer than Lingayats. Kannur had not only had an affair with a Peasant girl but had insulted Peasant youths, and indirectly, their caste.

The caste headman of the Peasants in the big village of Kere—he was then in his eighties—told me that he once received a complaint against a Brahmin who had had an affair with a Peasant girl and a child had been born of the union. The case was considered by the elders of Kere and they eventually decided to let the Brahmin off with a fine. The Brahmin had shown enough meekness towards the Peasant elders and this was a factor which induced them to let him off lightly. The girl was not punished as her paramour was from a higher caste and she was only subjected to a tongue-lashing.

The above incident occurred in the 1920s or earlier when village opinion had tacitly accepted the idea of castes being unequal. However, if a similar incident had occurred in the 1940s, it would have probably provoked a different reaction from Peasant elders. Deterrent punishment might have been inflicted on the Brahmin to make clear that the days of Brahminical superiority had ended.

'I shall . . . . your wife' was one of the worst abuses in the villagers' vocabulary. But rich landowners from the dominant and other high castes used it frequently against their tenants, debtors and servants. The latter had just to put up with it. But even in 1948 there were a few individuals who showed their resentment and anger when abused in the time-honoured way. One morning, when Kulle Gowda and I were walking along the rough track leading to Edagai village, we ran into the local Smith who was walking in the opposite direction. The Smith stopped Kulle Gowda and told him about a fight that he had, a day or two previously, with the Peasant headman of the village. The Smith and the headman were talking about something when suddenly the latter said, '*Ninna hedtina* . . . .' ('May I . . . . your wife!'). At once the Smith lost all control of himself and by the time he came to, he found that he was lying on top of the headman and that his hands were bloody. The Smith was truly a mighty man, tall and big-built, and all muscle and bone. He showed his right hand —it was large and calloused over with the daily use of heavy hammers, axes and other tools. He did not seem the least bit regretful at having beaten up the headman. In fact, there was unconcealed satisfaction at having taught the headman a lesson that he would not forget.

In another neighbouring village, the powerful headman experienced a shock to find the poor Peasant whom he had abused, replying,

'If my wife is to be .... by you, your wife should be .... by a Harijan.' The headman controlled with great effort his mounting anger and kept silent. The man whom he had abused was a member of the largest Peasant lineage in the village and there were several powerful men in that lineage who would have loved to make common cause with him against the headman. It was likely to become an inter-lineage incident.

One reason why the abuse stirred up its recipient so violently was that it attacked a man in a most sensitive area, viz. his maleness. Only when a man was deficient in maleness would he allow his wife to sleep with another. That was at least the belief. On the other hand, the man who slept with somebody else's wife had not only enjoyed the experience but had injured another man's maleness. An excess of maleness was something which one boasted about (at least to one's peers) whereas deficiency in it was humiliating. The cuckold had to hang his head in shame in village society. The only course open to him to vindicate his honour was to kill, in a moment of anger, his wife and her lover. Men who had committed such crimes were spoken of with approval if not admiration.

'Keep' relations had an explosive potential, and the cautious man looked for a widow or divorcee, as relations with her did not involve injuring a husband's maleness. However, the concerned kinsfolk, and village elders made efforts to get her married but they were not always successful. It was particularly difficult to find a husband when the woman had three or four children by her prior marriage. In course of time, however, she found a lover. He might be a widower or divorcee, or someone who merely wanted a second string to his conjugal bow. Public opinion recognized that the woman needed to have her sex gratified. She had the choice of being a mistress or whore. A whore was a threat to the morals of the entire village, while a mistress provided gratification to a widower, unhappily married man or powerful landowner.

As I said earlier, there was near-unanimous opinion in Rampura that only one village elder, a man in his sixties, had been faithful to his wife, and I found it both cynical and difficult to believe. Perhaps the villagers were only trying to impress upon me the rarity of faithfulness among husbands. I could not help asking myself why men who liked to brag about their sexual adventures expressed unqualified respect for a chaste elder. Perhaps they felt that the highest ideal of marriage was mutual faithfulness, an ideal which was too high for comfortable living. But when someone actually lived up to it they could not help admiring him. Incidentally, Rama, the super-human hero of the epic Ramayana, was a model of husbandly faith-fulness: mutual faithfulness was a high Sanskritic value.

Men and women were expected to behave in certain recognized ways, and departures from them were commented upon. For instance, a wife lacking in modesty, and who talked freely outside the house and before other men was dubbed a *gandubiri* (behaving like a man). A *gandubiri's* husband was embarrassed about his wife's reputation and the reflection it cast on his own ability to control his wife. Each man liked others to think that he controlled his wife. It is also prob-able that each man believed that he did.

Kobli was not a typical wife. It was reported that she had even beaten her husband once thus reversing an important element of the husband-wife relationship. Karage Gowda narrated to me how during a transplanting season Kobli came and held his hand on the pretext of seeking shelter under his umbrella. (I had the impression that my friend was indulging in a bit of fantasy or reading too much into an accidental touching of hands). He equated it to 'pulling him by the hand' which really was an invitation to him to sleep with her. As stated earlier, a man was expected to take the initiative in sex relations, and a woman who ignored this rule and made advances was certain to be the subject of much comment. And perhaps Karage Gowda was led to believe that Kobli was making advances to him because of her reputation. Several leaders were alleged to have had affairs with her. She was also reported to have seduced a youth or two. Her husband was believed to be inadequate.

All *jita* servants in the village excepting one was a male. But the exception illuminated the rule. Nadu Gowda had a 'sheep woman' (*kuriyavalu*) whose contract described her as a *jita* servant. It was her duty to drive her master's flock every morning to pasture and bring it back in the evening. And the 'sheep woman' not only kept the company of boys but behaved like them, even climbing trees. She was also strong. She was short, squat and ugly. A few of her com-panions were her lovers and one of them died of venereal disease.

The villagers were puzzled but amused by the phenomenon of someone who was biologically female but socially male. I was unable, however, to share their sense of amusement. I was repelled by the 'sheep woman': apart from being markedly ugly she seemed mentally retarded.

Even more significant was the arrival of a hermaphrodite from Hogur. 'She' was a Muslim by faith and 'she' was dressed like a local Muslim woman, with a skirt, blouse and a loose cloth draped over the skirt like a sari. Her face had a few days' stubble on it but the hair on her head had been allowed to grow like a woman's. It had also been oiled, combed, and tied in a knot just above the nape of the neck.

Mrs Karim, my neighbour, had taken the hermaphrodite to her house. Several women gathered round her and I could hear much feminine chatter and laughter. It was obvious that the hermaphrodite was a source of considerable amusement to the women. I later discovered that while she was at Mrs Karim's house the women had redone her hair, given her some food and betel leaves to chew.

Mrs Karim shepherded the hermaphrodite to a few houses including mine. And I found her sitting on my verandah at the centre of a group of Muslim women while a few men hung about outside. The hermaphrodite's face was wreathed in smiles, frequently showing her teeth reddened with betel leaves. My reaction to the hermaphrodite was, however, worse than my reaction to the 'sheep woman'. The incongruity between the sari and the groomed hair contrasted with the stubble on the chin. I could not understand why the women found her company so enjoyable. The men regarded her with amusement and wonder. She was a negation of two of the most cherished values of men, potency and aggression. But she could be allowed to move freely with their women. The women found her entertaining because she had characteristics of both men and women. And at the same time she was safe.

What distinguished a marriage from a 'keep' relationship was that children were essential to complete the former. A kept woman was expected to give sexual satisfaction, and sometimes also food but rarely children. A mistress with children was likely to become absorbed in her children and seek to protect their interests at the expense of the children by the wife. Any attempt by the mistress to confer legitimacy on her children by demanding marriage was certain to provoke serious opposition from not only the wife and other kinsfolk but the local community. When a wife was barren the husband felt justified in taking another wife. But no such justification existed when the mistress was childless.

It was not only the husband but his entire lineage which had a stake in his wife's fertility. Only if she produced sons could the ancestral land be cultivated. If, on the other hand, she gave birth only to daughters then one of the sons-in-law would have to become a surrogate son through the institution of *manevanthala* (corruption of *manevalathana*). The birth of children was an important step in a girl's becoming an effective member of her husband's household. Till that time there was always the possibility of the husband marrying a second wife. Only when children were born to the daughter-in-law did her husband and his parents all obtain common objects of love. The wife had also proved that she was fertile and had ensured the continuity of her husband's lineage (*vamsha* or *pilige*). She could exercise some power over her in-laws through her children. It was motherhood which really put the seal on a woman's acceptance in her husband's household.

Women had a dread of sterility. Calling a woman 'barren' (*goddu, banjer*) was one of the worst abuses just as an allegation of impotence had a similar connotation for the husband. Arduous pilgrimages were undertaken by married couples to obtain children. The high incidence of infant mortality added to the anxiety regarding children.

I have made the point that the villagers had a deep conviction that all normal human beings were subject to the basic biological drives. Only true sanyasis had conquered them. In this connection, a distinction is perhaps necessary between performing religious functions and being in ochre robes. Villagers were aware that priests were often this-worldly, and they discussed the career of a priest in the same way as they did a landowner's, trader's or artisan's. They would even point out, without any attempt at cynicism, how a man's devotion to a particular deity, temple or pilgrimage had contributed to his worldly prosperity. Worldly prosperity was promoted by religiosity and not antithetical to it. Occasionally the villagers made fun of a priest's greed. But a man in ochre robes was a different proposition altogether. He was holy, and he could rise above the demands of the body. Sanyasis had conquered sex, and they could subsist on the leaves of some plants and fresh air, cure diseases normally incurable, convert base metals into gold and even make themselves invisible. The older villagers had heard of sanyasis who possessed supernatural powers. The appearance of a sanyasi, his gestures, talk, food, etc. were reported in such a way as to suggest the existence of supernatural powers.

I wondered how individuals who were as keenly intelligent and hard-headed as the villagers could suspend their disbelief so willingly when confronted with sanyasis in ochre robes. It was obvious that it was the result of the internalization of certain values deeply imbedded in the culture, and even the shrewdest and the most sceptical of intelligences were under its influence. In this connection, I remember being asked by Kulle Gowda to go and see a young sanyasi who lived in a cave near the village. The sanyasi was none other than his second son by his first wife and I had my own guess as to the factors which had driven him to don ochre robes. I was far from keen on meeting him. But not so Kulle Gowda. He seemed eager to take me there. He seemed to me totally free from any embarrassment, or an awareness that the domestic environment had a share in driving the man to fleeing life. As far as Kulle Gowda was concerned, the sanyasi was someone whom I should meet in the course of my work as the recorder of everything that went on in the village. I refused to meet the sanyasi. My sense of my vocation was not as highly developed as Kulle Gowda's.

CHAPTER VI

Relations Between Castes

1 Introductory

IF THE Rampura villager's relation with the external environment was mediated through agriculture his relations with other human beings was mediated through caste. But it was caste in the sense of *jati*, the small local endogamous group and not in the sense of the broad all-India category of *varna*. One of the first questions asked of a visitor was about his *jati*, and the villagers regarded that bit of information as essential in order to learn about his occupation, diet and life-style. How they behaved towards him also depended to some extent on his *jati*.

When, however, the visitor was from a different linguistic region, learning his *jati* did not make much sense. For instance, I was accompanied by a student during my second trip to Rampura in 1962. My friends were curious about his social origins and I explained to them that he was a Bania from Baroda in Gujarat. I had to explain further that Bania referred to the trading caste in Gujarat. The villagers knew the Banajigas, the local trading caste, and the urban Komati were usually referred to as *shettaru* in Mysore. The Banajigas spoke Kannada while the Komati spoke Telugu. My student spoke Gujarati and a certain amount of Hindi. His dress was a long *kudta* (or *jubba*) and a pair of white pyjamas. Pyjamas were locally associated with Muslims but the fact the student wore homespun *khadder* suggested strong leanings towards the Congress party. In other words, the student's language and dress made it difficult to place him in the same category as any local caste. The villagers were eventually content to regard him as an outsider, Hindu and vegetarian. He was also an educated man, and my student. The fact that they could not talk to him in Kannada bothered them. They occasionally used me as an interpreter.

As I have described earlier, the older villagers cast me in the role of a Brahmin and landowner. By so doing, they were able to make me behave towards them in certain predictable ways, and they in turn were able to regulate their behaviour to me. I may have spent many years in Bombay and abroad (*sime*) but that did not alter my caste or my belonging to a landowning family. I had, like everyone else, to be categorized, and without categorization, regular relations were impossible.

Every caste had a traditional occupation and the various castes of a region were mutually dependent. The fact that money played a minimal role in the traditional economy of the village helped to stress the inter-dependence of the members of different castes and classes. A townsman like me could not help being impressed, even in 1948, at the popularity of barter in the internal economy of the village. Linked to this was the villagers', at least the older villagers', attitude to cash. Money was to be hoarded, lent at interest, or converted into land, house or jewelry when enough had been accumulated. A five or ten rupee note was not changed into smaller notes let alone coins for fear that it would be spent.

A man inherited an occupation, and the skills and secrets involved in its practice were transmitted to him by his father, uncle or older brothers. There was a feeling that the traditional occupation was the proper or natural one for members of the caste, and there was pride in the skill required for it as well as a sense of its importance. Everyone had it though Peasants had it more than the others.

When the members of different castes met and the talk veered round to their occupations there followed a heated argument as to the relative importance of each—rather like a meeting of scholars from different disciplines each of whom is profoundly convinced that his own is the crucial one.

A term of abuse occasionally heard in the village gave an inkling of the villagers' attitude to traditional occupation. When someone was clumsy in doing a piece of work he was likely to be reprimanded by an elder, 'What is it you are doing, you *addakasabi*?' *Kasubu* was occupation, and a person referred to his hereditary occupation as *namma kasubu* (our occupation). The speaker expected everyone to know that he was proficient in *his* hereditary occupation and that outsiders could not be expected to be equally proficient. *Addakasubu* meant literally 'cross occupation', i.e. an unnatural occupation. An occupation which was not hereditary in the caste was an unnatural occupation. The corollary of proficiency in a hereditary occupation was clumsiness in a non-hereditary occupation.

Among the Hindu castes, at the annual festival of Gowri (the wife of Shiva and the mother of Ganesha), the tools used in the hereditary occupation were worshipped. The festival came soon after the end of the hectic period of sowing and transplanting rice, and the tools deserved the thanks of those who had used them. The next hectic period came at least a hundred days later when the ripe crop was ready for harvesting. After harvest, the cattle were thanked.

But the impression of immutable, hereditary occupations which the above gives is not quite correct, for not every caste was able to make a living by practising its occupation, and agriculture and trade of some sort were common to all. For instance, several members of the artisan and serving castes in Rampura practised agriculture or trade either wholly or along with their traditional occupation. Only a few Shepherd households reared some sheep, and five or six households continued to weave *kamblis* (coarse woollen blankets). The others were whole-time agriculturists. The richer of the two Toddy-man households owned some land, a toddy shop and a half-share in a cloth shop. The senior brother also worked as a tailor at the shop.

I came across a peripatetic band of well-diggers who told me that they were originally Washermen but a switch as far-reaching as that was most unusual. In the neighbouring villages of Kere and Hogur, many Fishermen had become agriculturists and market gardeners. The Fishermen of Hogur were well-known for the skill and industry with which they cultivated their small plots of land.

While occupational specialization resulted in the interdependence of castes, hierarchical ideas, especially as expressed in endogamy and the restrictions on inter-dining, emphasized their separation from each other. Hypergamous ideas did occur in southern Mysore as elsewhere but they were not elaborated as in Kerala, Gujarat, Rajasthan, or in nineteenth-century Bengal. Caste endogamy was the rule, and until the thirties the smallest local *jati* was usually the unit within which marriages occurred. This was particularly true of the lower castes. But during the forties, and more especially during the post-Independence years, marriages increasingly ignored the smallest sub-divisions within the main *jati*. Thus while a Shepherd (*kuruba*) still married another Shepherd, the sub-divisions separating them were often ignored. Jumping across sub-divisions was more common among the higher and more populous and educated *jatis*.

A caste or *jati* was also a commensal group in the sense that food cooked by any adult member of the caste was acceptable to all the others. This should be distinguished from cases where there was only one-way movement in cooked food (and also drinking water). Here the acceptors of food were ritually inferior to the givers. Sometimes, the *men* of two different *jatis* such as Peasants and Shepherds ate food cooked by each other while the women did not. (At the huge collective dinners food was usually cooked and served by men volunteers. Within the household, however, it was the women who cooked.) However, this has to be distinguished from true symmetry which occurred only within a *jati*, or in its smallest unit. But here one very rarely came across individuals, priests or the very orthodox, who accepted cooked food only from their wives.

The maintenance of the separateness of castes and of the structural distance between them was achieved through the ideas of purity and pollution. A caste was pure in relation to a lower caste and impure in relation to a higher. The higher caste was prohibited from accepting cooked food or drinking water from the lower, let alone have connubial relations with it. In extreme cases, as between a Brahmin and Harijan, a minimum physical distance had to be maintained. Violation of the rules governing the acceptance of cooked food and water, and other forms of contact, resulted in the member of the higher caste being polluted. In such cases, he was required to undergo purificatory rites. I shall discuss the part played by purity and pollution ideas in intercaste relations in Section 3.

2 Hierarchy

The idea of hierarchy was present everywhere. Each man belonged to a caste which formed part of a system of ranked castes. Particular elements of culture such as diet, occupation and custom and ritual were distinguished as higher and lower: thus there was a higher as well as a lower diet, and superior as well as inferior occupations. Animals, vegetables, plants, grain, timber and fuel were also distinguished as higher or lower. A good breed of cow, for instance, was praised as *'olle jati'* (good *jati*) while a poor breed was dismissed as *'kilu jati'* (lower *jati*).

Pride in one's caste was common, and along with it went a slighting of the other castes and their customs. A Peasant, for instance, would cite a proverb commenting on the unreliability of the Smiths (*waja nanna magana aju goju*), and another criticizing the interminable disputations of the Shepherds. A Shepherd, on the other hand, mentioned a saying about Peasants that the money earned by them was squandered in paying fines presumably to caste or village assemblies. A proverb expressed the exasperation of invitees invited to Lingayat dinners: the food was served only after an elaborate worship of Shiva which paid little heed to the guests' hunger. The Brahmins were criticized for their incapacity to do manual labour, their love of ease and over-attention to food.

However, when in a humorous or self-critical mood, a man criticized his own caste, or joined others in criticizing it. Shepherds were not only notorious for disputing endlessly but for their lack of subtlety. Stories exemplifying either quality were told by the others. One evening Chenna, an elderly Shepherd leader, gave the headman and Nadu Gowda an account of a big Shepherd wedding in Mysore from which he had just returned. Several leading politicians and other important persons from the caste had attended the wedding. Mutton curry had been cooked in an immense cauldron to be served to the several hundred hungry guests. As the vessel was lifted from the stove and placed on the floor, the bottom suddenly gave way, and in a trice, the mouth-watering curry was all over the kitchen floor. The headman started laughing and said, 'After all, Shepherds!' Nadu Gowda and Chenna joined him in the laughter, and it was not easy to tell whose laughter was the heartiest. Chenna had the gift of being able to laugh at himself and there were several others like him in Rampura.

Sometimes self-criticism occurred in an exaggerated form and this was accompanied by praise of the virtues, real or imagined, of another caste. Thus I have heard Peasants commend the sense of unity of Fishermen and contrast it with their own divisiveness.

Occasionally, however, there was what appeared to be a more objective appreciation of the virtues or skills of another caste or other group. I came across individuals who pointed out to me the skill involved (for instance) in a particular agricultural operation, weaving or basketry. A few villagers praised the aesthetics of Muslim cooking and serving, and of their gift-giving.

However, caste was not the only area for the expression of hierarchical ideas. Landownership patterns were inegalitarian in as much as there were a few big landowners at the top, each of whom owned a sizeable quantity of land while at the bottom were a large number of landless labourers. In between were small landowners many of whom were also tenants, and they were followed by tenants. Many tenants hired themselves out as labourers during transplantation and harvesting.

A rich landowner commanded prestige just as a poor landless labourer excited in the more fortunate either pity or contempt. The former had also the capital to invest money in profitable enterprises. Typically, a rich landowner lived in a substantial house with an open, central courtyard, and was creditor to a large number of people while a landless labourer lived in a tiny hut or on the verandah of someone's house. He had to borrow money from others to survive but he was such a poor risk that it was very difficult for him a find a creditor.

There was a certain amount of overlap between the twin hierarchies of caste and land. The richer landowners generally came from such high castes as Brahmin, Peasant and Lingayat while the Harijans contributed a substantial number of landless labourers. But a few members from low castes such as the Smith, Oilman and Toddyman owned reasonable amounts of land while several Peasants and Shepherds were without land. Such lack of overlap between the two hierarchies produced interesting consequences. For instance, there were two households of Toddyman in Rampura, one comfortably off and the other very poor. As stated earlier, members of the former household commanded respect as landowners and had been placed in the second category of contributors to village festivals while in the third category were included several Peasants, Shepherds and other higher castes. In contrast to the wealthier household, the poor one was socially almost invisible. It consisted of a husband who did odd work for a landowner while his wife wove mats from dried toddy-palm leaves. The two lived on someone's verandah. While poverty did not alter caste status, there was very little communication between the two households. Thammayya, the head of the better-off household, talked to me once or twice about a really wealthy fellow-casteman's household in Mysore, and how they worshipped a miniature representation, in gold, of a toddy-palm tree (*Boswellia thurefera*). The members of the household were somewhat westernized, and prominent in public life. It was obvious that Thammayya admired them. He would probably have liked to emulate them but it needed wealth and sophistication which were beyond him.

Ideas of hierarchy derived from the *varna* model of five-layered India-wide castes are not only too simple and clear-cut but misleading in understanding the caste system as it operates at the village level.[1] To mention a glaring example of the lack of fit between the all-India category of *varna* and the strictly local, though omnipresent, category of *jati*, one has only to consider the Shudra. According to the *varna* system, the Shudras are fourth in the rank-order of castes, just above the Untouchables who are said to be beyond the pale of the system. Applied at the local level, the Shudra is a blanket category for a whole range of disparate *jatis* from prestigious, landowning Peasants (who have, in places, passed off for Kshatriyas) to artisan and servicing *jatis* one or more of which were just above the Untouchability line. There was no comparison, for instance, in the social standing of the Peasants and Shepherds on the one hand and the Swineherds and Basketry-makers on the other. Again, in the *varna* system there was no place for the Lingayats who claimed to be at least the equals of Brahmins.

Even of the five all-India castes, the fifth one is regarded as being outside the system. And there is no doubt about the exact position of each in the hierarchy. In the *jati* system, however, only the two extremes of the hierarchy are fixed with any degree of firmness and there is ambiguity regarding the position of all the others. Frequently, there is some difference between claimed and conceded rank, such difference being occasionally long-standing. Dissensus regarding the ranks of particular castes was part of the dynamics of the *jati* system.

The view of caste as a ladder-like hierarchy expressed in *varna* prevents the understanding of *jati* which is basically local. While uncertainty as to mutual rank is a marked characteristic of the middle regions of the *jati* system, it is not restricted to them. Even the popular idea that the Brahmins occupy the top position in the hierarchy needs to be modified. Brahmins are not a single homogeneous group but a congeries of similar-yet-different *jatis*. For instance, a large number of castes, including of course other Brahmins, will not accept food or water handled by the Marka Brahmins (also known as Hale Karnataka).

Marka Brahmins were not present in Rampura but many villagers, especially the older ones, had come across them in villages which they had visited. Several *jatis* in the village, the Lingayat and Peasant among others, felt that they could not accept cooked food, drinking

[1] For an analysis of the relation between *varna* and *jati* see my essay 'Varna and Caste' in *Caste in Modern India*, Asia Publishing House, Bombay, 1962, pp. 63–9.

water or even lime paste for betel leaves or snuff, from a Marka Brahmin.[1] As an illustration of the attitude of the villagers towards Markas, I was told the story of a group of Rampurians who were on a brief visit to Kannambadi village where they did not know anyone. Walking in the blistering afternoon sun had tired them, and their throats were parched. They saw an orthodox Brahmin, resplendent with caste marks, sitting on a verandah, and requested him for some water. He went in to get it. In the meanwhile, a passer-by told them that it was a Marka household. The visitors at once took to their legs before the kind host returned with the water. The story caused much amusement.

That the gap between claimed and conceded status can be both wide and long-standing was proved by the example of the Smiths. In southern Mysore, the Smiths were referred to as Acharis or Wajaru. Within the category of Acharis, the term Akkasale referred to workers in precious metals, Badagi to Carpenters who were also Blacksmiths, and Kanchugara to Brass and Copper workers. But these occupational divisions did not represent endogamous groups. For the latter, the Smiths were divided into three categories, Shivachara, Kulachara and Matachara. The first two were vegetarians and teetotallers, the first being stricter than the second, while the third ate meat and drank liquor. The Shivachara category was mentioned by my informants but there were no representatives of it in Rampura while there were those of the other two. It was, however, interesting that the Carpenter-cum-Blacksmiths were very largely Kulacharis while the workers in precious metals were all meat-eaters and liquor-drinkers. In other words, in spite of statements to the contrary, occupation, style of life and endogamy all overlapped considerably among the Smiths.

The Smiths were found all over South India, and their attempt to raise themselves up in the caste hierarchy through Sanskritization was an old one. In the towns, they called themselves Vishwakarma Brahmins and wore the sacred thread. But it looked as though the Smith attempt had only roused the ire of the other castes. The various

---

[1] Powdered lime (*chunam*) was mixed with water to make a paste which was applied on the back of betel leaves and then eaten with sliced arecanut. In this part of the country, arecanut was eaten only after the nut had been sliced, boiled with *Catechu indica*, and dried.

Lime paste was also used, in minuscule quantities, by snuff-takers to knead tiny lumps of moist tobacco to powder.

artisan and servicing castes were critical if not hostile to the Smith claim to be superior to them. Two arguments were cited against the Smith claim, one being their love of meat and liquor and the other, their being grouped among the 'Left-hand' castes. It was alleged that even some Kulachara men drank on the sly, and in the toddy-booth, the Harijan, Swineherd, Muslim and Smith all had to drink out of the same mugs. The Smiths were also subjected to symbolic as well as real disabilities as they were a 'Left-hand' caste. Thus while the 'Right-hand' castes had twelve pillars to their wedding *pandals* (awnings with plaited coconut thatching and supported by stout bamboo poles), Smiths were allowed only eleven pillars. They were not allowed to perform weddings within the village. They performed them at pilgrim-centres or in villages or towns where they were represented in some strength and had temples to their caste-deities, Kali and Hanuman.

No 'Right-hand' caste, including the Harijan, accepted cooked food or drinking water at the hands of the Smiths. Smiths were not permitted to walk on the village streets with their sandals on. The Peasant headman of Kere described to me an incident which had occurred in his village during the World War I years, and which pointedly brought home to me the hostility of the 'Right-hand' castes to the Smith. A rich Smith from Mysore had lent nearly Rs 5,000/- to his debtors in Kere, and in those days it was a large sum. He walked in one afternoon wearing *chadavu* which were slip-on sandals of red leather with toes curving upwards and inwards. In those days, *chadavu* were a status symbol worn by rich men from the high castes. The *kulavadi* (or *cheluvadi*), the traditional Harijan (Holeya) servant of the high castes, became very annoyed at the Smith's sporting the slippers, and belaboured him till he became unconscious.

It is significant that the *kulavadi* coming from the oppressed *jati* or Holeyas should have taken it upon himself to punish the Smith. And the offending Smith was no ordinary person—he was an out-sider and town-dweller, and had lent money to a few leading lights of Kere. But the *kulavadi* ignored all this and looked upon him as a member of the 'Left-hand' group who had no right to take on the symbols of the high castes in the 'Right-hand' group. It gave him an opportunity to punish a member of a higher caste.

Even in 1948 elderly villagers repeatedly talked to me about the low ritual rank of the Smiths and the stigma that attached to them as a result of their inclusion in the Left-hand group of castes. The disabilities, real and symbolic, from which they suffered were cited as evidence of their low rank. One particular symbolic disability was mentioned by several people: they not only had to have 'one pillar less' (*ondu kamba kadime*) but they were 'one colour less' (*ondu banna kadime*) than the 'Right-hand' castes. The term for colour, *banna*, is a corruption of the Sanskritic *varna* which originally referred to the division of Hindu society into five ranked categories. (The term *banna* is also used, very rarely though, for caste.)

But in spite of the general view that the Smiths were of low rank I found that they had moved upwards ritually and this was brought home to me during the Rama Navami festival (1952) when the headman made gifts to married women from Smiths and Brahmin castes. Rama was worshipped elaborately on each of the ten festival days and special dishes were cooked and offered to the deity. The expenses of each day's worship were borne by one of the better-off villagers. On the headman's day, the dishes cooked were even more elaborate than those cooked on the other days, and in addition, he gave gifts of cloth (for making blouses) to five high caste wives. He probably did this in memory of his wife who had died nearly a year ago. As mentioned earlier, widowhood was an inauspicious condition, and there was a strong belief that women who had done good deeds in their previous incarnations predeceased their husbands. A wife who had predeceased her husband was worshipped (*muttaide puje*) on certain occasions such as a wedding. Five married women were invited and shown ritual respect and given gifts of cash, blouse-cloth, fruit, flower and betel leaves and arecanuts.

The women who were honoured by the headman were the Rama priest's wife, the unmarried daughter of the Brahmin postmaster, and three Smith wives. I was surprised to find that the Smith wives were included among those honoured. I could not help recalling a dispute which had taken place in a satellite village of Kere many years ago in which a Peasant had been punished by the village elders for allowing a young girl from a friendly Smith family to take part in a wedding procession in his household. Along with Peasant wives, this girl had carried a *kalasa* (a metal vessel filled with water and its mouth stoppered with a coconut, and with betel or mango leaves stuck between the inner rim of the vessel and the coconut). A *kalasa* was regarded as sacred, and worshipped.

It was unheard of to let a Smith girl participate in a Peasant wedding procession. Someone had complained to the elders of Kere saying that the participation of the Smith girl in the procession had polluted all those who had attended the wedding and that the man responsible ought to be punished suitably. The matter was settled only after the wrongdoer had apologized to the elders, undergone purification, and paid a fine.[1]

The inclusion of the three Smith wives in the ritual performed on the occasion of the Rama Navami showed that the situation in Rampura in 1952 was radically different from that in the dispute just described. There were at least three more Brahmin wives in Rampura but they were either unavailable that day, or thought that it was beneath them to go to the temple and receive the gifts. Lingayat wives were also absent but this was probably due to their reluctance to visit temples of Vishnu.

In striking contrast to the kind of hierarchy conceptualized in *varna*, uncertainty as to relative rank characterized the hierarchy as it operated at the grassroots level. Besides, the hierarchy had its strictly local features. Thus it was not surprising to find occasionally the respective ranks of the local sections of a single *jati* varying in different villages. For instance, Barbers in Rampura seemed to enjoy a ritual privilege which was denied them in Kere and a few other villages—at least that was the view of Kempayya, the Washerman, who had the reputation of being the veteran of many caste disputes involving abstruse points of customary law.

One of the crucial rites at the weddings of the higher castes was *dhare* at which the bride was given as a gift by her parents to the groom. This was symbolized by each close relative of the bride and groom pouring a little milk over the bride's cupped hands which held a coconut resting on a few betel leaves and arecanuts. It was necessary for the groom's hands to be touching the coconut as well as the bride's hands to signify his acceptance of the gift.

Among the Rampura Peasants it was customary for a Barber to hold a vessel below the hands of the bridal couple to collect the poured milk. He received a gift for his services but even more important was the fact that he was given a role in the wedding ritual of Peasants.

It was Kempayya's contention that the Barber's was a polluting caste, and that he had no place inside the wedding *pandal* or booth. He cited a judgement of some law court which had declared that the

---

[1] See my 'The Dominant Caste in Rampura', *American Anthropologist*, Vol. 61, February 1959, pp. 1–16.

right to hold the milk-bowl belonged to the Washerman and not to the Barber. The latter had quoted in support of their claim a copper-plate inscription from Conjeevaram in Tamil Nadu while Washermen had produced a similar inscription from Keragodu in Mysore District supporting their stand, and the judge had held that as far as Mysore State was concerned Keragodu had to be given precedence over Conjeevaram. Kempayya said that the dispute in question had occurred when he was a boy, and he did not know the details. He also did not know the names of the rulers (or other authorities) who had recorded their decision on copper-plates.[1]

Many years ago, during one wedding season, Kempayya had managed to assert his right to hold the milk-bowl but the Barbers had appealed against it to Nadu Gowda's father, who was then the caste headman, and he had upheld their claim. Kempayya was bitter about the decision. He had strong feelings about the position of his caste, and he disliked Barbers intensely.

I discussed the question of the mutual ritual rank of the Barber and Washerman with Nadu Gowda. He did not agree with Kempayya's view that the Washerman was not polluting while the Barber was. Was the Washerman pure when he washed menstrual saris? He was impure just as the Barber was when he carried his *hadapa* (box in which he kept the tools of his trade).[2]

Relations between Kempayya and the Barbers were not friendly even in 1948. While he did wash their clothes he did not visit their homes to collect the washing as he did with the other castes. They had to take their washing to him. On their side, the Barbers did shave Kempayya but did not visit him in his house.

The view of the caste hierarchy as it operated at the local level was then radically different from that expressed in *varna*. Mutual rank was uncertain and arguable, and this stemmed from the fact that mobility was possible in caste. In a few cases, the chasm between claimed and conceded status was so wide that no resolution was possible.

Ambitious castes, or local sections of them, tried to borrow the customs, ritual and life-style of the higher castes in an effort to move up. That was the way to be one up on one's structural neighbours.

---

[1] References to judgements of law courts and copper-plate inscriptions occurred frequently while discussing caste, rank and customs. But details regarding dates, places and exact contents were rarely forthcoming.

[2] The Washerman bathed after washing menstrual saris and the Barber after he had plied his trade. At least that was what they were expected to do.

The locally dominant caste was an obstacle to mobility for several reasons. In the first place, such mobility had the potential of threatening its own ambition if not position. Second, it could result in a chain reaction which could then lead to the suspension of the flow of services and goods from dependent castes. It was, however, helpless when a higher power such as the Rajah approved of the mobility, or a powerful sectarian movement swept the countryside attracting converts from low castes.

Disputes as to mutual caste-rank were conducted in a particular syllogistic domain. The kind of ritual which a caste had, its customs, myth of origin, and style of life all became points in the attempt to change its overall rank. The members of the caste stressed features which they thought supported their claim while their adversaries picked on unfavourable features. Thus Kempayya argued that Washermen had a high rank because they made things pure. (The Washerman caste's full name was Madivala Shettaru, and *madi* referred to ritual purity. The clothes which a Washerman took were impure or *mailige* but after he had washed them they became *madi*). However, after the Barber had shaved his customer the latter was impure, and he had to have a bath and wear fresh clothes to become pure once again. But Nadu Gowda countered these arguments by saying that the Washerman was no less impure than the Barber when, for instance, he washed menstrual clothes. And perhaps also when he washed the clothes of a family in mourning, or suffering from birth-pollution.

Since each of the many items of the culture of a caste had rank implications, their evaluations did not always converge. For instance, a caste's occupation might have rated high while its dietary was low. The problem was made more intractable by the arbitrary investment of a trifling difference in custom between two *jatis* with considerable rank implications. A summation of ranks in diverse areas was not possible. This led to members of the caste stressing features favouring high rank while others picked on unfavourable features.

The articulated criteria of ranking were usually ritual, religious or moral resulting in concealing the importance of secular criteria. The influence of the latter was, however, real. For instance, while landownership and numerical strength were crucial in improving caste rank, any claim to high rank had to be expressed in ritual and symbolic terms. But at any given moment there were inconsistencies between secular position and ritual rank.

The idea of hierarchy was a *leit motif* underlying every area of culture. I shall illustrate what I mean by reference to two important areas, occupation and diet.

Occupations were distinguished into high and low on the basis of several criteria: non-manual occupations were superior to manual ones, and in the latter, the defiling and sinful occupations were the lowest.

The superiority of non-manual occupations was derived from a dual source: First, the Brahmins did not do manual work.[1] They had mastered the complicated ritual which was performed at life-cycle crises, calendrical festivals and temple worship. It was in the context of the non-manual tradition of the Brahmins that the Rama priest's over-attention to agriculture provoked harsh as well as contemptuous comments from the villagers. Once a young village boy accompanied the Rama priest and me from Gudi to Rampura and he kept telling me about the priest's indifference to his temple duties and his devotion to farming. I felt uncomfortable and the priest was annoyed but the boy took no notice of our reactions. According to him, if the priest kept the temple doors open for a few hours every day and distributed *prasada* among the devotees, the temple was certain to become popular. That might also bring in some additional money and grain to him. The boy was trying to point out the benefits of piety.

Manual labour was regarded as low but it was real work unlike non-manual activity. It was the farmer's back-breaking work which produced food for everyone. The whole world depended for its sustenance on the labour of the farmer who himself got a pittance of what he produced thanks to the rapacity of the government, landowners, and the middlemen. Many others such as priests and mendicants had to be supported by his activity.

Even though farming was the most important occupation in the world, the better-off farmers were keen that their sons should obtain education and become salaried officials in the government, or doctors or lawyers. Obviously they were tired of supporting everyone by their labours and wanted to join the ranks of the parasites. If you cannot lick them, join them.

---

[1] Brahmins who did agricultural work were, however, to be found in Western Mysore. They were the Sankethis, who spoke a Tamil dialect, and they were well-known for their capacity for hard, manual work and agricultural skill. But they managed to combine it with an orthodox style of life and also love of Sanskritic learning and Karnatic music.

The behaviour-pattern of landowners was also conducive to the lack of prestige of manual work. Generally, landowners, especially the bigger ones, only supervised the actual cultivation of their farms by their servants, tenants, share-croppers and labourers. Supervision usually meant exercising the tongue: issuing instructions, shouting, abusing, threatening, and very occasionally, praising faintly, and in rare circumstances, even the vague promise of a distant reward.[1] When there were grown sons, fathers were relieved of even routine supervision. However, they continued to evince a keen interest in farm work and they controlled the purse strings. They ordered their sons about as though they were children. Occasionally, they visited their farms to find out for themselves how good the supervision was.

The degree of abstention from manual labour varied, however, from landowner to landowner. The biggest rural landowners emulated the urban upper classes and the latter in turn emulated or at least took their cues from the Mysore royalty. For instance, a few wealthy landowners in the region kept horse-drawn carriages, in imitation of the urban upper classes. Elderly villagers remembered that when the present headman's father made his occasional visits to Mysore in the first two decades of this century, he used to wear a close-collared jacket (*kotu*), a gold-bordered dhoti, worn the Brahminical way, red slippers and a gold-laced turban, a style of dress that was characteristic of wealthy and respectable citizens.[2]

Manual work was either skilled or unskilled, and a skilled worker in any area of activity commanded respect. I have mentioned earlier how the taciturn headman was moved to admire Koonana Javarayi's farming skill and hard work. Kulle Gowda, whose dislike of farming was well-known, was, however, respected for his skill with his hands. A young Potter immigrant from Tagadur bragged about the skill needed to lift, quickly and neatly, the hollow, tubular stem of beaten earth emerging from the wheel, after it had been severed from the wheel with a pin.

The Potter claimed that no non-Potter had fingers deft enough for the operation. I tried my hand at lifting the stem but made a mess

[1] However, in the 1920s, a few leading landowners such as Nadu Gowda's father and Melkote (Sr.) seemed to have had no reluctance to do manual work on their farms.

[2] When in Rampura, however, he wore only a gold-laced dhoti in the Brahminical way. This was probably supplemented by a shawl worn like a stole during cold or wet weather.

of it as the bottom part collapsed. My performance proved the Potter's point, and provided amusement to those present.

The young Potter's bragging about the skill involved in his traditional occupation brought home to me that there was a difference between internal and external perceptions in evaluating an occupation. But with outsiders like me, they also took the trouble to point out the skill involved in the traditional occupations of castes other than their own. They did not want me to think that rural occupations were unskilled.

When my Potter friend was expatiating on the skill involved in his craft his discourse was interrupted by the sudden arrival of an old Potter from a town about fifty miles away. He had received some training in a craft school during his younger days and could make a few pottery toys. He was urged to show his skill to me. He was a quiet man and in about half an hour he produced a few specimens of his art. We all admired them but my articulate friend's admiration reduced him to total silence. I was surprised by his reaction though I did not comment upon it. Even within the same caste unusual skill extracted a tribute from everyone.

Manual work was either clean or polluting, and polluting work lowered the rank of the caste which customarily did it. For instance, the continued care of the scavenging swine greatly lowered the rank of Swineherds. In fact, villagers had little contact with the local Swineherds, and this was only partly due to the distance of their settlement from the main village. Unlike the Harijans, they were not indispensable to the village economy, and social and religious life.

The majority of Harijans, men and women, worked as labourers on land owned by the others, and while this work was of low prestige it was not polluting. But the Harijans were also required to remove dead cattle (including buffaloes) from the houses of caste Hindus. Handling dead cattle, tanning their hides, etc. were highly polluting. It was these things which made them untouchables while the pig-eating Swineherd was not.[1]

Defiling occupations were distinguished from sinful ones. For instance, butchery was sinful, for the butcher killed sentient creatures

---

[1] But attempts by Harijans in this area to give up eating carcass-beef, beat the tom-tom at village festivals, etc. were met with fierce opposition from the higher castes, especially Peasants. It would have been difficult if not impossible to find others willing or able to take the place of Harijans, and in addition, an assured source of cheap labour would have ended for the landed, high castes.

for his livelihood. The regular butcher in Rampura was a Muslim and he had relieved the Hindus of the burden of a sinful occupation. Generally, a Hindu killed a sheep or goat only as a sacrifice to a deity or ancestral spirit. This was true even when a fowl was slaughtered, though sometimes it was done for an important relative or guest. Sacrificing an animal to a deity or ancestor spirit provided a religious justification for slaughter. It was then not a sin, and, moreover, the meat had become consecrated as *prasada*.

It was only at wedding dinners (*neravi*) that the slaughter of sheep was a secular act. If the host had Muslim friends or clients whom he wanted to partake of the dinner, he had the animal slaughtered by a Muslim according to Islamic ritual.

The day-to-day needs of the village were met by the lone Muslim butcher. Only the better-off villagers could afford to buy mutton once or twice a week while the others bought it less frequently. Fresh fish was even rarer than mutton. However, it was usual for villagers to keep stocks of tiny, dried fish (*sigdi*), and these, along with strips of pickled mutton (*kanda*), provided some variety to a monotonous diet.

The diets of different groups constituted a hierarchy. Thus vegetarian dietary ranked highest from a religious point of view. Vegetarians had to keep away from fish and eggs but were allowed to eat dairy products such as milk, curd, buttermilk and *ghi*. But even the vegetarians did not form a simple, homogeneous category; the strict amongst them kept away from onion and garlic, and certain 'Western' vegetables such as radish, beetroot and egg-plant (brinjal).[1]

Gradations were even more marked among non-vegetarians; there were those who ate mutton but abstained from the polluting fowl. And even the fowl-eaters kept away from domestic pork. At the bottom were the eaters of carrion beef. Each category of non-vegetarians considered themselves superior to those lower. This went so far that they even resented being asked whether they occasionally ate an item from the diet of a lower category.

Only the lower non-vegetarian castes drank liquor, almost invariably palm-toddy (*henda*), and less frequently, arrack (*sarayi*). Drinking

---

[1] Brahmins had a strong aversion to garlic and this was true even of those who ate onion. Non-Brahmins, on the other hand, liked both onion and garlic, and used them in their curries. There was an olfactory conflict between the two categories of castes.

lowered the status of the caste or family which consumed it. Toddy was extracted by the Toddyman who had a low ritual rank. In the toddy-booth which was patronized, among others, by Harijans, Swineherds and Smiths, the mugs were used promiscuously. While this argument made sense in terms of the beliefs of the people, I am inclined to think that it was a rationalization of the low position of the drinking castes. The primary factor was that drinking was a characteristic of the low castes, and to make matters worse, it went along with eating low meats in a ritually polluting environment.

Vegetarians regarded non-vegetarianism as sinful. The sanctity of all life, and especially sentient life, was a major value with them, and they held that non-vegetarians were responsible for the slaughter of the animals involved. The village doctor, a Brahmin, once told a few of us gathered on my verandah that on some days the first thing the headman did on waking up was to send a servant to the butcher with detailed instructions regarding the exact part of the animal from which he wanted his cut, and then ask the servant to take a bowl with him for some blood. After saying this the doctor shook his head and smiled to indicate his sense of horror.

It would not be wrong to state that the non-vegetarian castes' attitude to meat-eating was mixed. On the one hand, it made for strength and stamina while on the other it was sinful. Hindu castes in Rampura always took care to cook meat outside the kitchen and in vessels exclusively kept for the purpose. Even the stove was separate. Meat was also not cooked on certain days of the week, such as Monday, Friday, Saturday, New Moon Day and so on.

Among meat-eating castes, one occasionally came across the phenomenon of a lone vegetarian living with relatives all of whom were meat-eaters. In such cases, the man usually held a priestly office which required him to be vegetarian. He cooked his own food as he did not want to be polluted by eating food cooked by meat-eaters. The latter not only did not resent his exclusiveness but respected it, and even took a vicarious pride in his religious scrupulousness.

Meat-eating had a lower place than vegetarianism in Sanskritic ideology. It was, for instance, forbidden at all calendrial festivals and weddings. This ban was, however, *literally* interpreted by the villagers, meat being cooked on the day after the festival. Only a *si uta* (literally, sweet meal) was permitted at a festival and it meant including a sweet dish in the menu. The sweet was incompatible with meat.

Meat was, however, obligatory at the annual, non-Sanskritic propitiation of ancestors during the *pitru paksha* [the dark half of the lunar month of *bhadrapada* (September–October)] and at the periodical festivals of village deities who were usually propitiated with blood-sacrifices.

Ambitious non-Brahmin castes sometimes became vegetarians in an effort to move up in the hierarchy but did not always find it easy to keep it up. A certain amount of cheating regarding dietary practices was therefore part of the caste system as it operated. The Rampura Traders (Banajigas) provided an example of dual standards in their dietary: they had migrated to Rampura nearly six decades previously, and they were all followers of Vishnu, prominently displaying the sectarian symbol of *namam* on their foreheads. Their lineage deities were Narasimha and Cheluvarayaswami (both, forms of Vishnu) of Melkote, and Chamundi of Mysore. They owed religious allegiance to a Sri Vaishnava guru at Melkote who annually visited them.

All the Trader households in Rampura were descended from Narasimha who was in his mid-nineties in 1948. They claimed the status of Vaishyas and they did not eat food cooked by anyone except Brahmins.

One day, in the course of a discussion of the dietary habits of different castes, someone volunteered the information that the Traders were vegetarians. Kulle Gowda, who was present, suddenly became angry and shouted, 'My pubic hair, they are fine vegetarians! I have seen bones in their domestic garbage.' Shrewd observer that he was, Kulle Gowda had once noticed a few bones in the garbage thrown by a Trader household from which he had concluded that their claim to be vegetarians was a hollow one: Q.E.D.

I have already described how there was a hierarchy among non-vegetarians and how each caste made it a point to stress the kinds of meat it abstained from. Thus a mutton-eater would explain how he would be thrown out of caste if he ate the polluting pig, let alone the sacred cow. He might even try to drive home his and his caste's fastidiousness by explaining how his mother or grandmother did not permit fowls to be kept in the house because of their tendency to eat everything including ordure and to litter the floor with their droppings. (Fowls were not kept in coops except at night.) The tendency to conceal meat-eating was perhaps more frequent than what appeared at first sight. For instance, a Swineherd told me that while

Peasants in Rampura and Kere avoided pork strictly, Peasants elsewhere were more lax. He had himself sold pork to them.

Sometimes, however, people violated their dietary rules without seeming to be aware that they were doing so—at least that was the impression I got. For instance, Peasants in Rampura were emphatic that they did not eat the rat by which they only meant the domestic rat and not the field-rat.

I have described earlier that in a hierarchical system such as caste there was an emphasis on the exclusiveness of each unit and its separateness and distance from the others. But opportunities for mobility did also exist, and the emulation of the customs, ritual and life-style of the higher and more Sanskritized castes was a condition precedent for mobility. Emulation did also occur within the local section of a caste, the richer, more prestigious and Sanskritized households being imitated by the others.

At the source of the emulation, however, were such factors as the acquisition of wealth, especially landed wealth, and political power. Traditionally, improvement in the secular status of a caste group was followed by an attempt to claim a higher rank for it in the local hierarchy. This meant, among other things, the Sanskritizing of its customs, ritual and life-style. The Sanskritization of a caste's life-style was both essential for its upward mobility and, contrary as it may seem, a symbol of its high rank.

The fact of heterogeneity within each caste, greater among the higher castes but present everywhere, was significant for mobility. The poorer and less educated households looked up to their richer castefolk for models. The urge to emulate them was all the greater when they were in the same village.

Among the Peasants, for instance, there were three leading households, and they formed a hierarchy. The headman's household led the other two by a wide margin, and until 1952, Nadu Gowda's was ahead of Millayya's. The headman's sons were keenly aware of their leadership and derived considerable satisfaction from contemplating how the others tried to emulate them in whatever they did, viz. sowing a new seed, growing a new crop, starting a bus or lorry, or performing the Brahminical *shraddha* for a dead ancestor.

It was not only the Peasants who emulated the headman's household but the others as well. But in the case of the Lingayats, who claimed to be superior to Peasants, emulation was confined strictly to secular areas. Indeed, in matters of ritual it was the headman's household which emulated Lingayats as also Brahmins. A Lingayat ritual expert, from another village, occasionally visited the headman's house for performing special rituals. (The priests of the Madeshwara and Basava temples did not perform domestic ritual.)

It was understandable that only the better-off among the high castes tried to emulate the headman's household. The very wealth and influence of the headman put him and his household beyond the emulative reach of the poorest in the village: 'They can afford to do it but can we?' A poor man had to be content to live as the gods had kept him.

But emulation was not confined to members of the same caste living in the village. The headman himself, for instance, was influenced by a son-in-law who had a law degree and was in politics. His political influence had enabled him to start a couple of small industries in a town near his village, and it was not unlikely that he helped his father-in-law to obtain, in 1952, licences from the State Government to start two bus lines. The headman had another prosperous affine in Ooty (in Tamil Nadu) and this gentleman was an active trader and owner of a coffee estate. The headman's horizons were much wider than those of other villagers.

The desire to emulate the higher castes emanated from other sources besides local leaders and caste leaders outside the village. Many villagers, Peasants, Lingayats, Muslims and others, were familiar with Mysore and Mandya, and were directly influenced by urban styles of living.

The cinema was also becoming significant as a source of diffusion of urban ideas and culture. And it was not only those who frequented the towns who were exposed to it: 'touring talkies' (mobile cinema houses) visited Hogur, Kere and other big villages, and Rampurians took their familes to see the films. A permanent cinema was coming up in Hogur in 1948.

During the inter-War years, villages in the Rampura region had each a few leading Brahmin households. By virtue of the land they owned, their caste rank, and the contacts they enjoyed with visiting officials, many of whom were also Brahmins, they wielded an influence out of all proportion to their numbers. Their customs, ritual and style of life were emulated by the others.

The process of emulation became increasingly complicated in the thirties and subsequent years when the State Government pursued vigorously a policy of supporting the 'backward classes' which involved practising some discrimination against Brahmins in appointments to jobs, and in promotions, and allotting seats in educational institutions. Educated village youth could not help becoming anti-Brahminical. This period also saw the rapid rise to power of the Peasants and Lingayats. The richer Peasants and Lingayats became urbanized, westernized and Sanskritized, and provided models for emulation for their rural castefellows and others. Urban cinemas, restaurants and hospitals, and increased bus and rail travelling were factors favouring changes in the style of life.

Any reference to the emulation of the life-styles of superior castes and individuals would be incomplete without a reference to the headman's unique position in the village. He was a pace-setter as far as agricultural practices were concerned. He was thorough and modern-minded and yet at the same time cautious. He was also a pioneer in initiating new commercial activity. His life-style was more Sanskritized than that of the other Peasants. In this he had taken his cue from his parents, and especially his old mother.

I have thus far considered the hierarchical aspect of caste. I have tried to highlight the difference between two conceptions of caste, the all-India system of *varna* and the purely local system of *jati*. I have tried to argue that the main features of *jati* point to a system which permitted individual castes to move up or down, unlike the ossified *varna* system in which each caste-category occupied an immutable position.

When caste is viewed as a hierarchy, it is the distinctness of each group and its separateness and distance from the others that receive emphasis. But distinctiveness and distance go along with the interdependence of the different castes living in a village or group of neighbouring villages. The two are parts of a single system.

I have presented above an over-simplified picture of the situation as it existed in 1948. But no account, however simplified, can fail to mention the overlap between caste and land categories. The bigger landowners all came from such high castes as the Brahmin, Peasant, Lingayat and Shepherd while very many of the landless labourers came from the Harijans. The smaller landowners and tenants came from a variety of castes though even here certain castes such as the Basketry-makers, Washermen, Traders, Muslims and Harijans were either not represented or only poorly represented.

Traditionally, ownership of land and power over human beings—the two were frequently linked together—were significant sources of mobility. But they had to be supplemented by Sanskritization for mobility to be translated into caste terms.

3   Purity and Pollution

The distinctness of each caste and its distance from the others were maintained, in the last resort, by appeal to certain sanctions. Thus those who violated the rules governing the acceptance of cooked food between castes, or the rule of caste endogamy, were punished by the concerned caste council. Perhaps more important was the effect of the rules of pollution and purity which were instilled in people from their earliest years. Children were taught these rules in the household, kin group, neighbourhood, and in their travels and pilgrimages. Folktales and songs, disputes, and ordinary talk contained references to pollution and purity.

The settlement pattern of the village took note of the need to keep castes distinct though this was an ideal only insufficiently realized in practice. It may be recalled here that the village shifted from its original site on the southern embankment of the Big Tank to its present site in 1874 (*circa*) and perhaps the residential patterns of the old village could not be totally carried into the new.

Elderly Rampurians told me that the old village had an *agrahara* (street inhabited exclusively by Brahmins) at the end of which was the Rama temple. The Harijans had a street (*keri*) of their own at some distance from the others. In the new site, however, there was no *agrahara*, and the Harijan ward was separated from the rest of the village only by the Mysore-Hogur Road (see map facing page 10). Their separation was more symbolic than real in purely spatial terms but still the higher castes did not enter the Harijan ward.

Only some Muslims visited the Harijan ward freely. This was perhaps why the headman always sent messages to his Harijan workers through one or other of his Muslim clients, Karim, Nasar and Imamu. It was significant that Muslim houses were interposed between the Harijan and caste Hindu houses.

The Swineherds' huts were located far away from the main village settlement, and they had very little contact with the villagers. The adult Swineherds were tenants of the headman while a young boy drove the swine around everyday. One old Swineherd woman went round neighbouring villages begging and telling fortunes. This was a traditional occupation of Swineherd women.

The clustering of houses on the basis of caste (and kin) did occur in the village (see map facing page 10) though it was more prominent in some interior villages. The residential pattern in Rampura had been disturbed first by the emigration of all but one household of the Brahmins and finally by the various waves of Muslim immigrants.

Again, the domestic architecture was such that it enabled villagers to keep the required social distance with different castes. The middle-to-rich farmers lived in houses which had central courtyards open to the sky, and covered verandahs facing the street. The front verandah was the place where the men received friends and visitors. If the latter were equals, they sat on a mat spread on the verandah, and if they were close friends even the mat was dispensed with. (Or the host asked someone to bring a mat from inside but the friend sat down saying that he did not need one.) If the visitors were inferior, they either stood or sat on the bare floor while the owner sat on a mat. Visitors belonging to very low castes even stood on the street while talking to the owner sitting on the verandah.

Again, when lower castes had to come into a high caste house they used the backdoor, and avoided going near the kitchen, puja room (if there was one) and the bathroom, all of which were purer than other parts. Only close kinsmen were taken into the kitchen or that part of the house where the members ate. Even they had to be in a pure condition for the domestic altar was frequently located in the kitchen. The cauldron in which the bath water was heated was also pure and a bath cleaned as well as purified the bather.

Contact between different castes was regulated by the related ideas of pollution and purity, and 'contact' was defined culturally. Thus, traditionally an orthodox Brahmin considered himself impure (i.e. polluted) if he was very near a Harijan even though physical contact did not occur. But similar proximity did not result in pollution in the case of some other castes. The structural distance between different castes varied, and traditionally, each caste knew literally where it stood in relation to the others.

'Contact' had to be forbidden or regulated between castes in such other matters as accepting drinking water and cooked food, having sex relationship, and giving or taking girls in marriage, in an ascending order of seriousness. Two other types of contact need mention because they were looked upon as serious: beating another person with leather sandals, or spitting upon him, acts which resulted in the person beaten or spat on being outcasted automatically. Sometimes even the threat of being beaten with sandals or spat upon was enough to result in outcasting. Thus in a dispute between a Potter and a Lingayat priest,[1] a point which proved almost explosive was the Potter's abuse: 'May I . . . . the Priest's wife. May I . . . . his mother. I am going to beat him with my sandals, and I am going to beat him till five pairs of sandals wear out.' I have discussed earlier how serious an insult it was to tell someone that the speaker would copulate with the former's wife. Expressing a desire to beat another with sandals was also a grave insult though in a different way. The first abuse attacked his masculinity while the second polluted him, threw him out of his caste. In the subsequent discussions of the dispute which occurred, the gravity of the threat to beat the priest with sandals was mentioned again and again. It was not only an offence against the priest but his caste and the Priest himself stressed this.

Even though the mere expression of an intention to beat someone with sandals was regarded as equivalent to the *deed*, in actual fact there was a difference. In 'The Case of the Potter and Priest', for instance, matters would have taken a turn for the worse if the Potter had carried out his intention. The Priest would then have had no alternative but to undergo the purificatory ritual with all the expense, publicity and humiliation it involved. Actual beating would have forced all the Lingayats to come together against the Potter, and perhaps against the local Potters as a whole. Lingayats from neighbouring villages might have put pressure on the village elders to mete out deterrent punishment to the Potter. Even a physical fight between the two castes was a possibility.

Contact with another person's spittle was polluting, and the spittle of a lower caste member was more defiling than that of a caste-fellow. *Enjalu*, i.e. spittle, or food polluted by having come into contact with one's own or another person's mouth, aroused a sense of disgust.[2] A man who had suddenly turned against his patron was liable to be taunted, 'You ate my *enjalu* all these days, and now, look at you!' A man who had benefited from another was expected to be loyal, and disloyalty was immoral if not sinful.

---

[1] See M. N. Srinivas, 'The Case of the Potter and Priest', *Man in India*, Vol. 39, No. 3, July–September 1959.

[2] Among Peasants, Shepherd and similar castes, a mother often ate from the same dish as her young child. This was more frequent among the poor. But this was discontinued after the child had grown up.

While boiled or steamed food, or food fried in oil had to be prepared by one's own, equivalent or superior caste, food which was cooked with milk, butter or *ghi* (clarified butter) could be accepted from inferior castes. Milk, butter or *ghi* enjoyed a special status as they all came from the cow which was regarded as sacred. (The fact that the milk or butter frequently came from the buffalo was ignored.) But food cooked with water or involving the use of salt was easily pollutable. Such food was accepted only from superior or equivalent caste.

The intentional violation of a pollution rule was treated as more serious than an accidental one. The distinction was crucial in determining the kind of punishment to be awarded to the offender. While accidental violation might be punished with a light fine or even with a demand for an apology from the offender, intentional violation was punished with a heavy fine or even outcasting.

As a child grew up, it gradually learnt the complex rules of pollution and purity which governed behaviour relating to inter-caste relations, life-cycle crises, and finally, daily life. The rules were not only many but admitted of qualifications, exceptions and escape clauses depending upon the circumstances of each case. However, the villagers did not seem to experience any difficulty in guiding their lives by them. Indeed, the more orthodox villagers were so used to them that they found the behaviour of an 'emancipated' person like me puzzling, to say the least. The observance of the rules of pollution and purity had become, at least partly, the symbol of an ethical and religious life and villagers found it confusing to see me ignoring them.

On one occasion, when I had got off the bus at Rampura, one or two village boys volunteered to transfer my luggage from the bus to the Bullock House. I had a large bamboo basket with me and it contained some fried snacks which my mother had given me. One boy was about to lay his hand on the basket when another sharply asked him to stop. The second boy, who was a Shepherd or Peasant, whispered in my ear that the first was a Harijan, and had he been allowed to touch the basket, the contents would have become polluted. Not only had this not occurred to me but I was upset at the thought that the Harijan was hurt by the officiousness of the Shepherd boy.

I have narrated earlier how Laki, Rame Gowda's little daughter, was contemptuous of my ignorance of the rules of pollution and purity. She was then a little chit of a girl but she was already being trained for her future role as a member of her husband's joint family. Laki derived her name from one of the deities regularly worshipped by the headman's household, Lakshmi, the Goddess of Wealth. The Goddess was elaborately worshipped every Friday, the day considered sacred for her. No meat was cooked in the headman's house on Fridays, and every member had a bath before the main meal of the day.

On Fridays, it was Laki's responsibility to get the domestic altar ready for puja. She swept the puja room, decorated the space before the altar with *rangoli* designs, cleaned the vessels used in worship, and finally, got the lamps ready for lighting. She then bathed, lit the lamps, performed *puja*, and had her breakfast only later.

As I have said earlier, among the high castes, the rules of pollution and purity were drilled into children from very early in life. Thus a Brahmin child, barely two years old, would be told not to touch a member of another caste during a festival or *shraddha* in the house. Questions of purity and pollution even cropped up when little boys or girls were playing. As they grew up, children became acquainted with the application of the rules of pollution and purity in a myriad contexts and this was how the rules became internalized over a period of time. Failure to observe them resulted in a sense of discomfort if not guilt. I have heard educated Brahmins in Mysore mentioning how uncomfortable (*mujagara*) they felt because they were not able to take a bath immediately after having their hair cut in a Barber's shop. Many educated Brahmins rationalized the pollution rules as rules of health.

The internalization of pollution rules was supplemented by external pressures and sanctions. Older members of the household, neighbours and caste or village elders were all likely to express their concern or annoyance when a rule was broken or ignored. I have already mentioned the role of the headman's mother in making sure that every member performed his or her religious obligations. The headman tried to play a similar role in the village. But when a serious violation occurred and the matter could not be settled at the kin or neighbourhood level, the matter was reported to the leaders of the dominant caste who inquired into the complaint and awarded suitable punishment.

I shall now discuss briefly a few characteristics of pollution. In the first place, the normal condition of human beings was a mild form of pollution and most secular work was done in that condition. But such impurity was relative to the condition of a person at prayer or while performing other auspicious ritual. But it was less impure than that of a man affected by death or birth-pollution. (To make matters more complicated, the chief mourners who performed mourning rituals had to be in a state which was identical with extreme purity.) The variable states of purity and pollution were also caste-bound in the sense that a member of a high caste who was ritually impure owing to, for instance, having been shaved by a Barber would continue to be pure vis-à-vis a low caste man. But the situation was more complex as between structurally equivalent or near castes, and also according to the gravity of the pollution.

Generally, when a pure person or object came into contact with an impure person, the latter communicated his impurity to the former and not *vice versa*. A purificatory rite was essential to restore the lost purity and that rite was simple and inexpensive, or complex and costly, depending on the gravity of the impurity.

But there were some holy objects which could not be rendered impure. Thus millions of impure and sinful people who bathed in the sacred Ganges in the North or Kaveri in the South, became pure as a result of the bath. (Even the floating down of corpses in the Ganges did not sully the river.) Ritual purity was, of course, different from cleanliness.

Pollution was contagious: One summer evening, when the headman, Nadu Gowda and I were out for a walk, the headman wanted to slice a mango which someone had given him during the walk. But none of us was carrying a knife. Then a Swineherd tenant of the headman, who was standing nearby, suddenly produced a big knife from his shorts' pocket. The headman took it, and was about to slice the mango when a doubt crossed his mind. He returned the knife to the Swineherd telling him, 'I don't want your knife, you may have used it to cut up a pig.' The Swineherd protested that he never used it for such a vile purpose but the headman was firm in his refusal.

If the headman's suspicion was well-founded, the knife had retained its pollution from pig-slicing and no amount of washing would cleanse it. And it polluted every edible article with which it came into contact.

The above incident recalled to my mind the accusation by Mrs Tiffin, a landlady in Oxford, that her Indian lodger was a hypocrite. He was a non-vegetarian but he once refused cuts of lamb served by

Mrs Tiffin on the ground that the knife had been used previously to carve beef. Mrs Tiffin found her lodger's behaviour irrational. I tried to explain the logic underlying the refusal of the lamb but my expository powers came up against her sturdy common sense.

Theoretically, there was no limit to the contagion. Thus a man who dined with an outcasted castefellow became polluted and a source of pollution to others. In fact, occasionally, the number of polluted persons kept increasing through contagious contact, and at some point the elders had to have mass purificatory rites. The multiplex and intimate character of village ties did not permit the long-term exclusion of a sizeable section of the local population. But sometimes matters went too far to be remedied by the elders and a new *jati* was formed by the polluted.

Pollution-purity concepts were more pervasive and systematized among the Brahmins than the others, and next to them were the Lingayats. But, as I have stated earlier, in religious matters the richer Peasants and others tried to emulate the Brahmins or Lingayats or both. The existence of two sectarian orders, one Vaishnavite and the other Shaivite, among the non-Brahmin castes, was relevant in this context. The Dasayyas, who were Vaishnavite, and the Jogayyas who were Shaivite, were both mendicant priests, and they were to be found among a variety of non-Brahmin castes including Harijans. Recruitment to the orders was in theory voluntary though in actual fact family tradition played an important part in recruitment. In families which had a tradition of supplying recruits, at least one member from each generation was persuaded to join the order. Dasayyas were initiated by Sri Vaishnava (Iyengar) gurus while Jogayyas were initiated by Lingayat gurus. Both types of gurus had links with the monasteries of their respective orders.

In short, both Dasayyas and Jogayyas were instruments for the greater Sanskritization of the ritual of their respective families and the local sections of their castes. Dasayyas drew on the Sri Vaishnava model of Sanskritization while the Jogayyas drew on the Lingayat model.

Generally, priests had to observe the purity-pollution rules more scrupulously than the laity, and this was true of all the castes including Brahmins and Lingayats. Of the three Brahmin households in Rampura, two were lay while the third was the Rama priest's and he had to be more mindful of purity and pollution then the others. The same was true of the Madeshwara priests, and the oldest member of the priestly lineage, Thammayya, enjoyed a reputation for piety. Sannu once told me that he could not eat a thing before 10 a.m. each day because of his ritual duties at home and in the temple. There was a big puja room in the house which had portable images of Madeshwara, and several other sacred objects. Sannu's household was a large one with a few infants and the places dirtied by them had to be cleaned and purified. The women next attended to the cleaning and purifying of the puja room and the vessels used in worship. The women and Sannu then had their baths after which the morning puja began. Only after the morning puja in the house and temple had ended did Sannu have his breakfast.

Generally, the members of each caste had a temple of their own, the priesthood of the temple being vested in a particular lineage. (But the association of a caste with a temple did not mean that worshippers were only drawn from it.) The eldest son of the man holding the priesthood succeeded to the office after his father's death. Such a priest was termed *gudda*, and there was some variability, from temple to temple, in the duties of the *gudda*. In some temples, the *gudda* was required only to open the temple doors once a week or so and light the lamps. Sometimes, he had, in addition, an active role at the elaborate, periodical festival of the deity. But whatever the duties, a *gudda* was expected to lead a stricter life than a layman. A *gudda* who was a vegetarian, or meticulous about the observance of pollution and diet rules, was singled out for praise by the villagers just as a lax *gudda* was criticized.

Again, the older villagers were generally more pious than the younger. The difference in age frequently also implied difference in exposure to education, and to urban and political forces. Thus the younger, school-educated and politically-conscious Peasant youths were inclined to be disdainful of pollution rules. They were also critical of the older leaders' piety and contrasted it with their unethical conduct.

But I was surprised to find that on some occasions the rules of purity and pollution were violated. For instance, at the Rama Navami festival in the summer of 1948, a few village youths harassed the priest by trying to tug at his dhoti when he was distributing *prasada* (sanctified food-offering) after the elaborate morning *puja*. The priest was in a condition of high purity and if he was touched by anyone, including Brahmin devotees who were not equally pure, he would have become impure. Being touched by devotees from the other castes was even more serious. Everyone knew this, and a few Peasant youths who wanted bigger helpings of *prasada* tried to tug at the priest's dhoti. If they succeeded in their efforts the priest as well as the *prasada* would become impure resulting in his having to abandon the food-tray. Tugging at his dhoti would also result in the priest's being humiliated, a condition which the high-spirited youths relished greatly. The priest ran into the *sanctum sanctorum*, declaring that he was not going to distribute the *prasada*. The angry and perspiring priest set out immediately for the headman's house, and told him excitedly what had happened. The headman there and then decided on arrangements for the supervision of the *prasada*-distribution. From the following day onwards, one member of the headman's, and another from Nadu Gowda's, households remained with the priest till everyone had received his *prasada*. I may add here that antagonism to the priest distributing *prasada* was a common enough event in the villages, though the Rama priest got more than his share of teasing.

One night, two of my lanterns were suddenly sequestered by my neighbours. In answer to my questions, I was told, 'Just come along with us.' The party reached the Mysore–Hogur road, and then walked along it eastwards till they crossed the CDS canal. They turned right immediately afterwards following the loop of the canal till they reached a particular canal lock which released waters to a big feeder canal irrigating many acres of valuable land. The lock had been closed, and a big landowner was upset at the denial of water to his precious crop. Two servants of the landowner sat down on the bare ground on opposite sides of the lock and tried to open it with an illegal key. It was a big T-shaped key and had to be turned several times after the bottom of the T had rested properly in the groove meant for it. Turning the key, especially the initial turns, was a tough job requiring much strength, Each servant took hold of the end of either arm of the T and tried to push it towards the other. The lantern-holders stood close by and everyone shouted instructions and encouragement to the freely perspiring servants. At first it looked as though the task was beyond them but slowly the key began to turn. After the first few turns, it became easier, and finally, the canal gate opened, and foaming water gushed into the dry feeder canal. There was a great shout of triumph and the faces around me beamed with pleasure.

It was significant that one of the servants involved in the above incident was a Harijan while the other was a Peasant, and in the course of turning the key, they could not help touching each other many times over. No one even seemed to notice the fact let alone comment on it. Everyone was concentrating on the job on hand. It was obvious that whatever the rules governing inter-caste contact, even caste Hindu–Harijan contact, they were ignored in an emergency. This was again brought home to me during my second visit to Rampura in the summer of 1952. The fortunes of several of my friends and acquaintances had changed during the period 1948–52, and one of those who had moved up was Pijja, the young Harijan who had refused to be pushed around by the high caste landowners. He had been appointed a peon in the village school. The work was not arduous and carried a salary. It gave Pijja enough time to attend to his other interests including cultivating his land. But one of Pijja's more difficult tasks was to take the headman's grandson Shiva (about six years old) to school everyday. Shiva had a healthy hatred of the school and its cramping environment. On some days his hatred was greater than on others, and one fine morning he had to be forcibly carried by Pijja to school. Shiva had a lot of fight in him and protested vigorously, yelling with all his might and thrashing his arms and legs about but Pijja held him round the waist in a vice-like grip. Villagers came out on their verandahs, and watched the scene with unconcealed amusement. The yelling ended, however, after a sweating and hard-breathing Pijja had deposited the victim before the teacher for the day's instruction.

I did not hear any villager commenting on the impurity involved in the above contacts. It appeared as though contact produced pollution in traditionally-defined contexts and their modern analogues or extensions (e.g. Harijans being served tea in special cups in urban restaurants) but not where they promoted the interests of the powerful men of the dominant castes. In both the instances cited above, the interests of powerful men were promoted by contact while the priest was functioning in a totally traditional situation.

Ideas of purity and pollution were, however, weakening as a result of urban contacts, education and politicization. I have mentioned earlier how Sannu varied his behaviour according to the situation, and he was typical of the more urbanized villagers. His younger brother, Siddu, an educated man who stayed in a neighbouring town, once exhibited his contempt for pollution rules by asking a Muslim boy to bring him some drinking water and drinking it to the hilarious amusement of his friends.

The younger men who took an interest in local and regional politics generally belonged to the better-off households, and were at least literates. Ideas of equality had stirred their minds but they naturally found it easier to be convinced of their equality with the higher castes and classes than to concede similar claims made by those lower. To the best of my knowledge none of them showed any awareness of the contradiction inherent in their attitude. In one of my discussions with Kempu in the summer of 1952 I found him critical of the arrogance of Brahmins who referred to all non-Brahmins as Shudras. He then asked me whether I was ready to eat food cooked by Peasants. Village-style, I offered Kempu a counter-challenge. I told him that I would be willing to eat food cooked by a Harijan, and would he join me on the occasion? Kempu backed down at once and replied that I was quite different from other Brahmins.

It was symbolic that accepted hierarchical notions were broken by some urbanized youths on the occasion of the visit of the Finance Minister in the first popular cabinet in Mysore State. As was customary, the headman entertained the Minister and his entourage (officials, journalists and political hangers-on) to snacks and coffee. But prior to the scheduled reception of the headman, the youths who were opposed to him, sprung a surprise tea on the distinguished visitor. The tea and the snacks were prepared in the most popular teashop in the village, owned by a Peasant. Generally, food for visiting officials was cooked by the village accountant, a Brahmin, but the youths wanted to emphasize their modernity and equalitarianism. While the Minister, who, incidentally, was a Shepherd by caste, partook of the tea, his vegetarian officials, Brahmin, Lingayat and Jain, excused themselves on some ground or the other from the progressive tea.

In contrast, the headman had his food prepared by the Rama priest. Mulling over the events after the Minister's party had left the village, the headman expressed satisfaction at the success of his tea and the relative unpopularity of the youths'. His conservatism and diplomacy—he knew that the vegetarian officials preferred snacks made by a Brahmin—had paid off.

During the summer of 1952, I was told by a Brahmin landowner, an Iyengar of Kere, that a visiting State Minister, from his own subcaste, had chosen to stay in the home of a Peasant landowner, and to accept the latter's hospitality. The Brahmin was very angry that the Minister had let down the members of his caste in the village.

Again, in 1952, I saw a growing friendship between the headman's second son, Lakshmana, and Nadu Gowda's second son, Kempu. Both were ambitious, energetic and intelligent men, and they wanted to start new business enterprises in the village. (Lakshmana nourished, at least in 1948, political ambitions, but realized, like many other urbanized men in the villages, that the road to power was a long, hard, thorny, slippery and expensive one.) They knew only too well that political connections were needed to get the permits and licences for starting new enterprises. Kempu wanted to instal a rice-mill, the second one in the village, the first being Millayya's. Lakshmana, who knew some politicians and officials, took Kempu in hand, and the two went round meeting influential men. In the course of their wanderings they went to Hunsur, a town about thirty miles to the west of Mysore, and attended a dinner. Too late, Kempu discovered that the hosts were Muslims. He asked Lakshmana, and the latter advised him to take it easy: they were moving in high circles and they could not afford to be squeamish.

A typical example of the kind of challenge posed by the new political forces to caste and pollution occurred in the summer of 1954 in Devipura, a village near the sugar town of Mandya. I was visiting the village with an official-friend, and a Peasant leader was furious about the arrogance of the local Harijans. A day or two previously a fight had occurred in a neighbouring village between gangs of Peasants and Harijans, and several men had been injured. According to the Peasant leader, Harijans had begun to claim all kinds of rights: 'Today they will want to enter our temples, tomorrow they will want to marry our girls.' I tried to tell him that the Congress Party stood for equality and that the government wanted to abolish Untouchability. I also pointed out that it was millions of villagers like him who had voted the Congress Party into power. My lecture did not, however, convert him. On the contrary, it only made him angrier: 'Let the Congress leaders first give their daughters in marriage to Harijan men before asking us to admit them to our temples.'

4 Harijans

My shortcomings as a field-worker are brought home to me poignantly when I contemplate the Harijans and Muslims. I realize only too clearly that mine was a high caste view of village society. I stayed in a high caste area, and my friends and companions were all

Peasants or Lingayats. However, I did know a few Muslims and Harijans, and one or two Potters, Smiths and Traders but none of them as intimately as I knew my Peasant and Lingayat friends.

The Harijans deserve a separate section if only because they were treated differently from every other group in ritual matters. They were not allowed to worship in caste Hindu temples or draw water from caste Hindu wells. (Muslims were allowed to use Hindu wells.) They were also excluded from using the big tank and only the canals taking off from it were permitted to them. It was all right for water to flow from the high castes to Harijans but not the other way about.

Inconsistent as it may seem with the above situation, close economic and social relationships existed between Harijans and the others. While ritual exclusion was on the basis of caste, closeness was on an individual, or at best familial, basis. Many Harijans had been employed as *jita* servants by landowners from the high castes. In the course of performing their duties they went to all parts of the house excepting the kitchen, which was considered pure. Harijan servants were allowed by some high class masters to look after young children, and friends told me that they had seen Harijan servants fondling the children of their high caste masters.

Certain indispensable services were provided by the Harijans to the village community as a whole. Caste was recognized as a basic unit for administrative purposes by the pre-British rulers and this continued even under the British. Thus Brahmins were appointed as accountants (*shanbhog*), landowners from the locally dominant caste as headman (*patel*), and village servants (*chakra*) from Harijans. *Chakras* had been given land by the government as payment for the services they rendered. *Chakrahood* was hereditary like other offices and the amount of land which was given to the original appointee had been divided through successive partitions into minuscule bits among the present holders of the office. The main duties of the *chakras* were to assist the accountant and headman in the collection of land taxes, and act as messengers and town-criers at village festivals and other important occasions. Either in their role as *chakras* or Harijans—it was not always easy to distinguish between the two—they were called upon, during village festivals, to do chores such as whitewashing the outer face of temple walls, putting up *pandals* before temple doors, beating the tom-tom, and removing the leaves on which villagers had dined. Harijan women winnowed, and ground or pounded grain, and did other similar jobs.

Teams of Harijan women were employed by big landowners for performing such essential tasks as transplanting, weeding and harvesting. And during the off-season, they were employed to assist in constructing or repairing the smaller feeder canals, tie up pruned twigs, often thorny, into tiny bundles to be used as fuel, and for many other jobs. Landowners and others who undertook contract work for a government department or district board, employed Harijan women (and men) for canal and road repair. This meant gathering pebbles from fields, piling them up and breaking them into smaller bits, and carrying baskets of earth from one point to another on the road under repair.

The closeness of the bond that prevailed between the high castes and Harijans found expression in the *halemaga* (literally, 'ancient son') institution. But it had become defunct in 1948 and I could only get accounts of it as it functioned in the thirties and earlier. The master households came from such high castes as Peasants, Shepherds and Lingayats. The *halemaga* household had to perform menial tasks, similar to those performed by Harijans at the Rama festival, during a wedding in the master's household. The *halemaga* was also required to remove the carcass of a dead bullock or buffalo from the master's house. While the hide, horns and meat were the *halemaga's* he had to give the master a pair of sandals and a length of plaited rope to be used for the plough during wet weather.[1]

As mentioned earlier, a Harijan functionary called *kulavadi* (sometimes also called *cheluvadi*) was the custodian of an important symbol of the caste system of the region, viz. a big and long brass ladle on the broad handle of which were carved the symbols of each principal caste. Thus Peasants were symbolized by a plough and bullocks, Oilman by an oil-press and so on. Rampura did not have a *kulavadi* but Kere, the administrative capital of the *hobli*, did have one, and I expect Hogur had another.[2] The ladle's stem ended in a

---

[1] Occasionally, I came across the phenomenon of a caste claiming another, usually a non-local one, as its *halemaga*. Copper-plate inscriptions existing in some important place were usually cited in support of the claim. I suspect that in such cases the claim was meant to be evidence of the claimant caste's high status.

[2] There seems to have been some correspondence between administrative and social divisions in pre-British days, and traces of it could still be seen in Rampura and neighbouring villages in 1948. Thus the *hobli*, an administrative unit higher than the village and lower than the *taluk* (or *tehsil*), had its capital (*kasaba*), and the caste court at the *hobli* capital was superior to that at the village. But such

big and deep bowl, and at weddings, the bowl had to be filled with rice and given to the *kulavadi* along with a silver four-anna piece (*pavali*). A *kulavadi* living in a market-town was entitled to scoop out a ladleful of any grain or other produce piled up before a merchant's shop.

It was significant that the keeper of the material symbol of caste organization, the brass ladle, was the *kulavadi*, a Harijan, and a servant-cum-messenger of the village.

I have referred several times to the changes which were occurring among Harijans in the Rampura region soon after Independence. The passing by the Mysore Government of 'The Mysore Temple Entry Authorization Act, 1948' which came into force on 7 February of the same year was an appropriate response to Harijan expectations regarding the new place which they envisaged for themselves in the wider society. On the thirteenth day after Mahatma Gandhi's funeral, Harijans were persuaded if not forced by younger caste Hindu leaders to enter their temples in some villages near Rampura. This may have led the Harijan leaders to think that at least the younger caste Hindus were keen on abolishing untouchability. If so, they were in for a disappointment. For, when some time later, Harijans in a few villages including Kere and Bihalli stopped performing certain festival duties which they regarded as degrading, they were subjected to economic boycott and beaten up, and their huts burnt. Many of the younger men took the lead in punishing the rebels. One such man, Putte Gowda, a sturdy Kere Peasant, confided in me that he had worked for Harijan entry into temples on the thirteenth day, but when he found that the Harijans wanted to give up performing all their traditional services he became so angry that he joined the others in walloping them.

Putte Gowda seemed to have thought that the Harijans should have been satisfied with symbolic entry into temples on the thirteenth day of Gandhiji's funeral. Their subsequent efforts to shed customary duties were evidence of their arrogance, and of ingratitude to those who had led them into caste Hindu temples. They had mistaken a symbolic concession for a permanent privilege.

On their side, local Harijans had come into contact with leaders from their castes who told them that beating the tom-tom on festive

superiority did not extend to caste courts, if any, at the *taluk* and district capitals. Above the *hobli* court, there was another which was usually referred to as the supreme court (*andala gadi*).

occasions, removing the leaves on which the higher castes had dined at collective occasions and removing the carcasses of domestic animals from their houses, were degrading, and inconsistent with their self-respect as human beings. They were thus caught between the forces of oppression and liberation, the former firmly in the saddle while the latter was then only a hope.

Traditionally, Harijans largely worshipped the village deities who periodically demanded blood sacrifices. However, in 1948, Harijans in Rampura and a few neighbouring villages started Rama Mandiras (shrines for the worship of Rama), where were kept lithographs of Rama and a few other Sanskritic deities, and once a week, a few men joined and sang devotional songs. The Harijans had begun to celebrate Rama Navami as a big festival. They took out their own Rama Navami procession on the day following the high caste procession.

There was a *bhajan* room in Kulle Gowda's house and Peasant and other caste Hindu youths met there once a week in the evenings and sang devotional songs to the accompaniment of a harmonium and the clash of cymbals. Sometimes, the *bhajan* group went round the village singing songs, carrying the picture of the deity and a lighted lamp with them. The *bhajan* group was founded in the thirties, and probably provided the model for the Harijan group in 1948. I may add here that ward-based *bhajan* groups and Rama Mandiras had started becoming popular in Mysore and other towns since the 1920s.

The Harijans were also getting politically organized. There was a Harijan official in the Rampura region who was urging his caste-fellows to assert themselves. He was not popular with the Peasants and other caste Hindus. He later resigned from his job to enter politics. At the general elections of 1952 he stood as a Praja Socialist Party candidate for election to the State Legislative Assembly while the headman supported another Harijan candidate who was the nominee of the Congress Party. The headman coralled all the adult Harijans in the village and arranged for them to be taken in bullock carts to the polling booths in Hogur. When the results were announced it was discovered that the former official had won defeating the Congress nominee. The headman suspected that he had been cheated. Pijja was sent for and asked whether he and his friends had voted according to instructions. Pijja was shocked at the suggestion that they could have done anything else. He replied that everyone had put the mark exactly where the headman had asked them to. And he was surprised at the result. But the headman knew Pijja, and the latter knew that the headman knew.

While the old leader of the Harijans, Kullayya, was respectful of the distance between him and the higher castes, Pijja opposed those high caste men who tried to do him out of his due or slighted him. He was as unpopular with the higher castes as Kullayya was popular. But even Pijja's opponents recognized that he was clever, articulate, and combative, and that he could not be ignored. He was also talented: I was told that he was a skilled narrator of *prasanga*. A *prasanga* was a traditional story with a built-in problem or riddle— rather the story ended in a problem and the audience were asked to offer the solution. The latter called for an intimate knowledge of the epics, *puranas* or other mythology. When the audience failed to produce the answer, the narrator did. Pijja was also a poet who could compose a poem 'about a leaf in a whirlwind' and sing it to the strumming of his *eknada* (mono-stringed instrument).

Pijja was resourceful. As the village Barbers did not serve the Harijans, he bought himself a safety razor and a pair of scissors and used them on himself. He then provided barbering services to a few friends.

Pijja came to know that the Government had various schemes to help Harijans: For instance, there was a government-sponsored 'Grow more food' campaign under which waste land was granted to cultivators. Pijja had applied for a few acres of waste land, and his application, perhaps along with many others, was lying unattended in the *taluk* office at Sangama. Once Pijja went to the *taluk* office to find out what had happened to his application. The clerk whom he approached asked for a bribe of two rupees to push it forward to the Amildar, the head of the *taluk*. Not only did Pijja not pay but he went straight to the Amildar's office and prostrated himself before the bewildered official. After a minute or two, the Amildar asked Pijja to get up and tell him what he wanted. Pijja narrated the incident and asked how a penniless Harijan like him could get anything done if clerks did not look at his application before receiving a bribe. The clerk was fined, Pijja's application for land was supported by the official, and word spread around that Pijja was not a man to be trifled with.

Pijja had crossed swords with a few high caste villagers, and had proved himself to be more than a match for all except the most powerful. I remember a complicated dispute between him and Thammayya, Sannu's agnatic cousin, and the oldest male member of the Madeshwara priestly lineage. It went before the headman himself for settlement a fortnight or so before the Rama Navami festival in 1948. I may add here that the headman intervened at the instance of Thammayya who had the reputation of being a hard-working but somewhat slow-witted man who needed protection against Pijja. Pijja had brought a middleman along to speak for him but when he felt that the middleman was making a point against him (Pijja) he did not hesitate to squash him. He argued his case brilliantly, scoring off Thammayya with ease. In the end, he got everything he wanted. Two days after the hearing he even persuaded Thammayya to tear up the I.O.U. which he had signed, thus depriving his creditor and employer of the only clout he possessed. On hearing of this Nadu Gowda commented, 'Pijja was born without a (proper) father, he would do anything.' It was a vicious remark and I was surprised at Nadu Gowda's making it.

Pijja was also in conflict with the conservative elders in his caste. The latter were afraid of the power wielded by the landowners while Pijja was not. At least not to the same extent. Pijja wanted the older Harijans to accept his leadership. He represented the winds of change that were blowing in the wider society. I could not help admiring Pijja's courage and fighting qualities.

5   Muslims

The Muslims were the third biggest group in the village and they had close economic and social relations with the Hindus. The Muslims appeared as a homogeneous group to outsiders, and this was enhanced by the absence of any restrictions on inter-dining between their various sub-groups. Such an appearance was, however, deceptive as sub-group endogamy was preferred though not mandatory. Further, the sub-groups formed a hierarchy, the Sheikhs and Sayyads regarding themselves as superior to the others. It was significant that neither group ate beef, while the Dayire (pronounced Dhare) did. The venerable-looking Hakim Sab told me that 'eating cow was like eating one's mother'. Hakim Sab was extremely hierarchical in his outlook and had no hesitation in dubbing people high or low. For instance, he said that the Dhare were a low caste. When I asked him why a young girl in Mamu Sab's house was wearing a headband, he replied, 'It is not among us but only among low caste people.' I later learnt that the headband was in honour of the girl passing her first Arabic examination.

Hakim Sab was regarded as knowledgeable by everyone in the village and I therefore went to him to get an account of the customs, ritual and festivals of the local Muslims. He was a frail old man racked by a chesty cough, and my sessions with him were frequently interrupted by his coughing bouts. One of the features of Hakim Sab's interpretation of Islam was the emphasis he placed on the concept of purity (*pak*).[1] This together with his keen sense of hierarchy and his filial sentiments towards the cow, made one wonder how much Hinduism had gone into Hakim Sab's interpretation. But Hakim Sab also told me that a Muslim who put a *kafir* to the sword went to heaven. It did not occur to him that he was talking to a *kafir*.

Besides the Sheikh, Sayyad and Dhare, there were three other divisions, viz. Pathan, also called Moghul, Labbe and Pattegar. There was only one household of Pattegar and the head of the household practised his hereditary craft of making twisted cotton cord, an indispensable article of domestic use.

All the Muslims in Rampura were Sunnis. They were bilingual, being able to talk to Hindus in Kannada, and among themselves, a kind of Urdu.

As among Hindus, landowning households had a higher status than the others. If with this was combined a long period of stay in Rampura, that enhanced the status further. Those households which had a house and some land in the old village enjoyed special esteem in the eyes of the villagers.

Land seemed even more precious for Muslims than for the others as only a few of them could be included even among the second-level landowners. A good many Muslims were engaged in trade and commerce while a few others provided certain services and skills absent among Hindus. The fact that Muslims were prominent in non-agricultural activities drew adverse criticisms from Peasants who

---

[1] After writing the above I began to doubt whether my impression of what Hakim Sab had said was correct, and I decided to check it against the original diaries. I found that I had written: 'The concept of *pak* or purity is an obsession. Purity of body, clothes, mind, etc. is a prerequisite to religion. *Haram*: After intercourse with a woman, both parties must wash before having intercourse again. If a wash is not taken then the second intercourse has the status of adultery (*haram*). Proper intercourse is *halal*.'

thought that only agriculture was real work. According to the latter, Muslims made their living by *gilitu* (corruption of 'gilt', meaning polish rather than substance) and thus escaped the need to do hard work. Being poor and economically dependent on the goodwill of the Peasant landowners, Muslims had to be respectful to their patrons and this again was interpreted as an attempt to escape hard work by seeking the support of powerful men. It was true that unlike the poorer Hindus, Muslims, by and large, preferred trade and commerce to working as *jita* labourers and this was because they were less tied to land and had to be on the lookout for other opportunities presented by trade and commerce.

Occupationally, Muslims were the most diversified group in the village. Among them were to be found traders, contractors, brokers, tailors and tinsmiths. The only butcher, plasterer, the shoer of bullocks' hoofs, snuff-maker, and cotton cord-maker in the village were Muslims. Even those Muslims who had some land or were engaged in cultivation did some trade or brokerage on the side.

Trading again varied from keeping petty grocery stores to the occasional selling of seasonal fruits and hardware and plastic gewgaws at weekly markets in nearby villages. Shukoor kept a shop where he hired out cycles (by the hour) and petromax lamps for festive occasions, and sold bottled soda water. Karim, Dilli Sab and one or two others sold mangoes during summer: they bought the produce of an orchard when the fruits were still unripe, and harvested them later for sale in urban markets. The responsibility for keeping a watch on the orchard was the buyer's. The latter usually camped in the orchard till all the fruits had been harvested. He endured the discomforts of living alone in the orchard, and braved the flies, mosquitoes and other pestilential insects in the hope of a few hundred rupees' profit at the end of six to eight weeks. One Hindu confided in me, 'That kind of life is too tough for us. Only Muslims are able to stand it.'

Economically and socially, Muslims were dependent upon Hindus. This was exemplified by the fact that Muslim tenants leased land from Hindu landowners, Muslim debtors borrowed money from Hindu creditors and Muslim *jita* servants worked for Hindu masters.[1] Many Muslims were clients of Hindu patrons. Besides, Muslim economic activities were frequently geared to Hindu activities and

[1] No Muslim *jita* servant worked for a Muslim, and two Muslims had Hindu servants.

institutions. For instance, a Muslim trader bought jack fruits whole-sale at a weekly market in Tendekere village in order to sell them in Rampura at the 'Festival of the Fast' (*upavasada habba*). A ritual fast did not mean abstinence from all food but only from normal diet. On fast days, villagers ate dishes cooked from grains other than rice or ragi, and also fruits such as banana, jack and oranges.

The bridal processions of members of the richest households, and processions at the festivals of village deities included displays of fireworks and the fireworks man was generally a Muslim from Hogur. Shukoor's and Karim's petromax lanterns were also in demand at processions. Muslim artisans derived the bulk of their income from working for Hindus.

Muslims were also socially dependent on the Hindus, and in parti-cular on the leaders of the dominant caste. They were certain that the headman, Nadu Gowda and others could be relied upon to protect them from local harassments and indignities. According to one informant, Rampura Muslims were split into three factions, and there was little communication between the factions. Any dispute among Muslims, including disputes among close kindred, had to be settled by Peasant leaders. I myself witnessed two disputes among kin which needed the intervention of Peasants.

Relations between Hindus and Muslims were close. I was occa-sionally surprised at the intimate knowledge which some Muslims had of Hindu culture. Karim, for instance, was well informed about the divisions among Peasants, their wedding customs, etc. I have already mentioned Akbar Sab's interest in putting an end to my single-blessedness and the criteria he looked for in the bride would have won the approval of my Peasant friends. I found a few Muslims enjoying listening to gramophone records of dramas which were based on stories taken from the corpus of Hindu mythology.[1]

On the other side, some Hindus admired certain traits of Muslim culture. For instance, Rame Gowda praised the brevity, dignity and quietness of a Muslim wedding which was a striking contrast to the elaborate, noisy and chaotic Hindu counterpart. He thought that Muslims displayed and served their food aesthetically, while Hindus paid no attention to these aspects. He admired the vermicelli (*shamige*)

---

[1] At a higher level, one of the finest actors on the Kannada stage in the twenties and thirties was Peer who played leading roles in dramas based on stories from Hindu mythology. He was universally admired by the Hindus for the sensitivity with which be played those roles.

made by them. The many manual skills of Muslims, making flower garlands, fireworks, ability to repair gadgets, etc. were also admired. However, Muslim indifference to pollution was criticized. The village accountant and Sannu both claimed to have seen Muslims spitting inside their houses. Again, unlike Hindus, Muslims felt no hesitation in visiting the Harijan ward. They did not think that they became impure from such a visit. Karim's popularity with Harijans and the fact that some of them took their disputes to him for settlement were both regarded as odd by the accountant. He also added that Karim took pleasure in pulling the legs of Harijan women. He said this when Karim was present and the poor man was embarrassed.

Friendship cut across not only castes but religious divisions as well. The Potter Sannayya and Karim were such good friends that even their wives had become close companions. Their houses were close to each other, separated only by the width of Gudi street. I once asked the Potter how it was that he and Karim were great friends, and he replied that his father and Karim's father had both been good friends in the old days. In fact, soon after Karim's father moved into Rampura, he had two pairs of bullocks which were tied up in front of the Potter's house for many months. The Potter's family had kept a watchful eye on the bullocks.

Mrs Karim had several other Hindu friends besides Mrs Sannayya. Thus when her six-day old infant died she was visited by many women including the Shepherd Kobli. Kobli consoled Mrs Karim telling her that some women had had to bear the loss of grown sons who were cultivators and mainstays of their families. Mrs Karim should compare her lot with theirs and take courage.

Shukoor who owned the hire-cycle shop was a friend of Swamy, Nadu Gowda's son. Once Shukoor returned from a brief trip to a nearby town and immediately after, he went in search of Swamy. Shukoor explained to me that if he did not see his friend for a few days he became uneasy in his mind. Such declarations of affection were frequently heard between grown men. Friendship was a value, and when a quarrel occurred between friends each partner narrated how much he had done for the other, and how much he had had to put up with. Friends who had quarrelled did not speak to each other and I came across several cases of breached friendships. An enduring friendship such as that between Nadu Gowda and the headman was certainly exceptional.

Friendship was not a simple, homogeneous category, It was either a 'horizontal' relationship between equals, or 'vertical' between superior and inferior. Thus, while the friendship between Lakshmana and Kempu, both Peasants and sons of big landowners was horizontal, that between Swamy and Shukoor was vertical. Shukoor and Aziz (a tailor) obtained occasional monetary and other help through Swamy's goodwill, just as Karim and Nenne were helped by the headman.

The relation between a patron and client was a vertical one, and it was often very close. The closeness grew with the years, and gradually, an element of friendship emerged from that inhospitable, hierarchical soil. I shall give an example of it below.

Karim's father was persuaded to migrate to Rampura by the headman's father who needed a groom and coachman for his horse and coach. He was installed in a house belonging to the headman, and given some land on a share-cropping basis, as his was a large family. Karim, and his younger brothers, Nasar and Bachche, were residents of Rampura in 1948, and all of them were the headman's clients. But Karim appeared to be closer to the headman than the other two. (But by the end of 1948 certain strains had begun to surface between Karim and the headman's lineage.)

Karim owned 1.5 acres of wet land which he and his older son cultivated, and in addition, he was a share-cropper on an equal amount of land belonging to the headman. He also received the crop growing on a few plots in the headman's rice-land for the varied services he was called upon to render. It was through the headman's goodwill that he obtained contracts from government or other agencies to repair sections of the road or canal. In 1952, Karim's young son, Mahmud, had been employed as a conductor on one of the headman's buses.

Every evening Karim had to visit the Harijan wards in Rampura and Gudi to book casual labourers, men and women for the headman for the following day. The headman's need for labour varied from day to day, and it was only around dusk that he had a precise idea of his needs for the following day. In Karim's absence, Nasar or Imamu were asked to book the labourers but Karim enjoyed a rapport with the Harijans which was denied to the others.

Karim was trusted in a way no other client was. He was once sent to a village near Bilikere to investigate the economic and sectarian background of a potential groom for one of the daughters of the headman. It was early summer, before ripe mangoes had started coming into the market, and it was easy for Karim to pose as a mango trader. He contacted a few Muslims in the village to find out if he could buy the fruits of an orchard. As luck would have it, he secured a good orchard at a low price. He became so friendly with his local contact that the latter insisted that Karim should be his guest. Gradually, Karim revealed the real object of his mission to the host who assured him that the groom's father was a big landowner and that he was financially sound. He was also a 'proper' Peasant, and not a follower of either the Dasayya or Jogayya sect. Karim reported his findings to the headman who then decided to agree to give his daughter in marriage to the landowner's son. Karim narrated the incident to me with pride, and added, with a smile, that he had made a good profit from the orchard.

As stated earlier, during the 1948 monsoon, the headman suddenly contracted bronchial infection which he was unable to shake off. It was decided to take the headman to the hospital in Mysore and Karim was despatched in the morning to fetch a taxi from Hogur, and he returned with a jeep which was usually hired out for wedding processions. Both the headman's sons went with their father to Mysore and Karim was asked to sleep in the headman's house. Several Peasants, including the headman's kinsmen, commented on the fact that Karim had been asked to stay in the house and not any relative. It was a measure of the family's trust in Karim.

While relations between individual Muslim clients and their Hindu patrons was one of trust, the relations between Hindus and Muslims as distinct groups were marked occasionally by suspicion. And this was largely due to the forces operating in the wider society especially during the critical years of 1946–8 when the country was repeatedly shaken by the riots and violence which both preceded and followed the partition of the sub-continent into the two sovereign states of India and Pakistan. Sometime in 1946 there had been a communal riot in Channapatna town (to the north-east) resulting in the migration of several Muslims into Rampura. (The riots had resulted in the brutal murder of a poor Hindu schoolmaster and this was known to some villagers.) The more politically conscious villagers occasionally expressed their suspicions about the loyalty to India of some of the immigrants. A few Shepherd youths employed in a Bangalore mill visited Rampura during Ugadi, the new year festival, and they narrated with pride their role in a communal fight which had broken out in Bangalore in 1947. One of them told me that initially the Muslims had the better of the exchanges but this had been reversed later.

The Indo-Pakistani conflict over Kashmir began in December 1947 and continued into 1948. The bloody and bitter communal riots of north India had resulted in the assassination of Mahatma Gandhi on 30 January 1948. While Gandhiji's martyrdom brought Hindus and Muslims together the events preceding it did not. The marching of Indian troops into Hyderabad in September 1948 roused mutual hatred and suspicion. For instance, Khwaja, a village grocer, told his friends that the Nizam's army would beat back the Indian troops in no time. The Nizam was the world's richest man and he had a great army. Khwaja had only a picture of Mr Jinnah, the founder of Pakistan, in his shop, and none of either Gandhi or Nehru. After the successful police action in Hyderabad, he was reported to have gone on a fast.

Before and during the movement of troops into Hyderabad, some younger Peasants became excited at the attitude of Khwaja and a few others whom they considered to be pro-Pakistan. They believed that Muslims discussed political matters regularly after the Friday prayers at the mosque. The discussions were said to be anti-Indian in intent. Local Muslims were also supposed to be receiving advice regularly from their co-religionists in the cities.

While my relations with Muslims were cordial, none of them discussed politics with me or with other Hindus. I remember mentioning the death of Jinnah to Shukoor who responded with stony silence. He probably did not wish to say anything for fear of being misunderstood. But then even his silence was likely to be misunderstood given the political atmosphere of 1947-8. However, considering the crisis through which Hindu–Muslim relations were passing in the country as a whole the occurrences in the village were very subdued.

CHAPTER VII

Classes and Factions

1 The Land-based Hierarchy

I DISCUSSED in the previous chapter how the hierarchical system of caste operated at the grassroots level. Its complexity was compounded by its meshing in with another hierarchical system based on the possession of differential rights in land. There was a two-way relationship between landownership and caste rank. Traditionally, ownership of land conferred respectability and prestige, and this was translated into caste rank in course of time, and contrariwise, high ritual rank unaccompanied by landownership produced anomalous situations. As mentioned earlier, the secular Brahmin commanded more prestige than the priestly Brahmin who was frequently poor and dependent upon gifts from those who were better off.

Unlike caste, the hierarchy based on ownership of land was a secular one, and, in theory, everyone was free to acquire land though the higher castes had more resources as well as opportunities for it. It could also be safely presumed that the members of the higher castes, and in particular, the locally dominant caste, were opposed to land passing into the hands of the lowest castes who provided the main source of agricultural labour.

The pattern of landownership in Rampura was broadly typical of the entire country. There were very few households each of which owned twenty irrigated acres or more, followed by a substantial number which owned less than five such acres. The 'landowner' category was hospitable enough to include even those who had an acre or less of dry land. From the point of view of the villagers, a man owning ten acres of irrigated land was regarded as comfortably off while twenty represented wealth.

Those who owned less than five acres of land were frequently found to be leasing an acre or two from a bigger landowner. There was a large number of villagers who were only lessees of land. They paid the owners an agreed quantity of rice per acre after harvest. The quantity varied in each case. The lessees also hired themselves out as wage labourers.

At the lowest level of the land hierarchy were the landless labourers. But not all the landless were labourers. Among the artisan and servicing castes, the Washerman, Basketry-maker, Swineherd and Oshtama did not own any land. Nor did any Trader.

A significant characteristic of the land hierarchy was the overlapping of categories in the middle and lower regions: some landowners were also tenants, and some tenants did wage-labour.

Owning sizable quantities of wet land involved the owner in continuing relations with tenants, servants and labourers, and with members of the artisan and servicing castes. The tools that were commonly used in agriculture were simple, and this meant that even three or four acres of irrigated land called for continuing labour from two or three persons. And during transplantation and harvesting, there was need for more labour.

The bigger landowners, in spite of their resources, found it difficult to secure enough labour. The problem was made more acute as a result of status considerations which prevented the members of the richest households from personally working on land. They generally leased out a part of their land to tenants or sharecroppers in order to reduce their management problems. As pointed out earlier, it was also a device for obtaining additional and assured labour.

The members of the artisan and servicing castes working for a landowner were paid in grain during the annual rice harvest. The relationship was a long-standing one with at least the bigger landowners and was not easily repudiated. For instance, if a landowner dismissed his Barber, Washerman or Smith, the latter appealed to the village elders to have his customary rights restored. The elders inquired into the matter, and persuaded the landowner to take back the dismissed artisan, if the latter had not been guilty of egregious wrong-doing. The landowner's household was referred to as *adade kula* and prestige was attached to customary relationships and being paid in grain.

Land was the most important source of wealth, and the scarcity of wet land made it extremely precious. The tenant was expected to be grateful to the landowner for the benefit that had been conferred on him and was expected to periodically acknowledge his indebtedness.

The landowner stood in the relation of patron to those who regularly worked for him. Each big landowner had many clients who hailed from different agricultural classes and castes. If caste and class each cut village society into different and horizontal layers, one upon another, division into patron and client represented a different type of alignment, a vertical one bringing together people from diverse castes and classes. The bond between patron and client was at the basis of factionalism which was endemic in rural India.

Whatever the consequences for production, the tenant's position was easier when the landowner was not locally resident. For one thing an absentee landowner could not evict a tenant with the ease with which a resident landowner could. Second, an absentee landowner was only paid the grain that was due to him whereas a resident landowner extracted a share of the straw as well. It was also not unusual for him to claim a share in the small summer harvest of pulses.

The resident landowner was able to extract a higher share of the crop than his absentee counterpart. Where the resident landowner belonged to the dominant caste, the exactions were even greater. He demanded from each of his clients a day's corvée when the shortage of labour was at its worst. He demanded also other services. Finally, it was easier for a dominant caste landowner to evict a tenant than it was for anyone else.

Prior to the 1930s, many of the big landowners in Rampura were Brahmins. But they migrated to the cities to seek salaried jobs for themselves, and better educational facilities for their children. And over the years their connection with their ancestral village reduced itself to annual visits at harvest to collect rice. A few went further and entrusted the task of looking after their land to a local landowner, usually a Peasant. Urban expenditure including the cost of education and the need to pay substantial dowries for their daughters resulted in their being separated from their land. The pace of emigration increased during the thirties and forties depriving the rural areas of a crucial social and cultural element. Only two local Brahmin households were resident in the village in 1948, the *ayurvedic* doctor being only an official liable to be transferred.

In the early fifties there was a movement in the Rampura area, led by an educated Peasant, demanding greater rights for actual tillers as against landowners. It affected absentee landowners far more than resident ones. Since many of the former were Brahmins they thought that the movement was directed against them. I remember a talk with a Brahmin landowner from Srinivasapuram who complained that his Peasant tenants were harassing him with regard to his share of the crop. In the fifties I heard similar complaints from several others. But as against this I also knew some Brahmin landowners who continued to have happy relations with their tenants from the various non-Brahmin castes. I think the truth was that the land reforms favoured tenants against landowners but the resident landowners were better able to take advantage of them than absentee landowners. Generally the former came from one or other of the non-Brahmin castes while a good proportion of the absentees were Brahmins, Where the non-Brahmin landowners belonged to the locally dominant caste, the reforms did not affect them significantly.

In Rampura in 1948, Peasants owned more land than all the other castes put together. The three biggest landowners were the headman, Nadu Gowda and Millayya. Among Lingayats, the two priestly lineages of Madeshwara and Basava were the biggest landowners. The members of the Madeshwara lineage derived additional income from the annual fair of the deity held during Deepavali (October–November).

Before the CDS Canal was extended to bring the benefits of irrigation to Rampura and neighbouring villages, some pasture land was locally available, and this enabled the Shepherds to practise their traditional occupation of sheep-rearing and weaving woollen blankets. But with the extension of canal irrigation, the quantity of pasture land shrunk with the result that many Shepherds had to switch over to agriculture. Only a few households continued to weave blankets. Since they could not rear sheep, they bought wool from the biggest landowners each of whom kept a flock.

I have earlier listed the castes which did not own any land. I may add here that among the artisan and servicing castes, even the privileged few who could call themselves landowners did not own more than an acre or two each. And as already mentioned, several Harijans owned tiny bits of land as descendants of the original village servant. But the return from the land was nowhere near enough to make any difference in the relation between Harijans and high caste landowners.

In the case of other lower castes, however, landownership did make a difference to their social standing. I have earlier referred to the well-off Toddyman and the contrast in status between him and his poor castefellow. There were two Oilman brothers who had by their hard work, thrift, and honesty acquired some cash and bought land, and they were universally well spoken of. In the course of practising their traditional calling, they visited the great shrine of Madeshwara in Kollegal *taluk* (then in Madras State, now part of Karnataka) regularly, and everyone believed that their success was the result of their devotion to the deity. The brothers painted their foreheads with horizontal stripes of *vibhuti* every morning, and they had a miniature *lingam* tied round their necks.

I wondered whether the Oilman brothers were not on the road to becoming Lingayats. Historically, Lingayatism recruited its followers from a number of diverse castes from Brahmin to Harijan, and individuals, families and local sections of castes continue to get converted to the sect through a process of social osmosis. But by and large, Lingayats regarded themselves as a caste and the others reciprocated the view.

Coming as they did in regular contact with hundreds of devotees of Madeshwara, a considerable proportion of whom were Lingayats, and believing as they did that their worldly success was due to the deity's blessings, nothing was more natural than for the Oilman brothers to become Lingayats. Besides, the latter were a much higher caste than Oilman, and conversion meant upward mobility. However, vegetarianism and teetotalism were essential attributes of Lingayatism and the Oilman brothers would have had to change their dietary if they had not done that already.

The biggest landowners from the Peasant caste commanded the respect of everyone in the village excepting the members of the factions opposed to them. Even Brahmins and Lingayats had to behave deferentially towards them. This was poignantly brought home to me when one afternoon in the summer of 1948, I found the Rama priest sitting in the headman's inner courtyard and talking excitedly to the headman's mother. The priest had just heard that his son had passed the Lower Secondary examination, conducted by the Government of Mysore, in the first division, and the poor priest was beside himself with excitement. I can still remember him walking down Gudi street with beads of perspiration on his brow and a pinch of snuff held between the thumb and index finger of his right hand. The priest made a beeline for the headman's house and found a sympathetic, though perhaps somewhat deaf, ear in the headman's mother. (While the men were pleased with the news they did not have the patience to listen to the priest.) The latter sat uncomfortably on his toes—perhaps he felt that if he squatted on the floor his pure clothes would become dirty if not impure—and poured out his news and problems. Mysore was a distant (22 miles), unknown and expensive city. Where would his son stay if he joined a high school there? How to meet his expenses? Who would look after him? And so on. Every few minutes the priest addressed the old matriarch as *avva* (mother). His attitude seemed no different from that of the headman's clients except for the fact that he was treated with respect as a Brahmin and priest. A big Brahmin landowner, on the other hand, would have been seated on a mat in the front verandah and the headman or one of his adult sons would have listened to him with respect.

The fact that among the non-Brahmin castes the acquisition of land was sooner or later followed by Sanskritization (and nowadays also Westernization) of the style of life meant that an attempt was being made to translate wealth and prestige into caste rank. There were opportunities in pre-British India to acquire land and political power and the view that traditional Indian society provides an instance of a 'closed system of social stratification' is indeed neat though not true.

2   Patrons and Clients

Patron-client relationships stemmed directly out of possession of differential rights in land. All those who worked for a landowner, tenants, servants and labourers on the one hand, and members of the artisan and servicing castes on the other, tended to become his clients. A patron had several clients and some clients had more than one patron. In addition, a patron could change his clients over a period of time and *vice versa*.

Every patron wielded power and the more ambitious among patrons wanted to control the entire village. (In pre-British times, a very ambitious patron could aspire to be a chieftain.) He had to conduct himself in such a way that he won the support of as many people as possible. Every able-bodied man counted in a physical fight between rival factions (or villages). In the years before World War I, when communications were much poorer than they are today, it was usual for a patron to have a few strong men around him. Wrestling was a popular sport, and at least the larger villages had wrestling-houses (*garadis*) where boys exercised and wrestled under the guidance of older wrestlers (*pahelwan*). The products of the wrestling-houses were valuable recruits to the order of clients. Not only were their methods of persuasion effective where other methods had failed, but their very presence induced people to be reasonable.

A big patron attracted clients as a magnet attracted iron filings. The poor and the weak felt unsafe without a patron. The latter provided a source of livelihood as well as a sense of security. Forces in the local culture were such as to encourage the weak to seek protection from the strong. I have earlier narrated how Pijja prostrated himself before the Amildar and held his feet to make clear to the official that his protection was needed. Similarly, a client who desperately needed a patron's protection held his feet and the patron was expected to respond positively. Patrons, kings, and deities were all expected to protect those who sought refuge in them (*sharanagata rakshaka*)[1]. The deity Vishnu is usually shown with his right hand held down, palm outward, to symbolize the gesture of *abhayahasta* or protection to those who sought it.

Clients followed a particular style in talking to their patrons. This perhaps varied somewhat according to the patron's caste. For instance, in the neighbouring village of Kere, I heard a very old Peasant client frequently use the term *nimma pada* (your feet) while talking to his Brahmin patron. I also heard the patron being addressed as *budhi* (lord)[2]. But in Rampura, the headman was addressed by his clients in the singular with the suffix *appa* (father) invariably added at the end of the sentence. The headman's clients respected him, and were even scared of him, but the honorific plural was rarely used. Sometimes he was referred to as *Gauda* (Chief) but even then the honorific plural was not used. To many he was a relative, to a larger number the leader of the Peasants, and to everyone in the village, headman. The singular number used towards him was a sign of intimacy and not of lack of respect. A stranger like me, on the other hand, was addressed in the plural and it would be absurd to suggest that I came within miles of the headman where the villagers' respect

---

[1] A powerful man who continued to protect a corrupt follower was, however, criticized. In such a case, the term *sharanagata rakshaka* was used pejoratively. I have heard educated men criticizing a political or other leader for this quality. The tendency to play patron is widespread, and it includes the so-called modern sectors.

[2] Such usage was widespread in this area in the thirties, and it started disappearing in the forties.

was concerned. Perhaps my being a Brahmin was an additional factor in the use of the honorific plural. All officials, irrespective of caste, were also addressed in the plural.

When a client was in deep trouble and needed the patron's help, he appealed to the patron's protective impulses by likening him to a father: 'You are like a father to me and whom else can I turn to when I am in trouble?' Occasionally a protective, paternal role was thrust on a man. For instance, a client's friends might urge the patron that the client had no doubt done a wrong thing but who else could he go to? 'He has done a thing comparable to [a child] eating mud. You chastise him, you spit on him, you beat him with your sandals. You have every right to do it. But whom else can he go to, you cannot give up his hand now.' The friends would ask the client to fall at the patron's feet and assure the latter that the folly would not be repeated. In short, it was difficult for a big landowner to escape his culturally destined role of patron. If he persisted in his refusal to play that role, he courted unpopularity, and was dubbed a selfish man. His rival was certain to benefit.

In return for the economic benefits and protection which he received, the client was expected to obey the patron, do his bidding, and be loyal. According to the Kannada saying, it was rank ingratitude to think ill of a house in which one had eaten (*unda manege eradu bageyabaradu*). The ideal client worked for the prosperity of his master. In an emotional moment, a client might even say that he was prepared to lay down his life for his master. This was a fine sentiment to articulate but everyone recognized that it was not intended to be put into practice.

An ideal patron helped his client in every way he could. He interceded on the client's behalf with officials or local self-government bodies or co-operative societies, to secure for him a benefit or contract, introduced him to a lawyer or doctor, advanced him a loan to meet an emergency, and tried to influence decisions in his favour in disputes in which he was involved. The intervention of patrons on behalf of their clients was widely recognized and a source of corruption. I have narrated earlier how the verdict in Kannur's case altered radically overnight because a kinsman and client of the headman had to be tried for alleged rape. In another case Kempu was about to make a point which was relevant but restrained himself as he saw Rame Gowda's wink. The crucial point died on his tongue to the detriment of one party to the dispute.

A client turned to his patron in every kind of emergency. When Uddayya, a kinsman and client of the headman, came down with tuberculosis the headman helped him to consult specialists in the tuberculosis sanatorium in Mysore. Uddayya stayed in Bharata's house (the headman's youngest son) during the protracted consultations and his younger brothers were not keen to shift him to the sanatorium. In the end the headman had to tell the brothers firmly that they must shift their brother to the sanatorium, or some other place and that he could not stay in Bharata's house any longer.

A Shepherd client of Nadu Gowda had to visit Sathnur to attend the final session of the negotiations over his daughter's divorce. He wanted Nadu Gowda's advice as to what were the proper terms of the divorce to which he should agree. He and Nadu Gowda held a brief consultation on my verandah, and the latter asked the Shepherd whether he had taken with him the ornaments presented to the daughter at the wedding. The old Shepherd opened the mouth of his dirty cotton handbag and Nadu Gowda peered in. Satisfied, Nadu Gowda gave him permission to leave.

One of the Smiths working for the headman casually told the headman, as the latter was setting out for his evening walk, that he was going to get married in a few days' time. The headman took a minute or so to digest the news and then asked the Smith to chop up the remaining stump of a particular tree on his farm to be used for fuel for the wedding dinner. The Smith understood which particular stump the headman was referring to—perhaps he had helped saw the tree—and left, looking satisfied.

Besides having specific duties towards clients, patrons had certain general obligations. A big patron had to keep an open house: sudden visitors, whether officials, politicians, total strangers, holy men or pilgrims were not allowed to leave the village without having a meal or snack. Failure to be generous with food exposed the patron to criticism. He was accused of meanness, and any misfortune that happened to him was regarded as deserved punishment sent from above.

A patron had to indulge in lavish spending at weddings and funerals. In the years before World War I, a big village wedding lasted a week and arrangements were made for feeding hundreds of people. Dancing girls from Mysore or some other town were invited to dance before the guests. Villagers reminisced for years about the big weddings and funerals they had seen. A patron's importance was judged by the magnificence of the dinner, dance and fireworks, and the number and importance of the guests who had attended the wedding.

It would, however, be an over-simplification to view Rampura as divided into a few social pyramids with a big landowner at the top of each. While it was true that each landowner had his followers, many clients had more than one patron. And many poor villagers did not like to make their loyalties clear. Such clarification had the risk of incurring the wrath of patrons whose protection had been implicitly repudiated. The poor generally behaved deferentially towards all big landowners partly because wealthy men were respected, and partly because of the possibility that they were likely to prove useful. Only when factionalism had gone too deep was such ambiguity impossible: even to be seen talking to one patron or his client was likely to be interpreted as a suspicious, if not hostile, activity by the other patrons.

The headman was such a powerful figure that except for a handful of people bitterly opposed to him, everyone in the village was at least outwardly deferential to him. He was the village headman and he had power and influence. It was not prudent to be on the wrong side of him.

At the same time, however, there were two major power blocs in the village, one clustering around the headman and his lineage, and the other, around the God's House lineage of which the Nadu Gowda was the principal spokesman in 1948 and Millayya was a leading member. The latter lineage had more members than the headman's. The members of the God's House lineage had a great sense of unity and this expressed itself on the occasion of the annual festival of the two lineage deities who had a joint shrine in the village.

Many of the smaller landowners who were either clients or had client-like attitudes towards the big patrons were themselves patrons of a few who were very poor. In such cases, the relationship between patron and client was more egalitarian than that between a big patron and client. It seemed as though there were different orders of patrons just as clientship subsumed a range of dependency-relationships. There were tenants, *jita* servants, casual labourers and artisans and servicing castes, and there were also others who merely sought occasionally the patrons' advice and intercession. This fact was quite well known though rarely articulated.

3 Factions

The landownership pattern, and caste and lineage systems provided the basis for factions. The division of a village into two or more mutually opposed factions was a permanent feature of rural social structure. The number of factions as also the degree of factionalism varied from village to village, or in the same village over a period of time but a faction-free village was difficult to come across or even contemplate. Factions were different from other units of the structure in that membership was to some extent voluntary unlike with caste and lineage. The element of voluntariness did diminish, however, with an increase in the degree of factionalism.

When a village had a large enough population each faction subsumed several social pyramids each of which included a landowner and his clients. The leader of a faction was either its biggest landowner, or one of the biggest.

A faction was a 'vertical' group in the sense that it brought together individuals in different economic categories, and from different castes. The clients of each landowner in the faction had either direct relations with the faction leader, or had them mediated through an immediate patron. Factions were certainly a manifestation of inegalitarianism but they forged strong bonds between unequal partners and provided yet another countervailing force to the horizontal ties of caste and class.

As I stated earlier, when I moved into the village, I was told that unlike its neighbours, Rampura was faction-free. The villagers seemed to believe in what they had told me, and there was also some basis for their belief. For in villages like Kere and Hogur factions were long-drawn and ran deep. In comparison, factionalism was muted in Rampura. The Revenue Inspector (*shekdar*) of Hogur *hobli* told me that he liked Rampura because the leadership was strong and united, and this facilitated government work. But he was speaking in a relative sense as he was aware of the existence of young men who were opposed to the headman.

The situation which obtained in Rampura in 1948 was, however, a fairly recent one. For, during the time of the present headman's father, factionalism was rampant. He was only the leader of a powerful faction, and he had to contend with the sustained opposition of the leaders from the other factions. Two of his bitter foes were from God's House lineage, Nadu Gowda's father, and Mollayya (Sr.), father of Mari Gowda. Several villagers narrated to me instances of defiance of the headman's authority by them. As stated earlier, the God's House lineage was numerically far stronger than the headman's, and its leaders wanted to make it clear that nothing in the village could be done without their support.

Yet another opponent was Melkote (Sr.) who, though without the support of numbers, used his knowledge of the law courts to harass those whom he disliked. The villagers respected him for his agricultural and legal skills and his opponents had a healthy respect for him. He had been dead for several years when I started my field work in 1948 and the older villagers spoke of him with admiration. The fact that one who headed a tiny lineage and lacked any official position, could harass big leaders, was the thing they admired in Melkote (Sr.). Villagers had an aesthetic as well as intellectual interest in disputes.

The Brahmin landowners who were in the village till the late thirties did not seem to have been active in local politics. Perhaps they had already started looking outwards. I know, however, that in a few neighbouring villages a handful of Brahmin landowners did play a significant part in local politics and factions.

From my talks with elderly villagers, it appeared that if anything factionalism had been much stronger in the period before World War I, and this seemed to be true of the region as a whole. Each large village had a few leaders each of whom had a considerable following, and the relation between them was generally one of rivalry. In many cases, however, rivalry (*paipoti*) had developed into hatred (*hage, jiddu, muyyi* or *dwesha*). Hatred prompted each lineage to seize every opportunity to inflict an injury on the other. The injured then felt honour-bound to get even with the injurer (*muyyi tirisikolluvudu*). The lineage which failed to avenge an injury lost its face, its maleness, it was dubbed womanly or impotent, and it is not unlikely that it also started losing clients. *Muyyi* (also *jiddu*) or institutionalized conflict between two lineages was a recognized relationship.

Conflict between leaders could arise over such important matters as land, women and seeking influence with officials. An ambitious leader, in the course of enlarging the size of his farm, hurt several persons' interests, and one of the latter could seek the aid of a rival leader to get the wrong righted. Again, two leaders might want the same widow or divorcee as keep (*rakhavu*). Access to officials was crucial for aspirants to power especially in the pre-democratic days.

The key officials were the heads of the *hobli* (Revenue Inspector), *taluk* (Amildars) and *district* (Deputy Commissioner). The irrigation engineers and a few others were also important but villagers did not come into contact with them except very occasionally. In the pre-Independence days these officials had power and prestige and their favour was necessary for enhancing a villager's interests and harassing his enemies.

The conflict between leaders took different forms. Thus a dispute over land or castes, or even a case of abuse in which they were either directly involved or only indirectly through their clients, had the potential to explode into a violent fight between factions, or result in the eventual outcasting of a few persons by the caste council or a protracted suit in the law courts. When hatred increased to the point where it shut out all normal caution, it exploded into pitched battles between contending factions or in deliberate killing. The fighting and murder were usually carried out by the toughs who were at the beck and call of a leader.[1] However, leaders were not always cautious enough to avoid being directly involved in the killings that occurred.

There was a subterranean layer of violence in the social life of rural Mysore in the years before World War I. The peace which the British had established had not percolated fully into the village partly owing to the poor state of the roads and lack of resources for a police force that was large, efficient or mobile enough for the purpose. Officials whose business it was to administer villages knew which villagers were law-abiding and peaceful, and which were not. In the latter category were to be found some leaders who enjoyed a reputation for violence which went beyond their villages. There were old men in Rampura who remembered leaders in neighbouring villages who were alleged to have committed murders, and of whom ordinary folk were scared. These leaders were termed, half-jokingly, *palegara* (chieftain). In the pre-British days, *palegaras* abounded in every part of Mysore, and whenever there was a weak king, they tried to take advantage of the situation by expanding the territories under them.

Even until the 1930s, the police were seen only rarely in most villages. In fact, their arrival usually indicated that something terrible like a murder or riot had taken place. It struck terror in the hearts

---

[1] See, in this connection, N. Rama Rao's *Kelavu Nenapugalu* (Bangalore, 1954) for the description of the incident which led to Devarase Gowda, the headman of Saligrama village, being taken into police custody, pp. 272–89.

of villagers. Even in 1948, elderly villagers recalled two visits of armed policemen to Rampura, once a few years before the beginning of World War I and the other towards its end. On each occasion, the visit was in connection with a murder which had occurred elsewhere. But the visits had left a deep scar on the minds of the villagers and had become part of local folklore.

Indeed, before Independence, villagers were scared of the visits of officials. Nadu Gowda recalled with much amusement that, during his youth, it was usual for ordinary villagers to take to their heels as soon as they heard the blowing of the horn (*kombu*), trumpet (*kahale*) and the tom-toms which heralded the visit of the mighty Amildar. The horn and trumpet could be heard a mile away. Only the headman and a few brave villagers remained to welcome the Maharaja's representative. But the villagers had reason to fear the visit of any official. Apart from the demand for taxes, and lingering fears from a tradition of conscription of able-bodied men for the all-too-frequent local wars, villagers had an understandable interest in concealing from the visitor many of the things that had gone on in the village since his previous visit: a man may have been severely beaten in punishment for something he had done, a bloody fight may have occurred between two groups, a powerful man may have diverted water illegally into his fields, or lopped off the branches of a roadside tree and so on. Even a murder may have occurred. The two village officials, headman and accountant, in particular, had many things to hide from prying official eyes.

During the depression of the thirties, several Rampurians took to raiding convoys of paddy-carts travelling from Hogur to Mysore. Uddaiah, who was the leader of one of the raiding-gangs, described to me graphically how the raids were carried out. The raiders usually hid in the darkness of a grove (*tope*) by the roadside, and as soon as the signal (the simulated hooting of an owl, for instance) was given by a scout, the men fell on the convoy. It was usual to pick the rear end of the convoy. The driver was knocked out with a blow from a staff and the gunny-bags in which the paddy was stored were gashed with sharp knives. Baskets were held under each gashed bag to catch the paddy pouring in streams. I do not know how significant these raids were economically but they did provide an outlet for the energies of the village braves.

The raiders were to be found on all the roads radiating from Mysore City to the towns and villages around. They even operated five miles from the city on the Mysore–Seringapatam road, near the village Kalasthavadi.[1]

Under the Mysore Local Self Government Act, 1926, Rampura had a panchayat comprising leaders from the principal Hindu castes and Muslims. The official panchayat was entrusted with such duties as the provision and maintenance of village streets, drains and lights, and making arrangements for the removal of sewage. Its main source of income was a levy on each house, house-site and shop. The government gave each panchayat a grant equal to the sum raised by it from taxes.

Until 1947, the headman was nominated as chairman of the panchayat by the Deputy Commissioner of Mysore District. In 1947, however, Rampura was allowed to have an elected chairman. This gave an opportunity to a small group of young men all of whom were bound together by common opposition to the headman, to make a determined effort to seize the chairmanship. The astonishing thing was that the young men almost succeeded in unseating the headman. It was then that Nadu Gowda came to his friend's rescue. With folded hands, he requested the young men, whose leaders were members of his lineage, to give the old leaders one more chance. '*Namma mana kapadi*' (protect our self-respect), he pleaded. His appeal proved successful. After all, he was a respected elder of God's House lineage and had a reputation for being a man of integrity. The opposition gave way and the headman was elected chairman. The headman was unable to forgive the bunch of young men who came near to defeating him.

As it happened, the 1947 election represented the high point of the challenge to the headman's authority for the young dissidents broke up soon after the election. Japi was accused by his friends of arrogance, Sidu left the village, and demoralization set in.

In the wake of his precarious victory the headman made a series of brilliant moves to safeguard and strengthen his position. First, he had one of his grand-daughters married to Nadu Gowda's third son, Karagu. This sealed an old friendship, and drew the most important leader of the God's House lineage closer to him.

[1] Alan Beals refers to a similar situation in Namhalli, near Bangalore, in the depression of the thirties. See His 'Interplay among Factors of Change in a Mysore Village', in *Village India*, McKim Marriott (ed.), Chicago, 1955, p. 96. N. Rama Rao also refers to the existence of thieves who preyed on carts carrying paddy from T. Narasipur to Mysore in *Kelavu Nenapugalu*.

It is necessary to repeat at this juncture that there was a sudden and rapid development of bus and lorry traffic on the roads in the fifties. Landowners whose pockets were bursting with money from the wartime sale of rice and jaggery, and who wielded political influence in post-independent India, were seeking new avenues for investment. They found them in buses, lorries, rice mills and urban housing. Only a very few educated villagers thought of more sophisticated avenues of investment such as cinema theatres in the growing towns and small scale industries, etc.

Some time after I left the village towards the end of 1948, the headman thought seriously of investing some of his money in urban housing and buses. Getting licences for buses did not present any serious problem as one of his close relatives was an important politician. He succeeded in bagging licences from the government to ply buses on three routes. He began with two buses in 1950 and decided to make use of the third licence later. One of the two was in collaboration with his eldest son-in-law and the bus went through his village. His youngest son Bharata resigned his job to take over the other line. Even in 1952 only two lines were being operated but the headman was looking forward to starting the third route soon. It was to link Rampura with a town about sixty miles to the north-west from which the headman's ancestors had originally migrated. Piety, nostalgia and money were all mixed together in deciding on the third route.

After having made certain of the bus routes, the headman asked his friend and affine, Nadu Gowda, whether he would like to invest his savings in a rice mill. The headman offered to help him to secure a licence, and in other ways too. Nadu Gowda thought over the offer for a few days and then decided against starting a mill. His first son Swamy was a contented soul, and was against exerting himself too greatly to earn more money. But the second son Kempu was cast in a different mould. He was intelligent and ambitious. He was strongly in favour of starting a mill but he was overruled by the other two.

After Nadu Gowda had said 'no', the headman sent for Millayya, also a member of the God's House lineage, and a big landowner, and asked him whether he was interested in starting a rice mill. The headman and Nadu Gowda both assured Millayya of their help and cooperation in the enterprise. Millayya talked the matter over with his brothers. They were keen. The two richer households had not only left the field for them but were actually offering their cooperation. Millayya thought deeply over all aspects of the matter and finally agreed. The headman kept his word and lent him 20,000 bricks from his kiln as an earnest of his support. Later, he helped Millayya to get the necessary licence, etc.

Millayya's rice mill was erected much faster than expected. It soon proved to be a profitable affair. Millayya and his brothers benefited not only from the income but from a sense of achievement and enhanced status. A young smartie from Kere, Tammu, was brought in as clerk-cum-public-relations-man, and soon became a confidant of Millayya and his brothers. Kulle Gowda wangled for himself a job as the Food Depot Clerk from the government but his tenure was mercifully brief. It was his job to look after the paddy stores in the godowns of the mill—it belonged to the government, which procured it from landowners at prices fixed by it to be sold under its rationing scheme. Each sack of paddy milled at any mill had to be under a permit and the Food Depot Clerk had to keep an account of it. This was intended to prevent milling for the black market. Kulle Gowda's accounts as well as his stocks were in a deplorable state. He blamed the rats for the decrease in the stored paddy. He also winked at unauthorized milling. He had to be sacked, and Sannu took his place. Sannu was working in that capacity when I revisited Rampura in 1952. Sannu became a friend of Millayya's family. This probably resulted in coolness between him and Nadu Gowda's household but Sidu (Sannu's younger brother) and Swamy continued to remain firm friends.

Kempu, Nadu Gowda's second son, was upset that his father and Swamy had overruled him in the matter of starting a mill. The success of Millayya's mill showed clearly that his brother and father had underestimated the quantity of paddy available in Rampura and its neighbourhood. He began to think of installing a paddy huller which was not only much cheaper but easy to operate. He probably mentioned it to his close friends, and soon the news got around. One day, when he went into the big mill, he found Karagayya, Millayya's younger brother, telling no one in particular, 'I have no cash for my *bidi* expenses. I am thinking of starting a huller.' The barb went home and Kempu was beside himself with fury. In his conversations with me, Kempu kept telling me that this was what finally induced him to start another mill in the village.

Kempu's efforts at persuading his brother, Swamy, and his father, Nadu Gowda, to instal a mill of their own, succeeded this time. His task was made easier when a visiting official mentioned the existence of a foreign-made mill which was cheaper than the Indian. Kempu found out more about it: it cost only about Rs 6,000, and it could be installed in the building next to Nadu Gowda's grocery shop. The low cost of the machine and the fact that it was not necessary to build a separate building for it meant that the capital needed was reduced to a fourth of the earlier estimate.

It is necessary here to comment on the part played by Lakshmana in all this. He consistently encouraged Kempu in his desire to instal another mill. He pulled up Swamy, Kempu's older brother, for not showing any enterprise. He perhaps did this at Kempu's instance. When Swamy pleaded inability to call on politicians and high officials to get the necessary licence, Lakshmana retorted that everyone felt uneasy at the thought of visiting important people. But that feeling had to be overcome.

Lakshmana took Kempu to meet high officials and even three ministers of the Mysore Government. It was necessary to meet the latter to counter the unfavourable notes put up by the officials. For instance, a very high official whose recommendation was essential for obtaining the licence did not see the need for another rice mill in Rampura. Kempu was very annoyed, 'He was barely five feet tall and he was so arrogant.' Kempu even thought that his rivals had brought influence to bear on him. (Not for a moment did Kempu concede the possibility that the official was right in following the rules.)

Millayya was upset by Nadu Gowda's efforts to instal another mill. He felt that Nadu Gowda had, in the process, broken a solemn assurance which he had given to Millayya. While Millayya kept his feelings to himself, his brothers gave free expression to theirs. Meanwhile, Tammu, the smart clerk from Kere, went into action. Kere men were known for their combativeness and politicking. I expect he saw officials and politicians in order to prevent Nadu Gowda from getting a licence. He also wrote a letter to a Kannada daily in Mysore urging that the Government should not issue licences for cheap, foreign-made mills which were so wasteful. (He even mentioned the brand-name of Nadu Gowda's mill.) Its rice-yield was low, it had a higher proportion of broken grain, etc. He bought enough copies of the paper and distributed them in Rampura. (It is difficult to understand why he did this unless he intended thereby to curry favour with his boss.) I expect that he also sent copies to the concerned officials and ministers.

Tammu's campaign failed to prevent Nadu Gowda from getting a licence but it did sharpen the cleavages already present in God's House lineage. I am certain that on many a verandah there was excited discussion about Nadu Gowda's starting a new mill after his promise of support to Millayya in his expensive and risk-ridden venture. Kempu and even Swamy justified the decision saying that but for Karagayya's deliberate insult to Kempu the second mill would not have come about.

But the interesting thing was both the groups spoke well of the headman. Karagayya told me that the headman had been consistently helpful. It was he who had started them on a profitable enterprise, loaned them the bricks and also helped them in several other ways. They could not easily forget what he had done for them.

Kempu also praised the support given him by Lakshmana. Lakshmana accompanied Kempu everywhere and talked to officials and ministers on his behalf. He had really shown Kempu the ropes and the latter was grateful. Even Swamy showed appreciation of what Lakshmana had done for them.

During the summer of 1952, I had a few talks with Karagayya, and in one of them he was able to take a more detached view of the entire mill episode. He felt that left to themselves Nadu Gowda and Swamy would not have started another mill. It was Kempu who converted his father and elder brother to his view which resulted in Nadu Gowda's going back on his word. I do not think he mentioned the person who had offered moral and other support to Kempu.

Nadu Gowda did lose some ground among his lineage-mates and in the village as a whole between my first and second field visits (1948 and the summer of 1952). This occurred principally over the Reed Tank which was about a mile or so from the Big tank, and at a lower level. It received water from feeder canals above it, and in turn its waters were used by those who had land at lower levels. It was not a pucca tank like the Big Tank with a high embankment. It was a depression where the overflow waters from above collected, and the reeds choked its shores. But it was a useful tank, and many members of the God's House lineage owned land around it.

Several months after I left Rampura in 1948, a very influential official applied to the government for permission to bring the tank-bed under cultivation. He claimed that the land was a marshy waste, and that he could drain the marsh, though it was a costly operation, and grow food crops on the reclaimed land. (At that time there was a 'grow more food' programme in the State and people were encouraged to bring waste and barren land under cultivation.)

Such an application (*darkasth*) was usually referred in the first instance to the headman to find out if the village had any objections to such allotment of land. I was told that the headman had stated that there was no objection. What was equally surprising, Nadu Gowda had not intervened to protect the interests of his lineage-mates. To cut a long story short, the tank was eventually allotted to the official, who spent a large sum of money draining the tank and then he had trenches dug to bring down the moisture. I was told in the summer of 1952 that he was going to plant banana suckers in the nine acres of what the villagers regarded as top quality land. Sugarcane and, later, rice could also be grown there.

There was a feeling among many villagers that many small land-owners had lost an important source of water for their lands. Further, an outsider had been able to acquire the valuable land and not a local man. They blamed both the headman and Nadu Gowda for the loss, and they felt that at least Nadu Gowda ought to have protected the interests of his lineage-mates. It was significant that no one criticized Millayya for his silence. Perhaps it was due to Nadu Gowda's being regarded universally as the leader of his lineage and because of his great friendship for, and influence with, the headman.

In short, the God's House lineage was much less unified than in 1948. The split between Nadu Gowda and Millayya had become deep, and in the process each had moved closer to the headman.

Japi's two elder brothers, M. Mari and M. Kempayya, both had a reputation for being a law unto themselves. This was the view not only of the village establishment, but of the younger members of the God's House lineage, who considered themselves anti-establishment. During the summer of 1948 a huge straw rick of M. Mari was set fire to, and it was widely believed that it was the work of Muga, a servant whom he had dismissed. I came to learn of this only a few months after the event, and the speakers, members of the God's House lineage, thought that Mari's unreasonableness had invited the arson.

M. Kempayya was notorious for his usurious activities. He lent money to the very poor for short periods and charged them cent per cent interest. He was a strong man and a bully, and he beat up people who refused to pay on time.

When I visited the village in summer of 1954 I found that Mari and Kempayya had filed a criminal suit against the village panchayat for a breach in the embankment of the Big Tank which had affected their valuable banana crop. They argued that it was also a threat to their property itself. (I do not know how they blamed the breach on the panchayat as the maintenance of the embankment was not its responsibility. Perhaps a clever lawyer had found a means of involving the panchayat.)

The case was being heard in Mysore and this meant that one or the other member of the panchayat had to journey to Mysore to be present at each hearing. The brothers probably derived some satisfaction from the harassment they were causing the panchayat, especially its chairman, the headman.

I met the brothers on the Mysore–Hogur road near Shukoor's shop and they requested me to photograph something for them. They needed it urgently. I went along with them not knowing the trap I was about to fall into. They showed the breach to me and asked me to photograph it. I took a few photographs and I agreed to send the prints to them from Mysore. I walked back with them to the village and then went up to the headman's house to say goodbye to him before catching my bus. The headman pointedly asked me what I had been doing and I told him. He ticked me off for associating myself with such characters as Mari and Kempayya. I ought to have known better. I assured the headman that I would not have taken the photographs if I had known the facts of the case. Feeling miserable at the mess I had got into even during a fleeting visit, I caught my bus back home.

The point that I wish to make is that the pattern of factionalism had changed from 1947 to 1952. The process of the break-up of the unity of the God's House lineage had progressed steadily soon after the first election to the chairmanship of the village panchayat. Nadu Gowda proved to be consistently loyal to his old friend the headman. He stood by him during the election even though it meant he incurred the wrath of the young dissidents, and perhaps also of several other members of his lineage. The marriage between the headman's grand-daughter and Nadu Gowda's third son strengthened the friendship and further weakened the unity of the God's House lineage. The headman also won over Millayya, the second biggest leader of the God's House lineage, by helping him to instal a rice mill.

Kempu's success in persuading his father and elder brother to instal their own mill and the events leading to it, produced a deep cleavage between Nadu Gowda's and Millayya's households. Interestingly enough, each household drew closer to the headman in the process of installing its mill.

The brothers M. Mari and M. Kempayya were members of the God's House lineage but their dispute with the panchayat did not involve their lineage in any way. They were both unpopular even among their lineage-mates.

CHAPTER VIII

The Changing Village

1 Technological Change

LOOKING back, I find that I was lucky to have lived in Rampura at a crucial period in its history. In 1948, it still retained enough continuity with the past while the potential was building up for radical change. The biggest landowners, who had acquired considerable sums of money during the war years, were looking out for new opportunities for investment in the 1950s. Unlike their fathers and grandfathers they did not want to buy up more and more land.

When I revisited the village in the summer of 1952 it had already taken a few steps in the new direction and there was promise of further change. There were two rice mills, two buses and a 'complete' middle school. (It was an 'incomplete' middle school in 1948 and village children who wanted to take the Lower Secondary examination had to go to another village, or get private tuition.) A school building was being built and plans were ready for constructing a hospital. The number of buses on the Mysore–Hogur road had increased and many village youths were studying in Mysore in high schools or colleges. The richer men in Rampura were finding it necessary to visit Mysore frequently. It looked as though the day was not far off when Rampura would be a dormitory of Mysore.

In 1948, I had occasionally come across a housewife carrying, on a flat piece of cowdung cake, a few live embers which she had obtained from a neighbour's house. It was usual for neighbours to take live embers from each other. Starting a fire from scratch was a slow business especially as kerosene was scarce and expensive. Taking embers from another also had a symbolic significance: it meant that both the giver and taker were in relationship with each other and with others. When a man was guilty of a serious offence against local morals and customs he was ostracized by the village leaders who proclaimed by beat of drum that no one was to have a relationship with him. He was denied the privilege of taking live embers (*benki* = fire) and hot water (*bisiniru*) from the others. Taking live embers from neighbours had become much less frequent in 1952.

I have stated earlier that the preparation of food, of which cooking was a part, meant much drudgery for the housewife: with the staple grain, *ragi* for instance, it had to be ground into flour for cooking and this was monotonous and time-consuming with the stone quern then in use. Rice, which was next only in importance to *ragi* as a staple, was not an easy grain either. It had to be dehusked and this was done with a primitive pestle and mortar. A hole of suitable size scooped out of a block of granite served for mortar and this was imbedded in the floor while a four-foot-long stout wooden pole with an ironband at either end, served for pestle. Two women worked the pestle, each alternating with the other in perfect coordination, while a third minded the mortar. Scattered grain had to be pushed back, husked grain taken out, and new grain fed in. All the three did their jobs while singing a traditional 'pounding song'.

There was also the more complicated *kotna* combining a mixture of the principles of the pestle and mortar and see-saw. The *kotna* was accommodated in a long verandah or hall, and it was worked entirely by women. A pestle was fixed to one end of a ten-foot beam which formed an angle of about 15° with the floor. Below the pestle was the usual stone mortar imbedded in the floor. The beam was balanced on a two-foot-high post fixed to the ground. The free end of the beam was treaded alternately by two women, which caused the pestle to go up and then come down with force to hit the grain in the mortar. The women, who were treading the *kotna*, hung on to ropes suspended from beams supporting the roof. Another woman minded the mortar.

Only small quantities of paddy could be dehusked by the *kotna*. It was painfully slow, and the proportion of broken grain (*nuchchu*) was greater than in a huller let alone a proper mill. Only those who wanted small quantities of paddy to be dehusked used the *kotna*. During the War years, landowners who had small quantities of paddy for milling or who for various reasons did not want to go to a mill, took their paddy to the *kotna*. In 1948 Rampura had only two or three *kotnas*.

It was usual for landowners in Rampura to have their paddy milled in Hogur, which, as I have stated earlier, was the capital of the *hobli*, and both Hogur and Rampura lay in T Narasipur *taluk*. Landowners avoided the mills in Kere, even though it was as near as Hogur, for Kere lay across the district boundary. It was difficult enough to have one's rice milled in the same *taluk*. It did not even occur to the villagers to think of crossing the district to get anything official done except when they had to go to the Secretariat in Bangalore.

Japi, one of the young men of God's House lineage, was responsible for putting the quern and *kotna* out of commission. Towards the end of April, he bought a second-hand huller and flour-mill and had them installed in a walled-off portion of his living room. His decision to invest his resources in a huller and flour-mill called for daring as well as foresight, especially in view of the many confident forecasts of failure from several villagers. He was only a middle-range landowner and he did not have much cash to invest. But he did not subscribe to the local belief that village women would rather grind their *ragi* at home than take it to the flour mill, and that landowners would not, under any circumstances, take their paddy to a huller. Village women seemed to welcome the opportunity to escape the drudgery of spending long hours rotating the stone quern, and also, those who wanted their paddy milled urgently took it to the huller instead of *kotna*. Besides, no government permit was needed for hulling paddy. This was a loophole in the regulations governing the milling of rice, helpful both to those with small quantities of paddy and to black-marketeers. The prices obtaining in the black market were so high that landowners did not mind the relative inefficiency and slowness of the huller.

Japi took me home a day or two before the formal inauguration of his enterprise; he had walled off a section of his long living-room to house the machines, and he gave me an account of the trouble he had in getting them to Rampura and having them installed. He put on the switch and after a few preliminary and uncertain noises, the huller thudded into activity, and I felt as though the floor and the walls were shaking in sympathy. A few neighbours came in to see what was happening, and their faces broke into broad grins at the machine's coming to life. I was glad that I was not one of Japi's neighbours: the noise and the shaking would have been too much. But to the villagers the machine was a novelty and a very useful one at that. Japi had changed the lives of village women by removing a perennial source of drudgery. He was also responsible for the disappearance from the village of *ragi*-grinding folksongs, and of songs sung while women dehusked paddy over the indigenous husker (*kotna*). Japi was also cautious and knew when to pull out. In 1952, some time after Millayya's mill had come into existence and before Nadu Gowda had started his own, he sold his machines to an entrepreneur in another village. 'And for a profit', he grinned.

Before World War I, the principal means of transport was the ubiquitous bullock-cart. Grain, goods and human beings were usually transported in open carts drawn by pairs of bullocks. It was a slow mode of travel—the bullocks travelled at three or four miles an hour while the occupants sat hunched up inside enduring acute discomfort. The discomfort became torture when the journey was long and the roads were uneven, rutted and embedded with stones. Sometimes the men got out of the cart and walked to stretch their legs for a while.

In 1948, inter-village roads were in a wretched state. Even bullock carts could only use them with difficulty, and frequently even that only in the dry season. But in spite of the difficulties, bullock cart travel was popular during the dry months following the rice harvest. As I have said earlier, this was the season for weddings, festivals of village deities, pilgrimages, journeys to cattle fairs, etc. The journeys were welcome breaks from the dull and back-breaking routine, and took the villagers into the world outside. It was still a world dominated by rural concerns but urban forces were penetrating them increasingly.

The first buses began plying in the Rampura region in the 1920s. Not every entrepreneur who invested in buses prospered and this was particularly true of the pioneers. But bus travel became increasingly popular during World War II. Higher prices for agricultural produce put money into the villagers' pockets, and the villagers' contacts with urban areas increased significantly. The wartime buses were invariably crowded. Since petrol was scarce, charcoal gas was used as fuel, and breakdowns were common. Wartime transport conditions continued to prevail till 1950 or so.

But the situation changed rapidly between my first and second field-trips. When I returned to the village in 1952, I saw gleaming new buses, bigger than the ones they had replaced, plying the same routes. Several big landowners in the area had become owners of the new buses and lorries, and in a few villages, several men had come together to start 'cooperative bus services'. These activities were evidence of the villagers' ability to take risks, especially when it is remembered that the declared policy of the government then was to 'nationalize' road transport. Important and remunerative routes had already been nationalized, and the routes allotted to the 'private sector' were new, unproven and circuitous, and the roads, horrible. The government knew that it could not afford to antagonize totally the rural landowners on whom it depended heavily for votes, and allowing them to ply along some routes, and granting them licences for rice mills and other small industries, were the repayment.

The new enterprises not only taught new skills and changed the pattern of life of those involved in them but also their outlook in significant ways. They learnt the art of cultivating politicians and officials, and became familiar with governmental procedures. Running buses called for new organizational skills and accounting procedures, and dealing with lower officials whose palms needed greasing regularly. The richer village youth did not want to look after ancestral farms but enter the new and challenging world of trade, commerce and industry. The more educated youths dreamed of becoming members of the State legislature, and even ministers in the cabinet. In short, they had come a long way from the world of their fathers and grandfathers. The entrepreneurs gave jobs to their kinsfolk, castefolk and fellow-villagers, and this had the effect of drawing more people to them.

As I said earlier, the first man to own a cycle in Rampura was my friend Kulle Gowda. That was in the early thirties, and in 1948, there were three or four cycles, in varying stages of decay. This situation had changed in 1952 when Yantra, the mechanic who operated Millayya's mill, kept a shop where several new cycles were available for hiring by the hour. Several years later, the richest villagers were buying cars and motor cycles. One of them wrote to me in Delhi to help him buy a motor-cycle at the capital as the products of the factory in Mysore had been booked for a few years. Another village youth once saw me walking on a road in Mysore city and insisted on driving me home in his car.

In 1948, there were five sewing machines in the village, and they were owned by two traders, and one Fisherman, one Toddyman and one Muslim. Tailoring as an occupation did not involve loss of status presumably because it meant working with a machine and required new skills. (In neighbouring Kere, a Brahmin chaplain derived the bulk of his income from tailoring.) Another interesting feature of tailoring was that men tailors did not regard it as beneath their status to make blouses for women. In other words, tailoring cut across differentiation based on caste and sex, and in addition, it made manual labour, when accompanied by new skills and machines, respectable. It brought the men tailors into new relationships with women who were not their kin or caste. The chaplain-tailor of Kere, for instance, ran a 'chit-fund' in which most of the participants were his customers. His scheme prospered greatly for a while but only to collapse later, robbing many women of their hard-earned savings. The entrepreneur had to flee the village and settle in another.

Among the several changes which had occurred between 1948 and 1952 was the availability of electric power. It not only powered the two mills in the village but provided lighting to several homes. The latter had also radios. I saw transistors only in the sixties with college-going youths who had returned home for the holidays.

I have referred to the villagers' request to the visiting minister to make available to them, on a hire system, a tractor and bulldozer, owned by the government. Four years after the request was made a government-owned bulldozer was levelling six acres of land on the headman's farm. This piece was too high to be reached by the feeder canals but the bulldozer was able to remove enough soil to make it irrigable. The bulldozer stayed on the headman's farm for a few weeks as it needed frequent repair, and it made an impact on the villagers in the same way as Japi's huller. To see the monster machine pull down huge trees and cut through blocks of earth was an experience which they would not easily forget. Modern technology did indeed perform miracles and human labour appeared pitiful in contrast.

There was also progress in public health. Rampura had been included in the Hogur health unit, and one of the consequences of the inclusion was the periodical spraying of street gutters and walls with D.D.T. Plans were also afoot for the construction of a hospital.

2   Economic Change

There were two sources of irrigation before the extension of the C.D.S. Canal in the 1860s, one being the Big Tank, and the other being the Ramaswamy Canal, which hugged the river Kaveri. Both the sources irrigated only a little more than 200 acres of low-lying land while the considerable quantity of land irrigated by the C.D.S. (as it was referred to by the younger villagers) lay at higher levels. Again, though it was only an administrative matter, the land irrigated by the Ramaswamy Canal lay within the jurisdiction of Hogur and not Rampura.

Naturally, a greater quantity of land was under the dry crops in the pre-C.D.S. days. The crops grown were millets such as *jowar* and *ragi*, the various pulses, and oilseeds such as sesame and castor. Dry crops were totally dependent upon the monsoon rains, which were notorious for their unpredictability, and people in dry villages were both poverty-stricken and backward. This was a well-known.

The extension of the Canal, and the consequent shift to the cultivation of rice resulted in a severe epidemic of malaria.[1] The original village of Rampura was located to the south of the Big Tank, in the bottom of a trough as it were, while the extension of the C.D.S. Canal looped around the top of the rise in the land, irrigating all the land below it. Only the present village site of Rampura and the land around it did not come under any canal.

The decision to move the village to its present site was taken in the wake of the epidemic, the actual shift taking place in 1874. The Deputy Commissioner of Mysore District was an Englishman, and he located the village site on the top of the rise, to the west of the canal as it skirted the village before turning sharply east and making a beeline for Gudda. The villagers took all their belongings including their deities (excepting Basava) to the new site. The deities Rama, Sita, Lakshmana and Hanuman were accommodated in a small house till they were moved into the present beautiful temple.

Any attempt to explain the failure to move the Basava temple on the ground that it was too solid a construction, does not carry much weight, as the Rama temple, also of stone, was moved. Indeed, the dressed granite slabs were first dismantled to be used in the construction of the new temple.

In 1948, several villagers contrasted their present prosperity with the poverty of the inter-war years, 1918–1939. As described earlier, rice merchants from Mysore visited the village at every harvest and took away nearly half the produce to be adjusted towards the interest due to them. This was true of everyone including the biggest landowners. This state of affairs forced the leaders to introduce certain

[1] Malaria in epidemic form similarly affected Mandya district in the 1930s when it came under the Visweswariah canal system. The water stagnating in the fields, canals and feeders was a potent source of the disease, and only the antimalarial drugs of the forties, and D.D.T., helped to wipe out it. The economic prosperity and political importance of Mandya dates from the forties.

reforms such as cutting down by one the number of feasts to be given when village girls got married and the banning of gambling. In an effort to promote harmony and economy in one village they permitted the dropping of the complex ritual of the distribution of the 'big betel' (*dodda vilya*) at weddings on the bride's father agreeing to pay Rs 8.25 to the *panchayat*. The ritual invariably gave rise to bitter disputes: a guest's right to represent his village did not go unchallenged while to have it rejected amounted to loss of face before equals and betters. Tempers got frayed, each tried to outshout the other, and walking out of the assembly was not unknown. Matters of protocol were not taken lightly in the village. The prudent welcomed paying Rs 8.25 to escape an explosive and expensive ritual.

One of the important results of World War II was to bring about a greater integration of village economy and life with the national. A poignant instance of this was the sudden loss suffered by the sugarcane growers as the result of a steep fall in jaggery price.

Further, the surplus paddy of the villagers was taken away by the government at rates determined by it, and growers could only have the paddy remaining with them milled against permits. They had to buy the *ragi* they ate from local shops against ration cards. And so on.

Before World War II, villagers in Mysore generally preferred handling coins to paper money. In fact, ordinary villagers were not willing to accept high denomination notes. Even coins were examined carefully before being accepted. A proferred rupee coin, for instance, was first flipped into the air, and only when the recipient was satisfied with the music of the silver hitting the ground, did he accept it. Frequently the older and better-off villagers stashed away hoards of silver rupees, and those who could, converted their cash into gold.

But these habits began changing during the war years. Villagers had to accept paper money as there was an acute shortage of metal. The silver content of the rupee decreased fast and flipping rupee-coins disappeared as a habit. Villagers sneered at the government's parlous financial position saying, 'They have no silver or gold but only paper.'

The Kannada term for coin is *nanya* but the villagers used it on occasion as a synonym for culture or refinement (*najooku*). They were convinced that refinement had come to them with the irrigation canals. In contrast, people in 'dry' villages were still without *najooku* and *nanya*. Their style of life and speech were crude.

3 Political Change

I have referred earlier to the increasing penetration of rural areas by officials since the beginning of this century. This occurred side by side with the development of communications. The government was becoming more pervasive and also assumed new duties and responsibilities for the well-being of the people.

Independence, and the subsequent introduction of adult franchise, marked a radical change in the villagers' attitude towards officials. The previous obsequiousness and fear which characterized earlier behaviour was replaced by a sense of self-confidence if not power. This was especially true of the richer, more urbanized and younger villagers. The lower officials in particular felt the impact of new attitudes.

Independence and popular rule increased the power of politicians who tried to influence the decisions of administrators to promote their interests.[1] For instance, honest officials who failed to oblige them were attempted to be transferred while those who obliged them were given benefits in turn. They wanted contracts, licences and permits to be given to their relatives, clients, friends and caste-fellows. During the fifties Kannada journals and newspapers were full of references to the activities of 'Congress *pudharis*'. A *pudhari* was a broker or middleman in politics, a man who had cultivated the men in power and interceded on behalf of those in whom he was interested. He obliged both those whose cause he sponsored and the politicians whose aid he sought. And like all brokers he expected to benefit from his intercessions. And he did. The term *pudhari* was pejorative and people, especially villagers, complained about the activities of *pudharis*. They donned the uniform of white homespun dhoti, *jubba* and Nehru waistcoat and wandered from village to government offices and ministers' and legislators' homes, taking with them their *protégés*.

The visit of the State's finance minister to Rampura in 1948 was a landmark, literally speaking, in that it was the first time that so high a dignitary had walked its streets. According to the older villagers, the highest official previously to visit the village was the deputy

---

[1] Writing in the popular Kannada newspaper *Prajavani* in the fifties, N. Rama Rao summarized the changes which had taken place in the position of the *amildar* (official in charge of a *taluk*), saying, 'Then the lord (*dhani*) of the *taluk*, now, recipient of favours (*runi*) from low political touts'.

commissioner, the official head of a district. The minister's visit meant much work for the villagers. It was preceded by the visits of lower officials who demanded that village streets be cleared of logs, carts, stores of fuel, bricks, etc. They also wanted the street gutters to be cleaned, and the insides of houses to appear neat and tidy. (There was the possibility that a 'popular' minister might take it into his head to visit a village house: the ministers had a keen nose for publicity.) The officials wanted the streets to be sprinkled with water a few hours before the dignitary's arrival so that the convoy would not be choked with village dust. (They ignored the fact that the rest of his journey was going to be dusty in any case.) They saw to it that two welcome arches were erected on the Mysore–Hogur road, one by the Harijans and the other by everybody else. (It was customary for Harijans to erect a welcome arch and the officials encouraged them to put up one on this occasion too. But it later turned out that the minister expressed his anger at the 'separatist' tendencies displayed by Rampura Harijans, and the Muslims who wanted additional facilities for the Urdu school.)

During the first few years of Independence villagers became so used to visits by ministers that they affected indifference. Being hard-headed men they asked the question, 'What good have these visits done to us?' They contrasted the old days when the deputy-commissioner, the 'lord' (*dhani*) of the district, had the power to help them with the contemporary situation when ministers kept coming but nothing happened. A minister's visit threw the village off its usual routine and meant some expense and ceremony in addition. It also gave a chance to local malcontents to have access to high officials and even the minister. While the elite liked to hobnob with the high and the mighty, they wanted the privilege to be denied to the poor, and to their opponents.

During the summer of 1952 I remember having a brief discussion with Tammu, the smart young man who was helping Millayya run his mill. The papers had reported that Mr Hamumanthaiya, then Chief Minister, as saying that ability and qualifications had to be the sole grounds for recruitment to jobs in the government, and not the caste from which the applicants came. I thought that Mr Hanumanthaiya had made a wise and courageous statement but Tammu pointed out that the voters who had elected him wanted applicants to be recruited from the backward sections of the society. Mr Hanumanthaiya's desire to appoint men on 'British principles' would not succeed. Tammu's comment perhaps revealed a keener sense of grassroots political realities than mine, and Tammu was typical of the politicized village youth. The latter had grasped the fact that the voters' interests had to be respected by their elected representatives. They were also aware that they could influence their representatives to bring pressure on officials to give favourable decisions. They had a sense of power which they liked to display. The villager was no longer scared of officials but was learning to flex his political muscles. The time-honoured rules of the political game were beginning to change.

Independence and adult franchise also brought new ideas and aspirations to the villagers. I shall illustrate my statement by referring to certain changes which occurred in Lakshmana's style of life, and to one of my brief encounters in Kere.

I have already commented upon Lakshmana's shrewdness and political ambitions. He once expressed to me his deep regret at his lack of education: if only he had been a graduate he could have done so much. He was sharply critical of his younger brother Bharata, who, after getting a B.A., had settled down to a quiet, low-level job in the government. Lakshmana felt that Bharata should have gone into politics. (There was an unstated assumption among the politicized village youth that a B.A. was indispensable for a ministership. I remember a bus journey in the summer of 1952 when a Kere man was reading out from a newspaper the list of newly-appointed ministers in Mr Hanumanthaiya's cabinet, and as he read, he graded them on the basis of their being graduates or 'double graduates', the latter being those who had secured a law degree after their B.A. or B.Sc. Small town legal practice gave ample leisure for political activity.)

Certain changes occurred gradually, almost insensibly, in Lakshmana's clothes and hair style. That symbol of Sanskritic orthodoxy, the tuft at the crown of the head, was the first to be sacrificed on the altar of politics, and Lakshmana grew a crop. (I do not know what his father and grandmother had to say to this.) He bought a green Nehru jacket flecked with white, and wore it above his shirt when he was visiting Mysore or some other town to meet officials, politicians and others. He wrote a few letters to the Kannada papers in which he called himself vice-president of the *taluk*'s ryots' (cultivators') association. (I had not heard of his election or nomination to that august office.) He held a meeting of the ryots of the *taluk* and he invited a budding and well-connected lawyer-politician from Mysore to take the chair. Lakshmana took great pains to have an elaborate lunch cooked for the influential guest and other invitees. (There was a fish course, from fish caught in the rice-fields on the previous day, and chicken curry, besides, of course, rice and vegetables.) But the meeting did not go as he had wanted it to. At an early stage in the proceedings two members of the audience from different villages got into a heated argument which threatened to explode into a fight. The energies of the organizers had to be diverted to bringing about peace between the angry debaters. This incident perhaps taught Lakshmana that the path to power was not roses all the way. He did not give up trying to win influential friends but he conducted his activities in a lower key.

During the latter half of 1948 Lakshmana began to be increasingly absent from the village. He was either seen getting on or off a bus, and the villagers did not fail to notice it. Previous to his developing political interests he had told me, and perhaps one or two others, that he wanted to live in the farm house quietly, away from the noise and dust of the village, and close to the river Kaveri. Lakshmana was a good supervisor and he may have genuinely wanted to stay in the farm house but at that time there were rumours that he had differences with the other members of his joint family. There may have been opposition to his shifting to the farm house from others in the household, including his wife. It was at this juncture that he became deeply interested in politics.

When I returned to Rampura in 1952 I found that the new activities of his household gave Lakshmana ample opportunities to travel. Running bus lines was no easy matter and needed unremitting attention on several fronts: the taxes and cesses to be paid, inspections by brake inspectors and other officials, dealing with policemen and law courts, getting spare parts, supervising the activities of bus drivers and conductors, maintaining accounts and so on. There were also houses in Mandya from which rent had to be collected, and finally, there was the cinema theatre in Mysore which the family had bought. In addition, Lakshmana retained some contact with the Ryots' Association.

I knew a village leader in Kere who had studied up to the S.S.L.C. and developed political ambitions. He was a man of violent antagonisms, and headed a faction. He wanted to become a legislator and tried to secure a Congress ticket in 1952. But Kere had several graduates who had been in the freedom struggle and one of them was given the ticket. My friend contested as an independent and lost to the Congressman. But he refused to be discouraged—he was tough and persevering. He owned a rice mill and was wealthy and had some local influence. One blistering afternoon I walked from Rampura to his mill in Kere and asked him if he could kindly let me borrow some documents which I wanted. He was then attired in freshly-laundered *khadi*, and his white Gandhi cap was placed at a jaunty angle. He was about to get into his new, gleaming Ambassador car to go to Bangalore. Mr Hanumanthaiya, the Chief Minister, was celebrating Sathyanarayana Puja and my friend had been invited. I could not help thinking then of Max Weber who had stressed the otherworldly, 'soteriological' character of Hinduism!

On another afternoon, I met a few boys in my friend's large household and I asked one of them what he wanted to be when he grew up. One of the boys was slow to open up but I persisted. He gave way finally: 'I want to become a minister.' As soon as he had uttered these words, my host rushed to him and pinched him on both the cheeks in delight. It was only then that I discovered that the boy was my host's only son while the other boys were his brother's. The son was going to fulfil the father's ambitions.

In Rampura in 1948, inter-caste relations were on the whole co-operative if not friendly. This was facilitated by the fact that Peasants greatly outnumbered all the other castes, and also owned the bulk of the arable land. And the headman and Nadu Gowda working in close cooperation provided unified leadership. The non-Peasants, including the Muslims, depended upon the leaders to give them a fair deal.

But with the introduction of adult franchise and of the electoral principle into panchayats and other local self-governing institutions, tensions between the castes increased sharply. I have already mentioned how in the summer of 1952 the headman was angry with the Harijans for not voting for the candidate whom he wanted elected. And in Kere, my friend, the Peasant leader, was defeated at the election to the State legislature, and he asked the members of a Brahmin household to quit the village on their own or face the prospect of being driven out. The members of this household, shrewd and extremely resourceful, had worked actively for the rival candidate who was a local Peasant as also the candidate selected by the Congress Party. But he was living at that time in Bangalore and could not offer protection in day-to-day situations to his supporters.

I have narrated earlier the visit in the summer of 1948 by a Shepherd who had settled down as a landowner in Kuderu near Chamarajanagar, after retiring from his career as an actor in a well-known dramatic company in Mysore. The Shepherd was a large and amiable man, and after his arrival, he talked to the headman and a few others on a variety of matters. Everyone listened to him attentively, as he was talking to them about happenings in the world outside. After reminiscing briefly about his acting days and his present preoccupations, he commented on the way in which Lingayats in his area— Kuderu was a Lingayat-dominated area—oppressed the others. He added that Brahmins had many faults and had done several unjust things when they were in power but they had certain inhibitions stemming from their respect for *dharma*. But unfortunately the Lingayats in his region were free from these inhibitions. I waited for someone to contradict the visitor but no one did. I wondered whether my presence came in the way of the group expressing its opinions about the way Brahmins used to treat the others. It was not unlikely that the visitor's day-to-day experiences in a village where Lingayat landowners exploited the others made him take a friendly view of the distant Brahmins. (His experience would probably have been different had he lived in a Brahmin-dominated area.)

It is only fair to add here that Lingayats felt oppressed in places and areas where they were in a minority. A Lingayat principal of a college who hailed from Mysore district once told me that his was the only Lingayat village in a region dominated by Peasants. And he added jocularly, 'We are in Pakistan'. Castes which were numerically very small experienced a sense of insecurity especially in villages where the leaders lacked a sense of fairness. A member of a minority caste invariably referred with pride to a village (or small town) where his caste was represented in strength. In such a place, a few of the caste-fellows there were well off and influential. An important temple was frequently located there and attracted pilgrims. The periodical festivals in the temple provided occasions for caste leaders to gather and discuss matters of common interest. In the case of Harijans, however, their minority status was greatly compounded by untouchability and economic dependence on the dominant castes.

4 Cultural Change

When I was doing fieldwork, I concentrated my attention on recon-
structing the traditional social structure which made me less sensitive
to the factors making for change. This explains, at least partly, my
failure to realize that the attitudes of the villagers with regard to
disease, health and life-expectancy had changed because of the sharp
decrease in mortality from the major epidemics of plague, smallpox
and cholera. Plague and smallpox had almost completely disappeared
while cholera was both much less frequent and destructive. The last
occasion when cholera visited the village in epidemic form was in
1949. Prior to the World War II years, villages were visited by one
or the other of these epidemics every few years. Preventive measures
took time to reach the afflicted villages, and even when they were
available, backwardness and superstition came in the way of their
acceptance. The *amildar* was generally in charge of organizing the
medical and relief measures. When an epidemic struck a group of
villages in a severe form, he had to evacuate the inhabitants from
their homes and settle them in temporary huts erected at some distance away. They were allowed to move back only after the epidemic
had died out.[1]

Traditionally, a person suffering from one of the epidemics refused
to take modern medicine as it was thought to annoy Mari (called by
many names). As could be expected of a deity who presided over
these death-dealing diseases, she was quick to take offence, and a
patient's only hope of recovery, slender though it was, was to throw
himself entirely at her mercy. The twigs and leaves of the margosa
(*Melia azadirachta*) were good for a person suffering from any of
these epidemics, especially smallpox. Twigs were kept near his head,
he was fanned with the leaves, and they were put into his bath-water
when he had recovered from the disease. Only after a cleansing bath
could he visit the shrine of the deity. Offerings of rice flour mixed
with jaggery (*tambittu*), tender coconuts and betel leaves and nuts
were carried on a tray to her. The *tambittu* was shaped like a pyramid
with a flattened top, and sometimes, a depression was made in the
flattened top to make possible its use as a lamp: the depression was
filled with *ghi* and it provided fuel to burn a cotton wick light. The

[1] There is a graphic account of the *amildar's* using the shaman of a village
goddess in order to persuade villagers struck by cholera to move into a temporary camp in *Kelavu Nenapugalu*, pp. 354–8.

wick was allowed to burn itself out after which the pyramid was broken up and distributed as *prasada*.

Summer was the season for the epidemics and they invariably disappeared after the monsoon rains. The propitiation of the goddesses presiding over the epidemics was referred to as 'cooling' them (*tampu eriyuvudu*). The margosa was one of the trees which provided cool shade in summer and its leaves, twigs and oil were all believed to have medicinal properties. Margosa trees were frequently planted close to the temple of the village goddess, and the association between the goddess, tree and epidemics were close in the minds of people.

In 1948, the conquest of the killer epidemics, and of endemic malaria contrasted sharply with the failure to make maternity safer or less traumatic. No village woman went to a maternity hospital to have her baby delivered. A few rich villagers were able to secure the services of a midwife from either Kere or Hogur but most village women turned to their older relatives and friends for help during delivery. A woman felt most secure with her mother and this was why the first few confinements occurred invariably in her mother's house.

The headman's wife died during childbirth a few months before my return to Rampura in 1952 and the headman was naturally deeply affected by the event. She was his second wife and younger by several years, and the fact that her death was due to the midwife's incompetence made it all the more poignant.

One of my sad experiences in Rampura related to the death of an infant a few weeks after I had moved into the village. One day, all of a sudden, I heard a woman moaning continuously from the other side of the wall of my bedroom. Sometimes the moans were long and loud while at other times they were short and faint. There were even brief intervals when they were totally absent. This went on for two or three days. It slowly dawned on me that Mrs Karim, my neighbour, was having labour pains, and her relatives and neighbours were busy visiting her. One night in particular, the moans were more or less continuous and were marked by frequent screams. I was unable to sleep a wink. I could not do any work the following day and I remember thinking unkind thoughts about Mrs Karim. Why couldn't women deliver babies with less fuss and noise? Why couldn't they be more reasonable? My work had made me thoroughly self-centred but even I noticed that I was the only one who was so surly and ill-tempered about having his sleep disturbed by Mrs Karim's pains and screams. Either the others slept much better than I did, or did not consider the matter suitable for comment. In any case, I am fairly certain that they would have thought it only natural for a woman to moan and scream during delivery. They would also have been more considerate to a mother having labour pains.

The baby came at last and a day or two after its birth, I found a distracted Karim wandering around with the half-shell of a coconut. I asked him what the matter was. He replied that the baby was hungry and that he was trying to get some cow's milk for it. Several hours later I heard Mrs Karim's loud and hysterical wailing. I also heard her friends trying to console her. An occasion such as this cut across the distinction between Hindu and Muslim for a few callers were Hindus. But it was entirely a feminine affair. No man, not even a relation, called on her.

The village doctor was not popular. In fact the complaint was occasionally heard that he only bothered about a few rich people and not about the others. As long as the doctor was assured of the headman's protection, he could ignore the others. He played cards regularly with the headman, Nadu Gowda and Kulle Gowda's father and that made it clear to everyone that he enjoyed the protection of the most influential men. His wife was coaching two boys in the headman's household for the Lower Secondary examination. One afternoon he brought a few hot *chaklis* (fried savouries) for the headman to taste. They were made by his wife, and it appeared that her cooking was even better than her teaching. The doctor practised the time-honoured tradition of propitiating the powerful and oppressing the poor.

One afternoon a man from a neighbouring village arrived in his cart at the headman's house to obtain treatment from the doctor for some illness. The headman gave a glowing certificate to the doctor's skills and then the doctor stipulated that he would agree to treat him only if a certain amount was paid in advance and an equal amount after the cure had been effected. The ingredients of the medicine were costly—he listed a few of the ingredients, and the time it would take to prepare it. A bargain was eventually struck.

The better off villagers went to an ayurvedic doctor in Hogur who had a good reputation, or to allopaths in Mysore. They were all enthusiastic about injections. A typical statement was, 'I went to the doctor in Mysore and he gave me an injection. Even as the fluid went in, I felt its power. An hour later, all my pain had gone.' In other words, the injection worked like magic. Urban doctors knew this weakness of villagers for injections and gave their patients what they asked for.

In 1948, there were two schools, one an 'incomplete' middle school for Kannada-speaking children, and an Urdu school for Muslim children. The former was housed in the official panchayat building while the latter was accommodated in a single-room structure with a thatched roof. The Kannada school was co-educational and attended by students from every group except Muslims. Girls generally attended school till they were eleven or twelve when they were withdrawn and stayed at home till they got married.

There were, however, a few village youths who had been to college who wanted to marry educated girls. But even they did not want girls who were 'too highly educated'. Adult girls who had been to school were suspected of having had affairs, and they were also likely to consider themselves too superior for rural life.

The Urdu school had less than thirty students and only one teacher. The right of Muslims to be taught in Urdu had been recognized in princely Mysore but where this meant founding schools using Urdu exclusively, the resources were too meagre to provide satisfactory teaching. This was particularly true of Urdu schools in villages.

As stated earlier, even in 1948 Rampura had only an 'incomplete' middle school, and local students who wanted to sit for the Lower Secondary examination had either to go to villages which had 'complete' middle schools or to a private tutor in Rampura. However, in 1948, education was becoming popular, and the bigger landowners made it a point to send their sons to high schools in neighbouring towns.

Prior to 1948, Rampura had produced four graduates all of whom lived outside. It was only those who did not have the minimum education required for a government job, who stayed back in the village. These were the young men who were dissatisfied with the existing state of affairs. They were politically alert, and disliked agriculture, indeed, all forms of manual work. They wanted to engage themselves in trade and commerce, and start small industries. They found village life cramping, and hated its petty discriminations and notions of high and low. They wanted change.

I have stated earlier that Nadu Gowda and the headman went to school together—that must have been in the 1890s. In those days the only school in the village was the traditional *kooli matha*. The teacher was an Oshtama,[1] one of whose descendants, a boy of ten or twelve, was living in the village in 1948. All traditional schools were known for their liberal use of the cane, and even more barbarous forms of punishment which were meted out to unruly pupils. The teacher (*upadru*, a corruption of *upadhyayaru*) taught his pupils the three R's, and learning was synonymous with committing things to memory. The complex orthography of Kannada, rules of grammar, numerical tables, meanings of nouns, and poems and hymns, all had to be learnt by rote. Indeed, a good part of the time every day was spent with the teacher saying something and all the students chanting it after him. Advanced students had to learn to read, and understand the epics, and a few other classics.

The 'graduation' of students was marked by ritual. On the ninth day in the bright half of the month of *ashwini* (September–October) the graduating students were dressed in their best and went along the village streets singing and dancing. The songs sung on this occasion were referred to as 'Manoumiya Choupada' ('four-lined poems sung at Mahanavami') and some of them were irreverent if not hostile to the teacher. The man who had wielded the cane so liberally came in for rhymed abuse and scorn on the occasion of their emancipation. The songs and dances were regarded as entertainment and the houses before which the students stopped gave gifts to be handed over to the teachers.

The *upadru* was a poor man and each student had to pay an annual fee in cash and grain besides the customary gifts made on occasions such as initiation into writing. In spite of his poverty, the teacher was a highly respected member of the village community. The fact that he was usually a Brahmin added to the respect he commanded.

The incomplete middle school, like other schools of its kind in the area, celebrated the worship of two Hindu deities, viz. the Ganesha and Saraswati. The propitiation of Ganesha ensured the removal of obstacles in the path of everyone including students, while Saraswati was the goddess of learning. (In homes where the elders entertained educational ambitions for their children they were enjoined to worship Saraswati.) The annual *puja* of these two deities in schools was

---

[1] Oshtamas were also known as Satanis, and men from this caste were employed as priests in temples to Hanuman and Vishnu.

popular with the students partly because of the tasty *prasada* which was distributed among them at the end.

During the Dasara festival in 1948, I was invited by the headmaster of the school to preside over the Saraswati puja. I suspected that my friend Kulle Gowda had persuaded the headmaster to invite me, and I had no choice but to accept it though I had no idea of my duties as 'president'. At some point in the proceedings I was asked to make a speech. I mouthed the usual platitudes about the need to respect elders and teachers, and to regard manual work as respectable if not elevating. I also urged the children to do something for the village when they became responsible citizens. But even as I was saying my piece I felt that I was an impostor who had used the occasion to please the few older men in the audience. Anyway, if my own boyhood provided any clues, the boys were probably impatiently waiting for me to end my speech so that they could share the *prasada*. To bring the events to a conclusion, the headmaster asked the boys to sing the national anthem. I told myself that Independence had indeed made enough of an impact for the headmaster of a remote village school to have trained his pupils to sing it. The boys stood up and sang 'God Save the King' with a strong rural Kannada accent. Either the headmaster wanted me to appreciate his students' mastery of English, or he had not received an order from the Education Department informing him of the changes that had taken place in 1947.

Since the beginning of this century, significant changes had occurred in the villagers' material culture. I shall not, however, make an effort to describe all the changes but shall limit myself to changes in two items both of which concerned the body, and were visible, viz. dress and hair-style.

The traditional dress of the villagers was a white dhoti with a coloured border which was wrapped around the waist like a *lungi* but unlike the latter its two ends were not sewn together. It covered the body from the waist to the shins. It was worn in such a way that the right side came on top of the left unlike in the Tamil country where the left side came on top of the right. An upper cloth of coarse cotton, or a woollen blanket worn round the shoulders, completed the outfit.

In the irrigated villages of southern Mysore, this dress gave place to a uniform of shirt and shorts. It is not known when exactly this dress came into vogue. However, by the 1920s shirt and shorts made from coarse dark grey or blue material had become so popular that it was a symbol of a cultivator. This dress was made by urban tailors, the poorer among whom worked in tiny cloth shops in the side streets. The shirt was collarless and the sleeves did not taper at the wrist or have buttons. The shorts were tapering at the knee-caps or, in a few cases, the shins.

Only the richer and more sophisticated villagers wore collarless shirts with 'proper' sleeves with buttons and button-holes. They were usually made from plain white cloth, or white cloth with coloured stripes, and a *dhoti* worn in the Brahminical style covered the region below the waist.

But the younger and more urbanized villagers had gone back to the *lungi* style but their *lungi* was different from that worn by their grand-parents. It came down to the ankles, and the cloth was fine to the point of being translucent. They also wore long, full-sleeved shirts with butterfly collars. A thin towel was invariably draped over the left shoulder. Most of them also wore thin, factory-made, effeminate sandals unlike their fathers who wore heavy hand-crafted ones made by Harijan leather-workers in Malavalli. Nadu Gowda, for instance, got his sandals made by a particular cobbler in Mala-valli, and he said no pair lasted him longer than six months. He was a huge man and the village roads were not kind on footwear. He was contemptuous of fancy sandals and their owners.

In the fifties, there emerged a small group of village youth all of whom were studying in high schools and colleges in Mysore. They dressed differently from everyone else in the village. They wore bush shirts, narrow trousers and Hawaiian sandals made of foam rubber. They tended to congregate in the house of one or the other of their small group to listen to film music over the radio or transistor. The bulk of the villagers regarded them as a privileged lot, boys who were supported by the hard work of their parents or uncles or older brothers. It was expected that they would have salaried jobs or stay in one of the cities when earning their livelihood.

In comparison with the men's dress, women's dress had under-gone very little change—a phenomenon that was true of India as a whole, at least until 1970. The sari and blouse continued to be the standard dress of village women. But the saris were no longer bought in nearby fairs but in urban shops which displayed a variety of hand-loom and mill saris in different colours and patterns. Sophisticated silk saris from such well-known centres of weaving as Dharmavaram,

Conjeevaram and Arni, and from factories in Bangalore and Mysore were sported by rich village women at weddings and festivals.

Before World War II, a close-necked and full-sleeved blouse from thick, grey cloth was popular with village women, or at least the poorer ones. This gradually gave way to half-sleeved and wide-necked blouses made from attractive, factory-made cotton material, and silks for weddings and festivals.

In 1948, the western-style crop was fast replacing the traditional tuft among the men and only the older and more conservative villagers retained a tuft. The Barber welcomed the crop as it meant less work than shaving the head of a man except for the crown adorned by a tuft. Conservative villagers had their faces shaved only when their heads were also shaved. The separation of the face-shave from tonsure was the result of westernization. Prior to that it was part of the total shave of the head and face, and those who had only their faces shaved were regarded as guilty of breaking pollution rules. However, matters became more simple when the crop became popular: the head was trimmed once in four or six weeks while the face was shaved once a week or fortnight, or before visiting a town. One of the village Barbers opened an urban-style shop on the Mysore–Hogur road where anyone could get his hair cut or shave any time during the day on payment of cash. While the traditional Barber did not perform his duties on inauspicious days the shop Barber ignored the prohibited days and timings. All this signified a weakening of traditional rules but even then very few villagers (perhaps, none excepting Pijja) used safety razors. The better off villagers felt that self-shaving was polluting (or at least their women-folk thought so) and bothersome while the poor ones did not have money enough to invest in the equipment and the frequent change of blades it called for.

5 The State and Change

A long-range view of the changes which had occurred in Rampura revealed the crucial role played by the state. The economic development of the Rampura region was based on the two major irrigation canals, Ramaswamy and C.D.S., which were planned and executed by the Hindu rulers well before the establishment of British rule.[1]

[1] See *Mysore Gazetteer*, edited by C. Hayavadana Rao, Vol. V, Bangalore, 1930, pp. 696–8.

After the defeat of Tippu Sultan at the hands of the British in 1799, and the restoration of the state, although truncated, to the earlier Hindu rajas, the administrative system became modernized slowly. The new administrative system enabled the state to undertake and execute development tasks for which the traditional system was not suited.

But just as it was obvious that on a long-term view the state's efforts at development were successful, a short-range view highlighted only the defects and inadequacies in its efforts. Some at least of the deficiencies seemed integral to any effort at improvement given the highly stratified nature of the society in which the people lived. The richer, influential and better-informed households were the first to take advantage of the new opportunities and their interests frequently clashed with those of the poor. Worse, frequently the enhanced power and resources of the wealthy made possible the more effective exploitation of the poor. The former were quick enough to sense when a new institution or improvement was likely to make the poor less compliant or more demanding, and opposition to such an institution was the result. The government's efforts to help Harijans to have tiled instead of thatched roofs for their huts were foiled by the manner in which the headman dispensed the grants: he doled out tiny sums which the recipients spent on their pressing needs which included, in a few cases, toddy. It was common talk among the high castes that the Harijans had misused the money given to them for improving their huts. What else could one expect? The government's good intentions did not match its wisdom. Can anyone straighten out a dog's tail by tying a length of bamboo to it?

An egregious instance of the conflict between the rich and poor came to my notice in the incident of the transformation of a bull into bullock which I shall summarize here. Jogayya was an agnatic relative and client of the headman. In fact, Jogayya's lineage had a client-like relation to that of the headman's. One brother of Jogayya worked as a *jita* servant of the headman's while another brother's wife had worked for a few years as maid to the headman's mother. The headman was in the habit of asking one or other member of Jogayya's lineage to do a job or run an errand at short notice. The latter could not say 'no'.

Early in 1947 the agriculture department of the Mysore Government embarked on a plan of improving the cattle in the State by giving to selected individuals in different villages quality bull-calves. The donees were required to feed and look after the calves, and after they were old enough, use them for stud purposes for at least five years. The recipient of the bull was again required to charge only one rupee for each service during the five-year period after which the bull became his. At least, that was the government's plan.

As could be expected, the headman was given a fine bull-calf by the officials of the agriculture department. The headman took it and then passed it on to Jogayya, asking him to look after it well. If he did look after it for five years, the headman would see to it that the bull became his (Jogayya's). It was a good calf and would become a valuable bull in course of time.

In 1948, the bull was a fine-looking animal in 'active service'. I looked at the book in which Jogayya had listed the cows it had served. The cows had come from Rampura and several neighbouring villages. It looked as though the government's plan to improve cattle was going to be one of its more successful ones, assuming, of course, that Rampura's experience was typical.

Jogayya was one of those who used to drop in on me frequently and I found him a worried man. He was poor and the bull was expensive to keep. Besides green and dry fodder, the bull had to be given pulses and rice bran (*tavudu*) ground to a paste, and coconut and jaggery. He had looked after it as if it were his child. But he wondered whether it would not be taken away from him one day. There was no document to show that he was the donee and that it was he who was spending money and time in raising it. He had denied himself and his wife and children necessities in order to see that the bull got enough good food. Could I take a photograph of the bull with him and his son? It may come to his aid one day.

I admired the animal and I had long wanted to photograph it. But I had no intention of getting embroiled in a dispute between the headman and his relative. I took a few pictures of the animal with Jogayya and his son, but I do not remember passing on a print to anyone. In any case, no one thought that I was scheming to make trouble for the headman. The animal and its custodians posed before the Bullock House, within fifteen yards of the headman's house. My own guess is that the headman had not contemplated taking back the bull but Jogayya's was a suspicious nature.

When I returned to Rampura in 1952, one of the first questions I asked Jogayya was about the condition of the bull. He seemed awkward and ill at ease and then smiled an embarrassed smile. After a couple of minutes' silence he told me that he had a big bullock and he needed another to make a team (*jodi*). It was not easy to find another which matched. Most reluctantly, he had to have the bull castrated. They now made an excellent pair and would fetch a thousand rupees. Thus ended the government's scheme to improve the quality of cattle, at least as far as the Rampura area was concerned.

Patience of an almost superhuman character, deep cunning and an ability to mask one's real feelings and intentions, were the only weapons which the desperately poor and exploited villagers had in their struggle against oppressors of all kinds, local landowners, tax collectors and invading armies. If they were unenthusiastic about an innovation which urban officials and local or foreign experts had thought up, it was because the latter were insensitive to the full implications of the innovation at the village level. While the ploughman thought of how well the new blade penetrated the soil, the worms underneath may be pardoned for taking a different view.

Another instance of the government's well-intentioned efforts going awry came to my notice in 1948. There was a young official whom I shall call Jangama and it was his job to promote rural welfare. His duties were unspecific and he addressed himself to many matters, in particular, hygiene and sanitation. I met him a few times, and I was at first told that he was an 'enthusiastic' official. It was only later that I understood the implications of this euphemism. He had urged the villagers to remove the unsightly manure heaps along the road and pointed out how they attracted mosquitoes and flies, and polluted the canal waters which were used for drinking. The villagers heard him out but went on as before. It was convenient to have the manure heaps near the owners' houses where they could be protected from thieves. Even more importantly, in the homes of most people it was the duty of the wife or daughter-in-law to carry domestic and cattleshed sweepings to the manure heap, and no woman liked the idea of a long early morning walk with a loaded basket on her head. It was especially difficult during the monsoon when it rained for days on end.

The Deputy Commissioner of Mysore had planned a visit to Rampura, and Jangama came a few days previously to ask the villagers to remove the unsightly manure heaps on the southern side of the Mysore–Hogur road. But the owners of the heaps took no notice.

He became angry, and throwing caution to the winds, applied a lighted matchstick to two or three heaps. They were all dry and caught fire easily and a favourable wind fanned the flames. The villagers had certainly not expected a young official to be stupid and highhanded enough to set fire to their precious manure heaps. Enraged, they went after him to beat him up. Jangama ran into the school house and bolted the door from inside. The villagers dared him to come out. In the meanwhile, word reached the headman about the incident and he hurried to the school and asked the villagers to disperse. He made Jangama come out and then talked to him about the seriousness of what he had done on that day and the risks he had run.

Jangama had failed totally to appreciate the villagers' point of view regarding the manure heaps. He did not understand that a change in the style of life of villagers could only occur after agriculture had brought a measure of prosperity to everyone in the village, and the rules of hygiene and sanitation had become part of the school curriculum. To be fair to Jangama, he was doing only what was expected of him. The failure to appreciate the villagers' point of view stemmed from a much higher level in the government than his. Petty officials cannot be blamed for wrong policies.

CHAPTER IX

The Quality of Social Relations

1 Reciprocity

THE principle of reciprocity was basic to rural social life. I have discussed earlier its expression in agricultural work. *Muyyi* was the term used for exchange of labour, and it was resorted to when the need for agricultural labour was at its peak.

Muyyi had also other meanings. For instance, it referred to the cash contributions made by relatives and friends at a non-Brahmin wedding. At any village wedding, sitting near the bride and groom were two men, one noting down the contributions made to the groom's household, and the other, the bride's. The richer households had these lists faired in big, bound notebooks. Each contribution had to be returned at a wedding in the donor's house. Elderly villagers recalled that in the old days anyone who failed to return the contribution was visited by the donor's debt-collector or *jita* servant. Such a visit meant that the defaulter had tried to get out of a solemn agreement. Since the sum involved was usually small, the defaulter was shamed. Village gossips were certain to pass the information to their relatives and friends.

The obligation to return *muyyi* cast a heavy social burden on the richer households. One or other member of such households had to be always on the move during the wedding season to return paltry contributions. The headman's household were the worst sufferers in this matter. In 1948 and 1952, Lakshmana made frequent trips to villages near and far, after the rice harvest which ushered in the wedding season. Rame Gowda once confided to me that *muyyi* was outdated. His household had 'too many contacts' (*samparka jasti*) and it was not practicable to retain them. Indeed, some of the more educated and westernized individuals among the non-Brahmins made it a point to announce in their wedding invitations that *muyyi* and *tera* (bride-price) payments would not be received. They considered it embarrassing to receive and record the petty sums of cash made as *muyyi*, not to mention the trouble involved in repayment. *Tera* was denounced as the sale of a girl. The more sophisticated guests preferred to make gifts of silver tumblers, saris and dhotis and gadgets instead of cash. This was the general practice among urban Brahmins though close relatives sometimes gave cash. (Payment by cheque was more prestigious than cash.)

The principle of reciprocity also expressed itself in unfriendly contexts. For instance, a man who had received an injury from another felt bound to avenge himself (*muyyige muyyi*). For instance, if A's straw rick was set fire to by B, A thought that he had to set fire to B's straw rick or inflict some other damage on him. Otherwise, his honour, if not manliness, was felt to be at stake.

Reciprocity also guided relations between close friends and relatives but this was obscured by the articulated sentiment that where there was affection there ought to be no calculation of return. In such cases reciprocity lurked underneath, surfacing only in crises.

The idea of reciprocity underlay cross-cousin marriage as also the marriage of a man with his elder sister's daughter. A girl went out of her natal home at marriage to join her husband, and she did not get a share in the ancestral house and land. She only got some jewelry and clothes. However, when her grown sons and daughters married their mother's brother's offspring, some kind of reciprocity occurred.

Underlying the broad idea of reciprocity in marriage was a more specific expression. While anyone in the preferred category of relatives enjoyed an advantage over an outsider, among the relatives themselves a man's father's sister's, or elder sister's, daughter was preferred to his mother's brother's daughter. Such a marriage ensured the 'return' of the daughter of an outgoing female member to her maternal lineage. The loss of membership of her natal family which followed her marriage was compensated when her daughter came back. As the saying had it, 'the calf had to be brought back from the place where the cow had been given' (*hasa kotta kadeyinda kara tarabeku*).

Respect for the principle of reciprocity was not always easy, without emotional or other cost. For instance, in the summer of 1948 Millayya was under pressure from his younger brothers not to give his daughter (by his deceased wife) in marriage to Kulle Gowda's brother's son. Millayya's younger brothers pointed out that Kulle Gowda's brother was poor, while Millayya was one of the rich landowners of Rampura and his daughter could easily have married into a wealthy household. But then when Millayya had been given Kulle Gowda's sister in marriage *his* household was the poorer one, and it was therefore wrong for him to refuse to give his daughter when he was better off. Wealth and poverty were both transitory while moral rules were permanent. Many came to hear of the discussion among brothers, and Millayya was praised by one and all.

The preference shown for sons by the villagers was also based on reciprocity considerations. Traditionally, sons provided the best insurance against old age. They cultivated the family land and looked after their parents during old age. They also performed annual sacrifices to propitiate the dead ancestors which were essential for the latter's satisfaction and for the lineage's continued well-being. The continuation of the lineage (*kula, annatammike, peelige, vamsha*) depended on the birth of male heirs in each generation. The disappearance of a lineage was viewed as a disaster. It resulted in the ancestral land's alienation.

The non-vegetarian castes in the village propitiated their dead ancestors on the ninth day (*marnoumi*) in the dark half of *bhadrapada* (September–October) with offerings of cooked meat.[1] The richer households slaughtered a sheep on this occasion while the poor had to be content with offerings of fowl. It was a big occasion. Each year during the *marnoumi* Nadu Gowda distributed twelve *khandagas* (khandaga = 180 seers) of paddy as charity to the village poor and mendicants. It gave him much satisfaction and he was proud of the fact that he had not stopped it even during the war years when rationing was at its worst. The annual act of charity, according to him, ensured that the living members kept good health and that the ancestral land continued to prosper. It was also an expression of gratitude to those who had worked unstintingly for their descendants: 'Where would we have been if they had not worked for us so hard?'

Reciprocity had also its subjective side. An individual felt compelled to do, or abstain from doing, something, because he had received a favour in the past, or because of existence of a prior bond stemming from the membership of a kin-group, village, caste, class, sect or religion. The word *dakshinya* expressed the sense of obliga-

---

[1] A few of them, however, performed the propitiatory rites during the asterism, *makha*, which fell generally in August.

toriness which moved persons to act in ways which were contrary to their immediate feelings and interests. The power of *dakshinya* was felt by one and all, excepting of course the minority of deviants. However, underlying *dakshinya* was the fear that if one did not do what was expected of one, others would not do what was in turn expected of them. But that was not the whole of *dakshinya*. It lay at the root of socialization, if not of all inter-personal morality.

Even when a man was not well enough to partake of the dinner at a relative's house he went because of *dakshinya*. And if he felt like cutting it, his host was certain to say, 'Just sit before the leaf, and make a pretence (*shastra*) of eating. That is enough.' The host on his side had to be certain that he had made every effort to secure the guest's presence. *Dakshinya* required him to put pressure on the guest. What applied to a dinner invitation applied also to more serious matters such as attending a wedding or festival, undertaking a journey, advancing a loan, giving or accepting a girl in marriage, and making a gift. *Dakshinya* made people do all kinds of things and this was acknowledged in the mordant humour of the saying, *dakshinyakke basaraguvudu* (becoming pregnant because of *dakshinya*).

A man who defaulted on his obligation was likely to be talked about. And continued indifference to obligations gave him a reputation for unreliability. In a small and closely meshed community, a reputation for unreliability was likely to have disastrous consequences. He would find no one willing to give him a loan, sponsor him for a contract or commercial transaction, employ him as a tenant and so on.

The multiplex character of rural social bonds was also a factor in restraining people from reneging on their obligations. Thus a labourer who wanted to stop working for a landowner had to take note of the likelihood that he might need a loan in the near future. Similarly, a landowner who wanted to sack a tenant had to restrain himself because he wanted the tenant's son as a *jita* servant. A reputation for ruthlessness did not enhance the landowner's popularity, and there were other landowners who were likely to take advantage of it. The ruthless landowner lost men to rival factions. In a multi-stranded relationship, the snapping of any single strand was prevented by the existence of the other strands. To this had to be added the constraints stemming from the value attached to enduring social bonds. There was always a tension between an uninhibited pursuit of one's interests and conformity to the restraining norms which were the expressions of other people's interests or desires.

2 Hierarchy

As was made clear earlier, caste divided the villagers into different hierarchical groups, and the idiom of caste was extended to objects and even events in the external world to distinguish them into high and low. 'Are the five fingers equal?' was a rhetorical question that was asked whenever the government's intention to abolish untouchability was discussed. The inequality between the fingers on a hand symbolized inequality in God's creation, and the government's attempts to bring about equality were absurd and bound to fail. But paradoxically many of those who argued in this way found the Brahminical or Lingayat claim to superiority wrong and offensive.

While as between castes (or sub-castes) the idea of hierarchy was dominant, every man recognized some relatives and friends as his equals (*sarikaru*), and he was particularly sensitive to his image among them. Humiliation before them (*sarikara munde avamana*) was so grave a matter that at times it drove a man to desperate action.

The idea of equality also found expression, although indirectly, in occasional moralizing which was perhaps born out of envy. Thus a wealthy miser was criticized for his folly in behaving as though he was going to take everything with him on his head when he died (*ella tale mele hottukondu hoguttaneye?*). Lakshmi, the goddess of wealth, was notorious for her fickleness: a man who was favoured by her one day was likely to be deserted by her on another.

The villagers were aware that an individual's moral worth was not determined by caste: that is, that there were some very moral individuals among the 'low' castes and immoral ones among the high. There was a realization that character was different from caste but at the same time sentiments were uttered implying that the higher castes were (or ought to be) more moral. This was seen, for instance, in the lapses of a high caste man receiving more attention than those of a low caste man, though this was to some extent due to the former's greater visibility. Also, the existence of differential life-styles between the higher and lower castes was interpreted to mean that the former's was superior.

Sanyasis represented another expression of the equality idea. They were recruited from both high and low castes but they were all holy men entitled to universal respect. That, however, was only the ideal. In practice, the sanyasi's caste prior to his initiation was relevant in some ways, and in particular, in the composition of his followers many of whom came from his own, equivalent or lower castes. Where a sanyasi was the head of a monastery, the bureaucracy was particularly sensitive in matters of pollution and purity, and treated lay followers from lower castes differently from high caste followers. But a few sanyasis had truly cosmopolitan followings cutting across not only caste but religious divisions.[1]

There were also other expressions of inequality besides those arising from caste and landownership. Men were superior to women, and the older were superior to the younger. Some expressions of hierarchy, however, had not been institutionalized; the dark-skinned were regarded as inferior to the light-skinned, the uneducated to the educated, urban to the rural and so on.

The omnipresence of hierarchical ideas had led to the proliferation and refinement of the symbols of superordination and subordination. For instance, the different parts of the human body had superior-inferior connotations. From the point of view of mutual rank the head was the highest part of the body while the feet were the lowest. One of the deepest expressions of respect was the traditional act of salutation in which a younger man placed his head on the older man's feet: the most superior part of the former's body had come into contact with the lowest part of the latter's. Similarly, a devotee in a temple prostrated (*sashtanga namaskara*) before the icon. Prostrating at the feet of a deity or of a patron symbolized the devotee's or client's abasement before the deity or patron. Such abasement was regarded as essential for seeking help and protection. In addition, a devotee slapped his cheeks before the deity to express his repentance for sins of commission and omission. The left cheek was slapped with the right hand and *vice versa*.

A devotee in a temple took all *prasada* to both his eyes first before drinking, eating or otherwise disposing of it. Thus the camphor flame which was waved before the deity before being offered to the devotees, was touched, symbolically, with both hands which were then taken to the eyes. The *thirtha* (holy water) was received with

---

[1] My comments apply only to 'traditional' monasteries and not to a modern organization such as the Ramakrishna Mission.

both hands and then drunk, and afterwards, the hands were taken to the eyes and wiped on the hair. Similarly, a flower or *tulasi* leaf (*Ocimum sanctum*) given by the priest was taken to both the eyes before being tucked behind the right ear. Incidentally, receiving with both hands was obligatory. The use of only one hand was disrespectful while receiving with the left hand was forbidden. A child was taught never to put forward its left hand to receive anything.

The feet were not only the lowest part of the body but they came into contact with dirty and polluting things. Even in 1948, only a small number of men (and no woman) wore sandals in Rampura, and a villager usually went into his house after washing his feet. His wife brought him a vesselful of water to the door, and the man washed his feet on the steps. A wife who failed to do this was not doing her duty.

The bodily positions which men assumed *vis-à-vis* each other had hierarchical connotations. As mentioned earlier, it was considered improper for a younger or inferior person to sit while his superior was standing while the opposite situation was proper. An inferior did not sit even when the superior was walking a few feet away. One afternoon Nadu Gowda was sitting on my verandah while the headman was pacing the corridor below and Nadu Gowda told him jokingly, 'Why don't you go home?' The headman understood what Nadu Gowda was trying to say and replied, 'I don't mind your stretching your legs.' Nadu Gowda retorted, 'You may not, but what will the people say?' Nadu Gowda was the headman's senior by a few years but he still felt that he had to show respect to the head of the village.

When several men were sitting on a bench only the senior among them had the right to cross his legs. (The stretching of legs was allowed only when extreme age made prolonged folding of legs very painful.) If between two men, the superior was sitting with his legs crossed, the inferior usually sat on his haunches, and if the superior was sitting on a mat, the inferior sat on the bare floor. If the superior was sitting on the verandah, the inferior sat at a lower level, and sometimes even on the street itself.

In a group of men it was not difficult to spot the leader. The leader spoke and gestured differently from the others. When an important man such as the headman was a member of a group, the others would not look him in the face but look down or away. And, frequently, when an inferior was with the headman, his right hand went to the back of his head where it moved up and down in a scratching motion while the lips opened in a placatory simper before speaking. Once when I was walking with the headman and Nadu Gowda on the road forming the crest of the tank bund, we encountered Pijja on a cycle, returning after a visit to Butagalli. As soon as he saw us, he jumped down from his cycle, removed his sandals, took them in one hand, and stood to a side of the road making room for us to pass. Even though Pijja had the reputation of being a rebel, he behaved like any other Harijan. Even non-Harijans who were in an inferior position had to remove their sandals and headgear before a superior.

Individuals who were economically and socially inferior seemed only too ready to agree with their superior, and flatter him when an opportunity presented itself. Agreeing with a superior and flattering him were approved if not prescribed ways of getting on, and every patron attracted one or more flatterers.[1] It is my impression that such flattery sounded more imposing in Sanskritized Kannada with frequent references to deities and incidents from Indian mythology than in plain, rustic speech.

The headman asked me to go over to his house one morning to meet the elderly Brahmin accountant of Hogur and his son. Much of the land owned by the headman lay inside the Hogur boundary. After I had been introduced to him, I invited him to have coffee and snacks in my house. I thought that I owed that courtesy to the headman's guests. I was taken aback to find the accountant responding to my well-meant invitation with a snub: 'We don't lack anything as we are in the house of goddess Lakshmi herself. We have had fruit and milk and our stomachs are full.' From the way the old man put it my invitation appeared as an unfavourable comment on the headman's inability to offer satisfactory hospitality to his guests. I sensed some hostility in the old man's reply—a feeling which was confirmed when I met him some time later in his house in Hogur—and more

---

[1] The Maharaja of Mysore had professional flatterers (*hogalu bhattaru*) whose duty it was to proclaim his titles on state occasions. They went ahead of the elephant on which he sat during processions proclaiming his titles every few minutes. It is difficult to establish a direct link between institutionalized flattery at the princely level and the tendency of richer landowners to attract flatterers but it cannot be dismissed as accidental as it is one of the several instances of the correspondence between the two levels. Such correspondence points to the widespread desire to imitate royalty even in the days of poor communications.

important, I felt upset that I may have given offence to the headman by my thoughtless invitation.

Failure to show deference to the rich, powerful and old was to invite their wrath. Sarcasm was the first weapon used but sometimes a threat was also packed into it. For instance, 'How is it you are seen here? You must have lost your way', was simple sarcasm while, 'You must be wanting something, you are too busy to wander aimlessly' contained the threat that the man would not get what he wanted as he had not been available when he was wanted. Taunting (*hangisuvudu*) was cruder than sarcasm, simple or packed, and taunting meant that the taunted was being taken to task for not reciprocating. He had not given anything in return for the favours he had received. If even then he did not mend his ways he was certain to be punished. Such punishment took a variety of forms. If he was a tenant or sharecropper, his contract was not renewed, other landowners were told not to encourage him, pressure was brought upon his creditor to press for repayment of loans, and he even ran the risk of being accused of stealing someone's crop or letting loose his goats or bullocks on a neighbour's land.

But occasionally an inferior did stand up for his rights before a superior. I have seen poor and humble villagers shouting loudly before the headman when they feared that their side of the case was being ignored. Indeed, I used to marvel at the patience with which the headman listened to the ranting of disputants. I had expected him to be brusque and authoritarian but I found him allowing a man to make his point in his own way. Perhaps he wanted each disputant to have the satisfaction of stating his case before he gave his verdict. The implementation of the verdict of a village court depended largely on the support it obtained from the people and on its appearing reasonable to everyone.

The rich and powerful had also duties which included hospitality to visitors to the village. Visitors usually arrived withou tnotice but they were invariably invited to a meal, and when they belonged to a superior caste the raw ingredients of a meal were supplied to them. No mendicant arriving at mealtime went hungry. The gifting of food (*anna dana*) was meritorious, and correspondingly, the failure to give it to the poor and hungry, a sin. Even those regarded as misers did not like to turn away a guest or mendicant arriving at mealtime. One of the worst criticisms of a rich man was to say that he turned away those who came hungry.

The advantages for travellers and visiting officials of the existence of such hospitality in villages which did not have inns and hotels are obvious. Even more important was the belief in the meritoriousness of sharing food in a system in which a few owned a great deal of arable land while the others lived on the margin of subsistence. During famines, which regularly visited the countryside, each big landowner took it upon himself to distribute some *ragi*-gruel to the starving. The feeding of hundreds of people at the weddings and funerals of the rich enabled the poor, who often had to go hungry, to have a free meal at which they could gorge themselves. Rice, which was a luxury for the poor, was served at such dinners, though with balls of *ragi*-dough. A good landowner walked along the rows (*pangti*) of squatting diners and made sure that each got enough to eat. (This had also its public relations side.) A full stomach had a special importance for those to whom it was not an everyday affair. The virtues of undereating make sense only to the overfed. The poor remembered the weddings of the rich principally by the kind of meals that had been cooked, and whether they were served as much as they wanted to eat or not.

The poor were exploited, and frequently mercilessly, by the rich. Or perhaps it would be more correct to say that the conditions of work accepted as normal in the village were harsh and exploitative. The only course open to a poor man who felt exploited and oppressed by a rich man was to curse the latter: 'May his house be ruined' (*avana mane halaga*), 'May his wife become a widow' (*avana hendati mundeyaga*), etc. There was a belief that when a poor man cursed a rich man out of the depths of his bitterness and hatred (literally, *hotte uri* or 'stomach fire') the curse would take effect. This was seen strikingly in the fear of a poor widow's curse, which, as described earlier, took the form of a long dirge. Thus two 'sanctions' were available to the poor against the rich: one was to curse, and the other, to run away.

3   *Face*

The word *moka* (from the Sanskrit *mukha*) or face was heard frequently in conversation. It stood for a person's image before others and for his self-respect. It was one of his most important possessions. He had to behave in such a way that he was able to show his face to one and all and not have to hide it. When a man, or those intimately associated with him, did something wrong he felt he was unable to show his face to others, especially equals. When a man insulted another at a wedding, festival or other public occasion, his face was 'broken' before everyone (*ellara edurige moka muridubitta*). It was an insult which he could not get over easily. A man who was aware that he had committed a serious wrong was said to look as though 'his face had been beaten with sandals' (*moka ekkadadalli hodeda hagittu*). Similarly, a man who had managed to make some money by selling his sugarcane crop at a profit, or had just got married, was teased by his friends: '[Your] face has acquired a lustre' (*mokakke kale bandubidtu*). Similarly, an official who exercised power revealed it in his face (*mokadalli darpa ide*). Gentleness (*sadhu*), badness (*ketta-tana*), etc. were all discernible in a man's face.

Another term that was heard frequently was *mana* which meant self-respect. A man with a keen sense of self-respect was referred to as a *manishta*.[1] He need not be rich. A comment that was heard occasionally was, 'We may be poor but we value our self-respect' (*navu badavaragirabahudu adare manadinda baluttiddeve*). Similarly a rich man did not have always a strong sense of self-respect. A *manishta* was driven to suicide (or even homicide) because he felt he had lost his self-respect. *Avamana* was the loss of *mana*.

A *manishta* kept his word, and he also discharged his obligations scrupulously. He paid creditors on time, and he gave the gifts he was required to. He did not easily brook an insult. If he was not strong or aggressive enough to react instantly to an insult, he showed his resentment by silent non-cooperation.

Insulting a person's family, caste and village amounted to insulting him. In the case of 'The Potter and Priest', the priest felt that his entire caste had been insulted by the Potter's declared intention to beat the priest till five pairs of sandals wore out. He pointed out there was only a small number of Lingayats in Rampura to take retaliatory action and they were dependent on the Peasants to safe-guard the honour of their caste.

A friend of mine who was connected with rural development work in Mysore in the early fifties narrated an incident which poignantly brought out how strongly a group of poor Harijans felt regarding their *mana*. He and his colleagues had been invited to a puja in the Harijan ward of the village, and the hosts, after preparing sweetened milk (*khiru*) for the guests, discovered that they had too few tumblers

---

[1] *Manishta* had two near synonyms in *gauravasta* and *maryadasta*.

and no one was willing to lend them a few more which they needed. At this the leader of the Harijans became so enraged that he emptied all the *khiru* into the gutter, saying, 'Where is our self-respect? We cannot even find enough tumblers for our guests.'

Individuals had also a sense of identification with their village and an insult to one's village had to be avenged like an insult to oneself, one's wife, one's family, etc. Disputes between villages did occur, and they were not always for material gains. The settling of inter-village disputes resembled international disputes in their tortuousness and sensitivity to issues of protocol. For instance, there was a dispute between some members of Kere and Bihalli at the annual festival of Madeshwara in Gudi in 1947, and the priests of the Madeshwara temple, and some leaders from Rampura and Hogur were all concerned to bring about peace before the Ugadi (Kannada new year festival generally falling during March–April) in 1948. A meeting was first fixed in Hogur but Kere leaders did not attend it as they felt insulted at being summoned to Hogur whose political and social standing was identical with Kere's. Both were *hobli* capitals, and each had the same kind of traditional court, viz. *kattemane*, for the settlement of caste and other disputes.[1] The meeting had to be finally held on neutral and sacred ground, viz. the open space outside the temple.

In brief, *mana* was a basic value, and everyone was sensitive about his self-respect including those who were desperately poor. I have referred earlier to the traditional ceremony of the 'big betel leaves' (*dodda vilya*) at which sets of betel leaves and arecanut pieces were distributed at the weddings of Peasants and other non-Brahmin castes, and how they were notorious for giving rise to disputes regarding mutual precedence. The order in which each set of leaves and nuts (*vilya*) was distributed had to respect the seniority principle, and any departure from it proved explosive. Each guest received *vilya* as a holder of a particular role, viz. temple priest, Maharaja's representative (*amildar*, the official head of the *taluk*), caste headman, village headman, Brahmin, or representative of each village in the region. It was the last category that gave most trouble; the credentials of each claimant to represent his village had to be beyond dispute, and in addition, there was the thorny question of mutual

[1] For a discussion of traditional caste and village organization in the Rampura area, see my 'The Dominant Caste in Rampura', *American Anthropologist*, Vol. 61, No. 1, Feb. 1959, pp. 1–16.

precedence among villages. It was not unknown for two men to claim to represent the same village, and in such a case, the one who had the better claim was given the *vilya*. This naturally enraged the defeated man. The matter of precedence between villages was even more difficult, and a decision taken at one wedding could prove to be a source of continuous trouble for the caste. The distribution of 'big betel leaves' was frequently marred by shouting and angry exchanges. The expense of this ritual as well as its explosive character was responsible for the decision of Rampura elders to permit fathers of local brides to opt out of the ceremony on payment of Rs 8.25 to the village council.

Quite apart from the distribution of 'big betel' at weddings, the giving of betel leaves and nuts to guests was a prescribed courtesy (*maryade*) on certain formal and ritual occasions. The failure to do so was an insult. During the fifties there was a bitter and protracted dispute in Kere where the dominant Peasants were divided into two factions, one supporting their caste headman's right to receive, on ceremonial occasions, two *vilyas* and the other consisting of all those who thought he should receive only one *vilya* like everyone else. Most villagers were drawn, willy-nilly, into the dispute, and one could not talk to a Kere man for five minutes without the dispute turning up in some form or other. The headman demanded two *vilyas*, one in his role as the headman of the Peasants of the entire Kere *hobli*, and the other as the leader of the Peasants of Kere village. Kere, as I have said earlier, had a number of educated and politicized men, and they thought that the headman's insistence on two *vilyas* was antediluvian and undemocratic. The headman was wealthy, had a record of service to the village, and wielded much local influence while a few of the educated leaders of Kere were active in politics outside the village. The dispute dragged on for years and I do not know how, if at all, it was resolved.

There was an ugly scene at the wedding, in 1947, of the head-man's daughter in which Ningu, a guest from Kere, well-known for his cantankerousness, walked out of the assembly (*sabha*) on the ground that he and all the other guests had been insulted. The 'insult' had occurred in the following way: As the wedding procession (*sabgast*) reached the Muslim area, a few Muslim leaders put jasmine garlands round the groom's and headman's neck as an expression of their regard for them. No one objected then but after the procession had returned home, Ningu got up and walked out complaining that the assembly had been insulted. According to Ningu, only the bridal couple had the right to receive garlands at weddings, and not anyone else. The headman, the chief host, should not have accepted the garland. By his acceptance, he had insulted the guests.

After walking out of the hall, Ningu walked to the gate of the Rama temple and sat down on a stone. The headman, Nadu Gowda and a few Muslim leaders hurried after him to pacify him and bring him back. Ningu had raised an explosive issue, and the headman's first task was to defuse it. He and his supporters assured Ningu that neither the Muslim leaders nor the headman had intended any insult to the guests. The Muslim leaders had only thought of showing their respect to the head of the village, that was all. After much coaxing, Ningu allowed himself to be led back to the wedding hall and the hosts heaved a sigh of relief.

There was a general belief in the village that in matters of precedence the Shepherds were really the most finicky group. There was the saying: *'kurubaranyaya kambligeddalu hididaru tiruvudilla'* ('Shepherds' disputes do not get settled even when the blankets on which they are sitting are being eaten up by termites'). The arbitrators and disputants sat on *kamblis* spread on the ground and the arguments about precedence went on and on oblivious of the infestation of the *kamblis* by termites. In temples controlled by Shepherds, the order in which the leaders were to receive *prasada* was strictly laid down and any departure from it gave rise to a protracted dispute. To be fair, this kind of dispute could have arisen in the temple of any other caste in the area and the Shepherds were only more thoroughgoing and exacting. If, for instance, a Shepherd leader was absent at the temple on an important occasion, when his turn for *prasada* came, the priest mentioned his name and sprinkled the *thirtha* on a pillar before passing on to the next devotee. Failure to do so was to invite trouble.

A man's self-respect was damaged when he was called a 'bastard' (*hadarakke huttidavanu*) before others, and far more seriously when he was spat upon or beaten with sandals. In the latter case, both the aggressor and victim were punished by the village and caste elders, the aggressor because he had committed a serious wrong, and the victim because he had been polluted, and could only be readmitted after an elaborate purificatory rite. However, with the introduction of British law, this type of wrong became actionable under 'defamation' which was significantly translated as *'mananashta'* ('loss of self-respect'). Defamation was resorted to by villagers to strengthen sanctions for traditional offences. This happened to coincide with the weakening of traditional sanctions with increased spatial mobility, urbanization and westernization.

4 Friendship and Enmity

Friendship (*sneha, dosti*) and enmity (*dwesha, vaira, hage, jiddu*) were both widely recognized relationships between individuals, families and lineages. Friends had frequent and pleasant interaction: they chatted together, went out on walks or journeys, ate in each other's houses, and occasionally, gave each other vegetables and fruits. With an enemy, on the other hand, there was a relationship of avoidance. When two men were not on speaking terms with each other they had a relationship of avoidance but this was still some distance removed from enmity. Enemies tried actively to harm each other in every possible way varying from malicious gossip, setting fire to straw ricks, diverting water from, or flooding fields and filing suits in law courts to plotting murder.

Sometimes, inherited enmity gave place to friendship, and an outstanding example of this was provided by the friendship of the headman and Nadu Gowda. It was significant that it was the village school which had brought the two together. The fathers of the headman and Nadu Gowda were illiterate, and were thus denied the opportunity which the sons had of coming together every day for several hours at school. The boredom of learning the complicated alphabet, the multiplication tables, etc., for several hours every day in a crowded and dingy room, and the fear of the tyrant with the cane were bonds which bound all the oppressed.

As explained earlier, considerations of reciprocity did prevail among friends though the rhetoric of friendship stressed only affection. But reciprocity did not have to be on a one-to-one basis, nor did it mean that a material good had to be reciprocated with another good. Friendship occasionally spanned economic divisions so that while one side gave goods the other gave time, labour and 'loyalty' (*niyat*). But too great a disparity in status changed friendship into a patron-client relation.

Friendship was more visible among, if not more characteristic of, men. Grown men did not experience any embarrassment in showing their affection for each other. Two friends who had met after an interval of a few weeks held each other's hands, or one put his hand over the other's shoulder, except among the middle-aged and old. On a few occasions my friends arrived suddenly on my verandah and announced that they felt like seeing me. They were a bit embarrassed to find me working but I assured them it was nothing urgent. I invited them to have some coffee before we all went out for a walk. My friends were pleased that I had pushed aside my work for them. The only one to grouse was Kulle Gowda, 'You go, by all means go, have a good time. I shall sit here and work.' He was not the one to allow his light to be hid by any bushel.

Needless to say, friendships occurred within the same sex. A friendly relation between a man and woman who were not kindred to each other, or more specifically, between whom sex intercourse did not constitute incest, was usually interpreted as a liaison. The concept of a platonic relationship did not make sense to the villagers. They were too biologically oriented for that.

Friendships did occur across the lines of caste though here, as in the case of cross-class friendships, there were structural limits. For instance, friendships between Brahmins, Lingayats or Peasants on the one hand, and Harijans on the other, were rare. Close relationship between members of one of the first three castes and Harijans invariably assumed the form of patron-client relationships. But I do know of friendships between Brahmins and Peasants, Lingayats and Peasants, and Brahmins and Lingayats. During the thirties I attended a wedding in Kere in which Mallayya, the Peasant friend of Seenappa, the Brahmin landowner-host, successfully 'persuaded' him to invite his (landowner's) cousin across the road. Seenappa was notorious for his obstinacy but Mallayya literally pushed him every step of the thirty yards or so between the two houses. Once or twice the host shouted at him, 'Mallayya, what are you trying to do? Don't force me to do what I don't like to.' But Mallayya handled Seenappa, his senior by at least a few years, and a Brahmin, firmly, like a father handling a wilful son. Seenappa finally reached the door of the cousin's house where he shamefacedly invited his relative to attend the wedding and bless the bridal couple. The incident provoked some mirth among the bystanders including Seenappa's relatives who commented, 'He listens only to Mallayya. None of us would have been able to persuade him to invite his cousin.'

Siddu, the Lingayat lawyer, and Swamy, Nadu Gowda's son, were close friends, but their friendship had to reckon with the pollution barrier. While Siddu was emancipated, his kinship group was orthodox, and as priests of the Madeshwara temple they were required to observe scrupulously the pollution rules. Swamy, his younger brother Kempu, and Japi used to visit Siddu in his big joint family house where he lived with his brothers and cousins. There was an immense wooden cot in the inner verandah of the house, and the visitors used to sit on it, leaning against the rolled up mattresses, while waiting for their friend to get ready to come out. But if Thammayya, the head of the lineage, saw the Peasant friends leaning against the mattress-roll, he insisted on its being washed. (Washing a mattress was neither easy nor tidy.) Only after a wash did it become pure enough to be used again by the members of the priestly household.

Siddu's wife was also a stickler for ritual purity. In the old days, she used to insist on her husband's having a bath after he returned from a walk with his Peasant friends. The latter came to know about it and protested vigorously to Siddu. Siddu, B.A., LL.B., was able to persuade his wife that he had to respect his friends' feelings. But he dropped visiting the Madeshwara temple in view of his departure from the regimen prescribed for the priests. He only broke his self-imposed rule during the annual festival when every member of the lineage had to perform some chore in the *sanctum sanctorum*. Even this he dropped after he started practising as a lawyer. His secular status was too high to permit him to be a priest.

However, pollution rules were beginning to be relaxed in 1948. The urbanized Peasant youth of the village resented Brahmin and Lingayat pollution-consciousness, and also their exclusiveness in food, drink, etc. By 1952 even the more conservative Peasants were offering tea or coffee instead of boiled milk to upper caste visitors. Cooked snacks were offered to old friends like me, and Peasant hosts tended to be generous in their hospitality. Still later, educated Brahmin and Lingayat friends were expected to dine with Peasants on occasions such as weddings. Any guest who refused to dine on such occasions offended the hosts. No allowance was made for a queasy stomach. The least he could do was to sit before the heaped up leaf and eat a little.

A few Brahmins had, however, developed a taste for meat and chicken curries, and when they visited their Peasant friends they insisted on getting non-vegetarian food which, incidentally, they never cooked at home. But their departure from tradition was not

always admired by their non-vegetarian friends. While it was understandable that conservative villagers should criticize meat-eating
Brahmins, it was surprising to find even the urbanized youth criticizing them for having forsaken all Brahminical principles.

Friendship was indeed a value for the villagers, more for men than
for women. Two good friends were said to be 'like brothers' (literally,
'like elder brother–younger brother', *annatammandirahage*). I heard
this expression several times and I could not help recalling the statement of an elderly English colleague who had told me that he and
his brother were very close and had written to each other every week.
He had added, 'We are very good friends.' That is, friendship connoted intimacy in England while in Rampura (as in rural India
everywhere), brotherhood conveyed intimacy. Adult brothers were
frequently at loggerheads with each other and this was well known
but apparently it was not enough to make a dent in the myth of
fraternal solidarity. (The popular belief that the girls who came in by
marriage into a family were responsible for its breaking up, was also
derived from that myth.)

Friendship was a valued thing and the longer its duration, the
greater was its value. By this test, the headman and Nadu Gowda
were indeed great friends. Nadu Gowda used to wax eloquent on this
subject but on this as on other subjects the headman was taciturn.
But he had genuine affection for Nadu Gowda, and the two spent
at least a few hours together every day. And as stated earlier, the
headman rarely went out of the village without being accompanied
by his old friend.

5　Gossip

Gossip (*harate*) was an important activity in the village, and certain
features of rural life such as nucleated settlement, the existence
of multiplex ties, limited spatial mobility, availability of leisure,
and the absence of regular recreation, all provided an ideal soil
for it.

The fear of being gossiped about did act as a sanction against
non-conformity. The words, 'the people will talk [about it]' (*jana
matanadikolluttare*), were familiar ones. But there was a small minority in every village which seemed indifferent to local criticism. Nadu
Gowda told me the story of the loose woman who was made to
undergo an elaborate and expensive ritual of purification before

being readmitted to caste. After she had bathed and worn new clothes, her tongue was singed with three kinds of needles, gold, silver, and iron, and she was given sanctified *vibhuti* by the guru who performed the purificatory ritual, to apply on her forehead. The woman, who was known for her tart speech, asked the guru whether it was not more appropriate to apply the *vibhuti* on the organ which had sinned instead of the innocent forehead. At the time I heard the story I was impressed by the villagers' ability to make fun even of things which they regarded as sacred. Its significance as showing the power of village society over confirmed violators of accepted norms came home to me only later.

The fear of gossip did not also restrain the Basava priest from doing what he wanted to. It was only when the Basava priest's mistresses tried to join the womenfolk of the Madeshwara lineage in cooking the dinner at the annual propitiation (*para*) in honour of the deity Basava that the headman had to intervene.

A man who was outcasted for flouting the rules of his caste and of the local community generally tried to get back into the fold after a while. He did this when he tried to find spouses for his grown sons and daughters. No one in the caste wanted to marry the offspring of outcasted parents unless they themselves wanted to be thrown out. The only way out was for the outcasted person to apologize to caste leaders for protracted defiance and beg them to take him back. This was done after he had paid a fine to the caste and undergone the ritual of purification and given a big dinner. Many a rebel, after years of defiance, crawled back into his caste when he wanted to marry his son or daughter. In other words, sub-caste endogamy enforced conformity.

Among those who were loudest in their condemnation of gossip were the rich and powerful: 'What work do they (the gossips) have? They sit on the verandah and criticize others.' The Revenue Inspector stationed in Hogur told me that officials had always to be sensitive to what the gossips on verandahs were likely to say. A State legislator once complained to Nadu Gowda that he dared not buy a new cycle for fear that gossips would say that it was a bribe from someone. (That he subsequently became wealthy is, however, another story.)

But while people in power claimed to be afraid of what the verandah critics said their actions often belied their words. The corruption of officials was a topic much discussed by all classes of villagers. The widely-held view was that with the arrival of popular government corruption had risen steeply and this was corroborated by officials who blamed politicians who interfered with the administrator's work to further their own ends. Ironically, homespun *khadi* had become, within a few years of Independence, a symbol of corrupt power instead of patriotism and self-sacrifice which it undoubtedly was during the freedom struggle when hundreds of Congressmen gave up their careers and courted imprisonment. During the early fifties, during one of my journeys by rail from Bangalore to Mysore, I was in a small third-class compartment, and at a wayside station, an elderly gentleman dressed in the uniform of a white homespun *kudta* (shirt), dhoti and Gandhi cap, entered our compartment. His clothes indicated that he was a Congress politician, and as soon as he got in, a volley of criticisms were hurled at the Congress. Corruption, the arrogance of power, indifference to people's welfare and many other sins were laid at its doors. The poor man, a rural landowner turned politician, and perhaps that too only at the district level, was a model of patience and good humour, and he did his best to answer his angry critics. He admitted some misdeeds, explained the difficulties of politicians and bemoaned the villainy of middlemen (*pudaris*). Soon, he had succeeded in establishing rapport with fellow-passengers, and the atmosphere in the tiny compartment was suddenly transformed into one of friendliness. All the passengers in the compartment were landowners, and I remember one of them, a young Brahmin from a village in Chamarajanagar, lifting his shirt and uncoiling from his waist several *ragi* plants, which had been wound round his dhoti like a belt. He strung out the plants, and measured them against his outstretched arms. They were indeed very tall plants, the tallest we all had seen. He explained that he had journeyed to a village near Bangalore to secure the seeds of this plant for his farm: the *ragi* plant was not only very tall but yielded more grain than other varieties. Everyone, including the Congressman, expressed their admiration for the *ragi*. The Brahmin farmer was delighted.

But I am digressing. The real point I wish to make is that I was taken aback at the swiftness with which the uniform of *khadi* had changed its meaning from self-sacrifice and patriotism to corrupt power. Everyone spoke of Congress *pudaris* and their misdeeds. They were everywhere, in government offices, educational institutions, law courts and hospitals. Along with the yellow press, which had proli-

ferated in the cities, the *pudaris* were among the less savoury con-
comitants of popular government.

There was, however, a well-known norm, honoured more in the
breach than in the observance, that gossiping was bad if not immoral. The saying *'madidavara papa adidavara bayalli'* ('the sinners'
sins lodge in the mouths of those who discuss them') was sometimes
cited to discourage gossip. There was also the argument of prudence
for abstaining from gossip. Everyone had something to hide from
the others, and it was wise therefore to keep one's mouth shut. Even
worse was the plight of those who pointed to the mote in someone
else's eye while ignoring the beam in their own. As the Kannada
proverb had it, 'there are holes in everyone's pancakes but in our
house, the pan itself has holes' (*ellara mane dose tootadare namma
mane kavaliyalle tootu*).

The men who kept to themselves and did not discuss others were
praised by everyone including the gossips themselves. Some amount
of verbal cannibalism was, however, an integral part of village life
and those who kept out of it were respected.

There was a strong feeling that the unpleasant things occurring
within a household should not be allowed to leak out. Every large
household had its own complicated politics and its share of deviant
behaviour, and neighbours and relatives tried to ferret out everything
that went on in it. Every head of a household had to put up with
hurts and insults from one or more members and learn not to complain about it. They were what was called in local parlance, 'blows
delivered inside the veil' (*musukina olagina guddu*). They were poignant, as the blows came from those closest to one, and therefore,
could not be discussed with even intimate friends. But when the pressure was too great a man's restraint gave way and he confided in
a friend.

While some people were inveterate gossips and a few abstained
altogether from gossiping, the others fell in between. The victims of
gossip certainly condemned it strongly but that did not prevent the
gossips from enjoying gossiping.

6 *Envy*

Envy was a familiar phenomenon. A villager who owned valuable
things such as a few acres of wet land, a pair of good bullocks, a
milch-buffalo, a gold wristlet or a fountain pen, expected others to

envy him and feared such envy. For instance, a villager whose new shirt got an accidental tear soon after it was admired by a friend was likely to remark, half in jest, 'What a foul eye you have! The moment you admired it, it tore.'

The eye (*kannu*) was an important locus of envy. A cow whose milk yield was high had burlap or cloth draped over its middle to conceal the udders from envious eyes. An attractive and intelligent child who evoked appreciative comments from relatives at a wedding or other occasion and became fractious soon after, was said to be suffering from *drishti* (or *kannu biddide*, i.e. someone's eye had fallen) or evil eye. The child's mother or other relative took in each hand a few chilis and salt crystals, took care to close the hands, and then waved them thrice before the child, after which the salt and chilis were thrown into the kitchen stove (*ole*). The chilis gave out an acrid smoke while the salt burnt. If the child became quiet soon after it meant that he (or she) had been really affected by someone's evil eye.

It was a rule of prudence, if not good manners, to refrain from praising another man's crop, orchard, house, cattle or child. For if any mishap followed the praise, the man who praised was certain to be credited with a bad or evil eye. A reputation for possessing an evil eye was no social asset. Everyone hid their valuable or attractive objects from him. Stories about the destructive powers of his eyes would do the rounds in the village, each narrator garnishing and improving the version he had heard.

The stomach (*hotte*) was another seat of envy. The envious experienced 'stomach fire' (*hotte uri*, or *hotte kichchu*) when anything good happened to someone they knew. Villagers frequently spoke of envious people resorting to malicious gossip or unfriendly action. A man whose straw-rick had been burnt down might exclaim, in bitter sarcasm, 'Their stomachs will now cool down' (*avara hotte tannagayitu eega*). The implication was that his straw-rick had attracted the envy of someone and its destruction must have given him satisfaction. Again, when a good bullock broke its leg during the agricultural season, the injured attributed it to someone's envy. He might then recall the latter's comment that the bullocks were fine animals, and that the price that had been paid for them was low. The owner of the bullocks would then reason that his good luck at the cattle fair had attracted the envy of the man in question.

The phenomenon of envy loomed large in the minds of villagers.

The 'haves' kept referring to the covetous eyes and burning stomachs of others which resulted in anonymous petitions (*moogarji*) to officials, malicious gossip, lawsuits, and in extreme cases to sorcery (*mata*). I must add, however, that sorcery was only very rarely mentioned, and there was no one in Rampura who had the reputation of being a practitioner of the black art.

One of the Traders in the village, Sappa, was busy constructing a 'modern' house-cum-shop after pulling down his old mud house. The building was of brick and mortar, and the front portion of the ground floor was to provide for two shops, one for groceries and the other for cloth. The rest of the house including the rooms on the first floor, above the shops, provided ample accommodation for Sappa and his family.

Sappa had built his house-cum-shop on the model of Traders' houses in towns. It was the first house in the village to have an upper floor, the first to have brick-and-mortar walls instead of mud ones, and finally, the first to be roofed with factory-made 'Mangalore tiles' instead of tiles made by local Potters. Sappa was not a rich landowner but a poor trader. But according to Sannu and a few others who talked to me, a poor man ought to know his place and stay there. He ought not to aspire to doing things which were beyond him. Tongues started wagging about Sappa's foolishness. Many knew that he was building the house on borrowed money, Rs 3000/- from Millayya and some more from creditors in Mysore. A villager sympathetic to Sappa told me that he had saved some money and and that it was not true to say that it was being built entirely on borrowed capital. Anyway, Sannu commented wryly that one of Sappa's creditors would eventually live in the house which he was taking great pains to build. Karagayya, Millayya's younger brother, said that Sappa was building like a townsman, paying for labour, and not like a villager who diverted his tenants and servants to do much of the labour. (He had not taken into account that Sappa was not a landowner with power over his servants and clients but only a Trader.) The village doctor, an inveterate meddler, criticized Sappa for the crest and motto which adorned the wall above the new shops. The crest consisted of two Indian flags, their handles crossing each other, and above them was the motto 'Shri Rama Sahayam', invoking the help of the deity Rama. The doctor told Sappa that it was wrong to mix up the national flag and Rama's name. The doctor was an 'educated' man, an urbanite and Brahmin, and poor Sappa got worried that he had done something wrong. The doctor then went round telling all and sundry what he thought about the Trader's crest. I found the doctor's behaviour childish and annoying, and in my annoyance, it did not occur to me to try and find out why he thought Sappa had done anything wrong. Was it because secular and religious symbols were being mixed up? The doctor may also have shared the widespread envy of Sappa, and also, he knew that the leaders of the village did not like Sappa's building a brick-and-mortar house. Voicing the sentiments of the rich and powerful gave the doctor satisfaction. That it also made him unpopular with ordinary folk did not seem to bother him.

It was envy which made villagers confidently predict that Japi's enterprise would be a failure. Again, envy lay at the root of the allegation made about every landowner that he had bought the land of poor Brahmins. It was true that by and large Brahmins had sold their land, and it had been bought by Peasants, but that was not the same thing as saying that everyone had prospered by buying Brahmin land at distress sales. Anyway, what was so wrong about buying it? How was it worse than charging 25 per cent interest to needy villagers or exploiting the labour of Harijans and very young boys?

A distinction may be made in expressions of envy on the basis of the social distance between the envier and envied. For instance, if one was rich and high caste and the other was poor and low, the latter commented on the meanness and exploitative nature of the former. If the rich man became ill or suffered a loss, then some poor man was bound to comment that 'God had showed [his anger with the rich man]' or 'What had been swallowed has now been vomited'. When one of Rame Gowda's eyes became infected during the latter half of 1948, Kulle Gowda told me that it was due to the family's black-market activities. Since every landowner had indulged in black-marketing, according to his resources and daring, the selection of one person for punishment seemed invidious. It was only explicable on the ground that the wealth and influence of the headman's family had attracted widespread envy.

Sometimes, a rich landowner was resentful of a tenant who was on the way up. The tenant had, by dint of hard work and saving over the years, bought a piece of land or built a house, and the landowner was then quick to detect signs of 'impertinence' or 'arrogance' in him. The owner perceived a threat to his future interests in the increasing prosperity of his tenant. The latter was likely to be accused of lacking in loyalty and gratitude, which was certain to drive the two further apart.

Envy from intimates, who were usually castefellows and relatives, and frequently also peers, presented a more difficult problem. An intimate came home frequently, talked to different members of the household including old women, was invited to share pot luck, and on rare occasions, his advice was sought. At the same time, it was recognized that peers and intimates were given to gossip and envy apart from the possible clash of interests.

All this resulted in an ambivalent attitude towards intimates and equals. They were the people with whom a man relaxed, whose presence and co-operation were essential on occasions such as weddings and funerals but there was need for wariness in dealing with them. Bad news had to be kept from them as they were likely to convey it to everyone, and it was likely to be distorted and exaggerated in the course of circulation. Good news could not be conveyed to them till it was beyond doubt as otherwise they may prevent it from becoming a fact. The relationship between a man and his intimates was a complex one and contained an important streak of conflict.

7 Sense of Humour

A sense of humour was an integral part of Indian village life even though anthropological studies show no evidence of it.

Mr Gorur Ramaswamy Iyengar is one of the leading humorists in Kannada, and his reputation is based entirely on the books he wrote on his beautiful, natal village of Gorur (in Hassan District) on the banks of the river Hemavati, a tributary of the Kaveri. While Mr Iyengar has an unfailing eye for the humorous incident and character, his writings are marked by nostalgia if not sentimentality, and this makes him miss the crudeness and cruelty which frequently flow through rustic humour. For instance, such physical shortcomings as stammering, lameness and muteness were occasionally the subject of 'humorous' comment. A half-wit was engaged in conversation solely for the entertainment his remarks provided to a small group of men who had time hanging on their hands. I have watched Kulle Gowda suddenly leave the work he was doing, to talk to the Rama priest's son-in-law, a man of subnormal intelligence, and whose freedom from any inhibitions in speaking about everyone including his relatives was a source of much amusement. Kulle Gowda asked him several questions, including one or two about the Rama priest, and the replies sent the small knot of men around into loud guffaws. The Rama priest and Kulle Gowda were old foes, and the latter got some pleasure from the obscenities hurled by the son-in-law at his father-in-law. Kulle Gowda also asked the son-in-law to carry a message to his former Peasant patron. The latter lived in a nearby hamlet, and Kulle Gowda and he had burnt the candle at both ends when they were much younger.

The damage suffered by an unpopular or unfair person gave widespread satisfaction, and the details of the incident were discussed and then passed on from person to person. Any trivial item of information was picked up and its humorous possibilities fully extracted. I wondered sometimes whether the disputes which occurred frequently were not a source of recreation for the villagers who saw in them welcome departures from the boredom of daily routine.

I remember the case of the widow whom her creditor Gulayya had tried to cheat. Kalamma the widow had borrowed Rs 50/- (Rs 5 in cash and the rest in paddy) from Gulayya, and when a year later, her son-in-law took the money to the creditor he was flabbergasted to be asked to pay Rs 150. 50 had been changed to 150 and when the creditor was to produce the document it was discovered that the addition was in green ink while the rest of the 'document', a sheet torn from a boy's notebook, was in blue. On seeing the document Kulle Gowda pronounced that there was only one man in the village who used green ink and that that was P. M. Lingayya. The latter was a trouble-maker, much disliked, and his providing proof of his involvement in cheating was relished by many. (Lingayya tried to get out of the awkward situation by saying that while the ink was undoubtedly his, he did not know who had used his pen.)

Both Swamy and Kempu took Kalamma's side against the creditor. This followed Nadu Gowda's advice to Kalamma not to pay the money to Gulayya. Kempu told Kalamma's son-in-law in the presence of Lingayya that the son-in-law and Kempu should split the Rs 50 equally between them and let Gulayya go to a court of law to recover his debt. That he dared not go to a court of law after the attempt to cheat was known and relished by all. Gulayya's patron had roundly abused him for trying to cheat a poor widow, and this also got to be known. It was said that Gulayya's clumsy attempt at forgery was prompted by the desire to please his mistress, who was related to Kalamma and hated her. The news of the liaison, and Gulayya's stupidity in putting himself in a position where he could be sued for cheating, his suddenly taking fright and trying to hide all documents with him out of a fear of police investigation, all caused much merriment.

However, village humour was not always tainted by cruelty. The general admiration for Mrs Karim's debating abilities, for instance, was the tribute which ordinary folk paid to virtuosity of no mean order. Some of the admiration was due to the fact that a woman, and a Muslim at that, was able to assert herself before an assembly of men which included the headman. It was a striking reversal of the role expected of the sexes, and it appealed to the villagers' sense of the absurd. The same reversal of roles occurred when the Harijan Pijja tied up his Lingayat master in knots before the village elders. His cleverness at argument, quick repartee and penchant for apt simile or metaphor, were all admired. Talent and virtuosity were always praised, and more so when found in unlikely places.

That the villagers' sense of humour was a genuine one was revealed by their ability to laugh at themselves on occasion. This was brought home to me on several occasions. Once Virabhadra complained loudly to me about someone who had stolen vegetables from his vegetable patch (*menasi madi*). I told him that there should be deterrent punishment for vegetable-stealers. Virabhadra, who had a contrary streak in him, asserted that it could not be done. When a man was caught red-handed he was likely to say that he helped himself to a few vegetables as he was in urgent need and could not find the owner. Had he found the owner, he certainly would have asked his permission first. Virabhadra then explained to me that it was not just anyone who stole. A farmer took vegetables usually from someone well-known to him. Taking vegetables from each other was therefore a sign of intimacy. As I heard Virabhadra explain, his original complaint appeared to me to be pitched in a high key if not altogether absurd. The same realization dawned on Virabhadra, and his dark round face split into a wide grin, his ear-rings offering a strange contrast to his impressive moustache. He had stalked into my verandah bursting with anger against the unknown thief only to depart like a boy who had had his hands suddenly stuffed with sweets.

Even the grave and silent headman rarely missed an opportunity of teasing M. H. Chenna, the Shepherd leader who was probably the headman's senior by a few years. He was not overwhelmed by the headman and this made possible the exchange of badinage between them. Chenna's grown sons had separated from him and were living with their wives. As the Marnoumi approached, Chenna planned to buy a ram at the Saturday market in Kirgavalu to be sacrificed for the meal (*ede*) in honour of his dead father. Chenna asked his sons to share the price of the ram as each of them was getting a share of the sacrificed meat. But the sons refused: it was Chenna's duty to offer a mutton-dish to his dead father and *not* theirs. Their turn to offer a sacrifice would come only after Chenna's death and not before. This was sound logic indeed though it did not seem to me appropriate to confront a living father with. The headman and Nadu Gowda admired the sons' logic and laughed heartily. Chenna soon joined them, and if anything, his laughter was heartier than that of the other two. Chenna had a big hooked nose, pointed chin, and his mouth was in a recess between the two. He had several teeth missing and as he laughed, he looked like a Walt Disney cartoon.

On another occasion, Chenna narrated an incident in his household which shocked me, though he and his friends, the headman and Nadu Gowda, regarded it as highly amusing. The fact that Chenna did not get along well with his wife was known to his close friends. This was responsible for his absence from Rampura for several weeks early in 1948 when he lived with his Vaishnavite guru in T. G. Koppalu, a hamlet seven miles away. Chenna found peace with his Guru and some of the peace might have come from marijuana-smoking to which the guru and his followers resorted occasionally.

On the occasion referred to above, the headman teased Chenna about his wife complaining to her friends about his still being a 'boy' (*hudugu*). I did not catch the meaning but later I was told that while Chenna continued to be ardent his wife thought they were too old for sex. Their sons and daughters were adult and married.

Chenna's urban son-in-law was visiting the village at that time and Mrs Chenna was solicitous of his needs, a fact which only exacerbated her husband's annoyance. To please her sophisticated son-in-law, Mrs Chenna made an urban, middle-class breakfast for him comprising *uppittu*, a savoury dish with broken wheat, and coffee. She took the hot breakfast to her husband who asked her what it was. When she answered him, he told her to pour the breakfast down her vulva. Chenna narrated all this calmly and cheerfully.

The headman and Nadu Gowda burst into loud guffaws on listening to this piece of conjugal dialogue, and as usual, Chenna joined his friends in the laughter. The three old men, laughing for all they were worth, in the middle of the street presented indeed an odd spectacle. I was the only quiet one and I was not certain whether it was proper for me to show my appreciation of Chenna's sense of humour. The guffawing old men were oblivious of the attention they were attracting from passers by. It was very unusual to see the headman so cheerful.

Even the poorest and oppressed villagers were not without a sense of humour. I cannot easily forget the laughter and the barbed humour of the headman's *jita* servants whom I saw every day for at least a few hours, and some of whom slept on the cowhouse verandah. While it was true that the laughter was marked among the boys, even the older men, excepting for Mada, all had their lighter moments. Savukana Ninga was an old Harijan and he had spent his entire life as a *jita* servant. Unremitting labour in all seasons and weathers coupled with continued hunger and malnutrition had so emaciated his body that it was a bag of skin and bones. He had a sharp, knife-like face with a hooked nose, and I can recall his leathery, unshaven, white-bristled face even now. Ninga narrated a few incidents from his life, and his humour stood out sharply against a background of poverty, misery and oppression.

One hot summer morning when I was walking along the CDS Canal, about thirty feet to the north of the bridge on the Mysore–Hogur road, I saw several workers, men and women, engaged in digging up silt to enable the smooth flow of water when water was let in, in June. This was an annual summer activity and it, like road repair, provided employment to some villagers during the leanest part of the year.

I stopped near the workers and started focussing my camera on them. One woman, who was carrying a basket of earth on her head, and perspiring freely in the sun, commented, 'Had we known that we were going to be photographed, we would have worn our good saris.' The comment provoked loud laughter. Villagers invariably wore their best clothes for the camera but they were not ideal for canal-digging!

A few men in the village were known for their freedom from normal inhibitions when talking to some women. Karim cracked loud jokes with the Harijan women who worked regularly for the

Headman. Sannu, the priest, was another and he was, on occasion, extremely obscene. For instance, he and Chari, the accountant, ran into Oilwoman Loki, sitting by the road and selling fried *vadas*. Sannu sat down and started teasing her. He asked her about the functions of each part of the female genitalia. After a while Loki got annoyed and said, 'Oh Priest, does your bottom itch?' The question was a warning to Sannu to shut up.

Kulle Gowda had a dry wit but it showed itself only with his equals and inferiors. When he was teased, he came out with a profanity or obscenity, or an astringent observation that amused those around him. He was also one of those men who talked freely to women though he did not go as far as Sannu.

A sense of humour probably enabled the poor and exploited to accept the conditions under which they were living, and it may also have been a substitute for more destructive expressions of interpersonal violence. But it is also possible that I am giving it far more importance than it really had. Another sociologist less desiccated and more compassionate might have given it a much less prominent place. And it is even possible that had I stayed among the Harijans instead of with the Peasants, I would have accorded a lower place to humour in village life. But as I write these lines I recall that Pijja and Savukane Ninga, both of whom were Harijans, had a keen sense of humour.

CHAPTER X

Religion

1 Introduction

I SHALL make only a few general remarks on religion in Rampura and shall avoid details. This is only making a virtue of necessity as this chapter, like its predecessors, is based entirely on my memory except for a small part of a section.

Foreign travellers, missionaries and administrators who have written on Indian religion have concentrated, by and large, on the exotic and sensational elements in it such as the multiplicity of deities, their bloodthirstiness and cruelty, fantastic shapes and forms, and their immorality; on the outlandish beliefs and customs, excessive ritualism and wasteful expenditure at weddings and funerals; and finally, on the sense of hopelessness, despair and fatalism, induced by the endless round of birth and rebirth. Westernized Indians have been, as a rule, critics and reformers of folk religion, and with rare exceptions, have dismissed it as 'superstition'. One hundred and fifty years of sustained attack on their traditional culture and religion have put Westernized Indians permanently on the defensive. This led to, among other things, an emphasis on those aspects of culture and religion which presented a 'good' image of India to foreigners and a denigration if not repudiation of the other aspects. Even attempts at reform seem to have been reinforced by a desire to present a decent cultural shop-window to foreigners.

The efflorescence in Indological research in the nineteenth century also led indirectly to downgrading folk religion. The translation of Indian scriptures and philosophical literature into English and other European languages, and the excitement which they caused in Western academic circles, brought considerable satisfaction to educated Indians. An overemphasis on the scriptural-theological dimension of Hinduism and it sects was the natural result.

Yet another factor worked towards the ignoring of folk religion. Educated Indians, by and large, hailed from the higher castes, and they had a built-in prejudice against ritual involving the bloody slaughter of animals, consumption of native, low-status liquor, and of fire-walking, hook-swinging and other cruel customs. It is not surprising that their accounts of religion underplayed these features and highlighted those which were flattering to the national ego.

If any category of scholars could have redressed the balance in favour of folk religion it ought to have been Indian anthropologists and sociologists. But unfortunately their success in this has not been conspicuous. For one thing, the study of religion did not become fashionable in the two disciplines until recent years. And even now religion is important only in the relation it bears, largely negative though, to two concerns which are felt to be paramount to developing countries, economic development and modernization. Further, leading Indian anthropologists and sociologists profess to be rationalists. In brief, the prevalent academic climate has not been conducive to treating folk religion seriously.

I have stated earlier that I had a visceral aversion to watching the spilling of blood, and to ritual involving cruelty to man and beast. But I was aware of my prejudices and considered them deficiencies in one wanting to study a sub-culture different from his own in some respects. But I did have an interest in ritual and religion though I wish I had had the time to make more systematic observations than I was able to. Above all, I had a deep respect for the religion of the people, and I had no desire to change it. When I examined my own faith, I found that it contained many elements which were present in the people's, and I did not regard this as something that I should be ashamed of.

Much has been said by foreign observers on the crippling effects, for individual and social endeavour, of the fatalistic ideology of Indians, in particular of rural folk. I wonder whether 'fatalism' did indeed have such effects on nineteenth century Indians, but if my own experience of Rampura in 1948 is any guide, it was likely that the foreign observers had misunderstood the part played by 'fatalism'. It came in handy usually as an explanation of a disaster that had already occurred and not as inhibiting present or future action. For instance, when a villager had lost a bullock at the height of the agricultural season, or his wife had died suddenly leaving behind young children, and then he or his friends explained his misfortune by reference to *karma* or *hane baraha*. *Karma* was only very occasionally used in its ordinary sense, viz. the kind of deeds a person performed in a particular incarnation (*janma*) determined the pattern of his life in the next. *Hane baraha*, the idea that what was written (by Brahma or fate) on the forehead would come to pass, was again used with reference to past events. I did not hear any villagers talking about Brahma, the Creator, recording each man's future on his forehead as soon as he was born, but a sudden misfortune or combination of misfortunes invariably prompted someone to refer to the 'writing on the forehead'.

Misfortunes were only too frequent in village India. The villager's pitiful resources, economic and intellectual, and his continuous struggles with the forces, natural and human, ranged against him, made him a frequent victim of disaster. The lack of any medical attention coupled with the total ignorance of the rules of sanitation made childbirth hazardous, and the frequent epidemics which carried off large numbers of people gave a chancy character to life. If to this were added undependable rains, insect and other pests, and vermin, extortionate landowners, usurious moneylenders and corrupt officials, we get an idea of the risks faced by farmers in growing a crop and the demands he had to meet. It was indeed a miracle that he managed to survive.

Living by immemorial custom offered a sense of security to the villagers but this was not without a price. Strict conformity was demanded from everyone, and the non-conformist who dared to violate custom ran the risk of being ostracized. Ostracism was particularly harsh in a small, face-to-face community where everyone knew everyone else. The community was also linked by agnatic, affinal, economic and other ties with neighbouring villages so that news travelled quickly along established networks.

Individuals were expected to spend as lavishly as they could on such occasions as weddings and funerals. The rich had naturally to spend far more than the poor. Failure to do so meant accusations of meanness or impiety. While tight-fistedness was the rule in everyday life, it had no place at weddings and funerals. The above norms were built into a villager from very early in life and internalized. Individuals were powerless to alter the value-system of the community. It could change, if at all, only as a result of the impact of powerful external forces as, for instance, when the leaders of the village introduced a few reforms in the thirties.

It is pointless to blame individual villagers for indulging in wasteful if not suicidal expenditure at weddings and funerals. It is understandable for foreign observers to be struck by the 'irrationality' of such behaviour but the same cannot be said of Westernized Indians who are themselves given to wasteful expenditure at weddings and funerals.

The villagers were heirs to a rich and complex religious life. The richer households among the Peasants usually had a more Sanskritized style of life than their poorer caste-fellows and this meant that they spent more time and money on their religious duties.

It is difficult to characterize the complexity of the religious life of villagers beyond stating that there was a multitude of deities and festivals, and that life-cycle crises were marked by ritual, which were sometimes elaborate as at marriage and death. The deities included gods as well as goddesses, some of whom demanded blood-sacrifices. The calendrical festivals were common to the region while some of them had even an all-India spread. The festivals of village deities were, on the other hand, purely local in character, and they generally lasted several days, and were frequently characterized by blood-sacrifices and by the performance of *pavadas* or 'miracles' in which the priest or other participant became possessed by the deity and answered questions.

There were also pilgrimages to the shrines of 'house deities', and to the great centres of Sanskritic Hinduism in south India.

Finally, no account of village religion would be complete without a brief reference to the phenomenon of possessions by deities and spirits (*gali*).

As stated above, marriage and death were marked by elaborate and complex ritual. Marriage itself began with the search for a bride and ended only when the wife joined her husband for good. Each step in this process was regulated by custom and interwoven with ritual. Mourning ritual began with death and ended only on the thirteenth day when a feast was given to relatives. The dead man (or woman) joined the body of apotheosized ancestors who were propitiated annually during the 'ancestors' fortnight' (*pitru paksha*) prior to the Dasara festival while among the Brahmins and a few other castes, the annual propitiation was on the anniversary of the actual day of death. The ritual surrounding birth ended on the eleventh day when pollution ended for everyone except the mother. The puberty of a girl resulted in her becoming impure for fifteen days at the end of which she was dressed in her best sari and jewelry, and made to sit on a wooden plank while women relatives performed some ritual, sang songs and offered her sweets and other good things to eat. As it was usual among the higher castes to have girls married before they came of age, consummation took place a few weeks after puberty. An auspicious day was selected by the astrologer for the ceremony, and relatives and friends were invited to a pre-consummation feast. The groom left his wife's bedside early in the morning, and stole away quietly to his house, without seeing any member of his wife's household.

There were variations between castes in life-cycle ritual, Brahmins, Lingayats and other Sanskritized castes spending more time and money on ritual than the others. The life of Brahmins in particular was permeated with ritual. Every Brahmin household had a domestic altar where *puja* was performed before the morning meal was eaten. Every adult Brahmin had to perform certain ritual acts daily (*nitya karma*), and besides, even acts like shaving, bathing, eating, defecating and urinating were accompanied by ritual. During the last few decades, however, the process of secularization had gone far enough to reduce the time spent on ritual as also the hold of ideas regarding purity and pollution. In 1948, for instance, of the three Brahmins in Rampura only the Rama priest lived like a Brahmin. The other two were preoccupied with their jobs. However, I should be surprised if they did not worship at the domestic altar every day before the morning meal.

I have discussed the ideas of purity (*maḍi*) and pollution (*mailige*) in my account of inter-caste relations. But these two linked ideas are also important in analysing life-cycle and daily ritual. But I shall not consider them here as I have discussed them at some length in my Coorg book,[1] and they apply more or less fully to the situation in Rampura.

The division of labour between the sexes expressed itself in ritual also. For instance, women cleaned the domestic altar and puja vessels, prepared the food or other article to be offered to the deities, and lit the lamps while the men performed the actual worship. This was particularly true of worship which was complex and lengthy among the Sanskritized castes. The priests, both those who were in charge of temples and the specialists in life-cycle ritual, were always men.

Older men and women were usually more ritual-bound than the younger, and the presence of an old woman in a household meant its

[1] *Religion and Society among the Coorgs of South India*, Chapter III, pp. 101-22, Clarendon Press, Oxford, 1952.

adherence to a traditional mode of life. There were several old women in Rampura like the headman's mother. The women adhered more closely to the rules of pollution and purity than the men, and the kitchen, which usually included the domestic altar, was the heart of the purity-pollution system. The women kept the men on the pollution track, and this was probably related to the fact that the social world of women was synonymous with the household and kinship group while the men inhabited a more heterogeneous world.

The subject of the complexity of village religion cannot be complete without a reference, however brief, to its 'underworld', viz. sorcery and witchcraft. Rampura in 1948 did not have a single sorcerer or witch though I did hear people citing the instances of individuals who had sought to acquire supernatural powers by spending nights in graveyards, digging up corpses, sitting on them and performing gory rites. But these were only stories which they had heard from someone or the other and no one in the village practised them. However, the bulldozer driver who was levelling the headman's land in the summer of 1952 was a practitioner of the black art. He even gave a black magic performance just as the wandering group of Garudigas had done in the summer of 1948. The bulldozer driver was a Tamil non-Brahmin. His powers so impressed the second son of the Basava priest, a maverick, that he enlisted himself as a pupil. Modern machine had also brought black magic to Rampura. (Students of modernization only emphasize the machine.)

2 The Many Kinds of Deities

The villagers propitiated a wide variety of deities from the high gods and goddesses of all-India Hinduism in their various manifestations, incarnations and identifications to local ones presiding over epidemics such as smallpox, cholera and plague, and others who had an intimate association with lineages and households. Indeed, the number and variety of deities seemed bewildering at first sight but was much less so if they were grouped into a few categories on the basis of well-recognized principles.

There was specialization among the deities and the degree of specialization varied from deity to deity. For instance, the deities presiding over epidemics were the most specialized of all and they were propitiated elaborately during epidemics or at their periodical festivals. It was their job to protect the village from the epidemics in return for propitiation. Before modern public health measures reached the villages, epidemics were frequent, killing substantial numbers. The generic name for the deity presiding over epidemics was Mari though she was also occasionally known by other names such as Kali. The Maris of different villages were distinguished by prefixing the village name to Mari. Thus the Mari of Kere village was known as *Kere Mari*. Sometimes she was merely referred to as *amma* or 'mother'.

As already described in Chapter IV, the rains, their occurrence at proper times and in proper quantities, as well as their failure, were a most important preoccupation of the villagers. Basava was the deity primarily concerned with rains since he was responsible for the welfare of cattle. Madeshwara of Gudi also came into the picture probably because he was regarded as very powerful. He was prayed to to ensure the safe delivery of cows. This function was perhaps derived from the fact that the main Madeshwara temple in Kollegal *taluk* was a centre for cattle trade during the four calendrical festivals (Shivaratri, Ugadi, Dasara and Deepavali) when villagers from far and wide flocked to it.

Other deities were also prayed to during a drought. The fact of caste was also relevant in this context, and I expect that Brahmins worried by the drought would pray to Rama or some other Sanskritic deity. In a grave crisis they would have the arduous *parjanya japa* performed by a group of Brahmins proficient in the ritual.

The continuity of the household was also of supreme concern to the villagers. This required that the women coming in by marriage were fertile and that the children born to them survived into adulthood and kept reasonable health. Without the household surviving, the family farm would lie fallow, thus underlining the link between human and chthonic fertility. One of the worst curses in the armoury of a villager, was 'May the *ekka* (*arka, Calatropic gigantea*) grow on your house'. The plant grew wild and one of the signs of a decayed house was the sprouting of the *ekka* plants all over the abandoned site. A more direct and less symbolic form of the curse was, 'May your house come to an end'.

Another category of deities concerned with the well-being of the household (and lineage) were the 'house deities' (*mane devaru*). I shall consider them later and rest content here with stating that if the 'house deities' proved unhelpful, the villagers approached any deity who they thought was likely to help. This kind of situation provided a door for the introduction of new deities, cults, and of even sanyasis, gurus, and charlatans who promised all sorts of benefits. I have referred repeatedly to the popularization, since the 1930s, of the cult of Tirupati Srinivasa. Again, in the neighbouring village of Kere I saw what was perhaps the beginnings of the cult of Sathyanarayana. This deity was popular over a great part of India, and propitiating him regularly by reading an account of his doings was believed to benefit the devotee both materially and spiritually.

Each temple in the village had a special association with a particular caste or group of castes. The Basava and Madeshwara temples, for instance, had Lingayats for priests, and attracted devotees from non-Brahmin castes. The latter part of the statement is, however, subject to two qualifications: Harijans were excluded from the temples of caste Hindus, and castes which were staunch followers of Vishnu had either nominal or no association with the Basava and Madeshwara temples which were Shaivite. There were at least three non-Brahmin castes which had a Vaishnavite orientation: one tiny household of Oshtama which traditionally supplied priests to Anjaneya (or Hanuman) temples; the Trader households which had as their lineage-deity Narasimha (half-man, half-lion), an incarnation (*avatara*)[1] of Vishnu, and finally, the Swineherds who had Srinivasa of Tirupati as their lineage-deity.

The division into Shaiva and Vaishnava sects was sharper in south India than in the North, and was found at different levels of the caste system. Among Brahmins, the Sri Vaishnavas (popularly called Iyengars) and Madhwas were both exclusive devotees of Vishnu while, among non-Brahmins, the Lingayats were exclusive devotees of Shiva. (Not long ago, orthodox Iyengars used to boast that they had never stepped into a Shiva temple.) Even when a whole caste or a section of it were not followers of a sect, individual households could develop an affiliation to a sect either directly or indirectly. Thus attachment to the Madeshwara temple resulted in increased contact with Lingayat priests, gurus and a Shaivite life-style, while association with a temple to Narasimha meant usually increased contact with Iyengar (or Madhwa) priests and a Vaishnavite lifestyle. Individuals from every non-Brahmin caste were free to join

---

[1] The deity Vishnu, who has the role of protector in the Hindu pantheon, incarnated himself repeatedly to crush evil forces which assumed the form of demons. Incarnations are not, however, confined to the mythic past: the pious believe that they occur whenever evil increases.

either the Vaishnavite mendicant order of Dasayya or Shaivite order of Jogayya. I shall discuss this later.

At the main village temple to Mari the priest (*gudda*) was a Peasant. (As mentioned elsewhere, the Harijans had a separate temple for Mari at which one of their castemen was priest.) This temple, like certain others in the village, was really active only on a few days in the year when a votive or other propitiation was taking place, or a regular festival was being held. For instance, the Mari temple at Rampura did not have an elaborate annual festival as at the Mari temple in Kere but was only propitiated when an epidemic of smallpox, chickenpox or cholera was about. In addition, any household in which a child was affected with chickenpox took the child to the temple after recovery, and worshipped the deity.

The duties of the priest in any one of these temples were not particularly onerous except very occasionally. Ordinarily the priest was expected to keep the earthen lamp in the *sanctum sanctorum* lit every evening, or on a particular day in the week, considered sacred to the deity. Sometimes, on the weekly sacred day, the priest was expected to have a bath, change into washed clothes and worship the deity before having his morning meal. I do not know how scrupulously such rules were observed in each case but I am certain that not every priest obeyed the rules expected of him. For instance, I do not remember the earthen lamp in the Mari temple being lit except on a few rare occasions, and it was in some ways an important temple. In this respect, the Madeshwara, Basava and Rama temples were different. The priests had to perform puja every morning and evening, though they, if they wanted to, abbreviated the service, and skimped on the offerings to be made. It may be recalled here that each grower gave the priest of each of the temples a headload of rice-in-the-straw and this was to ensure that the daily offerings were kept going everywhere. An honest priest offered a rice-dish every day to his deity, and he distributed at least some of it to the devotees present. Villagers felt that not only was the deity being deprived of something which was his due but the villagers of their share. Only at festivals and other special occasions was cooked food offered on a big scale but then additional collections were made for them. Here again, ordinary villagers complained of the meanness of priests who distributed minuscule portions to poorer devotees while taking care to send sizeable parcels to the leaders. The rule of reciprocity was being broken everywhere: between man and god, and between the priests and the villagers. I have a feeling that I heard complaints only about the Rama priest partly because villagers resented the attention which he paid to his land, and which, they believed, was at the expense of his other duties. On the other hand, the idea of Lingayat priests cultivating land did not appear grotesque.

The God's House lineage had a shrine to their tutelary deities in their ward, and an old member of the lineage was priest at the shrine. The deities had a reputation for fierceness and the priest was particular about bathing every day and lighting the lamps in the shrine.

The Rama temple had been endowed with two or three acres of rice land (far less than either the Madeshwara or Basava temple) and the priest had built for himself a hut on the vacant ground opposite the temple. The Rama Navami, marking the birth of the deity, was the most important of the annual festivals celebrated in the temple. It was next in importance only to the annual *jatra* of Madeshwara at Deepavali which attracted thousands of devotees from dozens of villages, and which brought in a considerable amount of money to the villagers in various ways. The priests were of course the biggest beneficiaries from the fair.

While in the old village the Rama temple had a close association with the Brahmins living in the *agrahara*, in 1948 it was the Peasant leaders who were in charge of it. They had raised the money to rebuild it: it was the most handsome building in the village, and it must have taken a few years to build it. The headman and Nadu Gowda personally supervised the collection of contributions, in cash and kind, for the Ugadi and Rama Navami festivals. The priest was aware of his dependence on the two leaders, in particular the headmen. If the priest was tolerated in the village it was because of the headman and Nadu Gowda.

It is likely that when the village had several households of Brahmins, some of whom were rich and influential, they controlled the Rama temple. But after their exodus to the cities, the temple came completely under the authority of the Peasant leaders, and its linkage with Brahmins was snapped.

The Madeshwara temple belonged really to Gudi people but as Gudi was a 'dry' and poor village, the priests had sought the patronage of the powerful leaders of Rampura. Sannu narrated to me how his grandfather moved from the tiny, ancestral hamlet of Chaudhary Koppal, located to the north of Gudi, to Rampura when the headman's father was a young man. The latter agreed to their staying in

Rampura and allotted them a site. Sannu told me that his grandfather heard the growl of a tiger at night during the first few nights of his arrival. Madeshwara rode a tiger, and the growls were interpreted as an auspicious symbol. The main temple to Madeshwara (of which the Gudi temple was an imitation) was situated in dense jungle, and the association of tiger and cobra with the awe-inspiring deity was only appropriate. But paradoxically the deity who rode a tiger, and whose hair was adorned by a coiling cobra, was also a protector of cattle. I did not inquire whether this came from the identification of Madeshwara with Shiva whose 'vehicle' is a bull (Nandi), or because of the cattle fairs held at the deity's festival, or because of both.

The linkage between Bire *devaru* (or Birappa, as he was popularly called) and the Shepherds was an intimate one, and the favourite animal for sacrificing to him was sheep. (Another way of stating the relationship was sheep: Shepherd: Birappa). Periodical festivals lasting several days at which elaborate ritual was performed, were held in honour of Birappa, and the Birappas of a region formed a hierarchy. Once in several years, a festival was held in which all of them were involved, and the ritual, which was even more elaborate than at the festivals of individual deities, reflected the hierarchy. A sharp sense of protocol between the deities characterized the festival which was in some ways like a drama, the processions of two deities meeting and then going to meet a third and so on.

There were temples to Birappa in neighbouring villages though not in Rampura. One of my neighbours, a very old man, was a priest (*gudda*) at one such temple. He was referred to as *Devara-guddayya* (literally, 'god's priest'), and he cooked his own food because he was a vegetarian while his daughter and her husband, with whom he stayed, were not. I used to see the old man, returning home in the evening after a day's work on the farm, with a headload of *jowar* stalks on his head. He was a man of few words, and he was respected for his vegetarianism and teetotalism. His only luxury was chewing betel leaves and nuts, which must have been an effort, for some of his front teeth had dropped out. Even though twenty-six years have passed, I can still recall his face, with its steel-grey, walrus moustache, lined with age and unremitting work and shining with sweat as he walked up, single-mindedly, to his house.

I have referred earlier to the discrimination to which the Smiths were traditionally subjected in this region. The caste deity of the Smiths was Kali, usually referred to as Kalamma, and only in towns or large villages in which they were represented in large numbers were there temples to her. (There was a Kali temple in Mysore, for instance.) Traditionally, Smith marriages were performed either at pilgrim-centres or in Kali temples.

Rampura, like most other villages in the region, did not have a Kali temple. But a few at least of the traditional disabilities had vanished as, for instance, was evidenced in the headman's households treating Smith and Brahmin married women on an equal footing during the Rama Navami festival.

Other castes in the village which did not have temples of their own were the Traders, Swineherds and Basketry-makers. The last-mentioned were really temporary immigrants who were expected to return to their home-town after spending a few years in Rampura. They seemed to be Vaishnavites in the sense that they were devotees of Srinivasa at Tirupati. The Swineherds had spent a much longer period in Rampura than the Basketry-makers, and also many households from other castes, but, for reasons mentioned earlier, they seemed marginal to village social life. They had come from Telugu-speaking areas adjacent to Bangalore, and if their names were any indication to their faith, they were Vaishnavites. The Traders were integral to the village economy and society and they were all Vaishnavites, the men colourfully indicating their allegiance by decorating their foreheads, every morning, with *namam*. Their names suggested that their 'house-deity' was Narasimha.

As stated earlier, the association of a caste or group of castes with a deity did not prevent them from seeking the aid of some other deity when it was necessary or expedient to do so. Thus during a smallpox epidemic everyone, including Brahmins, sent their offerings to Mari. I was told of Brahmins even making animal sacrifices to Mari through their non-Brahmin friends, though I personally did not come across any instance of it. I was also told of Muslims who sent votive offerings of milk and buttermilk to Madeshwara in thanks for the safe calving of their cows. Similarly Hindus, even urban, educated Hindus, visited the graves of Muslim *pirs* in the hope of having their wishes granted.

Castes whose temples were located outside the village did also develop an allegiance, over a period of time, to local deities and temples. It is here that the tendency of Hinduism to add any number of new deities to the list already worshipped, proved so convenient. Gradually, over the decades, the links with old deities became weakened as it happened with old friends with whom interaction had ceased. But when a member of the family died suddenly or fell seriously ill, or there was a series of inexplicable disasters, then an old man or woman in the kinship group asked the rhetorical question, 'What else could be expected when new water flushed out the old water, and old gods were no longer worshipped?' The afflicted family then visited the neglected deities, begged their pardon for long neglect. Old ties were renewed.

But when a caste had strong sectarian loyalties, or the basis of its formation was sectarian as with Lingayats, Sri Vaishnavas and Madhwas, there was a built-in resistance to worshipping deities from another sect. Similarly, Brahmins had a resistance to worshipping deities to which animals were sacrificed, and high non-Brahmins to deities who not only demanded meat but liquor. And, of course, caste Hindus did not worship a deity associated with Harijans exclusively.

3 The Character of the Deities

Deities differed from each other not only in their functions but in their personalities and character. This was particularly seen in the contrast between the mild, vegetarian deity Rama and the fierce Mari who was traditionally propitiated with the sacrifice of bull buffaloes. (Indeed, in those parts of South India where the male buffalo was not used as a draught animal, its only use was to be decapitated before Mari.) The villagers were so scared of Mari during an epidemic that they prayed to her to leave them and go away.

The propitiation of Mari during the hot summer months was called *tampu ereyuvudu* ('cooling her'). Her shrine was decorated with *margosa* (*Melia azadirachta*) twigs, and the margosa was well known for cool shade during summer. Married women (or virgins) carried trays each containing a green coconut (*elnir*), *kalasha* (a brass vessel containing some water whose mouth was stoppered with a coconut and a few betel leaves placed between the nut and vessel's rim) and *tambittu* (a dish of rice-flour sweetened with jaggery) and a set of betel leaves and arecanuts. Frequently, a hollow was scooped out in the flattened top of the rice-flour pyramid and filled with *ghi* in which a cotton wick was inserted and lit. This kind of lamp was generally made in fulfilment of a vow (*harake*), and the members of the household each ate a piece of the votive flour after the wick had burnt down.

Mari roused in her devotees craven fear and not love. and this fear rose to terror when an epidemic was actually on. Tradition-minded villagers afflicted with smallpox or cholera refused to take any allopathic medicine for fear that it would anger the deity further. Margosa twigs were kept near the patient, he was fanned with them, and after he had recovered, the leaves were put into the cauldron in which water was heated for his bath. It was only after this puri-ficatory bath that he visited Mari's temple to express thanks for his recovery. Mari was indeed an odd kind of 'mother' (*amma, avva, tayi*), one who killed her offspring right and left when she was angry with them. Mari was a different kind of mother from the human mother.

The villagers were afraid of not only Mari and other deities who demanded blood-sacrifices, but even of some vegetarian deities. For instance, Madeshwara evoked respect bordering on fear from his devotees. He was a celibate and misogynist. According to local tradition, the original site of the temple in Gudi was much higher than it is now, and the tower of the Chamundeshwari temple cresting the hill in Mysore was visible from there. Madeshwara was so in-censed at the sight of that offensive tower that he pressed the land down into a hollow from which it was invisible.[1]

Before World War II, pilgrimages to the main Madeshwara temple, in Kollegal Taluk in Mysore district, were undertaken on foot. Villagers trekked across miles of dense jungle in long convoys during the pilgrimage season. They had to carry their food with them, and drinking water was difficult to find. They had to be in a state of purity, and sex relations were tabooed during the pilgrimage. Hus-band and wife were required to address each other as 'brother' and 'sister', and women who expected to be in their periods before the journey had been completed did not undertake the pilgrimage.

I must digress here briefly. At various places in the book I have stressed the great hold Madeshwara had over the minds of villagers in Mysore and Mandya districts. The simple yet total faith which they had in the deity, and the risks they took in undertaking the pilgrimage to his main shrine—and many of them went every year —were most impressive. And the Madeshwara cult was the source of an ethic and world-view which was contrary to the villagers'

---

[1] The Sanskritic identification of the jungle deity of Madeshwara is neither complete nor clear. If it were complete, the goddess Chamundi (a manifestation of Parvati) would be his wife.

natural acceptance of the biological dimension of life. (There were similar cults elsewhere in south India, Shasta's in Kerala being an outstanding example.) This means that villagers were subjected to two contrary value pulls, one propelling them towards the total acceptance of the bodily appetites, and another, away from them. Hence the deep reverence in village culture—indeed in Indian culture as a whole—to the *sanyasi*, and holy man who had conquered his bodily appetites. Bodily processes symbolized and limited the human condition while conquering them was a mark of divinity.

The kind of relation that obtained between Madeshwara and the villagers was illustrated in an incident which occurred in the summer of 1952 when a new *teru* (elaborate wooden chariot in which the deity was taken out in procession at festivals and other special occasions) was being built. Much energy was spent in searching for the right kind of wood, and of course, at the cheapest possible price, and Sannu's older cousin, Thammayya, whose turn it was to be priest for the year, went round likely villages in his search of timber. He ended up by buying a big tree in Ganjam, and I shall pass over the problems of felling it and cutting its branches to suitable lengths and hauling them to the temple site. A carpenter with the necessary skill was brought in from another village for making the *teru*. But he had to have assistants, and Virachari, a local Smith, was asked to help him. He was an old man, and he had been running a temperature. At least, that was what he told Sannu's cousin when he was asked to assist the master-carpenter. But he nonetheless presented himself at the temple on the following morning. And he had a tale to tell. He found himself waking up before dawn, shivering and perspiring, for he had felt the sharp swish of a thin cane (*chadi*) across his back. He took some time to realize that it was only a dream but that did not help in preventing him from shivering with fright. He concluded that Madappa (that was how the deity was ordinarily referred to by the villagers) had been angry at his reluctance to turn up for work on the *teru*. He told all this to me later in the evening and I could sense the fear on his face even as he recalled the swish of the cane on his bare back.

The deity Srinivasa of Tirupati, to whom the richer villagers were fast developing an allegiance, had also a reputation for sternness. A promise made to him had to be kept and he did not treat broken promises lightly. He also granted favours to those who believed in him.

In contrast to Mari and Madeshwara, Basava was a mild deity. I do not have in mind here the fact that he was incapable of controlling his lecherous priest as such a charge could also be levelled at some other deities with a reputation for extreme sternness. (Indeed, in the wider society as a whole the corruption, cynicism and greed of priests was a part of the folklore.) I have in mind the villagers' belief that Basava had migrated to a temple in a village across the river because of anger over the priest's conduct. Basava had done a similar thing a few years previously. Going away from a place because one was angry was more typical of women than men, and that the symbol of unbridled masculinity, the bull, should behave like that only sharpened the paradox.

The sanction at the disposal of Basava was withholding rain but even here his was not a case of exclusive jurisdiction as, for instance, Mari's was over epidemics. Madeshwara, and even Rama, could be appealed to for rain.

However, Basava was not entirely without a stern element in him. I was told that during a cholera epidemic, several people heard, late in the night, the ringing of a cow bell and the sound of the ground being pawed by a bull to the accompaniment of angry snorts. A few men got up from their beds and went out to investigate the matter. Nowhere did they sight a bull. In the morning, they compared notes and concluded that Basava was angry and had to be propitiated.

I do not think a deity who was totally devoid of sternness could have won the allegiance of villagers. He was most likely to be ignored.

I must here refer to the concept of 'satya' (literally, truth) as applied to deities. A deity who answered the devotee's prayer had *satya*. I generally heard it mentioned in positive contexts and not in negative ones. That is, such-and-such a deity had *satya* while another had 'much *satya*' (*bahala satya*) but I did not hear of any deity as lacking in *satya*. Either this was due to the fear that such a charge might provoke the deity in question to retaliate, or because of an unstated assumption that all deities had *satya*. I can even imagine a situation in which a few devotees debated as to which of the various deities known to them had the greatest *satya*, but not one in which they debated the question of which deity (or deities) lacked *satya*.

Implicit in the idea of *satya* was the ability of deities to answer the prayers of devotees, to grant them the things they wanted such as good health, children, good harvests and money. In return for the sense of security and other benefits which they received from their deities, devotees propitiated them.

This way of stating things might appear crassly mercenary but it should be remembered that the ordinary villager was engaged continuously in a life-and-death struggle with his environment, natural and social, and his religion and gods had to be relevant to his struggle. He had no time for high-falutin theology. His reverence for the *sanyasi* who had renounced the world was undoubtedly genuine, but he did not consider it cynical to expect returns from hospitality and reverence to *sanyasis*. In popular thinking at any rate, *sanyasis* were credited with having powers which ordinary mortals did not.

4   House Deities and Sectarian Orders

The institution of house deities (*mane devaru*) had an importance even outside religion. When several households had the same house deity (or deities), it was frequently indicative of the existence of an agnatic linkage between them. This was useful in tracing links between the poorest sections of the village population which tended to have shallow genealogies. House deities were also useful in finding out the village from which a household or group of households had migrated to Rampura. For the bond between a household and its deities was a persistent one though the kind and intensity of contact varied from one household to another. It also varied according to the nearness of the original village, length of residence in the new village, the economic position of the household, and the kind of treatment which the household had received from the deity. In the case of the largest agnatic kin-group in the village, viz. God's House lineage, it was far more convenient to have a shrine built locally than for the thirty odd households to make the difficult journey every year. Another leading household which was otherwise scrupulous in the observance of its religious obligations, did not maintain any relation with its house deity except to name one of the sons after him, the reason being the death, many years ago, of a male child when the members were on a pilgrimage to the deity's temple. It was regarded as a particularly hostile act on the deity's part.

The intensity of the contact with the house deity varied from annual visits to once in every few years. But there were also some who had not visited their house deity for several years. Periodical visits were not, however, the only way of keeping contact with the house deity. For instance, an offering could be sent through a kinsman or friend. And even those who did not visit the house deity followed the custom of naming one of their children after him. At the hands of a man who had an intimate knowledge of the region, the names which regularly recurred in a genealogy provided clues to the identity of the house deity, and occasionally, to the lineage's sectarian orientation. There was also a negative rule regarding names: two living members of the household were not allowed to have the same name. Usually this meant the male child being named after the father's father (if the latter was dead), and the female child after her father's mother. In many genealogies, the members of alternate generations had the same names. But among the richer and more urbanized households names had begun changing. Such traditional names as Mada, Sidda, Beera, Kempa, Javara and Kala were giving way to Srinivasa, Ramaswamy, Narayana, Krishna, Srikanta and Shankara. (Interestingly enough, in the urban areas, the educated upper castes were busy changing from these names to secular name such as Ashok, Sanjay, Ravi and Mohan.)

With the non-Brahmin castes the house deity was frequently a village god or goddess demanding blood sacrifice. With some households, however, the house deity was a high god of Sanskritic Hinduism. Thus one Peasant household had as its deity Chenna Keshava of Belur and another, Narayana of Melkote. Where a Sanskritic god was the house deity, his consort was also worshipped, and her name was given to female children.

Under certain circumstances, a household sought protection from a new deity. The latter was referred to as '*mare bidda devaru*' or 'deity from whom shelter was sought'. Sometimes, the new deity completely eclipsed the old. Occasionally, new and prestigious cults were added to the old ones: I have referred to the increasingly popular cult of Srinivasa of Tirupati, and as the villagers' contacts with the wider world increased and diversified, there were likely to be further additions.

In fact, in the case of the richer and more influential families the cults observed were a layered whole providing an account of their religious evolution from the propitiation of strictly local village deities to all-India gods and *gurus* and sanyasis.

The household (and the lineage) was also the channel through which other religious traditions besides that of the house deity were perpetuated. I have earlier shown, for instance, how the special association between a particular caste and a temple was perpetuated through the household. This was not only true of the households which supplied one male member as priest (*gudda*) to the temple but of the others.

The household and not caste was the principal institution for perpetuating sectarianism. In fact, even the local section of a *jati* was not always homogeneous from a sectarian point of view. But where the entire caste was homogeneous, individual households did not have any elbow room except very occasionally when the head of a household came under the influence of a guru or monastery or temple belonging to a different sect. This had happened, for instance, with Shepherd Chenna whose caste was Shaivite in orientation but had come under the influence of a Vaishnavite guru. Nadu Gowda had also come under the influence of a Sri Vaishnava guru and monastery. The Oilman brothers had come under the powerful spell of a great Shaivite pilgrim centre. And so on.

Sectarian differentiation had occurred in Hinduism right from its earliest days, and during the medieval period, south India was the centre of some significant departures in doctrine. To begin with, the great Hindu theologian Shankara propounded the theory of *advaita* or monism (the idea that the individual soul was identical in nature with god, and that its eventual destiny was to merge in the latter). Ramanuja, coming two centuries after Shankara, had criticized *advaita*, proposed in its place *vishistadvaita* or qualified monism, according to which the individual soul did not totally merge in god but retained a sense of its identity even when united. Ramanuja was followed two centuries later by Madhwa, who advocated *dwaita* or dualism in which the individual soul and god were regarded as distinct entities. *Bhakti*, or devotion towards god, was far more important in the doctrinal systems of Ramanuja and Madhwa than in that of Shankara. Incidentally, Shankara was a devotee of Shiva while Ramanuja and Madhwa were both devotees of Vishnu.

Another significant development in the field of sectarianism came from Basava, the founder of Virashaivasm (militant Shaivism), popularly referred to as Lingayatism. Basava was roughly contemporaneous with Ramanuja, but he was not preoccupied with theological niceties and system-building. He was a forthright advocate of *bhakti* towards god (represented by the symbol of Shiva, the *linga*, which every Lingayat, male and female, had to wear round his neck), of the equality of all human beings irrespective of caste, and of the importance of manual labour for all. A corollary of the importance of *bhakti* was the downgrading of ritualism and of the authority of the scriptures, including the Vedas. Lingayatism was far more important than the three other sects founded by Shankara, Ramanuja and Madhwa, if judged solely by its influence on the masses, including those from the lower castes.

The perpetuation of sectarian ideology and practice was assured by the transformation of sects into castes, or a congeries of linked orders. Sectarian affiliation was a crucial principle of caste differentiation among Brahmins in south India while the Lingayats subsumed a number of caste distinctions which, however, are nowadays getting blurred under the impact of democratic politics. The monasteries of the four sectarian castes are presided over by *sanyasis* (referred to as 'Swamijis') who are highly respected by the people. Each sect has more than one monastery, the Lingayats having a large number of monasteries, especially in the northern and western parts of the State. While all the sects have an interest in popularizing their ideology, the Lingayats have been more active as well as more successful in their evangelizing efforts than the others. Entire castes, or sections of castes, have been absorbed into Lingayatism.

All this is preliminary to a brief description of the Dasayya and Jogayya which are two popular priest-cum-mendicant orders among the non-Brahmin castes in rural Mysore. The Dasayyas are a Vaishnavite order while the Jogayyas are Shaivite.

The order of Dasayyas was open to all men of the non-Brahmin castes, including Harijans. A hereditary guru from the Sri Vaishnava (Iyengar) caste performed the ritual which included branding the shoulders of the initiate with the twin symbols of Vishnu's conch (*shankha*) and discus (*chakra*), and teaching him a secret *mantra*. A Dasayya had a uniform, an elaborate one, consisting of a white gown, a coloured cummerbund, a turban, dhoti worn in the Brahminical way, a copper begging bowl slung from the shoulder (*bhuvanasi*), a conch shell for blowing, gong and striker, and a necklace of *tulasi* (*Ocimum sanctum*) beads. He decorated his forehead with the *namam*, and begged on days sacred to Vishnu in the Hindu calendar, such as Saturdays, especially Saturdays in the lunar month of Shravan (August–September). On such days he had to eat food prepared from the grain collected by begging. Among the non-Brahmin castes, a Dasayya was invited on such life-cycle occasions as naming ceremony, wedding, and death when he worshipped the symbols of his sect after which he was given a meal.

While the institution of Dasayya was ideally voluntary, there was a marked tendency for it, as for most things in the village, to become hereditary. At least one son joined the order to carry on the family tradition.

The guru visited his disciples once every few years if not annually. Such a visit was called *shishyarjane* as its main purpose was to collect cash and grain from disciples. It was also the occasion for initiating new candidates and to settle disputes among followers. When a village had several Dasayyas one of them was nominated the head and the guru generally functioned through him.

The guru had also inherited his position: he was a descendant in the agnatic line from one of the men whom Ramanuja, the founder of the sect, had entrusted with the authority to recruit followers. The authority and power of the gurus was therefore derived from their birth in branches descended from the original office-bearer and not from the head of any monastery. Each guru operated in a particular area, and on his death, his sons divided it among themselves. The right to work as guru in an area was treated like any other alienable property, being liable to be sold, mortgaged, rented or inherited. This was the case with other village offices also, religious as well as secular.

The Order of Jogayya was the Shaivite parallel of Dasayya. His uniform was an austere one consisting of a shirt, dhoti worn in *lungi* style, and turban, all ochre-coloured. The Jogayya's begging 'bowl' was a cloth-sling (*jolige*) suspended from the shoulder, the food and grain given by the people being deposited in the sling's bottom, Three horizontal *vibhuti* stripes decorated the Jogayya's forehead. Many a Jogayya had a repertoire of songs and stories about Shiva which he sang while keeping time with his cymbals. Some ballads were indeed long as, for instance, the one about Madeshwara, which could last several nights. A Jogayya frequently repaid hospitality by singing a religious song or ballad on the verandah of his host, and a few villagers sat round him listening, and incidentally, adding to their store of merit.

The initiation of an individual into the Order of Jogayya was carried out in a monastery, and the initiate (or his sponsor) had to pay the expenses of the rite as also a fee. The monastery had a hierarchy of officials the lowest (*chooradararu*) of whom visited villages to collect the annual fee payable by Jogayyas.

Even as recently as the 1930s, respectable Peasants did not like to marry into households which had a tradition of providing recruits for either Order and I was unable to find out why such households were considered inferior. Perhaps the reputation which Dasayyas and Jogayyas had for consuming liquor as part of their duties was responsible for the low esteem in which they were held. I was assured, however, that the consumption of liquor occurred only among those castes which already did so as a matter of custom. It was much more likely that the low status of Dasayyas and Jogayyas was due to their being required to perform priestly and mendicant duties. It is relevant to recall here that priestly households among Brahmins had a low status, and among priests, those who officiated at death were regarded as singularly low. Dasayyas and Jogayyas both had ritual duties at death, and at periodical ancestor propitiations. Again, Dasayyas and Jogayyas were regarded as low only among the landowning and trading castes, and not among the poorest sections of village society. To the latter, on the contrary, membership of the Orders provided a link with high caste organizations and resulted in the Sanskritization of customs and life-style, paving the way to social mobility.

5   Astrology

Astrology is woven into the fabric of Hindu religion as it is lived from day to day. I have already described the institution of reading the forecast for the coming year at the Ugadi festival, but I should add that the experts who prepared the almanac did not all follow a single system of calculation. There were different schools, and the cognoscenti argued among themselves as to which almanac was the most reliable. In princely Mysore, the Maharajah had his own astrologer, and the palace almanac commanded more prestige than the others. I wonder whether the authority of the Maharajah rubbed off onto the almanac.

The almanac also listed the asterisms (*nakshatras*) under which rain was expected as also the inauspicious periods (*Rahu kala, Gulika kala*) in each day of the week when no important or auspicious work was to be started.

An almanac was a necessity to an orthodox Hindu but in Rampura only the Brahmins, the priestly Lingayats and a few others had almanacs in their homes. When a poor and illiterate villager wanted to start an important job he found out from the Rama priest a suitable date and time for it.

But the Rama priest's knowledge of astrology was minimal, and those who wanted more expert advice had to seek it outside the village. Since only the Brahmins and a few others had their horoscopes cast at birth, the astrologer answered his clients' questions on the basis of the time of asking the question. (In the cities were to be found specialists whose income was derived mainly from practising this type of astrology. These astrologers were rated according to the reliability of their predictions.)

The life of the villagers was regulated by three calendars, the Julian, lunar[1] and solar. As already mentioned, one of the most important dates in the villagers' calendar was 10th June when the gates of the reservoirs were opened releasing waters into the irrigation canals. The village school, the government offices in the *taluk* and district capitals, and the shops and firms in the cities all regulated their activity principally with reference to the Julian calendar.

The agricultural, social and religious life of the villagers was largely based on the Hindu lunar calendar. I have already commented on the importance of asterisms in predicting the seasonal rains. A few of the older and more Sanskritized peasants knew the names of those which had unfailing association with rain. Most villagers and even some urban folk commented that such-and-such an asterism was certain to 'give' rain.

In the lunar year, the four months beginning with *ashada* (roughly from mid-June to mid-October) were inauspicious for performing weddings, house-warming and other ritual. They were the rainy months when Vishnu slept on his serpent-couch at the bottom of the ocean. He woke up four months later, on the eleventh day of the bright half of *kartika* which marked the coming of winter. The month of Pushya (January–February) was another inauspicious month for those who followed the lunar calendar.

The solar calendar was nowhere as important as the lunar for the religious life of most villagers. Only the Sankranti was based on it. However, Brahmins had to resort frequently to the solar calendar to perform some kinds of ritual. Offerings of sesame and water were

[1] Muslim religious life was guided by the Islamic calendar which was lunar but which differed from the Hindu lunar calendar in that there was no provision in it for a quinquennial intercalary month. But many village Muslims had knowledge of Hindu festivals, the dates on which they occurred, etc.

made to ancestors on the first day of each solar month (*sankramana*).
Rampura did not have a resident astrologer. In many villages of
the region, this role was performed by the hereditary chaplain
(*purohita*). Rampura's chaplain was resident in Hogur, and was not
easily accessible to local folk, that too the poorer ones. His place was
taken by the Rama priest whose competence did not extend beyond
consulting the almanac.

An old Lingayat priest, Shantiviraradhya, from another village,
enjoyed a local reputation for his knowledge of ritual and astrology,
and the headman and a few other Peasants and Lingayats consulted
him. The village elite had also access to experts in other villages and
in the towns.

Regulating social and religious life resorting to three calendars
appears extremely complicated but it was not really so. The seasons,
and the opening and shutting of the reservoir gates set the pattern
for agricultural activities while the almanacs printed in the cities
gave them the dates of their feasts, fasts and festivals. However, for
most villagers, the priest and astrologer made consulting an almanac
unnecessary. But the Brahmins found it necessary to consult the
almanac frequently.

6 Basic Religious Ideas

Certain ideas are basic to the understanding of the day-to-day religious life of the people in Rampura and neighbouring villages. It is
interesting that each of these ideas is a part of a linked pair. Thus
purity (*madi*) is linked with its contrary, impurity (*mailige*), wrong
conduct (*tappu*) with right (*sari*), justice (*nyaya*) with injustice
(*anyaya*), and sin (*papa*) with good or meritorious conduct (*punya*).
Another pair of linked ideas is *dharma* (moral conduct) and *karma*
(actions have consequences in subsequent incarnations), and it differs
from the other pairs in this that one is not opposed to the other.[1]
But this statement needs to be qualified: *dharma* in common parlance
means, among other things, good deeds, while *karma* is used for acts
which are wrong and even evil. According to the Kannada proverb
'*dharmakke kola katti karmakke mosale bittaru*' ('dig a pond and
gain *dharma*, and leave a crocodile in it and earn *karma*').

---

[1] The opposite of *dharma* is *adharma*, i.e. the violation of the rules of law,
morality and religion. *Adharma* is the antonym of *dharma* but it is a literary
term and used only very rarely in ordinary conversation.

I shall not discuss here the concepts of pollution and purity. They were fundamental to the organization of the social and religious life of the villagers but I must hasten to add that it was not possible to draw a clear line between the social and religious. In a sense, all social life was religious as it came under the sway of pollution and purity ideas.

Tappu and *sari* were again important, and each term had a range of meanings: *tappu* referred to technically incorrect action, violation of the rules of conduct (e.g. talking back to elders, or having sex relations outside marriage), or breaking a rule of ritual or religion (e.g. not offering blood-sacrifices to a dead ancestor). It also referred to a fine levied on a person for the wrong done. A caste or village elder was occasionally heard telling someone, somewhat aggressively, that when a particular rule was broken a fine had to be levied on the guilty person (*tappu vasuli madabeku*).

Sari meant 'correct' (way of doing a thing), proper (manners), appropriate (e.g. paying tit for tat), and also right in a moral sense. *Sari* also meant 'even' as opposed to 'odd' (*besa*) when referring to numbers. In that sense it also referred to sameness of level. When a person wanted to stress that a paddy-plot or the floor of a room was a perfect level he said '*sarisamawagide*'. *Sama* meant 'level' and *sari* was used as a prefix to emphasize the perfection of the level.

All properly brought up children were expected to have the power to discriminate between right and wrong. Implicit in such discrimination was the knowledge that choosing the wrong course of action had unpleasant consequences. For instance, a man who made passes at a married woman and got thrashed by the husband, became the target of gossip and scorn: 'The thing he did was like eating mud' (*mannu tinnuva kelasamadida*) and he deserved what he got. Another comment on such an occasion was 'whoever ate salt had to drink water' (*upputindare neeru kudiyabeku*) implying that the man ought to have stayed away from eating salt in the first place.

Villagers knew that the ability to discriminate between right and wrong was distinct from the actual choice of the right. Many a man chose the wrong course because of greed, lust or love of power. In fact, those who invariably chose the right were very few. They were referred to with respect bordering on reverence, and at other times with irreverence as 'Dharmaraya', after the eldest brother of the Pandavas, who never swerved from the right, and never told a lie.

Such conduct was admirable in one way but was impractical in that it was detrimental to one's interests.

A man who chose the wrong but got away with it, was a clever man while the one who got caught had to pay the penalty. In other words, in actual fact, not everyone who ate salt had to drink water. But this was as much due to luck as to cleverness. When his luck ran out, however, he was caught and punished. Hence the proverb that 'a thief's wife was bound to become a widow one day' (*kallana hendati endiddaru munde*).

Villagers were keenly aware that a rich man was able to escape punishment for his wrong deeds while a poor man did not. Money and power bought many a man's co-operation, compliance or silence. In any discussion of right and wrong villagers cited instances of rich men doing what they wanted to, without having to pay the price for it because they were able to frighten victims and witnesses, or bribed the police or other officials. The poverty of the poor was made worse by oppression by the rich. It looked as though moral maxims were meant only for the poor and the weak. But then something happened out of the blue and the rich man suffered a disaster or great disgrace, and villagers suddenly perceived the vulnerability of even the mighty before the justice if not the wrath of the gods. These events helped to reaffirm the faith of the villagers in divine justice and in the reality of moral rules.

Two other terms which were heard frequently in the villagers' talk were *nyaya* and *anyaya*. *Nyaya* meant 'according to law or rule, right, just, fair, moral' while *anyaya* was the opposite of *nyaya*. A point made by one of the parties to an argument may be fair or according to rule ('*adu nyayavada matu*', i.e. 'it is a just point') or outrageous ('*adu yava ooru nyaya?*', i.e. 'the rule of which village is it?'). It was not only the points and arguments advanced by disputants which were either *nyaya* or *anyaya* but the decisions of arbitrators. The corruptibility of arbitrators was a perennial theme of village life, and one of its functions, apart from any element of truth which it may have had, seemed to be to enable the defeated disputant to accept an unfavourable decision. Kinship links, and economic, sex and power considerations frequently distorted the procedures and decisions of village courts as some arbitrators themselves admitted occasionally.

Nyaya and *anyaya* were used freely in disputes, and disputes were frequent enough for sensitivity to the subtler points of customary law and procedure to be widespread among villagers. The disputes also provided occasions for the display of forensic skill and for besting old rivals. They were the intellectual equivalents of wrestling bouts with this difference that decisions in the latter were fairer as a rule.

Nyaya was also used as a synonym for a dispute that came up before arbitrators. Thus '*dodda nyaya biddubittitu*' meant that a big dispute involving difficult issues had arisen. As mentioned earlier, the Shepherds were notorious for their love of disputes, and sensitivity to questions of mutual precedence.

Dharma had both an ethical and religious referent. Its different meanings, 'correct', 'right', 'moral' and 'merit', all formed a continuum, and the same term connoted different things on different occasions. Similarly, even a term like *tappu* was capable of being used in a religious context: a man begged forgiveness from his god for a lapse (*tappu*) and paid a fine (*tappu kanike*) or performed some other action to atone for it.

The moral did not exist as a category independent from the religious, and one who violated a moral rule was also doing damage to his soul, and angering the gods. Thus deceiving another person was not only morally wrong but sinful. A trader who cheated his customers was inviting disaster upon himself or one of his family members. When the news of his cheating a customer got around, someone was bound to remark, 'will god keep quiet?' or 'does god keep his eyes shut?' Cheating defenceless persons like widows or minors, and embezzling village funds (*urottina hana*) or temple funds, was more heinous than ordinary cheating.

Looking at the situation from the religious side, certain sinful acts (and omissions) were also immoral. A son who did not perform his dead father's obsequies, or a priest who neglected his temple duties, was behaving unethically. This was compounded when the son had inherited property from the father, or the temple had been endowed with land. The rule of reciprocity had also been broken in such a case.

A man who had performed acts of *dharma* (*dharmada kelasa*) was respected by all. Having a well or pond dug near a temple, building a hospice (*chatra*), erecting bamboo and palmleaf booths (*aravattige*) for serving refreshments to pilgrims, and planting avenue trees for the benefit of wayfarers were all acts of *dharma* or *punya* (religious merit). The repair of a temple, and ensuring the performance of daily ritual by endowing it with land, were popular acts of *dharma*.

Dharma was also used in a relative sense varying according to status and role. Thus a king's *dharma* differed from his subjects', and each caste had its own *dharma*. A priest's *dharma* was different from a layman's, and a father's different from his son's. At the same time, there was also a common *dharma* which transcended differences of status and role.

Villagers, especially the older ones, saw the glaring discrepancy between the norms which they were taught in their childhood and the profound changes which had occurred in recent years. For instance, it was no longer true that all Harijans were landless labourers or village servants. Some were teachers in schools which were attended by high caste pupils, and there were also Harijan officials, lawyers, doctors, legislators and ministers. Many Brahmins had given up painting caste marks on their foreheads, shed their sacred thread, and even ate meat and drank liquor. Girls from Brahmin and other high castes no longer married before puberty but instead studied in colleges, and took up jobs outside the home. Some villagers thought that things were indeed topsy-turvy (*tale kelaku*, i.e. standing on head). The current (and absurd) idea that all men were equal was satirized in the local pun *onde mataram*. In 1948, I did not find a single adult villager, even among those under thirty, who thought that Harijans ought to be allowed to enter high caste temples or draw water from caste Hindu wells.

However, there was respect for such virtues as truth-speaking, honesty, kindness and sympathy for the poor, whomsoever they resided in. A Brahmin who was hard-hearted was criticized, 'What kind of Brahmin is he? He ought to have been a butcher.' Similarly, an honest and kind man belonging to a 'low' caste was respected and praised. But there was a belief that the higher castes possessed, or ought to possess, good qualities in greater measure than the lower.

But as mentioned earlier, common sense dictated that goodness or virtue ought not to be carried to excess. It was all right for a sanyasi or other holy man to speak the truth always, but not for ordinary men. That was suicidal. One certainly could not afford to tell an official or even a neighbour how much he had grown or sold. Losses and expenses had to be exaggerated, and yields and income reduced. In fact, even rich villagers dressed shabbily to give the impression of being poor. All this was part of the strategy of survival.

My discussion of *dharma* as I think it was understood by villagers might appear confusing but this was partly at least due to there being no hard and fast lines between its different meanings, 'correct', 'right', 'lawful', 'ethical' and 'meritorious'. Not infrequently it was used in different senses within the space of a minute or two. To make matters more complicated, though ethical and religious behaviour had a large overlap, it was possible to speak of a man's virtues without reference to their religious dimension and *vice versa*. For instance, a kind and honest man who was not ritually minded was contrasted with one who was very religious but exploited, economically and otherwi. e, those in his power.

Karma, which was paired with *dharma*, was a religious idea with far-reaching ethical implications. A man's present position was determined by the kind of life he had led in a previous birth (*janma*), and this was stressed especially when there was a hiatus between his qualities and his position. Thus a rich man who was mean and miserly was said to owe his wealth to the good deeds he had done in his previous incarnation. Similarly, a good man whose only son died prematurely had probably committed a grave sin in his previous incarnation. Such arguing from cultural hindsight was not infrequent. But it was interesting that the fear of misfortunes in a subsequent incarnation did not seem to have any effect on people's conduct in contrast to the fear of punishment, and the hope of rewards, here and now. God had in his hands the power to punish as well as reward, and if he wanted to command the loyalty of his devotees, he had to make a judicial mix of both like a good headmaster, or even a politician. He had also to make his presence felt by occasionally granting prayers. A god who was above the villager's concerns did not make sense. He may possess wonderful qualities but villagers wanted to know how he was going to be useful to them. Max Weber would have been disappointed in Rampurians: they were *not* soteriologists. Salvation was only the goal of saints and *sanyasis*. They wanted gods with whom they could bargain, and from whom they could obtain benefits. Even from saints and sanyasis they wanted benefits. They did not think it cynical to ask for benefits.

The idea of *karma* did not come in the way of undertaking activity initiative. As I have said earlier, *karma* was mostly used to explain misfortunes and calamities which had already occurred. Fear of punishment in another incarnation did not present itself as an immediate threat. It did not prevent the land-grabber from his continuing efforts to grab the land of the poor, the womaniser from coveting other men's wives, and the miser from levying usurious rates of interest. Any change in their style of life was more likely due to some sudden disaster or the influence of a guru or other holy man.

On any fair reckoning, villagers had to be regarded as activists. Considering their proneness to disasters of all kinds, their poverty and ignorance, and the fact that the planting of each crop was really an act of faith, it was indeed astonishing that they were activists. Withdrawal from all activity made more sense in their situation.

Karma did offer solace to the villagers in that it helped them to survive the all-too-frequent disasters. A drought may burn up seedlings, or torrential rain destroy the harvest, an enemy burn up the straw rick, or smallpox or plague take away the only son, but the villager continued his activity. *Karma* provided an explanation for the misfortunes which had occurred. But the importance of *karma* in preventing immoral action is open to question. However, other people's immorality provided an opportunity for gossips to lick their chops and sermonize. Gossip, which was abundant, provided an opportunity for the discussion and clarification of norms.

Papa (sin) and *punya* (religiously meritorious) were primarily religious terms but they also had ethical overtones. *Papa* referred to any sinful act but it was also an expression of pity or sympathy towards another person who was suffering or was deprived of a benefit or faculty. It is only with the former sense of *papa* that I am concerned here.

A sinful act might be related to a particular role of a man or woman, or it may be role-free. Thus a host who served more of a choice dish to one guest than to the others had committed the sin of *pangtibheda* or discriminating among the guests seated in a row. A paternal uncle who cheated his minor nephews of the property that was their due had abused a position of trust, and this was a graver sin than cheating a stranger.

There was a certain amount of castewise difference with regard to the perception of sin. Thus a Brahmin regarded all slaughter of animals as sinful since it involved the destruction of life while a meat-eating non-Brahmin regarded it as his religious duty to offer a blood-sacrifice to his dead ancestors or deities. Again, it was a sin for a Harijan to enter a high caste temple while it was a good thing for a high caste man to do so. (I am here referring only to traditional ideas.)

But there were also acts which were *papa* or *punya* for everyone, irrespective of caste, kinship, locality, class and sex. The sanctity of human life was a value which everyone had to respect. Visiting pilgrim-centres, feeding the poor, endowing land to temples, and digging wells and planting trees earned *punya* for all. Men who performed these acts were respected just as cheats, usurers and adulterers were disapproved of.

I must reiterate that what I have written so far about the basic religious ideas of the villagers is drawn from my experience of the 'touchable' Hindu castes. But I think that it is true of the Harijans also, though they are likely to regard with scepticism, if not reject, at least some parts of upper caste ideology and world-view. In this context, it may be pointed out that Sanskritized individuals in each caste articulated the ideas discussed above more clearly than the others. (Of course the clearest articulators of the ideas were not always well-known for putting them into practice.) Of the few Harijans whom I came to know reasonably well, Pijja was the most Sanskritized, and he expressed the ideas of popular Hinduism better than many a high caste man. Kullayya, the Harijan headman who was given to few words, was respected for his piety. It is not unlikely that these men were the vanguard of a more thoroughly Sanskritized culture for their caste as a whole. But the question then arises, what were the religious ideas of the less or least Sanskritized Harijans? Only an intensive study of the religious beliefs of the Harijans and other lowly castes would answer the question. Unfortunately, I did not feel the need to do it when I was in Rampura. In fact, with the limited time at my disposal, I could not concentrate on any single caste before gathering a modicum of information on each.

7 Man and God

Man and god, or to be more precise, men and gods, were in intimate relation with each other, and this relationship was characterized by inequality. Gods were powerful and could grant favours or cause disasters while men were weak and in dire need of protection from the myriad, hostile forces around them. The situation was much worse before modern medicine, communications, education and scientific methods of agriculture began to reach the villagers. The life of the Indian villager was indeed nasty, brutish and short, and if one may add, disaster-prone at every point.

Every landowner paid at harvest a headload of paddy-with-straw to each of the priests of the Basava, Madeshwara and Rama temples. These three temples were the richest and most prominent in Rampura. The deity Basava both represented and, in a sense, was in charge of the world of cattle and their welfare. In practical terms, it meant that they should be healthy and have enough fodder throughout the year. Since the most important sources of fodder were paddy and *ragi*-straw, *jowar* stalks and some green fodder during the rainy season, adequate rains at appropriate times were essential to keep the cattle well fed.

The deity Madeshwara was also a protector of cattle. Was not his 'vehicle' (*vahana*) the Nandi bull? He was the lord and master of Nandi.

Rama was a generalist among deities, people praying to him for pretty nearly everything they wanted. He was a good deity, and he did not evoke in his devotees the fear which Madeshwara or Mari did. He was also somewhat distant from the farmers' concerns. He was the god, *par excellence*, of the Brahmins, and of a few better-off Peasants and others.

As stated earlier, there was a division of labour among the gods, and villagers generally addressed their prayers to appropriate deities. Thus a prayer for the welfare of cattle was rarely addressed to Rama and never to Mari but to Basava or Madeshwara. Taking the Rampura region as a whole, men with skin diseases went on pilgrimages to the shrines of cobra-deities such as Mattitalayya, and the Subramanya shrine near Kalastawadi on the Mysore–Seringapatam road.

The deified spirits of male ancestors were propitiated annually, and the welfare of the living members of the lineage, and the farm, house and cattle were their concern. But these matters were also the concern of the house deities. Overlapping jurisdiction did, however, occur frequently, and in such cases, villagers took the safer path of praying to all the deities concerned.

From the foregoing, it is clear that villagers viewed their relations with deities in much the same way as they viewed their relations with each other. There was this difference, however, that the deities were vastly more powerful, and also more difficult to understand and predict than human beings. When one deity failed a devotee he approached another in much the same way as when one patron failed him, a client approached another.

Changes were occurring, however, in the religious world of the villager. New cults, deities, and gurus were swimming into the villagers' ken as a consequence of increased contact with urban forces and the mass media. For instance, I am fairly certain that over fifty years ago, only a few Rampurians, most of them Brahmins, had heard of the famous pilgrim centres at Tirupati, Madura, Rameshwaram and Banaras, and even among them probably not more than one or two had visited them. In those days, a pilgrimage to Banaras was regarded as a hazardous enterprise though much less so than in the nineteenth century when a pilgrim's successful return from it was a fortuitous accident.

It was only during the post-Independence years that Rampurians, like others in neighbouring villages, started visiting the major pilgrim centres in the State and outside. Improved health services had wiped out smallpox, cholera and plague, the epidemics over which the deity Mari in her various forms presided. The effects of these changes on the cults of village deities is important for study, and it is probable that the increased popularity of Sanskritic gods, ritual, and forms of worship was due to the forces mentioned above.

Reciprocity was a fundamental principle underlying the relations between man and god in the same manner that it was between human beings. To put it crudely, devotees expected to benefit from propitiating deities, and the benefits sought were health, wealth, children, good crops, victory over rivals, and a sense of security. They were also 'negative' in the sense of freedom from sickness and ill-health and from possession by evil spirits (*gali*, lit., 'wind', or *devva*, the opposite of *deva* or deity). Some deities were able to only grant one type of favour as, for instance, Mari or Basava whereas some others were more versatile like Rama and Madeshwara.

While the theologian conceived of god as immanent (*sarvantaryami* lit., inside everything), having knowledge of past, present and future (*trikalajnani*, lit., knowing three 'times'), ineffable (*anirvachaniya*) etc., the villager dealt with him as he dealt with his powerful patron or his Trader, Smith, Barber, Washerman or Potter. He wanted benefits and favours from the deities he propitiated. Sometimes he made a deal with a deity as when he made a vow promising to go on pilgrimage to his shrine if he was (for instance) cured of an illness, or his wife bore him a son. To remind himself of his vow, he took a piece of cloth, washed it, dipped it in a solution of turmeric, and after the cloth had dried put a coin in it and tied it to a pole in the kitchen roof. Sometimes after he had been granted the favour he had asked for, he made the pilgrimage.

A family shifted its allegiance from a traditional to a new deity when the former failed to grant a favour, or inflicted an injury while the latter proved to be helpful. Reciprocity underlay such a shift: the traditional deity had failed to observe the rules of the reciprocity game while the new one had. Reciprocity, or more appropriately, its content, varied from deity to deity, and this was contingent upon the personality and attributes of each deity.

When a devotee suffered a serious misfortune and his prayers to his deity were of no avail, he felt cheated. On occasion, however, he was so enraged by his deity's conduct that he abused him. When, for instance, the old priest of the Madeshwara temple, father of Thammayya, was arrested and taken to jail during the Ganjam revolt in the 1890s, his wife went to the temple, stood before the icon, and berated the deity, 'I will heap stones on you, I will heap thorny cacti on you.' Stones and cacti are the opposite of sweet-smelling flowers with which icons are decorated and worshipped. This incident was recalled nearly sixty years later.

In some cases, there were standard terms of abuse which angered devotees could use. Thus Shiva was addressed as '*makkalu tindukondavane*', i.e. 'You killer of children', referring to Shiva's destruction of Kama, the God of love. Rama was addressed as '*hendati kaledukondavane*', i.e. 'You who lost your wife', referring to Ravana's abduction of Sita.

It took me time to understand that opposition to a deity was a regular form of relationship like adoration or worship just as friendship and enmity were recognized forms of relationship among human beings. In this connection, it is significant that Hindu theology recognizes both adoration and opposition as legitimate forms of relationship with god. While most devotees chose the path of love and adoration, a few, very few, chose the path of opposition. A celebrated instance of opposition is provided in Hiranyakashipu, the puranic demon-chief, who was slain by Vishnu in his *avatar* as Narasimha (man-lion). Hiranyakashipu's hatred of Vishnu prompted him to prevent his young son Prahlada from worshipping him. According to folklore, Hiranyakashipu had the choice of attaining union with Vishnu through practising the path of love or opposition and he opted for the latter as it was the shorter. The path of love would have meant more incarnations (*janmas*) than the path of opposition. Approaching god through opposition is called *virodha bhakti* or adoration through opposition, and it is regarded as a closer relationship than that of love. In adoration through opposition, the devotee is unable to shake god out of his mind while in the other his mind could wander.

Rampurians lived in a theistic universe in the sense that everyone in the village believed that god did exist, or more precisely, deities, male and female, and spirits, did exist. I do not think that elderly Rampurians had come across an atheist in the course of their lives. Faith in a particular deity might have been shaken but that only prompted an individual to seek protection from another deity but not reject all deities. A rationalist and atheist simply did not make sense to Rampurians. The only two occasions when I found that I had annoyed my good friend Nadu Gowda were (1) when I expressed my preference to be a bachelor even though I was past thirty, and (2) when I refused to answer his questions about my religious beliefs, and instead, parried them with counter questions such as, why should people believe in god? It was one of those few occasions when I behaved with deliberation as I thought that it would be interesting to get Nadu Gowda's reactions to atheistic views. I persisted in my stupid cleverness, little realizing that I was annoying him in matters which were of profound concern. It was then brought home to me forcibly that where religion was concerned I could not count on Nadu Gowda's indulgence.

Nadu Gowda was in some respects an exceptional man but in certain others, as for instance his deep religiosity, he was typical of the villagers. Even Kulle Gowda, a non-conformist in many areas of behaviour, was religious but, characteristically, he wore his religion far more lightly than others. In fact, even those who were known for practising usury, lechery or deceiving others as a matter of habit, were not irreligious. But it was wrong to conclude from this that there was no relationship between morality and religion. Lechery and dishonesty, for instance, were both wrong and sinful. Those who broke the moral rules were aware of what they were doing, and in some cases at least, their religiosity might have been prompted by awareness of their wrong doing.

God existed, and evidence for this was available in the miracles that occurred in certain temples on certain occasions. For instance, many a villager narrated to me how, at the annual festival of the lineage goddesses of the God's House lineage, a party of devotees from the Salt-maker (Uppaliga) caste from a nearby village broke open a number of coconuts on their shaven heads. This was an old custom, and it was referred to as 'pavada' or miracle. How was it that these men were able to do it while ordinary men were not?

Another miracle was walking on nails (*mullamige*), or rather, walking with sandals through the soles of which were driven nails so that the sharp ends came into contact with the walker's soles. One of the priests of the Mikkere Virabhadra temple donned the *mullamige* during the Ugadi (New Year) festival when the deity's icon was taken to the Kaveri river for a bath. He walked about before the deity on the sandals, carrying an open sword in hand, and he answered questions put to him by devotees. (The questions related to health, birth of children, monetary problems, etc.) Several villagers told me about how painful it was to wear the *mullamige* and one young boy even challenged me to try them on. I did not accept the challenge: the nails were not only sharp but rusty.

The behaviour of some bulls (*basavas*) dedicated to the Shiva temple was also cited as evidence of the power of the deities concerned, and indirectly, of the existence of the latter. For instance, the bull dedicated to Mikkere Virabhadra (or of the deity Birappa of Hunjanakere) tried to gore a devotee participating in the festival, and it later transpired that the person in question was in a condition of impurity and ought to have abstained from attending the festival.

I must here pause to add that while the villagers cited supernatural events and happenings as evidence of the handiwork of god, they were not a credulous lot. They were shrewd, commonsensical and hard-headed, and this trait of theirs was seen repeatedly and in a wide variety of contexts. I shall illustrate what I mean by reference to a frequent form of divination, viz. the institution of flower-asking (*hu keluvadu*). There is more than one form of flower-asking but I shall confine myself to that which is common in Rampura.

When an individual, or a group of villagers wanted to take a decision and were unable to do so on the basis of the facts available or commonsense, or they wished to know what was likely to happen in the future on a matter of great importance to them, he or they went to a temple, and after worshipping the deity, prayed to him requesting that he 'give them a flower' (*hu koduvudu*). The priest was informed in advance, and he would have washed the deity and stuck water-wet flowers all over the icon before the arrival of the devotees. *Puja* was then performed, the last act in it being *arati*, the waving of lighted camphor (or cotton wick dipped in oil) before the deity. The priest then offered the light to each devotee who took both his palms to it after which he touched his eyes and then saluted the deity with folded palms. Then the leader of the party of the devotees formally requested the deity to give a flower. If a flower on the right half of the deity fell in response, it was interpreted as a favourable answer while a flower on the left side falling indicated a 'no'. However, if no flower dropped, it indicated that the deity did not wish to answer.

Since I was on very friendly terms with the villagers and I felt certain that they would not mistake me, I tried to point out that the fall of a flower which was stuck into a crevice cavity in the icon was governed by chance and that no significance ought to be attached to it. But I was told that the fall of any flower did not count but only of those which were wet and stuck firmly in. They explained to me that the *garbha gudi* (*sanctum sanctorum*) where the deity's image was housed was always without a window. The lighted lamp in that room along with incense sticks 'and camphor produced warmth and this resulted in the fall of flowers. But only the fall of wet and firmly stuck flowers was relevant.

Sometimes, however, after the deity had refused to give a flower at the first session, the devotees tried a second time, usually on the following morning. This was termed 'asking for a stale (or overnight) flower' (*tangalu hu keluvudu*). In such a case, only a flower which had been used on the previous day mattered and not any other.

Villagers assured me that they had, on rare occasions, witnessed flowers being 'thrown' (*eseyuvudu*) by the deity instead of merely falling. Sometimes a sceptical devotee even asked that a particular flower decorating the deity's icon be 'given' in indication of an affirmative answer. A great deal depended on the truth or power (*satya*) of the deity, the conduct of the priest, and perhaps also the faith of the supplicant.

To Rampurians, deities were as real as their friends, neighbours and relatives. However, relatives existed as human beings while gods existed sculpted in stone, wood or metal. (Some village deities inhabited even plain unhewn stones.) Each deity had his own personality, his special likes and dislikes, just like each villager who was not infrequently identified by his quirk or oddity.

The complexities of the flower ritual, and the reality and immediacy of deities to Rampurians, were brought home to me when in the summer of 1948 I accompanied a party of elderly villagers to the Basava temple to ask the deity whether the drought would be broken. It was a scorching afternoon, and we all trooped into the stone-paved compound of the Basava shrine. Each one of us had covered his head with a towel to protect ourselves from the heat and glare of the pitiless summer sun. Nothing I had witnessed in Brahminical temples, or even in Coorg, had prepared me for the 'interview' which followed between the villagers and the deity. Once or twice, the absurdity of the situation seemed overwhelming but I managed to keep a straight face, and more important, the earnestness of the villagers gathered in the narrow anteroom outside the *sanctum sanctorum* made a profound impression on me. I shall quote the 'interview', with slight alterations only, from my field-diary as a summary would fail to convey its quality:

Monday, 3 May 1948: Today some elders went to Basava to find out (ask the deity) whether it was going to rain (or not). Kulle Gowda's father, Nadu Gowda, Kobli's father and a few others comprised the party. Sannu joined later. On the way, I asked why Basava's temple had been chosen and not any other. I was told that was because it was the oldest. The Madeshwara temple belonged really to Gudi. The Rama temple was not either as old as Basava's or the department of rains did not come under Rama.

The Basava temple is in the old village site, and the temple has not been shifted like Rama's. Inside the temple is a stone pedestal on which sat Basava (figure of a recumbent bull). . . . On either side of Basava was a much smaller image of him. . .

The old priest's younger son substituted for his father on this occasion. The image had been washed etc., decorated with daubs of sandalwood paste, and flowers and *bilva* (*Aegle marmelos*) leaves, still wet with water, had been placed all over the face and neck. (Care had been taken to see that none was likely to slide down easily.)

It is believed that there is an intimate relation between Basava's *para* (feast) and rain. When (the first) monsoon rains occurred, the feast was given, and it is said that formerly rain followed the feast washing off the leaves used in the dinner.

After we went in, *puja* was performed, lighted frankincense (*dhupa*), and camphor were waved before the deity and then offered to the devotees. Flowers and *bilva* leaves were also given. (Sannu, his son, and I sat in the inner shrine while the others sat in the covered verandah outside.)

Kulle Gowda's father, Made Gowda, was asked to make the

request to the deity for a flower. I had imagined that everyone would stand up and bow silently beseeching almighty god for a sign which they could understand. But the proceedings were as different as possible from my expectations. Made Gowda stood up and said, 'You are famous as Rampura Basava. Do you wish to retain your reputation or not? Please give us a flower. We have not performed your *para* because of lack of water. Give us rain today and tomorrow we will perform your *para*.

'In Edagai, Kapi and other villages you are famous as Rampura Basava. It has rained all around us, in Hogur, Hundi, etc. Why has it not rained here? Tell us if you are angry. Why should you be angry with us? We have seen to it that you do not lack anything.' (Made Gowda here mentioned that there was something wrong with the priest which he would not mention then but later.)

Another elder almost barked, '*appaneyagali, yatakke kadastiya*' ('Give us your order, why do you torture us? Give it early.')

Made Gowda was irritated, 'Give us a flower on the left side if you so wish. Why do you sit still? Are you a lump of stone or a deity?'

Someone chimed in, 'He is only a lump of stone; otherwise, he would have answered.'

Made Gowda added, 'We will say that there is no god in the temple and that you have left the village'.

Someone else took a different line: 'We are not entirely dependent upon you. On 10 June, canal water will be released by the government. And anyhow it will rain a little later (after the south-west monsoon had set in). Even if it does not rain, we won't starve. Rampura people eat rice (grown with water from the irrigation canals) and not *jowar* (sorghum grown on wholly rain-fed land). So give us a flower.'

I sat in the inner shrine looking at the flowers. They seemed glued to the deity. There did not seem to be an earthly chance of any flower or leaf coming down. I wondered at the faith of these people. They were all in earnest (but) the atmosphere was not that of a group of men in awe of a great god but that of a number of reasonable men trying to coax a man lacking in good graces into right behaviour. It resembled a verandah scene where a dispute was being settled, and an unreasonable party was being told the right.

I asked the villagers whether if it rained that evening (after the deity's silence), they would conclude that Basava had given it. They said 'no'. . . .

Again, I told them that the flowers and leaves had been pressed into cavities (in the icon). They ought to have been loosely placed. They dismissed my idea. What was the point of placing them loosely? Only when firmly-placed flowers came down had the deity given them.

Made Gowda narrated to me an incident in his life when two of his grandsons contracted cholera and the doctor told him that they were as good as dead. Then his second son had a dream in which he saw a *bhairagi* (holy man in ochre robes following a Shaivite Order) who told him 'it is all right, go'. The son also heard bells ringing. Made Gowda went on the following morning to the Basava temple and asked for a particular flower. It fell at once and the grandchildren survived. . .

I then asked the elders what was the next step. They told me that they would visit the temple on the next morning to ask for a stale (*tangalu*) flower. The priest would stand outside the door, wave lighted camphor before the deity and then everyone would wait for a flower to fall. If no flower came down then it meant that the deity had left the village.

Abusing and taunting one's favourite deity was again understandable because it was common among people bound together by close ties and interests such as relatives, friends, masters and servants, and patrons and clients. A man who did not give a thing when he was asked might part with it when he was taunted, and taunting implied the pre-existence of close ties. The villagers' relations with deities paralleled in some ways their relations with patrons.

The fact that Basava was a deity to whom they had gone to plead for rain did not inhibit the villagers from speaking to him forcefully and uninhibitedly. The incident recalled to me the manner in which even the humblest villagers stood up for their rights when they felt that their rights were being trampled upon by somebody.

After the infructuous interview with Basava, a few younger Rampurians went to Madeshwara and asked him for a flower. The flower was given soon, and a heavy shower fell during the night. The grateful villagers quickly raised funds for a silk umbrella for Madeshwara, which had been promised him in return for rain, and took him out in a gala procession.

As far as the villagers were concerned the most important thing was that deities did exist, that they could be prayed to for obtaining certain desirable objects, bringing about desirable events, or avoiding or preventing the materializing of undesirable objects or events. Deities provided the necessary sense of security, and the source of hope for undertaking the multifarious activities essential for day-to-day living. But deities had to be worshipped, offered sacrifices, and made much of. Devotees had to be in a condition of ritual purity to approach and worship them. Failure to propitiate, make offerings, and observe the rules of purity and pollution was likely to result in punishment. However, the elaborate system of ritual, myth, belief and action which had been developed over the centuries to cocoon the villagers from all-too-frequent disasters, had set up its own anxieties, stresses, strains and guilt feelings.

CHAPTER XI

Farewell

As November progressed, I began to worry about the diminishing time available to me for work. I was expected to be in Oxford by the middle of January which meant that I had to reach there at least a week before. It was my first teaching job, and I was worried, to say the least, about my lack of preparation. But while in Rampura I could not think of anything else but the yawning gaps in my data. There was so much to be done. I went round during the day collecting information in a hectic way but when I went to bed I started thinking about the work still to be done and the unprepared lectures.

I had started my work in the village feeling strange, and wondering how it would go, but as the weeks went by, I felt that I had no reason to feel despondent. Information did not come in steadily but in sudden gusts, and after a while, I got used to the pattern. Village life, which at first seemed chaotic, gradually became more coherent. Perhaps more important was the fact that I enjoyed my work and my encounters with villagers from different castes and classes. True, there was always the feeling at the back of my mind that the time at my disposal was woefully short for studying so complex an entity as Rampura. My anxiety increased rather than diminished with such success as I had in the collection of data. I would list the number of things to be done in the coming week or fortnight and fret if I did not fulfil the targets I had set for myself. At times my anxiety reached a point when it prevented sleep and I usually solved the problem by running away to Mysore for two or three days. This had the effect of renewing my curiosity and zest.

In spite of frequent outbursts of anxiety, I enjoyed my field work. I was curious about everything concerning the villagers, and by and large, I liked them. I had mixed feelings about a few with whom I came into frequent contact but I tried, as far as possible, to see their point of view. I had a few close friends, and I liked talking to them, and being with them. I also knew that they liked me.

I felt a real affection for my village friends, and during my entire stay in Rampura, I cannot recall feeling the need for intellectual company. (I realize that this is also a comment on me.) My friends could discuss the events and institutions in the village with subtlety and humour which made me respect their intelligence. They understood that I wanted to learn about village life and institutions, and they took the trouble to answer my questions, however naive or ignorant they appeared. With only a few villagers such as Nadu Gowda, Sannu, Pijja, Washerman Kempayya and Hakim Sab did I have formal sessions at which I collected information on a variety of matters. With most others, my meetings were informal.

I suffered from two kinds of deficiencies in collecting information: I did not want to embarrass, let alone upset, my informants by asking them questions on financial, marital or domestic matters. Only if the informant himself touched on any of them, did I try to probe further. I usually obtained information on sensitive areas by keeping my eyes and ears open when people were talking, and by occasionally intervening with a question or two to give a focus to the talk. Even then, I took care not to appear nosey. I was aware that I was being circuitous but being endowed with a temperament which made me dread asking embarrassing questions, I had no choice. I am ignoring for the moment the likelihood of the villagers being put off by direct questions.

There was a considerable amount of gossip in the village about extra-marital sex relations and some of the reported liaisons were across the lines of caste. I felt that I should know about them and the only way to get the information was to ask my friends. But even with them I had to be circumspect as they could mistake me for being a garbage-collector which would have affected my standing with them. It was only when I was out walking with my friends that I asked them the questions which I wanted to, and after I had taken care to steer, as inconspicuously as I could, the conversation in the direction of my interests. I thought that I ought not to believe everything that I had heard or was told and that I should sift the chaff from the grain. Also, how could one get 'evidence' to substantiate a rumour? But my talks with my friends failed to yield the 'evidence' which I was seeking. My friends had of course heard the rumours which I had, and they believed them to be true. But the only thing I could conclude from all this was that rumours about extra-marital relations were widespread and widely believed in. This was only what was to be expected in village society where every bit of gossip moved along well-established networks and the networks of different individuals intersected at many points.

But the entire process of deliberately bringing out my questions about the seamy side of village life during walks with my friends made me uneasy. I felt that I was taking unfair advantage of them. Yet, on the other hand, I felt that I ought not to rest content with rumours, but seek certain information. I was bothered all the time about the propriety of what I was doing.

Perhaps one of the reasons why the villagers liked me was due to the contrast between their expectations about me, and my own behaviour: they had assumed that as an educated, urban and well-off (by their standards) Brahmin, I would behave like the officials who, during their brief visits to the village, met and talked with only a few leaders. In contrast, I went to everybody's house, talked with them, and took pictures. This they liked, and perhaps they did not appreciate enough the fact that I had to be informal with everyone in the interests of my work.

One of the results of knowing everyone in the village was a diffusion of my energies. I found it difficult to walk uninterruptedly from the Bullock House to wherever I had work. I had to stop and make conversation with my friends and acquaintances as otherwise there was the likelihood of their misunderstanding me. This was annoying but there was nothing to do but to put up with it. Sometimes, however, such chats yielded 'leads' about important matters which I had to follow up later. But whether they yielded information or not, they kept me in touch with a wider range of people than I had close relations with, and helped create a reservoir of goodwill for me.

The village represented a distinct olfactory world. Some smells were pleasant such as harvested paddy and jowar stalks, hedges, strawricks, and the smell of earth after the first rains. The smell of the Bullock House was, however, an acquired taste. I was used from childhood to cowdung smell—there was a colony of milkmen behind our house in Mysore—but living in the Bullock House, where eleven bullocks were tethered from early evening till the following morning, produced an overpowering stench of cowdung and cow urine, which was a phenomenon of a different order. There was no escape from this smell in the village for in most houses the animals were tethered in a part of the main living room. Anyone who had grown up in a village probably found the urban, middle-class home a sharp olfactory contrast. I did find the Bullock House smells overpowering to begin with but after a while I not only became used to them but even liked them.

Manure heaps also exuded a strong smell but strange as it may seem I did not find it unpleasant. I disliked them, however, because they attracted flies, mosquitoes and other insects. I remember a big manure heap at about a hundred yards to the north of Gudi, along the path to Kere. I had to pass by it when I walked to Kere, and I recognized it not by looking at it but by the smell issuing from it. It was a landmark for me, and not an unpleasant one.

But what I never got used to was the revolting practice of children defecating on the village streets. I hated walking on the village streets in the morning as I was certain to come across one or two children calmly defecating by the roadside. I welcomed the swineherds' pigs as they left the village cleaner unlike the dirty domestic fowls which only pecked at the piles of ordure and deposits of human phlegm on the road. This made me understand why the Sanskritized, non-vegetarian castes refused to eat fowl, and regarded mutton and fish as food of a higher order.

As my fieldwork progressed, I began to view the village and its environs more like a native than an outsider. Not only did I get used to smells, dirt, dust, heat, winds, noise, the insects and vermin, and the lack of privacy, I learnt to distinguish good land from bad and the various properties of the plants and trees commonly found in the area. I knew the life-histories of several individuals, the details of major disputes, and the main local events. In fact, I was occasionally able to correct my friends and acquaintances on matters pertaining to the village. There was an element of the show-off in me, and I was aware that my interventions would provoke someone to say, 'You know much more about our village than us.' This was a compliment no doubt but it was not free from a trace of concern. A few of my more knowledgeable friends told me that they had never imagined that I was going into every aspect of village life, and in the detail I did, and added, half-jokingly, 'Our secrets are now with you.' 'We don't know what you are going to do with all the information you have collected', and 'You can get many into trouble' were the other expressions which I heard occasionally. It was true that I knew of instances where individuals had benefited themselves at the expense of the government, but the last thing that I would have thought of doing was to harm those who had trusted me and given me of their friendship.

But not all the compliments of the villagers could convince me that I had done anything more than only scratch the surface as far as gathering information was concerned. In fact, paradoxical as it may appear, the compliments served only to remind me of my failures and of gaps in my data. But it was impossible to convey this to the villagers. But my conscience would not be lulled to sleep by the compliments even though sometimes I knew that I had in a way invited the compliments from them.

As my stay drew to a close I had also to worry about my social obligations. Word had got round that I would be leaving shortly, and I was stopped while on my rounds by everyone I knew' to be asked when I was going, how long I would be away, when I would return, etc. If I happened to drop a remark about English weather or food, I was certain to be detained longer. The villagers clamoured for more information, and after my exposition wondered how human beings could live in England. They might have been discussing Eskimos in the deepest Arctic.

My friends were sad at the prospect of my departure. They discussed every little detail of it, and told me repeatedly how they would miss me. They feared that I would forget them in the preoccupations of my work and social life. Would I write to them? It was enough if I wrote once a month about my safety and welfare. After all, I was going to a country thousands of miles away.

A few even asked me the price of an air-letter, and were shocked when I told them. The villagers were a frugal lot, and only wrote on postcards cramming as much information as they could into each. For instance, Nadu Gowda, who was extremely fond of his youngest son studying in a Mysore college in 1952, had instructed him to write once a month and only on postcards. But, quite inconsistently, he himself wrote me a few air-letters during the thirty months I spent in Oxford and I valued them as evidence of his great affection for me.

Nadu Gowda's son Kempu wondered why I had to go to a country so far away to get a job. Could I not get one nearer home? As far as he was concerned, it would be good if I became an officer in Mysore State, preferably as Deputy Commissioner of Mysore district. I would then be useful to him and others in the village.

Two friends who seemed particularly affected by my departure were Kulle Gowda and Nadu Gowda. The former's unhappiness was to some extent understandable. His self-interest was bound up with my continued stay in Rampura. I was a source of occupation and income to him. The occupation also gave him a sense of importance which was necessary for one who had come down in the world, and who was, in addition, vain. He was one of those who wanted me to write to him regularly. He kept nagging me, 'Once you get there you will forget us', but at the same time took care to see that I would have to write to him. He told me that he would keep copies of the documents which were drafted by him for those who sought his services as scribe, and record disputes. He intended doing a survey of Gudi, to which I have referred earlier, and this would also keep him in touch with me. As a parting gift I gave him a wrist watch. It was a foolish gift for I ought to have known that Kulle Gowda would part with it when he was next in need of money. A few villagers criticized the gift as they thought that I should have given something more valuable.

Nadu Gowda was the one most upset by my impending departure, and unlike Kulle Gowda, his self-interest was not bound up with my stay. If anything, I had made demands on his time and energies though in the process I had helped him spend his leisure, and perhaps also added to his entertainment. I could not help being surprised at the fact that we had become such good friends. Our friendship had grown steadily during the year, and was free from the occasional doubts and conflicts which had marked my relationship with the others. I had become very fond of the warm-hearted, grandiloquent and occasionally imperious and hierarchical old man. For several days before my departure, he spent hours on my verandah looking woebegone and telling me how bad he felt. He had even toyed with the idea of giving me an acre of wet land to induce me to settle down in Rampura. But he realized that I was 'as expensive as an elephant', and that an acre of land was pitifully inadequate.

I was touched by Nadu Gowda's generous thought, and I could appreciate what parting with an acre of wet land meant even to one who had over forty acres. But what I did not then realize was that it was the highest ever evaluation of my friendship, keeping in mind the fact that I had offered nothing in exchange. I wonder if the fact of my being a Brahmin had influenced him. He was the kind of man to whom a gift to a Brahmin would have appeared meritorious. He knew that my style of life was far removed from that of a pious Brahmin but I was a scholar, a profession which he probably associated with Brahmins. He once told me in his characteristic style, 'The kind of property you are acquiring lasts thousands of years unlike the property which we acquire.' He was, of course, referring to knowledge.

On the day before my departure, Nadu Gowda was sitting on my verandah leaning his heavy bulk against one of the dark-green modern pillars, carved by the village Smith. He was looking even more depressed than usual while I was busy packing. The headman walked across from his house, smiled a wise smile and said, 'I knew he was a "paper cap" (kagadada topi), and would leave us all one day. That was why I took care not to become too friendly whereas you observed no such caution. You see how his departure is affecting you.' It was an eloquent comment on the headman's nature, and also an explanation of why he had maintained a distance with me.

My last few days in Rampura were miserable. I was by temperament a stay-at-home but I had been forced to shift my residence periodically as a result of the profession I had chosen. The process of uprooting myself from a settled routine and established relationships with a known group of people was deeply disturbing, and in the present instance Rampura represented only the first stage in the snapping of my bonds. Leaving Mysore was going to be worse and then there was Bombay where I had several friends. The prospect of leaving the warmth and sun of Mysore for the cold and wet of an Oxford winter was not exactly exciting. (My previous winter in Oxford, the 1946-47 one, was the worst for several decades, and it was compounded by a power cut from 8 a.m. to 12 noon, and from 2 to 4 p.m.) As I thought of all this, I was full of self-pity. I envied the villagers who spent all their lives in one place, whose relationships were stable, and whose routines never varied, The village appeared a snug and cosy place, and lucky indeed were those who inhabited it even though they were ignorant of their good fortune.

My younger friends insisted that I should have 'tiffin' with them on the eve of my departure. The group included Swamy, Kempu, Siddu, Millayya's brother Karagayya, Congress Puttaswamy, and probably one or two others. They were the modernizers, and they got the tiffin prepared at Hotel Mollayya's teashop, the leading local teashop. Mollayya was a Peasant, and it was he who had prepared the snacks for the party given by the young dissidents to the visiting minister earlier during the year. My friends had done me proud: the thick chapatis literally dripped with pure ghi, and so did the sweet made with broken wheat. The best variety of bananas had been bought, and there were betel leaves and arecanuts after an oversweetened tea.

I tried hard but I could not eat more than one *chapati* and a few spoonfuls of the rich sweet. My friends assured me that everything was made with pure *ghi*, and that I should eat a little more. Were the dishes not to my taste?

I could not tell them that I did not have an appetite, and that rich food did not agree with me. The talk around me was hardly more to my taste: it was about my going away, my forgetting my poor friends in the village, and finally, did I know how long it would be before I returned home? All the questions that I was pushing away from my mind were being thrust before me.

It was sweet of my young friends to have given me a party, and I was deeply appreciative of their affection and kindness. As I returned after dark to the Bullock House and to my packing, the thought crossed my mind that I had not been given a party by the headman. Was he annoyed with me? I was certain that he would have heard of the party given by my younger friends and I did not know what he would conclude from it.

But soon I was too busy with the last stages of my packing, the brunt of which was being borne by Nacha, assisted by a few neighbours. Kulle Gowda walked in and out barking instructions to Nacha, much to the latter's annoyance. My furniture, bedding, vessels, etc., were being sent to Mysore in Karim's cart, driven by his son Alimia. An old tenant of my acquaintance from Kere, Kari Ninga, was travelling in the cart to make sure that the things would safely reach my house. It was going to be an all-night journey.

I was due to catch my bus at about 10 a.m. on the following day and I had to wait by the roadside with the luggage I was carrying with me. There was usually a scramble to get into a bus, and sometimes the bus arrived in Rampura overloaded, which meant that local travellers had to wait for another bus. As breakdowns were frequent, the timings of buses were not predictable.

I was suddenly summoned to the headman's 'office room' an hour or so before my departure. I went in to find that several men had already gathered there including the headman, his sons, Nadu Gowda and Karim. The room had been swept clean, and the chairs, benches and table had been dusted and rearranged. At the back, near the wall, was a table, and behind it were arranged three chairs, while the benches were arranged in front. The owner of the Brahmin teashop was making coffee and snacks in a corner, and I found the smell of coffee competing for supremacy with the more pervasive one of paddy in gunny sacks, and dust. I was invited to take the chair between the headman's and Nadu Gowda's, and as soon as I had sat down, the serious business of eating began. It was done with concentration. The teashop-owner was praised for preparing tasty snacks. My hosts did not neglect me either and pressed me to eat more. The teashop-owner was urged to look after me. But before we had finished with eating, music suddenly burst on our ears, music made by *nadaswaram* pipes and *dolu*. The musicians had come from Kere. The party must have been planned at least a day in advance. I felt mean at the uncharitable thoughts I had entertained about the headman on the previous evening. But I was not left to my reflections for long as Lakshmana suddenly stood up and made a speech praising me. It was a speech in the accepted style of farewell speeches: my virtues, real and not-so-real, were listed, the affection and esteem which the villagers had for me was stressed, as also the fact of my being missed, etc., etc. The end of the speech was marked by loud applause. A thick garland was produced from somewhere and Lakshmana put it round my neck and we did *namaskar* to each other. Karim followed Lakshmana, put a garland round my neck and poured a couple of handfuls of crystal sugar and almonds on my head. I stood up after the garlanding and confetti and thanked the villagers for their kindness and hospitality and for treating me as one of them.

As Lakshmana was speaking I suddenly turned to the headman and said, 'I feel terrible when I hear praise like that.' The headman replied, 'That is how the worthy feel.'

The bus arrived, and strangely enough, on time. But the headman's emissaries had told the driver that I was travelling and that a seat had to be reserved for me. The driver started using the horn to remind us that it was time. I panicked at the sound of the horn. I wanted to leave the room at once and run for the bus. But the headman asked me to take it easy. The bus would wait. I replied that the driver might become impatient and leave. Someone in the audience dared the driver to do that. They would see how he would visit Rampura again.

We continued to make small talk while the driver hooted the horn more persistently and I became more and more restless. After what appeared a long time we all got up and made for the door. Lakshmana instructed me to put on the garlands which I had deposited on the table. I obeyed him, and the procession formed outside on the street, with the musicians in front, followed by me, flanked by the headman and Nadu Gowda on either side, while the others brought up the rear. The musicians played for all they were worth, and the villagers got on to their verandahs to watch the procession. I felt very self-conscious as I saw the grinning faces on the verandah. It was a little more than a hundred yards to the bus but the journey seemed slow and protracted. There was a big crowd around the bus, and many villagers greeted me with the traditional good-bye: '*Hogibittu barutira?*' ('Will you go and come back?'). A front seat on the driver's row had been reserved for me, a tribute to the headman's power over the bus owner. I was standing near the front left wheel saying goodbyes when the driver told everyone concerned that he had really to be going. I got ready to climb into the bus when Lakshmana came and hugged me, north Indian style, with his right shoulder touching my left, and *vice versa*. He had his green Nehru waistcoat on, and like his dress, the bear hug which he gave me was also characteristic of the politicians.

I got into the bus at last and kept my hands folded in greeting as everyone around wished me farewell. The bus started after a great deal of stuttering and coughing. As the bus gathered speed I turned towards the Harijan ward where several men, women and children were watching our progress, and I greeted them. Suddenly I recognized, in the crowd, the emaciated and deeply creased face of Doni, my friend: 'Are you going away?' she cried out, and I started to reply. But the words choked in my throat. My self-restraint which had held so long threatened to give way and I turned my face away from her. At once, the small man sitting between me and the driver, whom I had not noticed so far, asked me, 'You must be an officer and very popular. It was a big send off.' I told him somewhat coldly that I was not an officer, and turned away from him, and looked on either side of the road. I wanted to be by myself for a while. It was going to be my last journey down that road for some time, and I wanted to drink in every detail of the vanishing countryside. The terraced rice-fields spread around me in all directions and clumps of trees were dotted about the rice-fields breaking what would have been otherwise a sheer stretch of paddy. The fields were in varying colours from green touched with yellow to gold and brown. The slightest breeze caused a ripple in the fields, and the plants swayed and bowed before returning to their vertical position. Occasionally, a gust of strong wind disturbed several plots momentarily ruffling the pattern of colours.

It was a sunny and breezy day, typical of the season and I wondered when I would be returning to the village. I feared that it would be many years and the thought depressed me. I tried to take my mind off my departure and take in the scenery. Feeder canals, clear and shallow, flowed rapidly through the fields, their banks lined with the *hongé* trees bright with shrill green leaves. The land dipped and rose, and went round sudden rises, while the bus rattled along, jolting us at every turn and twist, and dip and rise. Through it all I had brief and tantalizing glimpses of the shimmering Kaveri flowing in the distance.

Appendix I

The Hindu Calendar, Rain, and Agriculture

The Hindu calendar is divided into twenty-seven named fortnights, called *nakshatras* (literally, stars), and each *nakshatra* is in turn divided into four sub-periods called *padas* (feet). Traditionally, farmers took note of *nakshatras* in their agricultural activities—for instance, an old farmer told me that rice shoots transplanted during *Punarvasu* (5–18 July in 1948) would be ready for harvest in *Anuradha* (19 Nov.–1 Dec. in 1948). Again, rain is expected more during some *nakshatras* than in others. Rainfall is so certain to occur during *hastha* (26 Sept.–9 Oct.) that, according to a proverb, it extended its hand of protection to the farmer in the same way that Vishnu granted protection to those who threw themselves at his mercy. Vishnu is represented in his icons with his right palm facing the devotee, the fingers pointing downward. This position of the hand is referred to as *abhaya*, and is a characteristic of Vishnu, the protector in the Hindu trinity.

Even in the 1930s at the festival of *Ugadi* it was customary for a Brahmin priest or astrologer to read to villagers assembled in a temple the forecast for the year contained in the almanac. This was called *panchanga shravana* or 'listening to the almanac'. I shall quote below an extract from the almanac for the Hindu year of *Sarwadhari* (April 1948–March 1949) to give an idea of the content of a typical forecast. 'As Saturn will be king in the coming year, people will be troubled by drought, disease in some regions, thieves, robbers and officials. Only crops sown during the northeast monsoon (*hingaru*) will flourish. Since Mars will be minister, fires and armed clashes are indicated. The Moon will be Commander-in-Chief, and also lord of rain and cloud, and this means that some areas will have good rains, rich harvests, well-fed cattle, increased trade, and happiness for the people. Venus (*Shukra*), the lord of plants for the year, will ensure their good condition, and a good harvest. Mercury (*Budha*), the lord of grain, means poor rains, and higher prices for grains. The price of oilseeds and juicy articles (*rasa padarta*) is likely to increase as the Sun will be the lord of *rasa* (juice). The price of precious stones will, however, come down because Jupiter (*Guru*) will be their lord. Finally, as the deity Krishna will be the lord of cattle, rains will occur at appropriate times, and cattle and plants will flourish.'

The farmers had their own names for the more important *nakshatras*, usually corruptions of the hard-to-pronounce Sanskrit originals, though not always recognizable as such. Thus, *mrigashira* was referred to as *motadri*, *aridra* as *doddadri*, and *punarvasu* as *dodda husoon* (big *husoon*).

According to some old farmers, however, over the decades significant changes had occurred in the dates of some crucial activities such as transplantation. Thus Nadu Gowda told me that in his younger days rice shoots used to be transplanted in October, and not in July–August as was the practice in 1948. The October transplantation was probably a carry-over from the period before the extension of the C.D.S. Canal. *Ragi* was then the most important crop, and not rice. It was sown in June, and probably harvested soon after the stalks were cut in October. But as an increasing amount of land became irrigable enabling rice to be grown on it, *ragi* lost its importance. The acreage under *ragi* in 1948 was negligible, and *ragi* stalks cut in October had to wait till rice had been harvested and stored in the granaries.

I give below a list of *nakshatras* against corresponding dates for 1948:

NAKSHATRAS

	Name of Star	Dates	Comments
1	Uttarashada	11–23 January	
2	Shravana	24 Jan.–5 Feb.	
3	Dhanishta	6–18 February	
4	Shatabisha	19 Feb.–2 March	
5	Poorwabhadra	3–16 March	
6	Uttarabhadra	17–29 March	
7	Revati	30 March–12 April	
8	Ashwini	13–25 April	
9	Bharani	26 April–9 May	
10	Krittika	10–23 May	
11	Rohini	24 May–6 June	
12	Mrigashira	7–20 June	(Popularly called *Motadri*)

	Name of Star	*Dates*	*Comments*
13	Aridra	21 June–4 July	(Popularly called *Doddadri*)
14	Punarvasu	5–18 July	(Popularly called *Doddahusoon*)
15	Pushya	19 July–1 Aug.	(Popularly called *Chikkahusoon*)
16	Ashlesha	2–15 August	
17	Makha	16–29 August	
18	Pubba	30 Aug.–12 Sept.	
19	Uttara	13–25 September	
20	Hasta	26 Sept.–9 Oct.	
21	Chitta	10–22 Oct.	
22	Swati	23 Oct.–4 Nov.	
23	Vishakha	5–18 November	
24	Anuradha	19 Nov.–1 Dec.	
25	Jyeshta	2–14 December	
26	Moola	15–27 December	
27	Poorwashada	28 Dec.–9 Jan.	

The Hindu lunar calendar has an inter-calary month every four years, and this means that the corresponding Gregorian dates for each *nakshatra* vary from year to year. This should certainly have limited the use of the lunar calendar for the farmer. It is necessary to add, however, that the villagers also made use of the far more accurate solar calendar for performing certain rituals and festivals. The almanac gave lunar, solar and Gregorian dates.

The Gregorian calendar was becoming increasingly important in the lives of villagers, especially the better-off sections. The most important dates in the agricultural year were 10 June and 10 January, the dates when the canal gates were opened and shut respectively, marking the beginning and end of the rice season.

All government offices including post and telegraph, schools, colleges and hospitals, and stores and shops in urban areas regulated their activities by the Gregorian calendar.

Appendix II

The months according to the Hindu Calendar (lunar) for the year 1948 are listed below. 1948, like all Gregorian years, fell between two Hindu years which usually began on a date in March or April. Thus January, February, March and a part of April were included in the Hindu year Sarvajit, 1871, according to the Shalivahana era, while the remaining months of 1948 formed part of Sarvadhari, 1871. Each year had a name and there were sixty years in each cycle.

Margashira	13 December–11 January
Pushya	12 January–10 February
Magha	11 February–10 March
Phalguna	11 March–9 April
Chaitra	10 April–9 May
Vaishaka	10 May–7 June
Jyeshta	8 June–6 July
Ashada	7 July–5 August
Shravana	6 August–3 September
Bhadrapada	4 September–2 October
Ashwayuja	3 October–1 November
Kartika	2 November–30 November
Margashira	1 December–30 December
Pushya	31 December–29 January

Appendix III

List of Important Festivals in 1948

14 January	Makara Sankranthi
25 February	Festival of village Gods
	—Hatti Maramma, Ramagiriyamma, etc.
26 February	Karighatta Srinivasaswamy Car Festival
8 March	Maha Shivarathri
10 April	Ugadi
17 April	Ramanavami
17 July	Prathama Ekadashi (Upavasada habba)
27 August	Krishnashtami
6 September	Gowri and Ganapathy
19 Sept.–2 Oct.	Mahalayapaksha
3 October	Dasara begins
11 October	Ayudha puja
12 October	Vijayadashami
30 October	Madeshwara jatra
31 October	Narakachaturdashi
1–2 November	Balipadyami

Glossary

Aḍadé Periodic payments in kind to members of the artisan and servicing castes
Aḍadé kuḷa Landowning household which pays in kind to artisan and servicing castes
Aḍḍa kasabi Person practising a non-traditional occupation
Adharma Opposite of *dharma*
Agé pāti Nursery plot
Agrahāra Street inhabited exclusively by Brahmins
Ajjipālu Lit., grandmother's share, but actually the widow-mother's share in ancestral property
Aṇékaṭ Indigenous dam formed by building a masonry wall in the river-bed
Annadāna Gift of food
Aṇṇatammiké Lineage (see also *Vamsha, peeḷigé*)
Anyāya Injustice
Ārati Waving of light before a deity or human being
Aravaṭṭigé Booth where snacks and soft drinks are distributed to pilgrims
Āruwāsi Moisture in land
Āyurvēda Traditional Indian system of medicine

Bāgāyat Orchard land
Banjar Wasteland
Baṇṇa Colour or caste (corruption of the Sanskritic *Varna*)
Bhūmi tāyi Mother earth

Chakra Harijan village servant
Chāvaḍi Village council house
Chéluvāḍi Hereditary Harijan servant of the upper castes

Dākshiṇya Obligation, act prompted by a sense of obligation
Darkāsth Application
Dharma The moral code

Eḍé Food offered to deity or ancestor-spirit
Enjalu Spittle, or food polluted by coming into contact with spittle
Eru Plough

Garbha guḍi Innermost shrine in a temple
Gauḍa Chief
Gōḍu Alluvium
Gomāḷa Pastureland
Guḍḍa Hereditary non-Brahmin priest
Guttigédāra Tenant

Hagé Hatred

Haḷémaga Lit., hereditary ritual servant from a lower caste
Hobḷi An administrative unit lower than *tāluk*

Jagali Covered verandah
Jubba Shirt-like garment without collar and with pockets on either side

Kaḷa Threshing-yard
Kambḷi Coarse, woollen blanket woven by Shepherds
Kaṇaja Granary
Kasaba Capital town
Kasubu Occupation
Kaṭṭémané Caste court in a large village
Kesaru gaddé Slushy fields
Khaṇḍaga 180 seers (traditional unit for measuring paddy)
Khushki Unirrigated or dryland
Kooli maṭha The traditional one-teacher village school
Kula See *Vamsha*
Kuḷavāḍi See *Chéluvādi*

Maḍi Ritual purity
Maḍugikoḷḷuvudu 'Keep' (mistress)
Mailigé Impure
Māna Honour, self-respect
Mānanashta Loss of self-respect
Mané dévaru Lineage deity
Mānishta Man with a sense of self-respect
Maṭa Sorcery
Moogarji Anonymous petition
Muttaidé A woman whose husband is alive
Muyyi See *Hagé*. Also equivalent return, institutionalized conflict between two
  lineages

Nādaswaram Classical music played on pipes
Nāḍu Gowḍa Caste headman of the Okkaligas
Naivédya Offering of food to God
Nājooku Refinement
Nakshatra Asterism
Nāmam Caste-symbol of the Vaishnavas, especially Sri Vaishnavas (Iyengars)
Nāṇya Coin
Naṭi Transplantation
Niyat Loyalty
Nuchchu Broken rice, broken grain
Nyāya Justice

Osagé Consummation ceremony

Pāḷégāra Local chieftain in South India
Palla 100 seers

Panchānga   Almanac
Panchāyat   Village council
Pandal   Temporary awning erected on bamboo poles and with a roof of woven coconut fronds
Pangti   A row of diners
Pāpa   Sin
Para   A big vegetarian feast in honour of a deity
Patēl   Headman
Patta   Title deed
Pāvali   A silver four-anna piece
Peeligé   See *Vamsha*
Pie   1/192 of a rupee
Pitru paksha   The dark half of the lunar month of Bhadrapada (sacred for propitiating dead ancestors)
Prasāda   Consecrated food
Puṇya   Meritorious conduct
Puṇyāha   Purificatory ritual
Purāṇa   Traditional Hindu myths
Purōhita   Domestic priest or chaplain

Rāhu kāla   An inauspicious period of the day
Rakhāvu   See *Maḍugikoḷḷuvudu* (keep)
Rangōli   Designs drawn in front of the house each morning with powder made from a soft stone

Sabgast   Wedding procession
Sabhé   Assembly
Santé   Weekly market
Sārāyi   Arrack (distilled liquor)
Satya   Truth
Sauḍi   Waterman
Shānubhōg   Accountant
Shāstra   Science or system. Also symbolic and not effective action
Shēkdār   Revenue Inspector
Shrāddha   Ancestor propitiation
Sigḍi   Small dried fish
Sōdara māva   Maternal uncle
Suggi   Harvest season

Tāli   A gold ornament tied round the bride's neck by the groom at their wedding
Tāluk   Administrative division comprising a number of villages. (Also called *tehsil*)
Tampu   Cool
Tappu   Wrong conduct
Tappu kāṇiké   Pay a fine
Tari bhūmi   Irrigated or wet land
Tavaru mané   A woman's natal home
Téra   Bride-price

Thirtha Holy water. Sanctified water used in worship
Thōta See *Bāgāyat*
Tōḍa Field rat
Tombé Huge grain-container

Vaḍé A fried, savoury snack
Vaidika Orthodoxy
Vamsha Lineage
Varna Term for caste as an all-India category
Vasthi Seepage
Vibhūti Three horizontal stripes of sacred ash marked on the forehead. A symbol of devotion to Siva
Viḷya Collective term for a wad of betel leaves, arecanuts, etc., given on ritual occasions

Index